SEXUAL PRACTICE / TEXTUAL THEORY

SEXUAL PRACTICE / TEXTUAL THEORY:

LESBIAN CULTURAL CRITICISM

Edited by
SUSAN J. WOLFE and JULIA PENELOPE

BLACKWELL
Cambridge MA & Oxford UK

Introduction, editorial matter, and organization copyright © 1993
Susan J. Wolfe and Julia Penelope. Copyright © for all chapters rests
with the authors except for chapter 1: *Feminist Studies, Inc.*, University
of Maryland; chapter 3: *Signs* and the University of Chicago Press;
chapter 6: University of Tennessee Press; chapter 9: Southern Illinois
University Press; chapter 15: Cornell University Press; chapter 17:
Hypatia and Indiana University Press.

First published 1993

Blackwell Publishers
238 Main Street
Cambridge, Massachusetts 02142
USA

108 Cowley Road
Oxford OX4 1JF
UK

Library of Congress Cataloging-in-Publication Data
Sexual practice/textual theory: lesbian cultural criticism /edited by
Susan J. Wolfe and Julia Penelope
  p. cm.
Includes bibliographical references and index.
ISBN 1-55786-100-5 (Hbk) -- ISBN 1-55786-101-3 (Pbk)
  1. Lesbians' writings, American--History and criticism--Theory,
etc. 2. American literature--Women authors--History and criticism--
Theory, etc. 3. Lesbians--United States--Intellectual life.
4. Feminism and literature--United States. 5. Identity (Psychology)
in literature. 6. Women and literature--United States. 7. Lesbians
in literature. 8. Sex role in literature. I. Wolfe, Susan J.,
1946- . II. Penelope, Julia, 1941- .
PS153.L46S48 1993
810.9'9206643—dc20   92-33731
                                                        CIP

British Library Cataloguing in Publication Data
A CIP catalogue Record for this book is available from the British Library.

Typeset in Palatino on 10½ pt 12½ by Editorial Inc.
Printed in the USA on acid-free paper

Contents

Acknowledgments

A shorter version of Carolyn Allen's "Sexual Narrative in the Fiction of Djuna Barnes" previously appeared as "Writing toward *Nightwood*" in *Silence and Power* (1991), edited by Mary Lynn Broe, published by Southern Illinois University Press. Jeffner Allen's "Poetic Politics: How the Amazons took the Acropolis" was originally published in *Hypatia: A Journal of Feminist Philosophy* 3:2 (1988). Permission to reprint has been granted by *Hypatia* and Indiana University Press. "Toward a Definition of the Lesbian Literary Imagination" by Marilyn Farwell was previously published in *Signs: Journal of Women in Culture and Society* 14:1 (1988):100–118. Permission to reprint the essay has been granted by *Signs* and by The University of Chicago Press. Elaine Marks's "Lesbian Intertextuality" has been reprinted from *Homosexualities and French Literature: Cultural Contexts/Critical Texts*, 353–77, edited with an introduction by George Stambolian and Elaine Marks. Copyright © 1979 by Cornell University. Used by permission of the publisher, Cornell University Press. "Perverse Reading: The Lesbian Appropriation of Literature" by Bonnie Zimmerman was originally printed in "(En)Gendering Knowledge: Feminists in Academe," edited by Joan Hartman and Ellen Messer-Davidow, © 1991, by the University of Tennessee Press. Reprinted by permission. "What Has Never Been: An Overview of Lesbian Feminist Criticism" by Bonnie Zimmerman is reprinted from *Feminist Studies* 7:3 (Fall 1981):451–75, by permission of the publisher, *Feminist Studies*, Inc., c/o Women's Studies Program, University of Maryland, College Park, MD 20742.

List of Contributors

Carolyn Allen is associate professor of English at the University of Washington. She is currently completing a manuscript on representations of Lesbian sexuality in modern and contemporary fiction.

Jeffner Allen is associate professor of philosophy at State University of New York, Binghamton. She is the author of *Lesbian Philosophy: Explorations*, editor of *Lesbian Philosophies and Cultures*, and coeditor of *The Thinking Muse: Feminism and Modern French Philosophy*. She is active in the Society for Women in Philosophy and is on the Editorial Board of *Hypatia: Journal of Feminist Philosophy*.

Paula Bennett is assistant professor of English literature at Southern Illinois University, Carbondale. She is the author of *My Life a Loaded Gun: Dickinson, Plath, Rich and Creativity* and *Emily Dickinson: Woman Poet*. With Vernon Rosario, she is currently editing *Eros and Masturbation*, an anthology on the social, historical, and literary discourses of masturbation. She is also working on *Dickinson's Sisters*, a book on nineteenth-century women poets, ex Dickinson. Shakespeare is her hobby.

Erin G. Carlston is currently working on a doctoral degree at Stanford University and studying at the Université Paris VII on a Lurcy Fellowship. Her field is modernist literature, and her dissertation project is tentatively titled "Sapphic modernisms and the response to fascism."

Anne Charles is writing her doctoral dissertation at the University of Wisconsin on Lesbian expatriates. She teaches English and women's studies at the University of New Orleans.

Vilashini Cooppan is a graduate student in the Department of Comparative Literature at Stanford University. She has taught courses on pornography and on writing and identity. She is currently working on theoretical intersections between postcolonialism, feminism, and psychoanalysis.

Diane Griffin Crowder is professor of French and women's studies at Cornell College (in Iowa, not Ithaca). She lives with her partner and three cats, who all tolerate her passion for utopian fiction and murder mysteries. She is currently pursuing her research on the works of Monique Wittig. She has published studies on Wittig, Colette, Lesbian teaching, and the semiotics of the Lesbian body.

Sarah Dreher is a clinical psychologist, novelist, playwright, and Lesbian activist living in Amherst, Massachusetts. She has won numerous awards for playwriting, including the prestigious Alliance for Gay and Lesbian Artists in the Entertainment Industry Media Award. She has served as the only "out" member of Amherst's elective Town Meeting, and is cochair of the Amherst Civil Rights Review Commission. She devotes much of her time pushing to make the world safe for Lesbians.

Marilyn Farwell is associate professor of English at the University of Oregon. She has written essays on Virginia Woolf, Adrienne Rich, John Milton, and Lesbian literary theory, and she is currently working on a book on Lesbian narrative theory.

Judith Fetterley is professor of English and women's studies and director of graduate studies for the Department of English at the University at Albany, State University of New York. She is the author of *The Resisting Reader: A Feminist Approach to American Fiction* and *Provisions: A Reader from Nineteenth-Century American Women,* as well as of numerous articles on a variety of nineteenth-century American writers. With Joanne Dobson and Elaine Showalter, she founded Rutgers University Press American Women Writers Series. For this series she edited a volume of the short fiction of Alice Cary. She is the coauthor, with Marjorie Pryse, of *American Women Regionalists, 1850–1910* (Norton), and with Marjorie Pryse she is working on a critical study of the writers included in the anthology. She lives in Albany, New York, with her lover, her lover's two children, and her very own cat.

Linda Garber is the author of *Lesbian Sources: A Bibliography of Periodical Articles, 1970–1990,* to be published by Garland Press (Gay and Lesbian Monograph Series) in spring 1992, and the editor of *Teaching Lesbians:*

Classroom Practices and Politics, to be published by Routledge. She also has published articles in *The Women's Review of Books* and *Lesbian Ethics*, and she is currently completing a multidisciplinary anthology of writings in Lesbian studies. She is a Ph.D. candidate in the Modern Thought and Literature program at Stanford University.

Louise Kawada is a founding member of the Alliance of Independent Scholars (Cambridge, Massachusetts) and a free-lance violinist in the Boston area. She has published *The Apocalypse Anthology* (Rowan Tree Press, 1985) as well as articles on Whitman and on American women poets and their responses to nuclear issues. Currently she is researching and writing a longer work on Lesbian writers and their revision of comedic form.

Elaine Marks, Germaine Bree professor of French and women's studies at the University of Wisconsin–Madison, is author of *Colette* (1960, 1981) and *Simone de Beauvoir: Encounters with Death* (1973); coeditor of *Homosexualities and French Literature* (1979, 1990) and *New French Feminisms* (1980, 1981); editor of *French Poetry from Baudelaire to the Present* (1964) and *Critical Essays on Simone de Beauvoir* (1987); and author of numerous articles and book reviews on twentieth-century French literature and French women writers. She is currently completing a book on *The Jewish Question(s) in French Writing*.

Toni McNaron is a professor of English and women's studies at the University of Minnesota, where she has taught for twenty-eight years. The first chair of women's studies and the first director of the Center for Advanced Feminist Studies, Toni is deeply committed to feminist learning. Her publications include *Voices in the Night: Women Speaking about Incest* (1982), *The Sister Bond: A Feminist View of a Timeless Connection* (1983), and her autobiography, *"I Dwell in Possibility"* (1991). Her interests include gardening, travel, woodworking, and jogging.

Alice Parker chairs the Women's Studies Department at the University of Alabama. She has published on eighteenth-century French and francophone women writers, and she has edited, with Elizabeth Meese, two collections of feminist criticism and theory. Her recent work focuses on Lesbian texts, and she is finishing a book on Nicole Brossard.

Julia Penelope, having done her time in academia, is now a free-lance writer and linguist living in Massachusetts. She has coedited *The Original Coming Out Stories* (1980, 1989) with Susan J. Wolfe; *For Lesbians Only: A Separatist Anthology* (1988) with Sarah Lucia Hoagland; and *Finding the Lesbians* and *International Feminist Fiction* (1992) with Sarah Valentine.

With Morgan Grey, she coauthored *Found Goddesses: From Asphalta to Viscera* (1988), and she is the author of *Speaking Freely: Unlearning the Lies of the Fathers' Tongues* (1990) and *Call Me Lesbian: Lesbian Lives, Lesbian Theory* (1992). Her articles have appeared in numerous Lesbian and linguistics journals. She is working on an anthology on women and class, a feminist crossword book, and a history of Lesbianism. In 1993 Crossing Press will publish *Lesbian Culture*, coedited with Susan J. Wolfe. She enjoys cooking, gardening, weight lifting, and rock hunting.

Marthe Rosenfeld, born in Antwerp in 1928, grew up in Belgium and soon felt the effect of the rise of Naziism and the resurgence of anti-Semitism in Europe. A Jewish refugee in World War II, she considers herself fortunate to have been able to immigrate to the United States. Since the 1970s she has been teaching French and women's studies at Indiana University–Purdue University at Fort Wayne. She has published two articles on *The Lesbian Body* by Monique Wittig and an essay on the development of a Lesbian sensibility in the work of Jovette Marchessault and Nicole Brossard. As a Jewish Lesbian, she supports groups that promote Lesbian visibility as well as the survival of diverse cultures and ethnicities.

Linnea A. Stenson is completing her dissertation on the development of self- and community-identity in the Lesbian novel at the University of Minnesota in Minneapolis. She teaches literature courses at Macalester College in St. Paul, Minnesota.

Diana Swanson is assistant professor of women's studies and English at Northern Illinois University. She is currently working on a book about daughters, fathers, and narrative authority, focusing on the daughter-father relationship as a site for socialization into femininity and heterosexuality.

Susan J. Wolfe is professor and chair of English at the University of South Dakota. She has published a number of articles on linguistics, language and gender, and feminist aesthetics, and has contributed essays to several Lesbian anthologies. With Julia Penelope, she coedited *The Coming Out Stories* (1980) and *The Original Coming Out Stories* (1989). She lives happily out in the rural heartland with her lover.

Bonnie Zimmerman is professor of women's studies at San Diego State University and the author of several articles on Lesbian literature and theory and of *The Safe Sea of Women: Lesbian Fiction 1969–1989* (Beacon, 1990). She is still out after all these years.

Susan J. Wolfe and Julia Penelope

Sexual Identity/Textual Politics:

Lesbian $\left\{ \begin{matrix} \text{De} \\ \text{Com} \end{matrix} \right\}$ positions

We live in the postmodernist, poststructuralist (and, some would say, postfeminist) era, during a period when the term *Lesbian* is problematic, even when used nonpejoratively by a self-declared Lesbian. We can no longer speak as "individuals," it would seem; to do so is unforgivably naive and/or simpleminded. We can speak only as fictionalized "subjects," our individual identities existing only as the creation of (someone's) texts, or as the result of signification. In one hundred short years, German sexologists have "appeared" Lesbians in order to pathologize us and French poststructuralists have "disappeared" us in order to deconstruct sex and gender categories and to "interrogate" "the" subject.

Some academics have suggested that feminism and postmodernism have a great deal in common.

Theorists of postmodernism on both sides of the Atlantic similarly affirm that their movement shares a political agenda with feminism, inasmuch as to destabilize narrative relations between dominant and subordinate, container and contained, is also to destabilize the social and cultural relations of dominance and containment by which the conventionally masculine subsumes and envelops the conventionally feminine.

In the current jargon, both postmodernsim and feminism have "problematized gender relations," calling into question the "naturalness" of gender relations and seeing the relation between the sexes as the result of social forces, language, and/or power (Giroux, 28). Neither "man" nor "woman" is an ontologically stable object, an invariable category; both are constructed in history (Fuss, 3).

We will not quarrel with the idea that the term *Lesbian*, during the brief period when it has been used at all, has often been a term of opprobrium, not approbation – that it has been used linguistically to signify deviance and even monstrosity. Nor do we wish to fall into the kind of essentialism which would assume all Lesbians are "merely" Lesbians. We are members of different races, classes, ethnic groups; collectively Lesbians suffer from many forms of oppression.

On the other hand, postmodern philosophy, at least in the forms it has assumed within the halls of power (academic pedagogy, and aesthetic and critical theory) seems to us to threaten the erasure of real (or, as the postmodernists would say, "material") Lesbians. If identity is constructed by texts, perhaps there is no such person ("object") as a Lesbian, no (un-constructed) characteristic Lesbians share. If both texts and individual identity can be deconstructed, perhaps anyone, even a non-Lesbian, can "read as a Lesbian," as some have suggested. But if there is no Lesbian identity as such, then the statement that one is "reading *as* a Lesbian" is nonsense.

Postmodernist discourse seeks to displace liberal humanist notions of the self, the "bourgeois subject" (H. Foster, 77, cited in Waugh, 8). But as Waugh (8–9) notes, the unified self posited by liberal humanism was/is not a female self, much less a Lesbian one.

Subjectivity, historically constructed and expressed through the phenomenologi-cal equation self/other, necessarily rests masculine "selfhood" upon feminine "otherness." The subjective center of socially dominant discourses (from Descartes' philosophical, rational "I" to Lacan's psychoanalytic phallic/symbolic) in terms of power, agency, autonomy has been a "universal" subject which estab-lished its identity through the invisible marginalization or exclusion of what it has also defined as "femininity" (whether this is the non-rational, the body, the emo-tions, or the pre-symbolic). The "feminine" thus becomes that which cannot be expressed because it exists outside the realm of symbolic signification. Constituted through a male gaze and thus endowed with the mysteriousness of one whose *objective* status is seen as absolute and definitive. One . . . becomes a woman. . . .

In the dialectical relationship between traditional humanism and the postmodern anti-humanism emerging in the 1960s, women continue to be displaced. How can they long for, reject, or synthesize a new mode of being from a thesis which has never contained or expressed what they have felt their historical experience to be?

How indeed? How can women, much less Lesbians, rejoice in the de(con)struction of a unified self they have never been permitted (within patriarchal structures, including discourse structures) to possess. Initially unimpressed by the postmodernist discourse that purported to deconstruct gender and identity while continuing to relegate women to object status, feminist theorists began in the 1970s by adopting/adapting theories compatible with self-actualization.

In particular, it [feminism] emphasized the ideological production of "femininity" as the "other" of patriarchy and the need, therefore, for women to become "real" subjects and to discover their "true" selves. Thus, with a search for a *coherent and unified feminine subject,* began the deconstruction of the myth of woman as absolute Other and its exposure as a position within masculine discourse. (Waugh, 9)

The goal Waugh ascribes to feminism – that of seeking "an individual and collective identity," "a sense of agency and history for women . . . denied them by the dominant [male] culture" – is doubly compelling for Lesbian feminism. Lesbians, after all, have been marginalized both as women, and therefore subsumed within the category of the "feminine," and as nonwomen, departing markedly from stereotyped ("constructed") femininity. Like other doubly oppressed minorities (poor and working-class women and women of color), we have often been excluded from the category "woman" by feminist as well as patriarchal discourse, our real, material difference ignored. Waugh has noted that "one's experience of being a 'woman' or a 'man'" is not "simply the consequence of a 'false consciousness' which can be rationally deconstructed and thrown off. The basis of one's subjectivity as 'masculine' or 'feminine' is formed out of real needs and desires. . . ." (36–37). Shifting from Waugh's context to focus on Lesbian identity, we would contend that the basis of Lesbian subjectivity is likewise "formed out of real needs and desires," needs and desires that inform the unconscious and conscious development of individual Lesbians, despite the patriarchal values and discourses that eradicate us or render us invisible.

Lesbian theory, including critical theory, and Lesbian literary criticism (emerging a full ten years later than feminist literary criticism), has had the task of positing a Lesbian subject, experienced through a collective history and culture we have had to construct before we can begin to *de*construct Lesbian identity. That is to say, we have had to deconstruct the notion that women can be seen only in relation to men, and defined only in terms of male discourse, in order to create a position from which to speak and be heard by non-Lesbian feminist critics. Lesbian cultural criticism, including – importantly – Lesbian feminist literary criticism, occurred, to be sure, parallel to feminist criticism in general. It was published in *Sinister Wisdom,* it was featured in a special issue of *Margins* edited by Beth Hodges (1975), it was featured in panels of the Modern Language Association as early as 1975. But, as we and our contributors will argue in the first section of this anthology, no one seemed to be listening. Little was published, and nothing assembled in anthologies like this one or the recent book edited by Karla Jay and Joanne Glasgow (1990).

In the preceding paragraphs, we have turned to the terminology of deconstruction to suggest ways of challenging non-Lesbian views of Lesbian identity and culture. At the same time, we have suggested that poststructuralist theory and methodology, unless challenged by Lesbian feminist theory and politics, has as much capacity to destroy Lesbian identity as to construct it through deconstructing "gender." A number of those who contributed to this anthology have nonetheless found deconstruction to be a tool that can be put to Lesbian uses, a strategy capable of liberating Lesbian writers and readers. By fusing feminism with the deconstruction of identity, they have joined other poststructuralist feminists who redefine identity as a construct.

In adopting poststructuralism, however, Lesbians, if we have Lesbian feminist agendas, walk a precarious tightrope. Fuss (103–4) notes the problems deconstruction poses for feminists, quoting from Kristeva: "As Julia Kristeva ponders, 'what can "identity", even "sexual identity" mean in a new theoretical and scientific space where the very notion of identity is challenged?' . . . The fear is that once we have deconstructed identity, we will have nothing (nothing, that is, which is stable and secure) upon which to base a politics." It might be possible to adopt the position, as Fuss does, that "The deconstruction of identity is not necessarily a *disavowal* of identity," that "there must be a sense of identity, even though it would be fictitious," and that the view that identity is unstable and incoherent "could produce a more mature identity politics" (104). If this position were tenable in the face of social reality, it might be compatible with, and indeed conducive to, Lesbian, feminist, and Lesbian feminist political goals.

Giroux (29) argues that postmodern feminism has criticized, and even rejected, a number of assumptions central to postmodernism, including "the postmodern emphasis on erasing human agency by decentering the subject; in related fashion it has resisted defining language as the only source of meaning, and in doing so has linked power not merely to discourse but also to material practices and struggle." It should be evident to readers that the writers in this anthology have (implicitly or explicitly) incorporated such a critique even when they appear to deconstruct. As Lesbian theorists, they seek to clarify very real distinctions obscured by much postmodern discourse, to avoid "the postmodern tendency to portray the body as so fragmented, mobile, and boundaryless that it invites confusion over how the body is actually engendered and positioned within concrete configurations of power and forms of material oppression" (Giroux 34).

Postmodern feminism might well offer a grounded politics, as some theorists have suggested, preventing Lesbians and feminists from ignoring the multiplicity of individual identities and, therefore, of the possible factors determining relations of power and sources of oppression. Unfortunately, debates between poststructural and traditional theorists may have refocused feminist debate and Lesbian debate, forestalling social and political action, even as such debates have defused radical activism in academia. Zavarzadeh and Morton (61), for instance, argue that the poststructuralist emphasis on "self-reflexiveness," because it is couched in "textual, discursive, and significatory [rather] than in political terms," has resulted in a "language of *différence* [which] doesn't seem to have made any difference in academic practices." What is ignored by poststructuralism is "a politics that aims at questions of the access of disenfranchised groups to culture's bank of power/knowledge/resources: this is the 'deeper problem' (the structural, not merely significatory, character of oppressive and exploitative social relations). . . ."

As Lesbians, we cannot allow our concern with the politics of sexuality under patriarchy to become absorbed in the study of mere textuality. Nor can we afford to allow privileged patriarchal discourse (of which poststructuralism is but a new variant) to erase the collective identity Lesbians have only recently begun to establish. Recent events suggest that Lesbian identity, however multifaceted, is precarious – and not simply, as poststructural theorists might argue, because all identity is unstable.

For what has in fact resulted from the incorporation of deconstructive discourse, in academic "feminist" discourse at least, is that the word *Lesbian* has been placed in quotation marks, whether used or mentioned, and the existence of real Lesbians has been denied, once again, this time by those theorists and practitioners who would regard Lesbians as mere discourse constructs, the product of textuality, undetermined by sexuality. At the same time, our Lesbian colleagues inform us, deconstruction is now taught *as* feminist and Lesbian studies, displacing critical approaches that had sought to authenticate the identity of Lesbians and other women.

Outside the walls of academia, Lesbian identity and indeed Lesbian existence is threatened by assertions that Lesbians, like other women, "sleep with men"; by the insistence that the fight against AIDS (or, indeed, against anything but the oppression of Lesbians) is or should be the focus of our emotional, intellectual, and political energies; and by the verbal harassment of Lesbians at political rallies (now by gay men and bisexuals as well as by heterosexuals).

Poststructuralist discourse has become a dominant force in Anglo-American criticisms at the precise juncture in history when Lesbians, women of color, poor and working-class women, and others on the periphery of patriarchy have begun to find a literary and critical voice, to seek social and political equality, to become visible, to establish their identities for themselves, identities that had been denied them within patriarchy and patriarchal discourse.

The simultaneous emergence of Lesbian and other minority identities and cultures on the one hand, and of the poststructural deconstruction of the ideas of self, author, text, and identity on the other, may be mere coincidence. Given the historical erasure of Lesbians, however, the current trend within poststructuralist criticism to regard Lesbian difference as a discursive or textual construct, coupled with the very real denial or denigration of Lesbians outside the confines of "theory," emerges as a very real threat to Lesbians and their identities. To demonstrate the importance of a self-defined Lesbian identity to individual Lesbians, to the Lesbian feminist critique of patriarchy, and to the creation of Lesbian culture, we consider it necessary to review the position that Lesbians have occupied within patriarchy and its discourses.

Separately and together, we have wrestled with the notion of "Lesbian culture" for years. We have alternately hoped for it and despaired of it. A common culture assumes that there exists a community capable of transmitting its shared values and beliefs; to posit a community presupposes common interests and goals. But what, if anything, are or should be the goals and interests common to all Lesbians? Who, after all, is a Lesbian?

When mainstream American society condescends to notice our existence, it usually defines the Lesbian as a "homosexual woman," a woman whose sexual desires are directed toward other women, as though Lesbians constituted a not-very-interesting subspecies of the generic homosexual, read: nonmen. In a number of papers written during the 1970s, we suggested that such labeling relegates Lesbians to a subculture within a subculture, given that the terms *homosexual* and *gay* function (like *man*) only as pseudogenerics. In "Sexist Slang and the Gay Community: Are You One, Too?" (1979) we observed that, aside from differences in values and lifestyles within the Lesbian community, there were dramatic differences between the values and life experiences of gay men and Lesbians, as could be documented by the blatant misogyny (and homophobia) expressed in gay men's slang and humor.

Underlying our argument was a twofold assumption. First, we assumed that a Lesbian community would, or at least ought to, incorporate feminist values and develop a language for expressing them. On the other hand, we held to the belief that Lesbians, unlike non-Lesbian feminists, loved women and related to women, and only women, sexually. A Lesbian culture would, we felt (unlike most cultures), transmit as a primary value the worth of women and would view love between us as of central importance.

We were, in short, adopting a Lesbian feminist perspective in our criticism of gay men's language and in our critique of the concept of an inclusive "gay culture" – one that incorporated Lesbian culture. Bonnie Zimmerman, in "What Has Never Been: An Overview of Lesbian Feminist Criticism" (reprinted in this volume, pp. 33–54), claims that Lesbian literary criticism rests on the assumption that a Lesbian perspective is a unique one, one that challenges patriarchal culture:

. . . One set of assumptions underlies virtually all lesbian criticism: that a woman's identity is not defined only by her relation to a male world and male literary tradition . . . that powerful bonds between women are a crucial factor in women's lives, and that the sexual and emotional orientation of a woman profoundly affects her consciousness and thus her creativity. Those critics who have consciously chosen to read as lesbians argue that this perspective . . . assigns the lesbian a specific vantage point from which to criticize and analyse the politics, language and culture of patriarchy.

As Zimmerman notes, we (Lesbian feminist critics) must decide how inclusively or exclusively we define "Lesbians" in order to decide when a specific writer is a Lesbian writer or a text a Lesbian text. Throughout history we have, prior to the twentieth century, been erased, our existence denied. If we hold that sexual experience with another woman is central to Lesbian identity, we face excluding not only many writers and texts, but also the experience of the women among us who self-identify as Lesbians in the absence of that experience. We will reduce the canon of Lesbian literature to works written in the twentieth century, when Lesbian experiences have been expressed more openly.

Lacking a definition of *Lesbian*, lacking a clear sense of Lesbian identity, we find it difficult to create a Lesbian culture, "to provide lesbians with a tradition, even if a retrospective one" (Zimmerman, this volume, p. 41). Yet, as many of our contributors suggest, the establishment of Lesbian traditions, including a literary tradition, and of a Lesbian community (or Lesbian communities with a number of shared concerns and values), is important in allowing Lesbians to perceive ourselves at all.

An individual's identity, according to Erik Erikson (as cited by Susan Kupper, 27), is "how she perceives herself in comparison to others within her society, combined with the way she perceives that those others view her." Patriarchal society has viewed the Lesbian as a monster, a grotesque pervert; looking to others within *that* society cannot provide the Lesbian with a positive identity (self-concept). In patriarchal culture, heterosexuality is considered to be the "natural" form of sexual expression for women, so that Lesbians and Lesbianism are either unmentioned or condemned, by literary critics and theorists as well as psychologists.

The Eriksonian definition of identity views a society as a group of people holding mirrors, each determining her own identity according to the image of herself in a mirror held by someone else. (This concept of identity is developed by McNaron, this volume, pp. 291–306.) Perhaps identity is constructed by such an infinite regression of individuals glancing into the mirrors held by others, each ignoring the image of herself in the mirror she holds, except to compare her own image with her images of everyone else. In that case, we ask that Lesbians hold up the mirror for other Lesbians, each comparing herself with the other Lesbians as she perceives them.

In compiling this collection, we have therefore restricted its contents to contributions by Lesbian authors, realizing that that is a controversial decision – one which, in conjunction with the focus of the anthology, might result in the book being termed a "separatist" book. To the extent that the work as a whole is an attempt to define ourselves and our values for ourselves; a critique of patriarchal values as expressed in literature, literary theory, and criticism; an expression of a variety of Lesbian vantage points from which to invoke Lesbian culture – to that extent, it is a separatist book. We would like to make clear at the outset, however, that not all our contributors would identify themselves as separatists.

We began this anthology precisely when the tenets of postmodernism, a central force in Continental critical theory for the past two decades, had also become a primary force in North American critical theory, and poststructuralist (post-?)feminist theory began to replace traditional feminist theory in American criticism. Because postmodernist theory denies that a unified self – an inner essence capable of achieving selfhood through action – exists, some feminist theorists have expressed concern that postmodernism may be inconsistent with feminist goals. In *Feminine Fictions: Revisiting the Postmodern*, Patricia Waugh (1989) argued that postmodernism may offer little to women seeking to actualize themselves, seeking a unified identity beyond the feminine as constructed within patriarchy, the Woman as Other. Postmodernist theory therefore seems to offer still less to Lesbians, whose existence has only been rarely, and then selectively, acknowledged by patriarchal societies.

Foster (1984:78) argued that the "loss" of subjectivity is no great loss for women at all, cast as they have been as the Other, an object whose difference from men was the source of male subjectivity:

For what is this subject that, threatened by loss, is so bemoaned? Bourgeois, perhaps, patriarchal, certainly – it is the phallocentric order of subjectivity. For some, for many, this is indeed a great loss – and may lead to narcissistic laments about the end of art, of culture, of the west. But for others, precisely for Others, this is no great loss at all.

Postmodernism gained widespread acceptance among Western intellectuals precisely at the time when those "constructed" as Other by those with power sought liberation. Just as women, Lesbians, gay men, and racial minorities rose to challenge their marginalization and to define themselves as subjects, the white male intelligentsia declared that subjectivity was a fiction. Thus, we disagree with Foster that the "loss of subjectivity" is no great loss for those of us previously constructed as "Other"; the erasure by the powerful of subjectivity elides the possibility of our ever attaining subjecthood.

Poststructuralist rhetoric insists that "impersonal relations of power" have constructed the identities of those who have been marginalized, but its rhetoric obscures the fact that, if there are "relations of power," some are more powerful than others. Those who benefit from "relations of power" are hidden within the abstract nouns used to describe these "relations." In the passage quoted above, for example, Foster (1984) referred to "the phallocentric order of subjectivity," an order created *by* men *for* men, to ensure that agency, including the right to structure language and discourse, remained a male prerogative.

Retaining that prerogative, poststructural theorists (also largely male) have now declared that identity and subjectivity are constructed "in" society and "in" discourse. Within the social constructionist and deconstructive paradigms, then, identity is merely a "construct." Lesbian identity, in particular, is said to be a "fiction" created by nineteenth-century sexologists.

As linguists, we are troubled by the conflation of two senses of the word *identity* in such theories. Clearly, there were women who loved women and who expressed their love sexually before Lesbian sexuality was pathologized by nineteenth-century sexologists. The *identity* constructed by sexologists, then, was an *image* of the stereotypical Lesbian, an image designed to discourage Lesbian sexual activity and to sustain male control of women's sexuality (by insisting that male-controlled heterosexual behavior was the only available outlet for women's sexuality). As Lesbians, we seek to establish a self-determined identity – a sense of self confirmed through connections with others and transmitted through common culture(s) – for Lesbians, one that affirms our material identity, grounded in our sexuality.

Our decision to edit this anthology presupposes that Lesbian identity *exists.* That is, we grant Lesbians "ontological status," assuming that, whatever discourse may say about us (Lesbians), we exist, materially, outside of discourse. As the preceding discussion suggests, this assumption, which might have seemed a trivially obvious fact two decades ago, has been challenged by poststructuralist thought. Slightly more than a hundred years ago, sexologists had to establish some notion of Lesbian identity, when Western culture doubted that Lesbians existed, in order to establish that Lesbians were a pathological category.

Therefore, to ask "*Who* is a Lesbian?" is a question neither irrelevant nor frivolous. In fact, some attempt to identify our Lesbian selves is essential to an anthology of Lesbian criticism. Such a work claims implicitly that one or more critical perspectives exist that are unique to Lesbians, and therefore presupposes that Lesbians share characteristics that identify us as such. Yet, as Bonnie Zimmerman points out in *The Safe Sea of Women* (1990b:50), "There are no simple, 'common sense' answers to such a question." As is obvious by this point, as editors we have rejected the alternative approach, the decision not to identify a specifically Lesbian perspective on the (to us, spurious) grounds that identity is constructed, and that, therefore, anyone can read or write as a Lesbian.

A Lesbian may choose *not* to write as a Lesbian; that is, she may refuse to reveal the reality of her Lesbian experience in her writing. A non-Lesbian cannot *choose* to write or read *as a Lesbian*. The non-Lesbian may produce a work or a reading that is empathic or compatible with a Lesbian sensibility, but s/he does not share in Lesbian experience. Non-Lesbians do not know what it is like to grow up as a Lesbian, to live as a Lesbian, to love as a Lesbian, to think as a Lesbian. A heterosexual man who decides to write a book or poem *as though* he were a Lesbian will produce only something written by a heterosexual male imagining that he is imagining/thinking/writing like a Lesbian. The thought process during composition is quite different: his material identity is non-Lesbian, and he performs a process of translation, transmuting his own imaginings into a product that may resemble a Lesbian work, or what others may accept as a Lesbian work. The so-called "Lesbian" pulp novels of the 1950s, for example, were sometimes written by men under assumed women's names.

For centuries, men have produced literature *about* Lesbians, about how men think Lesbians think, how men imagine Lesbians behave *as* Lesbians, how men imagine it might feel to be a Lesbian. But these are not works within a *Lesbian* literary tradition. Nor can a heterosexual woman write about Lesbians as a Lesbian would. In *Women of the Left Bank* (1986) Shari Benstock intended, judging from her preface, to produce a nonhomophobic, nonmisogynist book. Yet, as Anne Charles illustrates in "Two Feminist Criticisms: A Necessary Conflict?" (this volume, pp. 55–65), Benstock's treatment of the "mannish" Lesbians in her study is unguardedly "lesbophobic," as though she were unaware of how Lesbians might read and interpret her descriptions.

While it may be possible for heterosexuals to read and write about Lesbians empathically, we maintain that responding empathically to Lesbian (or to any other) experience is not the same as *having* the experience oneself. We would argue that each person reads within the limits of what s/he knows, and that includes what s/he "knows" of others' experiences, which is, of necessity, secondhand. A heterosexual who sits down to read a Lesbian novel reads it first as a heterosexual, and then, perhaps, by some imaginative extrapolation, as s/he thinks some Lesbian might read it. This does not necessarily mean that, because differences among individuals exist, people are doomed to read and write only for themselves. In fact, people regularly read texts created by others with widely different experiences, and do so with varying degrees of pleasure. Nonetheless, they enjoy engaging with the different perspectives that frame such texts. Further, each reader brings to her/his reading a mixture of ignorance, curiosity, confidence, and preconceptions.

Lesbians have been reading heterosexual texts since we started school and understand them perfectly well, although we may feel excluded from some of the attitudes they express and some of the experiences they describe. Similarly, non-Lesbian readers do not read or interpret Lesbian texts in the same ways that Lesbians do. Indeed, some measure of the pleasure to be derived from reading lies in the challenge of grasping and interpreting other points of view, and, sometimes, integrating that information.

Talking about whether a text is Lesbian or not, identifying a writer as Lesbian, or undertaking the project of producing something to be read as "Lesbian literary criticism," all assume some means of establishing Lesbian identity. Borrowing the framing question from Sue Lanser (1979), Bonnie Zimmerman, in "What Has Never Been: An Overview of Lesbian Feminist Criticism" (this volume, p. 37), introduced the issue as one of inclusion versus exclusion:

> We are . . . concerned about developing a unique lesbian feminist perspective or, at the very least, determining whether or not such a perspective is possible. In order to do this, lesbian critics have had to begin with a special question: "When is a text a 'lesbian text' or its writer a 'lesbian writer'?" (Lanser 1979:39). Lesbians are faced with this special problem of definition: we presumably know when a writer is a "Victorian writer" or a "Canadian writer." To answer this question, we have to determine how inclusively or exclusively we define "lesbian." Should we limit this appellation to those women for whom sexual experience with other women can be proven?

As editors for an anthology of Lesbian literary criticism, we have to explain how we identify those we include as members of the category "Lesbian." This is not, however, as simple as the form of the question suggests. A "Victorian writer" is one who lived during that literary period; a "Canadian writer" is one who has lived most of her life in Canada or was born there. Lesbians, however, have no readily apparent temporal or spatial means of identification; and making sexual activity the only, or primary, criterion of Lesbian identity is problematic (given that such activity cannot always be confirmed, particularly for earlier historical periods, and given that some Lesbians, like some heterosexuals, decide *not* to act on their desire).

Initially, it might seem attractive to confine the use of the label *Lesbian* to self-identified Lesbians, and to conclude that a Lesbian text is a text written by a self-identified Lesbian. Yet many authors we might wish to identify *as* Lesbians did not identify themselves as such. Some women who have had sexual relationships with other women never consider themselves Lesbians; some lived during periods when neither the term nor the concept was available. Moreover, like Lesbians generally, a Lesbian writer, regardless of the cultural context in which she wrote, may regard a Lesbian relationship as an interruption in her otherwise heterosexual life, or view her relationship with another woman as anomalous. Djuna Barnes, for example, denied that she was Lesbian, claiming she was merely in love with Thelma Wood, a specific woman. More recently, Holly Near claimed she was a "Lesbian" despite the fact that she was in an active heterosexual relationship with a man.

These examples indicate two things. First, Lesbian identity cannot be based solely on one or more sexual acts, because the experience of Lesbian sexual intimacies is not limited to lifelong Lesbians. Many women experience Lesbian attractions whether or not they act on them. Second, there is no one kind of Lesbian. Instead, because each of us comes to our Lesbianism at different times and in different circumstances, there must be several bases for terming a woman a "Lesbian."

When the lives of Lesbian writers are examined, questions of identity are further affected by the social and cultural contexts in which they wrote. A writer may have lived her entire life as a Lesbian, yet never produce an identifiably Lesbian text. Moreover, since heterosexuals of both sexes have written about Lesbians (just as Lesbians have written about heterosexuals), a text with Lesbianism as its subject matter cannot necessarily be termed a "Lesbian text." Rather, it is Lesbian identity itself, and the modes of perception that accompany it, that determine the focus of texts.

To proceed, then, to a consideration of a specifically Lesbian criticism, a critical perspective that can be identified as uniquely Lesbian, is to make ourselves increasingly open to challenge. We must anchor our definition of Lesbian writers, readers, and critics firmly in a definition of *Lesbian*, and determine just what we mean by "Lesbian identity." We will offer a brief history of the term *Lesbian* before offering our own definition.

The issue of Lesbian identity is a comparatively new one, and still largely argued among Lesbians ourselves. The term dates back to the late nineteenth century, when the sexologists, responding to the first wave of women's liberation, needed to label a behavior they wanted to stigmatize. Until then, there were no words to name love between women. Because the sexologist assumed that heterosexuality was natural and good, while Lesbianism was correspondingly unnatural and perverted, they sought answers to the questions "WHAT is a Lesbian?" and "WHY do Lesbians exist?" Their views on Lesbianism are obvious from the labels for Lesbians that were coined in the late nineteenth century: *homosexual, invert,* and the sex-specific *Sapphist* and *lesbian*.

The strangely late appearance of these labels in public discourse deserves some comment here. The *Oxford English Dictionary (OED)* fails to list the word *Lesbian* in the body of the dictionary, but defines it in an archaic sense in the supplement. Even modern dictionary-makers persist in giving as their first definition "an inhabitant of Lesbos," as though that were the primary sense of the term, with the definition "a female homosexual" as the second or third sense. Havelock Ellis, the German sexologist, is generally credited with introducing the term *Lesbian*, in *Sexual Inversion* (1897); but he was in fact quoting a Professor Platt, who used the word *Lesbian* in the entry on Sappho he wrote for the eleventh edition of the *Encyclopedia Brittanica*. Although the *OED* lexicographers ignore *Lesbian*, there is an entry for *Sapphism*, for which the earliest citation is 1890. This does not mean, however, that there were no women-loving women before the last decade of the nineteenth century, but rather that the label appeared only when the sexologists decided to identify those in need of their "cures." The *OED* defines a *Sapphist* as "one addicted to Sapphism"; Sapphism is defined as "unnatural sexual relations between women."

Interestingly, the word *heterosexual* postdates all the terms for same-sex love, a fact that points to a newly developed self-consciousness about sexuality in general, at least in Western culture under Christianity. (Prior to the end of the nineteenth century, sexualities were either "natural" or "unnatural.") *Heterosexual*, in fact, first appeared in 1901 and referred to an "abnormal or perverted appetite toward the opposite sex," but the opprobrium intended by the label did not have the same long-lasting consequences for heterosexuals. *Heterosexual*, although the newer term, shed its early stigma, for reasons that should be obvious.

For many centuries, then, it suited patriarchal cultures and the men who governed them more or less to ignore love between women. So unspeakable was the idea that women could and did love each other passionately that male literary scholars felt quite justified in changing Sappho's female references to their male counterparts (as though she might have made a mistake). The appearance of labels to denote explicitly same-sex love radically altered public discourse about sexuality. Perhaps the most quoted scholar on the subject of sexuality and its entry into public discourse is Michel Foucault, whose *History of Sexuality* (1978) has already had a significant, if implosive, effect on the issue of Lesbian identity.

Foucault's reconstruction and description of the "history of sexuality" reflects an obtuse disingenuousness that borders on misrepresentation. Contrary to the presentations of feminists who have taken up Foucault's reorganization of the discourse on *sexuality*, he spent little time examining how women's sexuality was formulated by successive generations of male speakers, and failed to mention Lesbianism at all. If he had not been cited, however briefly, by so many feminist and Lesbian feminist literary critics of the past decade, we could ignore him entirely.

Foucault's project is nothing less than a conceptual upheaval, a reorientation of how we ask questions about sex and sexuality in Western societies. He rejected the idea that sex has been "repressed" in Western culture, and reframed the issue.

The central issue . . . [is] to account for the fact that it [sex] is spoken about, to discover who does the speaking, the institutions which prompt people to speak about it and which store and distribute the things that are said. What is at issue, briefly, is the over-all "discursive fact," the way in which sex is "put into discourse." (11)

However, as his agentless passives suggest (*said, put*) his "history of sexuality" failed even to suggest *who* "does the speaking" or *how* sex "is put into discourse." In fact, he later enjoined his readers not to ask such questions. Not only did he neglect to point out that the public discourse he examines was (and remains) the domain of white, male heterosexuals, and that it was *their* discourses he discussed; he failed to observe that his is simply one more white, male, European treatise on how the rest of us have misunderstood the significance of that discursive tradition in our own lives.

Yet Foucault's central thesis is unassailable: To say that sex has been "repressed" in Western discourse is to misperceive and misunderstand how male sexuality, and heterosexuality, as perceived by men, have shaped Western societies. Far from censorship of talk about sex, "there has been a constant optimization and an increasing valorization of the discourse on sex" (23) over the past three centuries:

Not only were the boundaries of what one could say about sex enlarged, and men compelled to hear it said: but more important, discourse was connected to sex by a complex organization with varying effects, by a deployment that cannot be adequately explained merely by referring it to a law of prohibition. A censorship of sex? There was installed rather an apparatus for producing an even greater quantity of discourse about sex, capable of functioning and taking effect in its very economy.

What Foucault did not say, did not want to say, is that "talk about sex" is really male heterosexual discourse that assumes "women as objects" as its focus. From the Victorian gentleman's club to the locker rooms of today, women need not be explicitly mentioned in "talk about sex." Rather, men discuss sex as something that they achieve – as "getting laid," "getting some action," "finding a piece." It is a discourse in which women as objects, as bodies, as parts of bodies, are merely the implicit scenes of male activities. Beneath the decorous public layer of religious and judicial discourses vilifying all varieties of sex, including nonreproductive hetero-sexuality, is the pornographic literature of sex, which Foucault called the *ars erotica* (57). That is, while men condemned sex in discourse at official and institutional levels, they elaborated and pursued it through "unoffi-cial," concealed discourses, which multiplied and flourished outside the "new . . . propriety." Although Foucault granted that sex had to be "sub-jugated" (by someone) at the level of language in order (for someone) to control it (17), the examples he cited, as well as those he omitted, empha-size the obliqueness of his approach.

Without question, new rules of propriety screened out some words: there was a policing of statements. A control over enunciations as well: where and when it was not possible to talk about such things became much more strictly defined; in which circumstances, among which speakers, and within which social relation-ships. Areas were thus established, if not of utter silence, at least of tact and discre-tion: between parents and children, for instance, or teachers and pupils, or masters and domestic servants. (17–18)

Someone defined the boundaries of talk about sex "more strictly" and "es-tablished" the relationships in which the "new propriety" was to be ob-served (by someone else?). Foucault's failure to name *who* performed these discursive acts served his larger rhetorical purpose: directing our attention away from male control of both discursive and sexual acts and the corollary exclusion of women as agents in discourse and sex. Notice-ably absent from his list of "tact and discretion" is any reference to the rules of discourse on sex obtaining between women and men, although one might think that talk about sex would be more common in a marital relationship than, say, in one between "masters and domestic servants."

In fact, these omissions were quite purposeful on Foucault's part. His silence on such points was essential to the credibility of his undertaking. He signaled his awareness that at least some of the proprieties he alluded to are sex-specific, because men have power and use it to subjugate women. When he advanced what he called "cautionary prescriptions" (rather than "methodological imperatives"), he dismissed the observable sex-specific social reflexives in discourse about sex:

We must not look for who has the power in the order of sexuality (men, adults, parents, doctors) and who is deprived of it (women, adolescents, children, pa-tients); nor who has the right to know and who is forced to remain ignorant. *We must seek rather the pattern of the modifications which the relationships of force imply by the very nature of their process.* (99; our emphasis)

Foucault invited his readers to join him as the "we" engaged in this disarming analysis. Questions regarding who has the power in discourse, who benefits from keeping another group ignorant – these questions, Foucault asserted, are misleading. Likewise, he forbade us to "imagine" how men have structured discourse:

> . . . We must not imagine a world of discourse divided between accepted discourse and excluded discourse, or between the dominant discourse and the dominated one; but as a multiplicity of discursive elements that come into play in various strategies. It is this distribution that we must reconstruct, with the things said and those concealed, the enunciations required and those forbidden, that it comprises; with the various and different effects – according to who is speaking, his position of power, the institutional context in which he happens to be situated – that it implies; . . . (100)

We were ordered not to notice that someone had identified which discourses they would accept or exclude; we were not to notice that male discourse dominates or that men subjugate women's discourse. Yet the words themselves betray the reality Foucault ordered us to remain ignorant of. "*His* position of power" and *his* place within and "institutional context" are accidental; they simply "happen." "We" are not coconspirators in Foucault's project, but the abstract *we* "forced to remain ignorant."

What Foucault went to great lengths to construct is a fortuitous history, one in which male domination is reduced to a happenstance intersection of "relationships of force" in which some discourses (men's) are privileged while others (women's) are silenced. The language of his treatise (successfully, apparently, concealing what he wished to hide) was intended to charm us into acquiescence. Yet, if we examine Foucault's discourse for what he said and what he did not say, "the things said and those concealed," we find a pattern of descriptions without agency, a universe of activities, specifically *sexual* (read: *heterosexual*), in which we are to understand only that someone did or said something, but in which – and by means of which – the actual, if unnamed, white, male agents of all this talk are "concealed," indeed erased.

The case Foucault chose to exemplify his analysis is telling and bears on the issue of Lesbian identity. In order to illustrate how discourses are the multiple outcomes of "various strategies," he chose the introduction and stigmatization of homosexuals by the sexologists.

> There is no question that the appearance in nineteenth-century psychiatry, jurisprudence, and literature of a whole series of discourses on the species and subspecies of homosexuality, inversion, pederasty, and "psychic hermaphrodism" made possible a strong advance of social controls into this area of "perversity"; but it

also made possible the formation of a "reverse" discourse: homosexuality began to speak in its own behalf, to demand that its legitimacy or "naturality" be acknowledged, *often in the same vocabulary,* using the same categories by which it was medically disqualified. There is not, on the one side, a discourse of power, and opposite it, another discourse that runs counter to it. Discourses are tactical elements or blocks operating in the field of force relations; there can exist different and even contradictory discourses within *the same strategy;* . . . (101–2; our emphases)

On the one hand, Foucault accurately observed that homosexuals could not begin to argue for their naturalness or petition heterosexual societies for acceptance *until* the sexologists had named and identified them, although he cast the abstract noun, *homosexuality,* as the putative agent of speak. But, on the other, what is it when specific individuals, all of them male, take it upon themselves to describe and stigmatize a group – in this instance, homosexuals – if *not* "a discourse of power"? This is not the result of "various discourse strategies" but a response from a group already deprived of the right to speak by the group empowered to name them in the first place.

And there is disingenuousness in Foucault's choice of this illustration and the way he used it. As he presented it, the only "change" introduced by the sexologists was to transform the sodomite, "a temporary aberration," into a species, the homosexual (43). As his discussions make clear, Foucault focused on *male* homosexuality because it suited him to do so. But the sexologists themselves were equally concerned, if not more so, with the "female invert," with Lesbianism. Ellis, in fact, suggested that "the earliest case of homosexuality recorded in detail occurred in a lesbian" who was burned at the stake for sodomy in 1721 (1897:195). If "discourses are tactical elements or blocks operating in the field of force relations," as Foucault asserted, the partiality of his presentation makes clear that he, too, employed discourse tactically so that his readers would accept his views without challenge.

There were, in fact, Lesbians who joined with gay men in the "reverse discourse" that Foucault mentioned, but their relation to the pronouncements of the sexologists and their role in the "reverse discourse" were problematic precisely because they were women. As Sheila Jeffreys pointed out in *The Spinster and Her Enemies,* "Contemporary male gay historians have seen [Havelock Ellis] as performing a service to male homosexuals by breaking down the stereotype that they were effeminate. For women the service he performed was quite different" (1985:106).

As part of their self-imposed task of categorising varieties of human sexual behavior, the sexologists of the late nineteenth century set about the "scientific" description of lesbianism. Their description has had a momentous effect on the ways in which we, as women, have seen ourselves and all our relationships with other women up until the present. They codified as "scientific" wisdom current myths about lesbian sexual practice, a stereotype of the lesbian and the "pseudo-homosexual" woman, categorising women's passionate friendships as female homosexuality and offered explanations for the phenomenon. Male writers of gay history have tended to see their work as sympathetic and helpful to the development of a homosexual rights movement since they explained male homosexuality in terms of innateness or used psychoanalytic explanations which undermined the view of male homosexuality as criminal behavior. (105–6)

Since Lesbianism was not a crime in Britain at the time the sexologists were writing, their contribution to our understanding of Lesbian identity cannot be seen as positive in the same way. While sexologists were debunking the stereotype of gay men as effeminate and creating the species "homosexual," they were simultaneously making of the corresponding Lesbian stereotype a "scientific" fact. Sheila Jeffreys (1985:106) illustrates this from Havelock Ellis's *Sexual Inversion* (1987):

When they still retain female garments, these usually show some traits of masculine simplicity, and there is nearly always a disdain for the petty feminine articles of the toilet. Even when this is not obvious, there are all sorts of instinctive gestures and habits which may suggest to female acquaintances the remark that such a person "ought to have been a man". The brusque energetic movements, the attitude of the arms, the direct speech, the inflexions of the voice, the masculine straightforwardness and sense of honour, and especially the attitude towards men, free from any suggestion either of shyness or audacity, will often suggest the underlying psychic abnormality to a keen observer.

In the habits not only is there frequently a pronounced taste for smoking cigarettes, often found in quite feminine women, but also a decided taste and tolerance for cigars. There is also a dislike and sometimes incapacity for needlework and other domestic occupations, while there is some capacity for athletics.

When we factor in aspects of discourse about sexualities, such as the sexologists' obsession with defining and categorizing Lesbianism, and note Foucault's silence about it, his grand enterprise turns out to be yet one more male entry into "the process" of those "relationships of force." Nor can there be any doubt about the purpose of his project to derail, again, the feminist attempt to disrupt the white male heterosexual's domination of the world of discourse and the language of identification.

Foucault's treatise on "the" discourses of sex and sexuality is so abstract and partial that it successfully conceals much of what he intended it to, and his project has all but succeeded in dismantling the discourse of Lesbian feminism by omission and elision. But there are other ways to describe what occurred, and Foucault's choice to focus on the "repression" argument is only one fragmentary account with its own agenda.

In fact, hypotheses explaining the lateness of Western patriarchies to name Lesbianism as a "sexuality" and the time during which the labels and their definitions appeared have been addressed by several feminist scholars. Until the late nineteenth century, there was no such topic as "Lesbianism" in the public, political, male sphere of discourse. Sheila Jeffreys, citing the earlier work of Carroll Smith-Rosenberg (1975) and Nancy Sahli (1979) on "smashing" and quoting an excerpted letter from Geraldine Jewsbury to Jane Welsh Carlyle, observed that "Historians could not fail to notice the expression of [such] sentiments ['romantic friendships']. They tried to ignore them or explain them away so that they could not be allowed to challenge their heterosexual account of history" (1985:103). In fact, romantic friendships between women had been actively encouraged up to this time, and "Men tended to see these relationships as very good practice for their future wives in the habit of loving" (Jeffreys 1989:19).

This male beneficence abruptly stopped when women began to create other lives for themselves beyond the heterosexuality constructed for them. In *Surpassing the Love of Men* (1981), Lillian Faderman suggested that the increasing possibility that women could live independently of men, a turn of events traceable to the nineteenth-century women's liberation movement, threatened male hegemony and the institution of marriage that bound women to them in mandatory heterosexuality: "If they [women] gained all the freedom that feminists agitated for, what would attract them to marriage? Not sex drive, since women were not acknowledged to have one. . . ." (237). For the male psyches threatened by the spectre of economically independent and politically active women, "the sexologists' theories . . . came along at a most convenient time to bolster arguments that a woman's desire for independence meant she was not really a woman" (Faderman, 238). As Jeffreys (1989:20) described this period of transition, "Emotional relationships between women were harmless only when women had no choice to be independent of men, and became dangerous when the possibility of women avoiding heterosexuality became a reality."

In order to make credible this new threat to heterosexual domesticity, the sexologists created the "pseudohomosexual," "a woman who did not necessarily fit the masculine stereotype, had been seduced by a 'real homosexual' and led away from a natural heterosexuality, to which it was hoped that she would return" (Jeffreys 1985:108). "Real" lesbians, according to the sexologists (like Krafft-Ebing and Havelock Ellis), were "born that way," whereas the "pseudohomosexual" was a "natural" heterosexual temporarily seduced away from men by a "real one." By positing a transitory category between the innate sexualities of Lesbians and their heterosexual sisters, the sexologists were able to stigmatize not only the nineteenth-century feminists who smoked and disliked needlework but the women who, until then, had freely enjoyed passionate romantic friendships free from male comment or censure.

Through the defining of any physical caresses between women as "pseudo-homosexuality" by the sexologists, the isolation and stigmatising of lesbianism was accomplished, and women's friendships were impoverished by the suspicion cast upon any physical expression of emotion. (Jeffreys 1985:109)

Historically, men have controlled "talk about sex" and its meaning, both in public and in private. With isolated exceptions, such as Sappho and the Lesbians mentioned pejoratively by Martial, Lucian, and others, all women had been assumed to be heterosexual until the end of the nine-teenth century, when it suited men's political purposes to codify and stig-matize any and all intense female relationships explicitly, but especially those in which the physical passion of like to like might be acted upon.

Since then, Lesbians have lived under siege. Not surprisingly, the sexologists grounded their definitions of *Lesbian, invert,* and *homosexual* on the expression of genital sexuality, simultaneously locking several Lesbian generations into their discourse framework and erecting a physically intimidating barrier be-tween those who act on their feelings and those who do not, between Lesbians and "heterosexual women." For more than a hundred years, women have hid-den from themselves on one side of that protective wall. Others, like ourselves, whether they called themselves "Lesbian" or not, vaulted the wall and began to create the texts examined in this anthology.

As we have said, an adequate description of Lesbian identity must be based on more than specific sexual activities, as important as they are. "Being a Lesbian" means more than touching and being touched by women. Living "as a Lesbian" involves more than sexual intimacies and orgasmic rushes. We cannot forget that Lesbians, like heterosexual women, can choose celibacy, can choose not to act on their emotional and sexual feelings. Are they "real" Lesbians? We would say "yes."

There is a time in a Lesbian's life when she becomes aware of the wall, the line between "them" and "us," and considers its height, its breadth, and the strength of her desire. She takes her own measure, and she says either "I must jump now" or "Perhaps this will pass." Whichever choice she makes, her life becomes a battlefield on which she confronts the threats and lies of what men have said and continue to say about women, our sexualities, and what our actions "mean" in their world. Even if she marries and bears children, as many Lesbians did in the past and still do today, her mind knows what she will not reveal to anyone else.

Yet, in spite of the evidence of history, in spite of the evidence of our experience, we find self-identified Lesbian feminists who insist that there were no Lesbians prior to the late nineteenth century only because the label *Lesbian* did not exist. One such writer is Ann Ferguson, whose definition restricts the term *Lesbian* to those of us who have lived in the twentieth century and then further excludes the majority of twentieth-century women we would consider Lesbians:

[A] lesbian is a woman who has sexual and erotic-emotional ties primarily with women or who sees herself as centrally involved with a community of self-identified lesbians whose sexual and erotic-emotional ties are primarily with women; and who is herself a self-identified lesbian. (1982:153–155)

We gain insight into the purpose of Ferguson's definition of *Lesbian* when we examine the three premises on which her definition is based, each of which reflects an assumed meaning for all words expressing *identities*, as well as the naive belief that language necessarily expresses experience:

1. A person cannot be said to have a sexual identity that is not self-conscious;

2. It is not meaningful to conjecture that someone is a Lesbian who refuses to acknowledge herself as such;

3. A person cannot be anything unless others can identify her or him as such.

In an attempt to "do justice" to some modern ideal of "what a Lesbian is," Ferguson produced premises that are ahistorical and ignore the confusions Lesbians face when we sort our experiences and feelings and attempt to describe them. When we consider the varieties of Lesbian experience and the many ways we know ourselves in the world, Ferguson's premises, and the definition they buttress, leave us empty-handed. What, for example, does "self-conscious" mean? What about the "new" Lesbian who has only acknowledged to herself that she is a Lesbian but has not yet acted on the knowledge? What about women who unself-consciously love other women because no one has told them they "should not"? What about the Ladies of Llangollen? Is there any way of determining whether or not they were "self-conscious"? Ferguson's use of self-consciousness as a "proof" of one's Lesbianism makes her first premise as unenlightening as arguments that require "proof" of Lesbian sexual activity.

Likewise, her use of the verb *refuse* narrows the second premise so that it applies only to women who know other Lesbians exist. This premise is rigidly twentieth-century in its applications, even as it excludes Lesbians who are geographically or socially isolated. It is meaningless to say that Sappho or Rosa Bonheur "refused" to acknowledge their Lesbianism, and the term ignores Lesbians who reject categorization. More viciously, it erases the lives of all the women who were executed and otherwise perse- cuted because they loved other women *before* a label existed to categorize their "crime" specifically. Ferguson's second premise is accurate only when the woman in question has had the option of knowing that she is a Lesbian (because the concept and the language to identify it have been available to her) and has, in addition, been so highly visible that someone would know whether or not she "refused to acknowledge" her Lesbian- ism. Moreover, while Ferguson may consider it meaningless to conjecture about which twentieth-century movie stars, writers, or politicians might be Lesbians, precisely because their high visibility makes them most likely to "refuse to acknowledge" their Lesbianism, such conjectures are neces- sary elements of Lesbian attempts to establish and maintain our historical continuity, which is always in danger of erasure (even by other Lesbians).

Finally, Ferguson's third premise is vulnerable to disproof by numerous counterexamples, because it presumes that identity is, as in Eriksonian theory, determined by the recognition of others, whose identities must in turn be confirmed by us, the endless mirroring we discussed earlier. Who are the "others" who must be able to identify us? If a Lesbian is passing for heterosexual and only her lover knows she is a Lesbian, is she a Les- bian? Suppose a closeted Lesbian lacks the requisite lover and no one else knows she is a Lesbian? Such tests as Ferguson's ignore the social and economic conditions Lesbians face. This sort of definitional leveling de- nies our historicity.

Moreover, Ferguson's premises exclude from the category *Lesbian* women who are Lesbians but deny it, and those who remain closeted all their lives and maintain secrecy about their identity, yet they admit to the category bisexuals and women who claim to be Lesbians for some period of time. What about "hasbeans," women who have decided, after years of living as Lesbians, that they are now heterosexual? If they satisfied all of Ferguson's criteria for two years and then decided they loved a man, were they "real" Lesbians for just those years or only "passing through"?

If we apply this "definition" rigidly, we may include as Lesbians mem- bers of Natalie Barney's Paris salon, perhaps the Daughters of Bilitis (1957–1972), and the post-Stonewall Lesbian groups that have come and gone since 1969. Ferguson's definition would probably exclude Billie Jean King and Geraldine Jewsbury, as well as the many Lesbians still living in cultural and social isolation, some of whom have never heard the word *Lesbian* or, because of their circumstances, are unable to find other Lesbi- ans to whom they might relate.

Certainly, Lesbian identity is partially a social construct. How we per- ceive and understand ourselves is a result of accumulated experience. Our self-concept itself is shaped by the age at which we first think of ourselves as Lesbians; the information on which we base our identification; where we live; the autonomy we have; how mobile we are, and so on. When we factor in differences in class, race, religion, and ethnic backgrounds, the contrastive potentials multiply. There can be no doubt that Lesbians differ from one another in numerous ways, in how we perceive our Lesbianism, and how we choose to act or not act on those perceptions, but that fact does not make some of us "real" Lesbians and others "unreal."

If our identities are socially constructed to some degree, there is one significant aspect of Lesbian identity that cannot be overlooked or discounted, and that is what other writers have called our "invisibility." It is not true, as Ann Ferguson has claimed, that "It is false that lesbians are invisible in our society." She maintains that the word *Lesbian* denotes "quite visible lesbians, e.g., working class butches, those who appear to act like men as well as to have sex with women" (1990:74).

Even if one grants Ferguson's assumptions, focusing on the negative and limited denotation of the word *Lesbian* does not contradict the fact that most Lesbians spend portions of our lives invisible to ourselves as well as to others. Because some of us heard the word *Lesbian* applied to "quite visible" Lesbians as we were growing up, many assumed (erroneously) that we "could not be" Lesbians because we did not *look like* the individual to whom the label was applied. That stereotype, handed down from Ellis and his cohorts, has served to coerce some Lesbians into heterosexual relationships, just as some heterosexual women have lived as Lesbians for part of their lives because they did fit the stereotype.

Invisibility is part of the social construction of a Lesbian identity because so many of us, especially if we were born before 1970, developed our identities in an informational vacuum. To understand the Lesbian experience, one must somehow imagine what it would be like growing up into an identity that is unmentionable in any positive or helpful context. As the heterosexual agenda becomes clearer and clearer and its requirements and strictures become more and more insistently coercive, Lesbians have very few options, none of which are attractive. Of course, we have the option of remaining silent about what we are feeling, the option probably chosen most frequently. We keep our dismay and discomfort to ourselves.

Worse, even our silence may only buy us time. A parent may find and read a diary or journal, or a precious bundle of letters and notes hidden under underwear in a dresser. Or one of us may finally decide she can no longer remain silent, and out of her frustration may muster the courage to confess her feelings to a girlfriend, setting painful and humiliating consequences in motion. This is "invisibility." It is not a rhetorical fabrication. It is real. It is the silence imposed on each of our Selves, on each Lesbian who instinctively rejects the identity displayed, coerced, imposed by everyone and everything in her life. It is intended to destroy a Lesbian's sense of Self, and more often than not, succeeds in doing so.

But some survive. Some of us have lived to tell our stories, to create Lesbian texts, to read Lesbian texts, even (audaciously) to write commentaries and criticisms of Lesbian texts. All of these activities must be pluralized, multiplied, complicated, and pluralized again, because there is no single, narrow, one-sentence definition of "The Lesbian." The sexologists may have been the ones to name us, but we create ourselves. Out of a mishmash of disinformation, misinformation, and outright lies, each Lesbian constructs some story about who she is and who she might someday be; and she approaches her literature, if she is lucky enough to stumble upon it, with that construction, looking for additional pieces of her story.

We began this anthology in the hopes that we and our contributors might contribute to the growing number of Lesbian texts that exist to affirm Lesbian sexuality and Lesbian cultures. We dedicate it to Lesbians everywhere, past, present, and future.

PART I

Lesbian Identity in Feminist Literary Criticism: The Necessity for Lesbian Feminist Literary Criticism

Introduction

When the anthology *Feminist Literary Criticism: Explorations in Theory*, edited by Josephine Donovan, appeared in 1975, contributor Cheri Register could state confidently that there were three "distinct subdivisions" of feminist criticism:

(1) the analysis of the "image of women", nearly always as it appears in works by male authors; and (2) the examination of existing criticism of female authors. . . . The third type still needs formulating. . . . It is a "prescriptive" criticism that attempts to set standards for literature that is "good" from a feminist viewpoint. (2)

The first of these approaches, exemplified by Kate Millett's *Sexual Politics* (1969), Mary Ellmann's *Thinking about Women* (1968), and Simone de Beauvoir's earlier *The Second Sex* (1949), focused on the misogynistic portrayal of women in literature by men, analyzing negative images of women and the limited roles available for women in literature imposed by sex-role stereotypes. The second approach, closely related to the first, examined male critical evaluation of female authors. Both were concerned primarily with what men had said about women.

The feminist appraisal of existing criticism of female authors led to the (re)discovery and revaluation of such authors as Charlotte Perkins Gilman, Kate Chopin, Gertrude Stein, and Kay Boyle, and to arguments for their inclusion in the dominant literary canon. Many feminist critics, perceiving that this "add-on" approach to the canon was theoretically naive (suggesting, as it did, that there was something sacred in the conception of "literature" as a compilation of "great" works created by "authors"), eventually joined poststructuralist critics in challenging the assumptions that had first constructed the canon and the literary critical tradition. At the same time, an alternative feminist approach sought to establish a female tradition in literature comparable to that which had been established for male authors.

The "prescriptive" approach outlined by Marcia Holly (1975) demanded "authenticity" in the literary depiction of female characters and male-female relations. Holly argued that writers were responsible for establishing "real" character motivations and for identifying gender-specificity in their work, while feminist critics were responsible for observing when female characters were inauthentic, expressing "an understanding that literature has failed generally to create authentic female characters" (45). In stipulating consciousness raising as a necessary precursor to feminist criticism and to the creation of authentic literature, Holly saw herself as developing a foundation for a feminist aesthetic, one that would counteract existing stereotypes and transform culture and society. Donovan (1975:76) summarized the role of feminist criticism, which she, like Holly, saw in terms of its power to transform culture:

Not only, however, are we involved in the recognition of new "paradigms" (following Thomas Kuhn's terminology); we are, as feminists, involved in their creation. The new feminist critic is not "disinterestedly" describing cultural phenomena in the tradition of academic liberalism. She is (and knows herself to be) politically motivated by a concern to redeem women from the sloughbin of nonentity in which they have languished for centuries. Her procedure, then, is to propose a critique of the literary and critical structures that have held women in a condition of lesser reality in both the past and the present. The determination of what those structures are derives more perhaps from feminism as a political theory than it does from theories of literary criticism.

Noting that the contributors to *Feminist Literary Criticism: Explorations and Theory* had looked largely to "androgyny" as a transformative paradigm, Donovan nonetheless conjectured that the nascent Lesbian feminist movement might play an important role in developing a feminist aesthetic:

Radical feminists and lesbians have been in the forefront of the women's movement in seeking the patterns that identify women as a separate cultural group. Out of these as yet embryonic tendencies may emerge a feminist, feminine, aesthetic. (1975:77)

An examination of feminist critical theory a decade later indicates that Donovan's optimism about the possibility of developing a unified "feminist, or feminine" aesthetic was illfounded; and that, for reasons detailed by Marilyn Farwell (this volume, pp. 68–70), the concept of "androgyny" was not only inadequate but, like other metaphors for creativity, grounded in male sexuality and its presumptions. Despite the emergence of a "generation of lesbian feminist literary critics" during the late 1970s, noted by Zimmerman (this volume, p. 33), neither lesbian criticism nor lesbian feminism seem to have had a significant impact on feminist criticism or feminist theory as a whole. While contemporary feminists have insisted that feminism and feminist criticism must respond to differences among women, their practice has been to honor these differences by mentioning them as they move on to issues considered more theoretically "important" – the deconstruction or construction of gender, author, subject, identity; *difference* as a set of verbal possibilities or as constructed by discourse: *l'écriture feminine*. Initially, however, feminist literary criticisms simply ignored the existence of Lesbian criticism and viewed Lesbian authors and characters, when they noticed them at all, from a heterosexual perspective:

> The perceptual screen of heterosexism is also evident in most of the pioneering works of feminist literary criticism. Ellen Moers's *Literary Women*, germinal work as it is, is both homophobic and heterosexist. Lesbians, she points out, appear as monsters, grotesques, and freaks . . . but she seems to concur in this identification rather than calling it into question. . . . Perceptual blinders also mar Spacks's *The Female Imagination*, which never uses the word "lesbian" (except in the index). (Zimmerman, this volume, p. 35)

Charles's essay in this volume, "Two Feminist Criticisms: A Necessary Conflict?," suggests that a large number of contemporary non-Lesbian (but) feminist critics as well as mainstream (nonfeminist) critics continue either to overlook Lesbianism or to pathologize it, although more subtly than has been done in the past. Charles contends that Shari Benstock "evoke[d] pathology" in *Women of the Left Bank* (1986) by first polarizing the Left Bank Lesbians into those who adopted "the Barney-Flanner model of lesbian behavior" and those, who, like Radclyffe Hall, engaged in "cross-dressing" and, presumably, assumed "male" identities, and then praising Barney as unique among Lesbians of the period because her "life is distinguished by a remarkable emotional maturity and the absence of self destructive impulses" (Benstock, 292).

Charles documents Benstock's tacit approval of Barney's "ideal of feminine beauty," an acceptance of sex-role stereotyping that ultimately led both Barney and Benstock to reject "the dress and behavior of 'mannish' lesbians" (this volume, p. 60).

Summarizing reviewer responses to Benstock's book, Charles finds that only Lesbian feminists have addressed the issue of Benstock's lesbophobia in *Women of the Left Bank*, a lesbophobia that accounts for her (Benstock's) implicit acceptance of the lesbophobia expressed by patriarchal psychologists and by some of the Left Bank Lesbians she quoted. Charles concurs with Doughty (1987) that, in general, non-Lesbian feminist criticism fails Lesbian readers by failing to interrogate literary and critical texts grounded in the fear and/or hatred of Lesbians.

Zimmerman's (1981) pioneering overview of Lesbian feminist criticism, first published in *Feminist Studies*, has since been reprinted in *Making a Difference: Feminist Literary Criticism* (1985), edited by Greene and Kahn. We reprint it here not only because it remains one of the best examples of

Lesbian feminist criticism, but also because it exemplifies work within a "self-conscious literary tradition" that acknowledges and incorporates the problems of identification and definition central to Lesbian feminist theory itself.

We are more concerned about developing a unique lesbian feminist perspective or, at the very least, determining whether or not such a perspective is possible. In order to do this, lesbian critics have had to begin with a special question: "When is a text a 'lesbian text' or its writer a 'lesbian writer'?" (Lanser 1979:39). Lesbians are faced with this special problem of definition. . . . We have to determine how inclusively or exclusively we define "lesbian." Should we limit this appellation to women for whom sexual experience with other women can be proved? This is an almost impossible historical task. (Zimmerman, this volume, p. 37)

By 1981, Zimmerman found evidence that Lesbian feminist critics were indeed moving toward developing an aesthetic, as Donovan had hoped in 1973. Contrary to Donovan's prediction, however, lesbian poetics, aesthetics, imagery, and literary style – and the study of them – had diverged from non-Lesbian feminist criticism and its mainstream aspirations, both of which seem unable (or unwilling) to take on the complex issues addressed by Lesbian feminist writers. This noticeable omission in much feminist criticism has created a gap between theories of literature and literature itself, because Lesbian authors continue to produce a literature that challenges the "known" and addresses the "unknowable."

As we write a decade later, Lesbian feminist criticism has continued to focus on Lesbian identity as a context for the creation and interpretation of literature. Much non-Lesbian feminist criticism has instead adopted poststructuralist approaches developed by Continental (chiefly French) male theorists, hoping to show how language, or discourse, or texts, inscribe and construct gender. Since most poststructuralist approaches equate the "feminine" with the corporal, the nonrational, and/or the presymbolic, seeing "her" as the (nonspeaking) Object, feminist writers and critics employing poststructuralist concepts must try to wrench them from their patriarchal moorings or must celebrate the "fact" that, as women, they write (from) the body. Most Lesbian feminist critics have found such theories incompatible with expressing a positive Lesbian identity, for patriarchal stereotypes of femininity and femaleness privilege heterosexuality.

Farwell's "Toward a Definition of the Lesbian Literary Imagination," which first appeared in *Signs* in 1988, reviews the controversy surrounding Adrienne Rich's and Monique Wittig's uses of the Lesbian as a metaphor for female creativity. The metaphor appears to challenge the traditional Western (patriarchal) view that male sexuality alone, or at best an androgyny contingent upon male-female duality within a heterosexual model, is at the root of all creativity. Farwell further rejects the use of the mother as a metaphor for imaginative creativity, since this metaphor likewise relies ultimately on the patriarchal assumption that both female sexuality and female creativity are confined to biological reproduction.

Farwell (p. 66) observes that *"Lesbian* is one of the few words in our language, if not the only one, that privileges female sexuality," and that the metaphoric connection of the Lesbian with creativity powerfully counters the images and metaphors of creativity that have privileged heterosexuality by equating creative production with biological reproduction. She also summarizes the controversy generated by the Lesbian as metaphor and, more generally, by "generalized, less sexually dependent definitions" of Lesbians proposed by contemporary writers. Conflict of opinion over such definitions has arisen not only because they ahistoricize Lesbian existence and ignore specific differences among Lesbians (p. 67), but because as a metaphor, lesbian, like the other metaphors,

trades on similarities and differences between tenor and vehicle. . . . In abstracting from the literal experience, the metaphor gains a wider range of meaning but loses specificity and, of course, loses some connection with its source – lesbians. A woman who is a lesbian, then, may not necessarily be a metaphoric lesbian. . . . (p. 73)

Analyzing the work of Rich and Wittig, Farwell demonstrates the manner in which each separates or connects sexuality to the metaphoric Lesbian. Though the two "depend on different and, at times, radically opposed philosophies of language, they also have important elements in common, elements that deconstruct Western sexual metaphors for creativity and point to the possibility of female autonomy" (p. 79). Perhaps more importantly, by "removing the male from the audience, text, and authorial stance, [Rich and Wittig move] the woman writer from the margins to the center of her own language" (p. 79). As both are Lesbian theorists whose positions on the Lesbian metaphor for creativity are here analyzed by a Lesbian critic, we further suggest that Lesbians have been placed (by Farwell as well as by Wittig and Rich) at the center of discourse about literary theory, creativity, and Lesbian identity – a position from which to begin to speak about Lesbian culture.

Assuming the materiality of both body and text, Farwell states (p. 78), Wittig incorporates sexuality into her definition of Lesbian as metaphor, but views the power of Lesbian sexuality as emanating from the Lesbian rejection of patriarchal definitions of *woman*. The Lesbian repudiates, crosses, lives outside of all categories and boundaries. From this position Wittig's lesbian lovers release sexual *and* creative energy, because the power of the word and "the pleasures of the female body are intimately related" (Marks, p. 287). Having soared beyond the boundaries of patriarchal sexuality and discourse, the Lesbian speaker is free, in the words of Farwell, to "forge a textuality/sexuality of her own, with its own reality and language" (p. 78).

For Farwell, *Lesbian* encompasses a process of imagining a world into being, one in which patriarchal categories are erased, and males are no longer central in the text, or to the text as author or reader. The privileging of Lesbian subjectivity and Lesbian sexuality makes for new images, new language, new space. Farwell regards sexuality as "the core of the metaphor" (p. 79), just as we have seen sexuality as the core of Lesbian identity. The projection of Lesbian sexuality onto and into the text transforms textuality, by providing new images and symbols, as well as by providing for new relations between women. "The writing of the text" then becomes, as Farwell says, "an act that affirms self in community with others" (p. 80).

1

Bonnie Zimmerman

What Has Never Been:
An Overview of Lesbian Feminist Criticism

In the 1970s a generation of lesbian feminist literary critics came of age. Some, like the lesbian professor in Lynn Strongin's poem, "Sayre," had been closeted in the profession; many had "come out" as lesbians in the women's liberation movement. As academics and as lesbians, we cautiously began to plait together the strands of our existence by teaching lesbian literature, establishing networks and support groups, and exploring assumptions about a lesbian-focused literary criticism. Beginning with nothing, as we thought, this generation quickly began to expand the limitations of literary scholarship by pointing to what had been for decades "unspeakable" – lesbian existence – thus phrasing, in the novelist June Arnold's words, "what has never been" (Arnold 1976:28). Our process has paralleled the development of feminist literary criticism – and, indeed, pioneering feminist critics and lesbian critics are often one and the same. As women in a male-dominated academy, we explored the way we write and read from a different or "other" perspective. As lesbians in a heterosexist academy, we have continued to explore the impact of "otherness," suggesting dimensions previously ignored and yet necessary to understand fully the female condition and the creative work born from it.

Lesbian critics, in the 1980s, may have more questions than answers, but the questions are important not only to lesbians but to all feminists teaching and criticizing literature. Does a woman's sexual and affectional preference influence the way she writes, reads, and thinks? Does lesbianism belong in the classroom and in scholarship? Is there a lesbian aesthetic distinct from a feminist aesthetic? What should be the role of the lesbian critic? Can we establish a lesbian "canon" in the way in which feminist critics have established a female canon? Can lesbian feminists develop insights into female creativity that might enrich all literary criticism? Different women, of course, answer these questions in different ways, but one set of assumptions underlies virtually all lesbian criticism: that a woman's identity is not defined only by her relation to a male world and male literary tradition (a relationship brilliantly dissected by feminist critics), that powerful bonds between women are a crucial factor in women's lives, and that the sexual and emotional orientation of a woman profoundly affects her consciousness and thus her creativity. Those critics who have consciously chosen to read as lesbians argue that this perspective can be uniquely liberating and provide new insights into life and literature because it assigns the lesbian a specific vantage point from which to criticize and analyse the politics, language and culture of patriarchy:

We have the whole range of women's experience and the other dimension too, which is the unique viewpoint of the dyke. This extra dimension puts us a step outside of so-called normal life and lets us see how gruesomely abnormal it is. . . . [This perspective] can issue in a world-view that is distinct in history and uniquely liberating. (Boucher 1977:43)

The purpose of this essay is to analyse the current state of lesbian scholarship, to suggest how lesbians are exercising this unique worldview, and to investigate some of the problems, strengths and future needs of a developing lesbian feminist literary criticism.[1]

I

One way in which this unique worldview takes shape is as a 'critical consciousness about heterosexist assumptions' (Bulkin 1978:8). Heterosexism is the set of values and structures that assumes heterosexuality to be the only natural form of sexual and emotional expression, "*the* perceptual screen provided by our [patriarchal] cultural conditioning" (Stanley 1979:4–5). Heterosexist assumptions abound in literary texts, such as feminist literary anthologies, that purport to be open-minded about lesbianism. When authors' biographies make special note of husbands, male mentors, and male companions, even when that author was primarily female-identified, but fail to mention the female companions of prominent lesbian writers – that is heterosexism. When anthologists ignore historically significant lesbian writers such as Renée Vivien and Radclyffe Hall – that is heterosexism. When anthologies include only the heterosexual or nonsexual works of a writer like Katherine Philips or Adrienne Rich who is celebrated for her lesbian or homoemotional poetry – that is heterosexism. When a topically organized anthology includes sections on wives, mothers, sex objects, young girls, ageing women, and liberated women, but not lesbians – that is heterosexism. Heterosexism in feminist anthologies, like the sexism of androcentric collections, serves to obliterate lesbian existence and maintain the lie that women have searched for emotional and sexual fulfillment only through men – or not at all.

Lesbians have also expressed their concern that the absence for many years of lesbian material in women's studies journals such as *Feminist Studies, Women's Studies* and *Women and Literature* indicates heterosexism either by omission or by design. Only in 1979 did lesbian-focused articles appear in *Signs* and *Frontiers*. Most lesbian criticism first appeared in alternative, nonestablishment lesbian journals, particularly *Sinister Wisdom* and *Conditions*, which are unfamiliar to many feminist scholars. For example, in *Signs'* first review article on literary criticism (1975), Elaine Showalter makes no mention of lesbianism as a theme or potential critical perspective, not even to point out its absence. Annette Kolodny, in *Signs'* second review article (1976), does call Jane Rule's *Lesbian Images* (1975) "a novelist's challenge to the academy and its accompanying critical community," and further criticizes the homophobia in then current biographies, calling for "candor and sensitivity" in future work (Kolodny 1976:416, 419). However, neither this nor subsequent review articles, even as late as 1980, familiarize the reader with "underground" sources of lesbian criticism, some of which had appeared by this time, nor do they explicate lesbianism as a literary theme or critical perspective. Ironically, during the 1970s more articles on lesbian literature had appeared in traditional literary journals than in the women's studies press, just as in preceding years only male critics felt free to mention lesbianism. Possibly, feminist critics have felt that they will be identified as "dykes," and that this would invalidate their work.

The perceptual screen of heterosexism is also evident in most of the pioneering works of feminist literary criticism. Ellen Moers's *Literary Women*, germinal work as it is, is both homophobic and heterosexist. Lesbians, she points out, appear as monsters, grotesques, and freaks in works of Carson McCullers, Djuna Barnes (her reading of *Nightwood* is at least questionable), and Diane Arbus, but she seems to concur in this identification rather than calling it into question or explaining its historical context. Although her so-called defense of unmarried women writers against the "charge" of lesbianism does criticize the way in which this word has been used as a slur, she neither condemns such antilesbianism nor entertains the possibility that some women writers were, in fact, lesbians. Her chapter on "Loving Heroinism" is virtually textbook heterosexism, assuming as it does that women writers articulate love only for men (Moers 1977:108–9, 145). Perceptual blinders also mar Spacks's *The Female Imagination*, which never uses the word "lesbian" (except in the index) or "lover" to describe either the "sexual ambiguity" of the bond between

Jane and Helen in *Jane Eyre*, or Margaret Anderson's relationship with a "beloved older woman." Furthermore, Spacks claims that Gertrude Stein, "whose life lack[ed] real attachments" (a surprise to Alice B. Toklas), also "denied whatever is special to women" (which lesbianism is not?) (Spacks 1976:89, 214, 363). The latter judgment is particularly ominous because heterosexuals often have difficulty accepting that a lesbian, even a role-playing "butch," is in fact a woman. More care is demonstrated by Elaine Showalter, who in *A Literature of Their Own* uncovers the attitudes toward lesbianism held by the nineteenth-century writers Eliza Lynn Linton and Mrs. Humphrey Ward. Showalter does not, however, integrate lesbian issues into her discussion of the crucial generation of early twentieth-century writers (Woolf, Sackville-West, Richardson, and Lehmann, among others; Radclyffe Hall is mentioned but not *The Well of Loneliness*), all of whom wrote about sexual love between women. Her well-taken point that modern British novelists avoid lesbianism might have been balanced, however, by a mention of Maureen Duffy, Sybille Bedford, or Fay Weldon (Showalter 1977:178, 229, 316). Finally, the word "lesbian" does not appear in the index of Sandra Gilbert and Susan Gubar's *The Madwoman in the Attic;* the lone reference made in the text is to the possibility that "Goblin Market" describes "a covertly (if ambiguously) lesbian world" (Gilbert and Gubar 1979a:567). The authors' tendency to interpret all pairs of female characters as aspects of the self sometimes serves to mask a relationship that a lesbian reader might interpret as bonding or love between women.

Lesbian critics, who as feminists owe much to these critical texts, have had to turn to other resources, first to develop a lesbian canon, and then to establish a lesbian critical perspective. Barbara Grier, who as Gene Damon reviewed books for the pioneering lesbian journal *The Ladder*, laid the groundwork for this canon with her incomparable but largely unknown *The Lesbian in Literature: A Bibliography* (Damon et al. 1975). Equally obscure was Jeannette Foster's *Sex Variant Women in Literature*, self-published in 1956 after having been rejected by a university press because of its subject matter. An exhaustive chronological account of every reference to love between women from Sappho and Ruth to the fiction of the 1950s, *Sex Variant Women* has proven to be an invaluable starting point for lesbian readers and scholars. Out of print almost immediately after its publication and lost to all but a few intrepid souls, it was finally reprinted by Diana Press in 1975 (Foster 1975). A further resource and gathering point for lesbian critics was the special lesbian issue of *Margins*, a review of small press publications that appeared in 1975, the first issue of a literary journal devoted entirely to lesbian writing. In 1976 its editor, Beth Hodges, produced a second special issue, this time in *Sinister Wisdom* (1975, 1976). Along with the growing visibility and solidarity of lesbians within the academic profession, and the increased availability of lesbian literature from feminist and mass-market presses, these two journal issues provided a starting point for the development of lesbian feminist literary criticism.

The literary resources available to lesbian critics form only part of the story, for lesbian criticism is equally rooted in political ideology. Although not all lesbian critics are activists, most have been strongly influenced by the politics of lesbian feminism. These politics travel the continuum from civil rights advocacy to separatism; however, most, if not all, lesbian feminists assume that lesbianism is a healthy lifestyle chosen by women in virtually all eras and all cultures, and thus strive to eliminate the stigma historically attached to lesbianism. One way to remove this stigma is to associate lesbianism with positive and desirable attributes, to divert women's attention away from male values and towards an exclusively female *communitas*. Thus the influential Radicalesbians essay, "The Woman-Identified Woman," argues that lesbian feminism assumes "the primacy of women relating to women, of women creating a new consciousness of and with each other. . . . We see ourselves as prime, find our centers inside of ourselves" (Radicalesbians [1970] 1973:245). Many lesbian writers and critics have also been profoundly influenced by the politics of separatism, which provides a critique of heterosexuality as a political institution rather than a personal choice – "because relationships between men and women are essentially political . . . [they involve] power and dominance" (Bunch 1975:30). As we shall see, the notion of "woman-identification," that is, the primacy of women bonding with women emotionally and politically, as well as the premises of separatism, that lesbians have a unique and critical place at the margins of patriarchal society, are central to much current lesbian literary criticism.

II

Unmasking heterosexist assumptions in feminist literary criticism has been an important but hardly the primary task for lesbian critics. We are more concerned about developing a unique lesbian feminist perspective or, at the very least, determining whether or not such a perspective is possible. In order to do this, lesbian critics have had to begin with a special question: "When is a text a 'lesbian text' or its writer a 'lesbian writer'?" (Lanser 1979:39). Lesbians are faced with this special problem of definition: we presumably know when a writer is a "Victorian writer" or a "Canadian writer." To answer this question, we have to determine how inclusively or exclusively we define "lesbian." Should we limit this appellation to those women for whom sexual experience with other women can be proven? This is an almost impossible historical task, as many have noted, for what constitutes proof? Women have not left obvious markers in their private writings. Furthermore, such a narrow definition "names" lesbianism as an exclusively sexual phenomenon – which, many argue, may be an inadequate construction of lesbian experience, both today and in less sexually explicit eras. This sexual definition of lesbianism also leads to the identification of literature with life, and thus can be an overdefensive and suspect strategy.

Nevertheless, lesbian criticism continues to be plagued with the problem of definition. One perspective insists that "desire must be there and at least somewhat embodied. . . . That carnality distinguishes it from gestures of political sympathy for homosexuals and from affectionate friendships in which women enjoy each other, support each other, and commingle their sense of identity and well-being" (Stimpson 1981:364). A second perspective, which might be called a school, claims, on the contrary, that "the very meaning of lesbianism is being expanded in literature just as it is being redefined through politics" (Smith 1977:39). An articulate spokeswoman for this "expanded meaning" school of criticism is Adrienne Rich, who offers a compelling inclusive definition of lesbianism:

I mean the term *lesbian continuum* to include a range – through each woman's life and throughout history – of woman-identified experience; not simply the fact that a woman has had or consciously desired genital sexual experience with another woman. If we expand it to embrace many more forms of primary intensity between and among women, including the sharing of a rich inner life, the bonding against male tyranny, the giving and receiving of practical and political support . . . we begin to grasp breadths of female history and psychology which have lain out of reach as a consequence of limited, mostly clinical, definitions of "lesbianism." (Rich 1980:648–49)

This definition has the virtue of deemphasizing lesbianism as a static entity and of suggesting interconnections among the various ways in which women bond together. However, all inclusive definitions of lesbianism risk blurring the distinctions between lesbian relationships and nonlesbian female friendships, or between lesbian identity and female-centered identity. Some lesbian writers would deny that there are such distinctions, but this position is reductive and of mixed value to those who are developing lesbian criticism and theory and who may need limited and precise definitions. In fact, reductionism is a serious problem in lesbian ideology. Too often, we identify "lesbian" with "woman," or "feminist"; we equate lesbianism with any close bonds between women or with political commitment to women. These identifications can be fuzzy and historically questionable – as, for example, in the claim that lesbians have a unique relationship with nature or (as Rich also has claimed) that all female creativity is lesbian. By so reducing the meaning of "lesbian," we have in effect eliminated lesbianism as a meaningful category.

A similar problem arises when lesbian theorists redefine lesbianism politically, equating it with strength, independence, and resistance to patriarchy. This new political definition then influences the interpretation of literature: "If in a woman writer's work a sentence refuses to do what it is supposed to do, if there are strong images of women, and if there is a refusal to be linear, the result is innately lesbian literature" (Smith 1977:33). The concept of an "innately" lesbian perspective or aesthetic allows the critic to separate lesbianism from biographical content – which is an essential development in lesbian critical theory. Literary interpretation will, of course, be supported by historical and biographical evidence, but perhaps lesbian critics should borrow a few insights from textual criticism. If a text lends itself to a lesbian reading, then no amount of biographical "proof" ought to be necessary to establish it as a lesbian text. Barbara Smith, for example, interprets Toni Morrison's *Sula* as a lesbian novel, regardless of the author's affectional preference. But we need to be cautious about what we call "innately" lesbian. Why is circularity or strength limited to lesbians, or why is love of nature or creativity? It is certainly not evident that women are "innately" anything. And while it might require a lesbian perspective to stress the dominant relationship between Nel and Sula ("All that time, all that time I thought I was missing Jude"), the critic cannot ignore the heterosexuality that pervades this novel.

Almost midway between the inclusive and exclusive approaches to a definition of lesbianism lies that of Lillian Faderman in her extraordinary overview, *Surpassing the Love of Men: Romantic Friendship and Love Between Women.* Faderman's precise definition of lesbianism provides a conceptual framework for the four hundred years of literary history explored by the text:

"Lesbian" describes a relationship in which two women's strongest emotions and affections are directed toward each other. Sexual contact may be a part of the relationship to a greater or lesser degree, or it may be entirely absent. By preference the two women spend most of their time together and share most aspects of their lives with each other. (Faderman 1981:17–18)

Broader than the exclusive definition of lesbianism – for Faderman argues that not all lesbian relationships may be fully embodied – but narrower than Rich's "lesbian continuum," this definition is both specific and discriminating. The book is slightly marred by a defensive, overexplanatory tone, caused, no doubt, by her attempt to neutralize the "intense charge of the word *lesbian*" (Rich 1979a:202); note, for example, that this charged word is omitted from the title. Furthermore, certain problems remain with her framework, as with any that a lesbian critic or historian might establish. The historical relationship between genital sexuality and lesbianism remains unclear; nor can we easily identify lesbianism outside a monogamous relationship. Nevertheless, despite problems in definition that may be inherent in lesbian studies, the strength of *Surpassing the Love of Men* derives partly from the precision with which Faderman defines her topic and chooses her texts and subjects.

This problem of definition is exacerbated by the problem of silence. One of the most pervasive themes in lesbian criticism is that woman-identified writers, silenced by a homophobic and misogynistic society, have been forced to adopt coded and obscure language and internal censorship. Emily Dickinson counselled us to "tell all the truth / but tell it slant," and critics are now calculating what price we have paid for slanted truth. The silences of heterosexual women writers may become lies for lesbian writers, as Adrienne Rich warns: "a life 'in the closet' . . . [may] spread into private life, so that lying (described as *discretion*) becomes an easy way to avoid conflict or complication" (Rich 1979a:190). Gloria T. Hull recounts the moving story of just such a victim of society, the black lesbian poet Angelina Weld Grimké, whose "convoluted life and thwarted sexuality" marked her slim output of poetry with images of self-abnegation, diminution, sadness, and the wish for death. The lesbian writer who is working class or a woman of color may be particularly isolated, shackled by conventions and, ultimately, silenced "with [her] real gifts stifled within" (Hull 1979:23, 20).

What does a lesbian writer do when the words cannot be silenced? Critics are pointing to the codes and strategies for literary survival adopted by many women. For example, Willa Cather may have adopted her characteristic male persona in order to express safely emotional and erotic feelings for other women (Russ 1979; Lambert 1982). Thus a writer some call antifeminist or at least disappointing may be better appreciated when her lesbianism is taken into account. Similarly, many ask whether Gertrude Stein cultivated obscurity, encoding her lesbianism in order to express hidden feelings and evade potential enemies. Or, on the other hand, Stein may have been always a declared lesbian, but a victim of readers' (and scholars') unwillingness or inability to pay her the close and sympathetic attention she requires (Secor 1979).

The silence of "Shakespeare's [lesbian] sister" has meant that modern writers have had little or no tradition with which to nurture themselves. Feminist critics such as Moers, Showalter, and Gilbert and Gubar have demonstrated the extent and significance of a female literary tradition, but the lesbian writer developed her craft alone (and perhaps this is the significance of the title of *the* lesbian novel about novel writing, *The Well of Loneliness*). Elly Bulkin's much-reprinted article on lesbian poetry points out that lesbian poets "have had their work shaped by the simple fact of their having begun to write without knowledge of such history and with little or no hope of support from a woman's and/or lesbian writing community" (Bulkin 1978:8). If white women can at least imagine a lesbian literature, the black lesbian writer, as Barbara Smith demonstrates, is even more hampered by the lack of tradition: "Black women are still in the position of having to "imagine," discover and verify Black lesbian literature because so little has been written from an avowedly lesbian perspective" (Smith 1977:39). Blanche Cook points out further that all lesbians are affected by this absence of tradition and role models, or the limiting of role models to Hall's Stephen Gordon. She also reminds us that our lesbian foremothers and networks were not simply lost and forgotten; rather, our past has been "erased," obliterated by the actions of a hostile society (Cook 1979).

It would appear, then, that lesbian critics are faced with a set of problems that make our work particularly delicate and problematic, requiring caution, sensitivity, and flexibility as well as imagination and risk. Lesbian criticism begins with the establishment of the lesbian text: the creation of language out of silence. The critic must first define the term "lesbian" and then determine its applicability to both writer and text, sorting out the relation of literature to life. Her definition of lesbianism will influence the texts she identifies as lesbian, and, except for the growing body of literature written from an explicit lesbian perspective since the development of a lesbian political movement, it is likely that many will disagree with various identifications of lesbian texts. It is not only *Sula* that may provoke controversy, but even the "coded" works of lesbian writers like Gertrude Stein. The critic will need to consider whether a lesbian text is one written by a lesbian (and, if so, how do we determine who is a lesbian?); one written about lesbians (which might be by a heterosexual woman or by a man); or one that expresses a lesbian "vision" (which has yet to be satisfactorily described). But, despite the problems raised by definition, silence, and coding, and absence of tradition, lesbian critics have begun to develop a critical stance. Often this stance involves peering into shadows, into the spaces between words, into what has been unspoken and barely imagined. It is a perilous critical adventure, with results that may violate accepted norms of traditional criticism, but it may also transform our notions of literary possibility.

III

One of the first tasks of this emerging lesbian criticism has been to provide lesbians with a tradition, even if a retrospective one. Jane Rule, whose *Lesbian Images* appeared about the same time as Moers's *Literary Women*, first attempted to establish this tradition (Rule 1975). Although her text is

flawed, relying too much on biographical evidence and derivative interpretations and including some questionable writers (such as Dorothy
Baker) while omitting others, *Lesbian Images* was a milestone in lesbian
criticism. Its importance is partially suggested by the fact that it took five
years for another complete book – Faderman's – to appear on lesbian literature. In a 1976 review of *Lesbian Images*, I questioned the existence of a
lesbian "great tradition" in literature, but I now think I was wrong
(Zimmerman 1976). Along with Rule, Dolores Klaich in *Woman + Woman*
(1974) and Louise Bernikow in the introduction to *The World Split Open*
(1974) have explored the possibility of a lesbian tradition, and recent critics such as Faderman and Blanche Cook, in particular, have begun to define that tradition, who belongs to it, and what links the writers who can
be identified as lesbians. Blanche Cook's review of lesbian literature and
culture in the early twentieth century proposes "to analyze the literature
and attitudes out of which the present lesbian feminist works have
emerged, and to examine the continued denials and invalidation of the
lesbian experience" (Cook 1979:720). Focusing on the recognized lesbian
networks in France and England that included Virginia Woolf, Vita Sackville-West, Ethel Smyth, Gertrude Stein, Radclyffe Hall, Natalie Barney,
and Romaine Brooks, Cook provides an important outline of a lesbian cultural tradition and an insightful analysis of the distortions and denials of
homophobic scholars, critics, and biographers.

Lillian Faderman's *Surpassing the Love of Men*, like her earlier critical articles, ranges more widely through a literary tradition of romantic love
between women (whether or not one calls that "lesbian") from the six-
teenth to the twentieth century. Her thesis is that passionate love between
women was labeled neither abnormal nor undesirable – probably because
women were perceived to be asexual – until the sexologists led by Krafft-
Ebing and Havelock Ellis "morbidified" female friendship around 1900.
Although she does not always clarify the dialectic between idealization
and condemnation that is suggested in her text, Faderman's basic theory
is quite convincing. Most readers, like myself, will be amazed at the
wealth of information about women's same-sex love that Faderman has
uncovered. She rescues from heterosexual obscurity Mary Wollstonecraft,
Mary Wortley Montagu, Anna Seward, Sarah Orne Jewett, Edith Somer-
ville, "Michael Field," and many others, including the Scottish
schoolmistresses whose lesbian libel suit inspired Lillian Hellman's *The
Children's Hour*. Faderman has also written on the theme of same-sex love
and romantic friendship in the poems and letters of Emily Dickinson; in
novels by James, Holmes, and Longfellow; and in popular magazine fiction of the early twentieth century (Faderman 1978a, 1978b, 1978c, 1978d).

Faderman is preeminent among those critics who are attempting to establish a lesbian tradition by rereading writers of the past previously as-

sumed to be heterosexual or "spinsters." As the songwriter Holly Near expresses it: "Lady poet of great acclaim / I have been misreading you / I never knew your poems were meant for me" (Near 1976). It is in this area of lesbian scholarship that the most controversy – and some of the most exciting work – has occurred. Was Mary Wollstonecraft's passionate love for Fanny Blood, recorded in *Mary, A Fiction*, lesbian? Does Henry James dissect a lesbian relationship in *The Bostonians*? Did Emily Dickinson address many of her love poems to a woman, not a man? How did Virginia Woolf's relationships with Vita Sackville-West and Ethyl Smyth affect her literary vision? What was the nature of Alice Dunbar-Nelson's affection for other women? Not only are some lesbian critics increasingly naming such women and relationships "lesbian," but they are also suggesting that criticism cannot fail to take into account the influence of sexual and emotional orientation on literary expression.

In the establishment of a self-conscious literary tradition, certain writers have become focal points both for critics and for lesbians in general, who affirm and celebrate their identity by "naming names," establishing a sense of historical continuity and community through the knowledge that incontrovertibly great women were also lesbians. Foremost among these heroes (or "heras") are the women who created the first self-identified lesbian feminist community in Paris during the early years of the twentieth century. With Natalie Barney at its hub, this circle included such notable writers as Colette, Djuna Barnes, Radclyffe Hall, Renée Vivien, and, peripherally, Gertrude Stein. Contemporary lesbians – literary critics, historians, and lay readers – have been drawn to their mythic and myth-making presence, seeing in them a vision of lesbian society and culture that may have existed only once before on the original island of Lesbos (Klaich 1974; Harris 1973; Rubin 1976). More interest, however, has been paid to their lives so far than to their art. Barnes's portraits of decadent, tormented lesbians and homosexuals in *Nightwood* and silly, salacious ones in *The Ladies' Almanack* often prove troublesome to lesbian readers and critics (Lanser 1979). However, Elaine Marks's perceptive study of French lesbian writers (1979) traces a tradition and how it has changed, modified by circumstance and by feminism, from the Sappho of Renée Vivien to the Amazons of Monique Wittig.

The problem inherent in reading lesbian literature primarily for role-modeling is most evident with Radclyffe Hall – the most notorious of literary lesbians – whose archetypal "butch," Stephen Gordon, has troubled readers since the publication of *The Well of Loneliness*. Although one critic praises the novel as "the standard by which all subsequent similar works are measured," most contemporary lesbian feminists would, I believe, agree with Faderman's harsh condemnation of it for "helping to wreak confusion in young women" (Vincent n.d., Faderman 1978b). Such an extraliterary debate is not limited to lesbian novels and lesbian characters; I am reminded of the intense disappointment expressed by many feminists over George Eliot's disposal of Dorothea Brooke in *Middlemarch*. In both cases, the cry is the same: why haven't these writers provided us with appropriate role models? Blanche Cook may be justified in criticizing Hall for creating a narrow and debilitating image for lesbians who follow; however, Catharine Stimpson's analysis of the ironic levels of the text and Claudia Stillman Franks's demonstration that Stephen Gordon is a portrait of an artist deepen our understanding of this classic, suggesting that its hero and message are highly complex (Stimpson 1981; Franks 1982; see also Newton 1984). In looking to writers for a tradition, we need to recognize that that tradition may not always be a happy one. It encompasses Stephen Gordons alongside characters like Molly Bolt in Rita Mae Brown's *Rubyfruit Jungle*. Lesbians may also question whether or not the incarnation of a "politically correct" but elusive and utopian mythology provides our only appropriate role model.

As with Radclyffe Hall, some readers and critics have been strongly antipathetic to Gertrude Stein, citing her reactionary and antifeminist politics and her role-playing relationship with Alice B. Toklas. However, other critics, by carefully analyzing Stein's actual words, establish that she did have a lesbian and feminist perspective, calling into question assumptions about coding and masculine role-playing. Cynthia Secor, who has developed an exciting lesbian feminist interpretation of Stein, argues that her novel *Ida* attempts to discover what it means to be a female person, and that the author profited from her position on the boundaries of patriarchal society: "Stein's own experience as a lesbian gives her a critical distance that shapes her understanding of the struggle to be one's self. Her own identity is not shaped as she moves into relation with a man" (Secor 1978:99; also 1982a and 1982b). Similarly, Elizabeth Fifer points out that Stein's situation encouraged her to experiment with parody, theatricality, role-playing, and "the diversity of ways possible to look at homosexual love and at her love object" (Fifer 1979:478). Recently Fifer suggests that Stein pursued the two contradictory goals of concealment and exposure of her personal life (Fifier 1982). Deirdre Vanderlinde finds in *Three Lives* "one of the earliest attempts to find a new language in which to say, 'I, woman-loving woman, exist'" (Vanderlinde 1979:10). Catharine Stimpson places more critical emphasis on Stein's use of masculine pronouns and conventional language, but, despite what may have been her compromise, Stimpson feels that female bonding provides Stein with a private solution to a woman's mind-body split (Stimpson 1977; also Burke 1982; O'Brien 1984).

Along with Stein, Emily Dickinson's woman-identification has drawn the most attention from recent critics, and has generated considerable controversy between lesbian and other feminist critics. Faderman insists that Dickinson's love for women must be considered homosexual, and that critics must take into account her sexuality (or affectionality). Like most critics who accept this lesbian identification of Dickinson, she points to Susan Gilbert Dickinson as Emily's primary romantic and sexual passion. Both Faderman and Louise Bernikow thus argue that Dickinson's "muse" was sometimes a female figure as well as a male (Faderman 1978a; also Morris 1981). Some of this work can be justifiably criticized for too closely identifying literature with life; however, by altering our awareness of what is *possible* – namely, that Dickinson's poetry was inspired by her love for a woman – we also can transform our response to the poetry. Thus Paula Bennett daringly suggests that Dickinson's use of crumbs, jewels, pebbles, and similar objects was an attempt to create "clitoral imagery" (Bennett 1977). In a controversial paper on the subject, Nadean Bishop argues forcefully that the poet's marriage poems must be reread in light of what she considers to have been a consummated sexual relationship with her sister-in-law (Bishop 1980; see also Patterson 1951; Morris 1983).

Feminist critics working on other major literary figures, particularly the early twentieth-century modernists, increasingly uncover evidence of the impact lesbian love had on their literary production. For example, Louise DeSalvo analyzes how the love shared by Virginia Woolf and Vita Sackville-West enabled them "to look inward and backward together, to reexamine a past that was difficult for each of them to deal with alone": a process of interspection that "is preserved in the score of literary works that they wrote while they were lovers and loving friends" (DeSalvo 1982:214). Similarly, the work of Susan Friedman and Rachel Blau Duplessis explores the "sexualities" – both lesbian and heterosexual – of H.D. (Friedman and Duplessis 1981; Friedman 1983). It is becoming evident that many women writers, especially in the twentieth century, can be understood only if the critic is willing and able to adopt a lesbian point of view.

IV

The establishment of a lesbian literary tradition, a "canon," as my discussion suggests, has been the primary task of critics writing from a lesbian feminist perspective. But it is not the only task to emerge. For example, lesbian critics, like feminist critics in the early 1970s, have begun to analyze the images, stereotypes, and mythic presence of lesbians in fiction by or about lesbians. Bertha Harris, a major novelist as well as a provocative and trailblazing critic, considers the lesbian to be the prototype of the monster and "the quintessence of all that is female; and Female enraged. . . . A lesbian is . . . that which has been unspeakable about women"

(Harris 1977:7). She offers this monstrous lesbian as a female archetype who subverts traditional notions of female submissiveness, passivity, and virtue. Her "tooth-and-claw" image of the lesbian is ironically similar to that of Ellen Moers, although from a lesbian rather than heterosexual point of view. But the very fact that Moers presents the lesbian-as-monster in a derogatory context and that Harris presents it in a celebratory one suggests that there is an important dialectic between how the lesbian articulates herself and how she is articulated and objectified by others. Popular culture, in particular, exposes the objectifying purpose of the lesbian-as-monster image, such as the lesbian vampire first created by LeFanu's 1871 ghost story, "Carmilla," and revived in early 1970s "B" films, as a symbolic attack on women's struggle for self-identity (Zimmerman 1980).

Other critics too have analyzed the negative symbolic appearance of the lesbian in literature. Ann Allen Shockley, reviewing black lesbian characters in American fiction, notes that "within these works exists an undercurrent of hostility, trepidation, subtlety, shadiness, and in some instances, ignorance culling forth homophobic stereotypes" (Shockley 1979:136). Homophobic stereotypes are also what Maureen Brady and Judith Mc-Daniel find in abundance in recent commercial fiction (such as *Kinflicks, A Sea Change, Some Do,* and *How to Save Your Own Life*) by avowedly feminist novelists. Although individuals might disagree with Brady and McDaniel's severe criticism of specific novels, their overall argument is unimpeachable; contemporary feminist fiction, by perpetuating stereotyped characters and themes (such as the punishment theme so dear to prefeminist lesbian literature), serves to "disempower the lesbian" (Brady and McDaniel 1980:83). Lesbian, as well as heterosexual, writers present the lesbian as Other, as Julia Penelope Stanley discovered in prefeminist fiction: "The lesbian character creates for herself a mythology of darkness, a world in which she moves through dreams and shadows" (Stanley 1975:8). Lesbian critics may wish to avoid this analysis of the lesbian as Other because we no longer wish to dwell upon the cultural violence done against us. Yet this area must be explored until we strip these stereotypes of their inhibiting and dehumanizing presence in our popular culture and social mythology.

Lesbian critics have also delved into the area of stylistics and literary theory. If we have been silenced for centuries and speak an oppressor's tongue, then liberation for the lesbian must begin with language. Some writers may have reconciled their internal censor with their speech by writing in code, but many critics maintain that modern lesbian writers, because they are uniquely alienated from patriarchy, experiment with its literary style and form. Julia Penelope Stanley and Susan Wolfe, considering such diverse writers as Virginia Woolf, Gertrude Stein, Kate Millett and Elana Dykewoman, claim that "a feminist aesthetic, as it emerges out of women's evolution, grounds itself in female consciousness and in the unrelenting language of process and change" (Stanley and Wolfe 1978:66). In this article the authors do not call their feminist aesthetic a lesbian feminist aesthetic, although all the writers they discuss are, in fact, lesbians. Susan Wolfe later confronted this fact: "Few women who continue to identify with men can risk the male censure of 'women's style', and few escape the male perspective long enough to attempt it" (Wolfe 1978:3). Through examples from Kate Millett, Jill Johnston, and Monique Wittig, she illustrates her contention that lesbian literature is characterized by the use of the continuous present, unconventional grammar, and neologism; and that it breaks boundaries between art and the world, between events and our perceptions of them, and between past, present, and the dream world. It is, as even the proponents of this theory admit, highly debatable that all lesbian writers are modernists, or that all modernists are lesbians. If Virginia Woolf wrote in nonlinear, stream-of-consciousness style because she was a lesbian (or "woman-identified"), how does one explain Dorothy Richardson, whose *Pilgrimage*, despite one lesbian interlude, is primarily heterosexual? If both Woolf and Richardson can be called "feminist" stylists, then how does one explain the nonlinear experimentation of Joyce or Robbe-Grillet, for example?

Nevertheless, the suggestive overlap that exists between experimental writing and lesbian writing is leading to a rethinking of the literary meaning of lesbianism. If it is difficult to define authoritatively a lesbian writer or a lesbian style, it may be more fruitful to ask how lesbianism functions as a sign within the text. Bertha Harris and Barbara Smith, as discussed above, attempted to locate an inherent lesbianism in texts not intended to be read as lesbian. Many other critics are turning to the self-defined lesbian literature produced since the late 1960s, using it as a laboratory in which to explore the notions of a lesbian aesthetic, a lesbian imagery and symbolism, a lesbian ethics and epistemology.

Among the most interesting work is that being done on the French novelist and theorist Monique Wittig. Her literary project has been to shape a "lesbian writing" that locates the lesbian subject outside the male linguistic universe. Using the language and concepts of contemporary French feminism, critics have shown how Wittig attacks phallogocentrism by "overwriting" metaphors, "translating" cultural myths, and "restructuring" genres. As a writer and theorist, argues Diane Griffin Crowder, Wittig unites the realms of language and politics: "'Lesbian writing' is a tool for transforming the female subject's relation to all cultural systems which are, by definition, political" (Crowder 1983:131). In the neat conclusion to her study of *Le corps lesbien*, Namascar Shaktini defines "*Ecriture lesbienne* [as] a *coup d'écriture*" (Shaktini 1982:44; also Rosenfeld 1978; Wenzel 1981).

Other critics also demonstrate how lesbian writing transforms the traditional elements of fiction and poetry, creating new paradigms in the process. Marilyn Schuster carefully analyzes the way in which Jane Rule, a stylistically conservative novelist, subverts traditional symbols of western culture in order to tell a true story about lesbian lovers (Schuster 1981). Catherine Stimpson's historical and thematic study of the lesbian novel from the 1920s to the 1970s explores two patterns, the "dying fall" and the "enabling escape," used by lesbian novelists to respond to the stigmatization of homosexuality (Stimpson 1981:364). My own work on the lesbian novel of development illustrates a similar pattern of repression and liberation, as well as demonstrating the similarities and differences between lesbian and traditional *Bildungsroman* (Zimmerman 1983; also Gurko 1980).

Studies of lesbian poetry, in particular, suggest the emergence of a lesbian poetics. Elly Bulkin first traced the various sources of contemporary poetry and analyzed the "range of lesbian voices" (Bulkin 1978:10). Mary Carruthers, in asking why so much contemporary feminist poetry is also lesbian, observed that the "lesbian love celebrated in contemporary women's poetry requires an affirmation of the value of femaleness, women's bodies, women's sexuality – in women's language" (Carruthers 1979:301). In a more recent article, Carruthers deepens her concept of a lesbian poetics. She identifies a "distinctive movement in contemporary American poetry" that she names "Lesbian poetry" because

the "naming and defining" of this phrase is its central poetic preoccupation. These poets [Adrienne Rich, Audre Lorde, Judy Grahn, and Olga Broumas] choose to deal with life at the level of metaethics – its social, psychic, and aesthetic underpinnings, which are articulable only in myth; their metaethics takes its structure from a complex poetic image of lesbian relationship. (Carruthers 1983:293)

For these poets, love for and between women forms the basis of a "common language" replacing patriarchal discourse (see also McDaniel 1978; Diehl 1980; Clausen 1982; Libertin 1982).

Carruthers is a notable example of a critic searching out the ethical imperative of contemporary lesbian writing. Such also is the intention of Sally Gearhart and Jane Gurko, in an essay that compares the success of lesbian and gay male writers in transforming heterosexual ideology. The authors claim that, in contrast to gay male literature, lesbian literature "does express a revolutionary model of sexuality which in its structure, its content, and its practice defies the fundamental violent assumptions of patriarchal culture" (Gurko and Gearhart 1979:3). This article, admirable in many ways, also illustrates one danger inherent in the attempt to establish a lesbian vision, paradigm, or value system. In the attempt to say *this* is what defines a lesbian literature, the critic may be tempted to read selectively, omitting what is foreign to her theory. Most contemporary lesbian literature does embrace a rhetoric of nonviolence, but this is not universally true; for example M. F. Beal's *Angel Dance* and Camarin Grey's *The Winged Dancer* are hardboiled detective novels, and *Le corps lesbien* is infused with a violent eroticism that is, nevertheless, intensely antipatriarchal. Violence, role-playing, disaffection, unhappiness, suicide, and self-hatred, to name a few "taboo" subjects, all exist within lesbian culture, and a useful criticism will have to effectively analyze these as *lesbian* themes and metaphors, regardless of the dictates of ideological purity.

V

As lesbian feminist criticism has developed over a decade, it has changed, and it has changed the criticism of others. Lesbian criticism was originally influenced primarily by the politics of lesbian separatism. This position is exemplified by a statement from *Sinister Wisdom,* a journal that developed a consistent and articulate separatist politics:

"Lesbian consciousness" is really a point of view, a view from the boundary. And in a sense every time a woman draws a circle around her psyche, saying "this is a room of *my own,*" and then writes from within that "room," she's inhabiting lesbian consciousness. (Desmoines 1976:29)

The value of separatism, which has always provided the most exciting theoretical developments in lesbian ideology, is precisely this marginality: The notion that lesbians exist "on the periphery of patriarchy" (Wolfe 1978:16). Separatism has provided criticism, as it has lesbian politics, with a cutting edge and a radical energy that impels us forward rather than allowing us to slip backward from fear or complacency. Those critics who maintain a consciously chosen position on the boundaries (and not one imposed by a hostile society) help keep lesbian and feminist criticism radical and provocative. Understandably, those critics and scholars willing to identify themselves publicly as lesbians have also tended to hold radical politics of marginality. Exposing oneself to public scrutiny as a lesbian may in fact entail marginality through denial of tenure or loss of job, and those lesbians willing to risk those consequences often have a political position that justifies their risk.[2] But, increasingly, lesbian criticism has developed diversity in theory and approach, incorporating the insights of Marxist, structuralist, semiotic, and even psychoanalytic criticism. Although lesbians, perhaps more than heterosexual feminists, may mistrust systems of thought developed by and associated with men and male values, our work is in fact richer and subtler for this incorporation.

At this time, lesbian criticism and cultural theory in general must continue to grow by developing a greater specificity, historically and culturally. We have written and acted as if lesbian experience – which is perceived as that of a contemporary white middle-class feminist – is universal and unchanging. Although most lesbians know that it is not, we too often forget to apply rigorous historical and cross-cultural tools to our scholarship. Much of this ahistoricity occurs around the shifting definitions of lesbianism from one era and one culture to another. To state simply that Mary Wollstonecraft "was" a lesbian because she passionately loved Fanny Blood, or Susan B. Anthony because she wrote amorous letters to Anna Dickinson, without accounting for historical circumstances, may serve to distort or dislocate the actual meaning of these women's lives (just as it is distorting to *deny* their love for women). There are also notable differences among the institution of the *berdache* (the adoption by one sex of the opposite gender role) in Native American tribes; *faute de mieux* lesbian activity tolerated in France (as in Colette's *Claudine* novels); idyllic romantic friendships (such as that of the famous Ladies of Llangollen); and contemporary self-conscious lesbianism. It may be that there is a common structure – a lesbian "essence" – that may be located in all these specific historical existences, just as we may speak of a widespread, perhaps universal, structure of marriage or the family. However, in each of these cases – lesbianism, marriage, the family – careful attention to history teaches us that differences are as significant as similarities, and vital information about female survival may be found in the different ways in which women have responded to their historical situation. This tendency toward simplistic universalism is accompanied by what seems to me to be a dangerous development of biological determinism and a curious revival of the nineteenth-century feminist notion of female (now lesbian) moral superiority – that women are uniquely caring and superior to inherently violent males. Although only an undertone in some criticism and literature, any such sociobiological impulse should be questioned at every appearance.

The denial of meaningful differences among women is being challenged, particularly around the issue of racism. Elly Bulkin has raised criticisms about the racism of white lesbian feminist theory:

If I can put together – or think someone else can put together – a viable piece of feminist criticism or theory whose base is the thought and writing of white women/lesbians and expect that an analysis of racism can be tacked on or dealt with later as a useful addition, it is a measure of the extent to which I partake of that white privilege. (Bulkin 1980:16)

Implicit in the criticism of Bulkin and other antiracist writers is the belief that lesbians, because of our experience of stigma and exclusion from the feminist mainstream, ought to be particularly sensitive to the dynamic between oppression and oppressing. White lesbians who are concerned about eradicating racism in criticism and theory have been greatly influenced as well by the work of such black lesbian feminist literary critics as Gloria Hull, Barbara Smith, and Lorraine Bethel (see Bethel 1982; Hull 1982; Clarke et al. 1983). A similar concern is not yet present over the issue of class, although the historical association of lesbianism with upper-class values has often been used by left-wing political groups and governments to deny legitimacy to homosexual rights and needs (see Kaye 1980). Lesbian critics studying the Natalie Barney circle, for example, might analyze the historical connections between lesbianism and class status. Lesbian critics might also develop comparisons among the literatures of various nationalities, since the lesbian canon is of necessity cross-national. We have barely explored the differences among American, English, French, and German lesbian literature (although *Surpassing the Love of Men* draws some distinctions), let alone non-Western literature. Recent articles on the lesbian coding in Colette's *The Pure and the Impure,* as well as those on Wittig, suggest, however, that we may soon see a truly international lesbian literary canon (Dranch 1983; Cothran 1981).

VI

As lesbian criticism continues to mature, we may anticipate the development of ongoing and compelling political and practical concerns. At this time, for example, lesbians are still defining and discovering texts. We are certainly not as badly off as we were in the early seventies, when the only lesbian novels in print were *The Well of Loneliness,* Isabel Miller's *Patience and Sarah,* and Rita Mae Brown's *Rubyfruit Jungle.* However, texts published prior to 1970 are still difficult to find, and even *The Well of Loneliness* is intermittently available at the whim of publishers. Furthermore, the demise of Diana Press, Daughters Inc., and Persephone Press (which were among the most active lesbian publishing houses) leaves many major works unavailable, possibly forever. As the boom in gay literature subsides, teachers of literature will find it very difficult to unearth teachable texts. Scholars have the excellent Arno Press series, *Homosexuality: Lesbians and Gay Men in Society, History, and Literature,* but, as Faderman's monumental scholarship reveals, far more lesbian literature exists than anyone has suspected. This literature needs to be unearthed, analyzed, explicated, perhaps translated, and made available to readers.

As lesbian critics, we also need to address the exclusion of lesbian literature from not merely the traditional but also the feminist canon. Lesbian literature has not yet been integrated into the mainstream of feminist texts, as evidenced by what is criticized, collected, and taught. It is a matter of serious concern that lesbian literature is omitted from anthologies or included in mere token amounts, or that critical works and MLA panels still exclude lesbianism.[3] Lesbianism is still perceived as an unimportant and somewhat discomforting variation within the female life cycle, when it is perceived at all. It may as yet be possible for heterosexual feminists to claim ignorance about lesbian literature, but lesbian critics should make it impossible for that claim to stand much longer. And, just as we need to integrate lesbian material and perspectives into the traditional and feminist canons, we might also apply lesbian theory to traditional literature. Feminists have not only pointed out the sexism in many canonical works, but have also provided creative and influential rereadings of these works; lesbians might similarly contribute to rereadings. For example, *The Bostonians*, an obvious text, has been reread often from a lesbian perspective, and we could reinterpret D. H. Lawrence's antifeminism or Doris Lessings' compromised feminism (particularly in *The Golden Notebook*) by relating these to their fear of, or discomfort with, lesbianism. Other texts or selections of texts – such as Rossetti's "Goblin Market" or the relationship between Lucy Snowe and Ginevra Fanshawe in *Vilette* – might reveal a subtext that could be called lesbian. Just as few texts escape a feminist re-vision, few might evade a lesbian transformation.

This last point – that there is a way in which we might "review" literature as lesbians – brings me to my conclusion: that in a brief period of a few years critics have begun to demonstrate the existence of a distinct lesbian aesthetic, just as feminists have outlined elements of a female aesthetic. Certain components of this aesthetic or critical perspective have been suggested by Judith McDaniel:

> Lesbian feminist criticism [or literature, I would add] is a political or thematic perspective, a kind of imagination that can see beyond the barriers of heterosexuality, role stereotypes, patterns of language and culture that may be repressive to female sexuality and expression. (McDaniel 1976:2)

A lesbian artist very likely would express herself differently about sexuality, the body, and relationships. But are there other, less obvious, unifying themes, ideas, and imagery that might define a lesbian text or subtext? How, for example, does the lesbian's sense of outlaw status affect her literary vision? Might lesbian writing, because of the lesbian's position on the boundaries, be characterized by a particular sense of freedom and flexibility or, rather, by images of violently imposed barriers, the closet? Or, in fact, is there a dialectic between freedom and imprisonment that is unique to lesbian writing? Do lesbians have a special perception of suffering and stigma, as so much prefeminist literature seems to suggest? What about the "muse," the female symbol of literary creativity: do women writers create a lesbian relationship with their muse as May Sarton asserts? If so, do those writers who choose a female muse experience a freedom from inhibition because of that fact, or might there be a lack of creative tension in such a figurative same-sex relationship?

Lesbian literature may present a unified tradition of thematic concerns, such as that of unrequited longing, a longing of almost cosmic totality because the love object is denied not by circumstance or chance but by necessity. The tension between romantic love and genital sexuality takes a particular form in woman-to-woman relationships, often articulated through musings on the difference between purity and impurity (culminating in Colette's study of variant sexuality, *The Pure and the Impure*). Lesbian literature approaches the theme of development or the quest in a manner different from that of men or heterosexual women. Lesbian literature, like lesbian culture in general, is particularly flexible on issues of gender and role identification; even *The Well of Loneliness* hints at the tragedy of rigid gender roles. Because of this flexibility, lesbian artists and writers have always been fascinated with costuming, since dress is an external manifestation of gender roles that lesbians often reject (see Gubar 1981). As we read and reread literature from a lesbian perspective, I am confident we shall continue to expand our understanding of a lesbian aesthetic and literary tradition.

This chapter has suggested the vigor of lesbian criticism and its value to all feminists in raising awareness of entrenched heterosexism in existing texts, clarifying the lesbian traditions in literature through scholarship and reinterpretation, pointing out barriers that have stood in the way of free lesbian expressions, explicating the recurring themes and values of lesbian literature, and exposing the dehumanizing stereotypes of lesbians in our culture. Many of the issues that face lesbian critics – expanding the canon, creating a nonracist and nonclassist critical vision, transforming our readings of traditional texts and exploring new methodologies – are the interests of all feminist critics. Since feminism concerns itself with the removal of limitations and impediments in the way of female imagination, and lesbian criticism helps to expand our notions of what is possible for women, then all women would grow by adopting for themselves a lesbian vision. Disfranchised groups have had to adopt a double vision for survival; one of the political transformations of recent decades has been the realization that enfranchised groups – men, whites, heterosexuals, the middle class – would do well to adopt that double vision for the survival of us all. Lesbian literary criticism simply restates what feminists already know, that one group cannot name itself "humanity" or even "woman." As Adrienne Rich suggests, "We're not trying to become part of the old order misnamed 'universal' which has tabooed us; we are transforming the meaning of 'universality'" (Bulkin 1977:58).

Whether lesbian criticism will survive depends as much upon the external social climate as it does upon the creativity and skill of its practitioners. If political attacks on gay rights and freedom grow; if the so-called "moral majority" wins its fight to eliminate gay teachers and texts from the schools; and if the academy, including feminist teachers and scholars, fails to support lesbian scholars, eradicate heterosexist values and assumptions, and incorporate the insights of lesbian scholarship into the mainstream; then current lesbian criticism will probably suffer the same fate as did Jeanette Foster's *Sex Variant Women* in the fifties. Lesbian or heterosexual, we should all suffer from that loss.

NOTES

1 This survey is limited to published and unpublished essays in literary criticism that present a perspective either sympathetic to lesbianism or explicitly lesbian in orientation. It is limited to *literature* and to theoretical and scholarly articles and books (not book reviews). The sexual preference of the authors is irrelevant; this is an analysis of lesbian feminist *ideas*.

2 The National Women's Studies Association in the USA now has a "fired lesbians" caucus, not all of whom would identify themselves as separatist. The most dramatic attack on lesbians in academia occurred at California State University, Long Beach, in 1981–82, resulting in the decimation of that institution's women's studies program.

3 For example, recent anthologies such as *Shakespeare's Sisters* (Gilbert and Gubar 1979b) and *Gender and Literary Voice* (Todd 1980a) include no articles on lesbian ideas or authors. *Women's Autobiographies* (Jelinek 1980) includes four articles on writers for whom lesbianism was clearly a significant aspect of the self, but the subject is addressed only in Annette Kolodny's article on Kate Millett (1980). At many points in *The Female Hero* (Pearson and Pope 1981), lesbian texts and concepts could have deepened and extended the authors' analyses. Many important essays of the past few years (Abel 1981; Homans 1983) develop theories about such subjects as female bonding and linguistic representation that beg for some attention to lesbian texts. It is encouraging to note that lesbian criticism seems to have influenced other critics. Two notable examples are *Archetypal Patterns in Women's Fiction* (Pratt 1981) and "Soldier's Heart: Literary Men, Literary Women, and the Great War" (Gilbert 1983).

2

Anne Charles

Two Feminist Criticisms:
A Necessary Conflict?

When I use the term "lesbian feminist" in this essay, I draw on Catherine Stimpson's definition of "lesbian." Thus lesbian feminism, in my view and for the purposes of this essay, must include an erotic component, and "a lesbian feminist" may best be defined as "a woman who includes the practice of same-sex eroticism in her political, psychological, and emotional woman-identification." One may write thoughtful and sensitive criticism from virtually any critical standpoint, of course. Yet I insist that the phrase "lesbian feminist criticism" refer to critical work produced by lesbians who openly and consciously bring their lesbianism and/or lesbian feminism to bear on their critical practice.

Besides the category of "lesbian feminist criticism," I propose a "mainstream" or "nonfeminist" grouping, and a "nonlesbian and feminist" kind of criticism. I postulate these critical clusters in full recognition of the problems inherent in the formulation of unitary constructs. Concerning lesbian feminist criticism in particular, however, it might persuasively be argued that it must be constituted before it can be refined.[1]

At the end of 1986, feminist nonlesbian critic Shari Benstock published a critical examination of the lives and work of twenty-two female expatriates (thirteen of whom were lesbians) who lived on the Left Bank in Paris during the first forty years of this century. I suggest that the feminist critical response to this work, entitled *Women of the Left Bank,* coupled with a lesbian feminist analysis – particularly of Benstock's treatment of lesbians – yields demonstrable evidence of the current conflict between lesbian feminist criticism and nonlesbian and feminist criticism. An examination of the book's reviews appearing in the mainstream media (briefly defined as those publications not explicitly aligned with feminism) provides useful insights as well.

Not surprisingly, Shari Benstock's scholarly reputation and connections earned *Women of the Left Bank* several short laudatory notices from mainstream review publications, which stress Benstock's contribution to Modernist scholarship. (The critic aims to place her twenty-two woman writers on the literal and metaphorical landscape of Modernism.) Though an unnamed reviewer in *Publishers Weekly* mentions the "sexually liberated lifestyles" (61) of Benstock's subjects, the reviewers in such journals as *Choice, Library Journal,* and *The New York Times Book Review* (where the work is included as a New Paperback) altogether overlook the subject of lesbianism. Length constraints may account for this omission, though, as we know, lesbian invisibility is a commonplace in the mainstream media.

Feminist critic Linda Wagner-Martin distinguishes herself from her colleagues writing in the mainstream, however, when in *American Book Review* she prefaces her praise of Benstock's project by declaring that "the usual tactic in literary history is to smother the issue of lesbianism" (13). Though this reviewer unreservedly applauds Benstock's demonstration that lesbianism was responsible for the "psychic and emotional health" (13) and increased productivity of many woman modernists, Ronald Hayman, writing in the *Manchester Guardian Weekly,* observes that "Shari Benstock might have written a better book if she had committed herself to the view that Natalie Barney took – that lesbianism is a psychically and artistically liberating force" (21). These reviews together clearly suggest that Benstock's treatment of lesbianism in *Women of the Left Bank* is open to interpretation.

At this juncture, though, I would like to examine three mainstream reviews that demonstrate that, despite the impact of various progressive movements in the last twenty years of U.S. history, lesbophobia continues to flourish in some segments of the mainstream critical community. And Shari Benstock's *Women of the Left Bank* predictably provokes responses in this quarter. Penelope Mesic, for example, in a notice in *Booklist,* reveals not only that the subject of lesbianism may be raised in short reviews, but that it may be raised more than once. Clearly irritated by Benstock's decision to discuss lesbian lives at all, in the first sentence of the notice Mesic snidely praises the critic's "tolerance for idiosyncratic sexual conduct and belief" (380). Later the reviewer condemns the book's lack of "impartiality" in terms that express disapproval of Benstock's sympathy for certain lesbians. As in her first sentence, Mesic noticeably avoids the word *lesbian* as she somewhat gratuitously rallies to the side of Ernest Hemingway by complaining that "When women's homosexuality is discussed . . . it is with gentleness and acceptance, but when the issue of Hemingway's latent homosexuality is raised, Benstock loses her sense of perspective, becoming almost catty" (380). The cause for Ms. Mesic's concern clearly is not respect for Ernest Hemingway's sexuality; rather she is made uncomfortable by what she perceives as sympathetic treatment of lesbians.

Two longer mainstream reviews of *Women of the Left Bank,* however, are particularly noteworthy in that they use a similar and curiously contemporary strategy to undermine lesbianism. Lachlan Mackinnon's "Lesbos-sur-Seine," published in the *Times Literary Supplement*, trivializes and undercuts Benstock's lesbian subjects variously. And in response to the suggestion that lesbianism may increase artistic and work-related productivity because "women support each other well" (285),[2] Mackinnon dutifully invokes the legacy of the sexologists' pathological model of lesbianism according to which lesbian relationships, as Celia Kitzinger explains, are marked by "exploitation of the partner and the self" (106). The relationship between Gertrude Stein and Alice B. Toklas, therefore, enables Mackinnon to pontificate in this regard that "exploitation may be part of any couple's existence, whatever their sexuality" (285). Curiously, Benstock's reading of the relationship between Natalie Barney and Liane de Pougy moves Jerrold Seigel, writing in *The New Republic*, to explain in a similar vein that "lesbian love can also be a form of domination" (33).

But the critics' choices to develop their suggestions of lesbian "domination" or "exploitation" by calling forth Natalie Clifford Barney's World War II fascist sympathies set them apart from other reviewers and provide a timely lesbophobic focus. To be sure, Barney's fascist leanings are as undeniable as they are openly acknowledged by feminist critics, including Shari Benstock. But to invalidate Barney, whom Benstock has designated her principal affirmative lesbian subject, by linking fascism to lesbianism is a master stroke of distortion which calls up the sexologists' early description of lesbianism as a physical or mental illness even as it may be counted upon to evoke contemporary horror of Naziism in many audiences.

That Barney's admiration of Mussolini and support of Ezra Pound's anti-Semitic broadcasts occurred when she was in her sixties (Jay 1988:35), and that her lesbianism began to be expressed when she was in her teens or early twenties (2–3), fails to prevent Jerrold Seigel from suggesting that her "antisemitic and fascist enthusiasms" may be "the negative dimensions of Barney's lesbianism" (34). Lachlan Mackinnon explores a similar avenue of persuasion by preposterously asserting that "if fascism is the aestheticization of politics, Barney's own aesthetics may have had something to do with it. Her lesbian poems had 'external forms' which were 'traditional, even clichéd,' an aestheticization of the erotic" (285).

Seigel and Mackinnon's strategy of undermining Barney's lesbianism by introducing and developing the pathological model of lesbianism is interesting because it is indirect. Celia Kitzinger accounts for the necessity for the indirection of their reviews when she explains that "the combined efforts of second-wave feminism and Gay Liberation have been sufficiently effective that the old conceptualization of lesbianism as pathology no longer carries the credibility it commanded from the early until the middle years of this century" (43).

But Seigel and Mackinnon illustrate clearly that the pathological paradigm of lesbianism has not been eradicated from critical discourse; it has just been driven underground. In some instances it has also taken on the contemporary guises of spiritual illness manifested in the lesbian-as-sinner (evoked by the fundamentalist right in the United States) or of political illness (in the postwar United States and elsewhere) expressed as the lesbian-as-fascist. Thus the critics at once evoke moral outrage against fascist sympathizers in World War II, extend the ensuing aversion to lesbianism, and personalize or individualize the morally offensive duality by connecting it with a prominent lesbian. By deliberately channelling the reader's response in this way, Seigel and Mackinnon invite us to envision Natalie Barney's relationships in particular and lesbian relationships in general as constantly threatened by "destruction, mutual defeat, exploitation, . . . oral sadistic incorporation, [and] aggressive onslaughts . . ." (C. W. Socarides, quoted in Kitzinger, 106). In short, by way of fascism, we are returned to the paradigm of lesbianism as pathology.

That this cluster of negative characteristics must be mitigated or disguised in segments of the mainstream media may be a good sign, though some would doubtless prefer clarity over indirection, outright offensiveness over elusive innuendo. And, to the extent that the bald image of the lesbian as unnatural or sick has been rendered unacceptable in critical discourse, we may credit, among others, lesbian feminists and those nonlesbian feminist critics who have brought an awareness of lesbian feminism to popular culture and into certain academic settings. One could even argue that Shari Benstock's decision to pay so much attention to lesbians in *Women of the Left Bank* has made one small inroad in the mass of critical discourse where lesbianism is either invisible or viewed (covertly or otherwise) as pathological.

What is particularly insidious about the pathological model, however, is that it surfaces in unusual ways in the most unlikely places. And, strangely enough, the paradigm of the sick lesbian may be discovered in *Women of the Left Bank.* In fact, Shari Benstock herself introduces it in chapter 1, explaining that the Barney circle was beleaguered by a "destructive and homophobic" self-image based on the work of the sexologists and "constructed around notions of illness, perversion, inversion and paranoia" (11). Though Natalie Barney dedicated her energy to combating this image, Benstock clarifies that many lesbians of the time internalized the pathological model with unquestionably damaging results. The critic also explains that "these interpretations of homosexual character traits among women of the Paris community still persist, even among lesbian feminist critics who rightly insist on the need for reexamination of the women in this time and place" (11). Clearly Benstock has done some research; and, taken at face value, her observations seem sound and informative. One may notice a slight emphasis on lesbians and lesbian feminists accepting the pathological model instead of on those who imposed it, but as Benstock identifies "the parent culture" as the oppressor, she seems to be on solid ground.

Shari Benstock is certainly correct in pointing to the fact that, though some social scientists and other "experts" may disguise their adherence to the paradigm, it continues to operate in current culture. And, as Celia Kitzinger demonstrates, drawing her material primarily from psychologists' publications in the 1960s and 1970s, the pathological model was favored openly not too long ago. After introducing the familiar image of "the lesbian as a shadowy creature haunting a seedy twilight world and enduring a life of unmitigated misery," Kitzinger lets the experts elaborate, as they describe lesbian life as "'the very antithesis of fulfillment and happiness' ([R.] Kronemeyer, 1980...)," "'lonely, difficult and unhappy...' ([F. E.] Kenyon, 1978...)," filled with "'frustration and tragedy' ([D. J.] West, 1968...)," and marked by the "'personal confusion, anguish and fruitless search for love which may be the products of maldevelopment' ([B. M.] Pattison, 1974)." Though C. W. Socarides touches on Freudianism when he affirms that "'agony, sorrow, tragedy, fear and guilt of both unconscious and conscious nature... pervades the homosexual's life' (1972)," and M. E. Romm employs a faint political nuance by observing of lesbians and gay men that "'the label "gay" behind which they hide is a defense mechanism against the emptiness, the coldness and the futility of their lives' (1965)" (Kitzinger, 100), the pattern that underlies all of these descriptions may be clearly observed.

Benstock again evokes pathology in describing women who failed to adopt "the Barney-Flanner model of lesbian behavior," which, she explains, "constituted a minority opinion among homosexual women of the Left Bank community, most of whom demonstrated that they had internalized both homophobia and misogyny" (115). The critic further informs us that Natalie Barney's efforts "to reverse the effects of self hatred" (292) among lesbians failed because though Barney's "life is distinguished by a remarkable emotional maturity and the absence of self destructive impulses... she was surrounded by women who turned against themselves..." (292).

Clearly Benstock sets up a polarity here, which she encapsulates under the heading "Lesbos Divided" (306). As Shari Benstock sees it, one kind of Left Bank lesbian (in the minority) is represented by Natalie Barney and Janet Flanner, and the other is represented by Radclyffe Hall and, to a lesser extent, Gertrude Stein. Of the relations between the most symbolic of each pair Benstock reports that "Barney was put off by Hall's assumed identity as 'John,' an image of denied womanhood that Barney both pitied and despised" (307).

Though Benstock's treatment of women in the Stein/Hall camp ultimately raises serious questions about the critic's own attitude toward
these women, one can also sense trouble from the very beginning when
Benstock declares in chapter 1 that

Barney herself objected to modes of lesbian behavior that seemed to confirm the
scientific theories then prevalent. In particular, she objected to any form of dress or
behavior that suggested homosexual women were really men trapped in women's
bodies. Therefore, she objected to cross-dressing, to the anger, the self indulgence,
and self pity that marked the behavior of many of her friends and to the need to
mime the male in dress, speech and demeanor. (11)

If Benstock's language in this passage implies that she shares Barney's
objections to cross-dressing, suspicions increase in the Stein/Toklas chapter as the critic explains that "female cross-dressing was indeed the mark
of self-contempt" (180), or that "photographs and self-portraits by such
Paris artists as Frida Kahlo and Romaine Brooks affirm the self-contemp-
tuous psychological subterrain supporting cross-dressing" (181). But it is
in the discussion of Romaine Brooks's portraits of women dressed in
men's clothing in the Natalie Barney chapter that Benstock really begins
to sound like proponents of the pathological paradigm: "The portraits expose devastating self-divisions presumably hidden by external poses, at-
testing to rather than disguising the divided psyche" (305). Of Brooks's
subjects' choice of dress, Benstock asserts that while cross-dressing may
free women, it also, and here the critic quotes Susan Gubar, "expresses the
mutilation inextricably related to inversion when it is experienced as perversion" (305). Alleging that the painter herself suffered "the effects of
self-division," and explaining that "in Brooks's work . . . the portrait reveals the painful results of self-castration," Benstock returns to the polarity that seems to dominate her thinking about lesbianism and avers that
"under Brooks's observant eye, these women no longer represent
Barney's notion of the ideal of feminine beauty, but rather betray that
ideal by choosing male costuming in which to cloak the effects of psychic
castration" (305).

Critical feminist and lesbian feminist readers might pause at this juncture to reflect on "the ideal of feminine beauty," which Benstock seems at
points to endorse as a favorable alternative to enactment of a "mannish"
lesbian role. Clearly this precept at once enforces sex-role stereotyping
and imprisons women in the narrow and destructive cultural expectation
of "how they should look" and act. And, as in *Women of the Left Bank*, implicit approval of this ideal is often accompanied by rejection of the dress
and behavior of "mannish" lesbians. In fact, Celia Kitzinger points to the
pervasiveness and contemporaneity of this connection by describing con-

demnation or insensitivity toward "mannish" lesbians as "one of the manifestations of the widespread and reactionary acceptance of male-defined 'femininity', rife in lesbian and feminist communities as well as in society generally . . ." (147).[3]

The corollary implication of this adherence to what Sue-Ellen Case calls "the heterosexist cleavage of sexual difference" (298) is that women conventionally considered "feminine" be approved and integrated into the larger feminist or cultural community. This gesture replicates heterosexual roles, of course, by validating the traditional dress and passivity conventionally associated with the "femme" role in lesbian relations and the "feminine" in heterosexual ideology. In addition, because "butch" lesbians in the dominant culture often represent lesbian resistance, and because the "butch-femme" dyad often signals lesbian sexuality, the simultaneous erasure or invalidation of the "butch" and affirmation of the "femme" lesbian participates in the twin suppression of lesbian autonomy and sexuality, a suppression that is one cause of the conflict I propose.

Of course signs of Shari Benstock's feminism surface throughout *Women of the Left Bank*. Her apparent endorsement of "the feminine" in discussions of cross-dressing, for example, is mitigated by other passages in the book where she seems to recognize the destructive potential of the concept. Similarly Benstock identifies the source of the link between "butch" lesbians and pathology as in the larger cultural environment rather than within the women themselves. But the question of origins concerning "butches" ultimately blurs in *Women of the Left Bank* as Benstock seems to shift her disapproval from what she sees as the negative behavioral and psychological features of cross-dressing to its practitioners. And, in her brief characterization of the Marquise de Belbeuf, the critic's prejudices inescapably manifest themselves as she blames the experience of lesbophobia not on those who perpetuated it, but on the marquise herself. Benstock declares:

Some prominent women . . . openly invited censure. The Marquise de Belbeuf became an object for woman haters, who considered her perverse and degenerate. Adopting male dress and forms of behavior, the marquise reversed the premises by which patriarchal society functioned, assuming for herself male privilege and power. Antagonizing influential elements of belle époque society, she put herself at risk. (48)

Feminists and lesbian feminists have heard this argument before. It is surprising and disturbing, nevertheless, to find the familiar tactic of blaming the object of oppression applied to a woman and appearing in the pages of a book of feminist literary criticism.

In a later discussion of the marquise, Shari Benstock seems to draw directly from Havelock Ellis's *Sexual Inversion,* in which, as Lillian Faderman (1981) clarifies,

Ellis established the mystique of the "true lesbian," a mystique which was subsequently accepted by many lesbians themselves who then became transvestites and "butches" because such behavior demonstrated ipso facto that they were the genuine article, that they must be taken seriously and not forced into heterosexual patterns. (244–5)

Benstock personalizes Ellis's paradigm and adds her own charges as she observes of the marquise that "her lesbianism was *real,* and she derided bourgeois society by making a burlesque of male dress and mannerisms. (She did to men what dandies did to women in hateful mockery)" (84; emphasis added). I have noted elsewhere that Benstock's parenthetical equation dismisses power imbalances between men and women and, therefore, as in all equations between differently empowered groups, is facile and highly suspect (Charles 1987:26). But what emerges at this point is the simple fact that Shari Benstock disapproves of and is made uncomfortable by those she perceives as "mannish" lesbians. In her treatment of the Marquise de Belbeuf and elsewhere, disapproval and discomfort slide into dislike and distortion. And there is no room for dislike and distortion in any treatment of any lesbian in any critical work.

One may argue somewhat persuasively that it is simply a problem of word choice or failure to distance oneself from lesbophobic sources. Certainly the text is peppered with unproblematized locutions like "Paris may have been tolerant of deviance" (47) or, of Barney, "Her 'emancipation' is evidenced by her blatant lesbianism" (271). And, though Benstock does acknowledge the lesbophobia of Susan Gubar's "Blessings in Disguise," for example, at some points in the book she seems to rely uncritically on Gubar's essay and simply reproduces the latter critic's prejudices through unproblematized direct quotation.

But these difficulties, of course, point to the larger problem in *Women of the Left Bank,* which emerges most clearly when Benstock's acknowledgment that the sick lesbian is a socially constructed and enforced stereotype pales against the unmediated reproduction and repetition of the pathological image of the "mannish" lesbian. In other words, Shari Benstock's personal prejudices against "butch" lesbians distort her treatment of these women in *Women of the Left Bank* and ultimately reaffirm the stereotype of the sick lesbian.

Writing in *History,* reviewer Francis Hartigan praises Shari Benstock's book and presents her credentials in the following terms:

Benstock handles her subject [lesbianism] well because as an established scholar of twentieth-century literature (particularly of James Joyce who was also an expatriate in Paris in this era), as editor of the *Tulsa Studies in Women's Literature,* and as former director of the Center for the Study of Women's Literature at Tulsa, she is well versed in literary, historical and feminist issues. (152)

The immediate question Hartigan's appraisal provokes at this juncture is "How can such a prominent feminist have written a lesbophobic book?"

Unfortunately feminist critical response to *Women of the Left Bank* fails to shed any light on this matter. In fact, the reviews of the book seem to reenact the lesbian/nonlesbian dichotomy, which appears in feminist criticism more than many of us would like to admit. Predictably, then, the only feminists who address the issue of lesbophobia of *Women of the Left Bank* are lesbian feminists.

In a short review in the *Gay Studies Newsletter,* I encapsulate the above analysis of Benstock's book and observe that the critic also expresses the popular lesbophobic discomfort with and disassociation from lesbian separatists, thus expanding her personal category of "unacceptable lesbians" (26). And Frances Doughty in *The Women's Review of Books* places Benstock's book in the context of critical and social history as she wryly and accurately observes of Benstock's treatment of "mannish" lesbians that "The mainstream's appropriation of an outgroup's experience by renaming and redefining it away from them is a form of oppression that feminists are not automatically incapable of committing" (7).

Doughty points to the division in feminist criticism of which Benstock's book is a manifestation, by noting that "A whole debate is developing among feminist scholars about – what? Basically, to put it in lesbian terms, I think it is about butches. But the discussion goes on with no reference to or understanding of what lesbian roles are or were or what they are about" (7). Doughty's language here deliberately disassociates her as a lesbian from the kind of feminist scholarship she describes.

I submit that this disavowal is a clear manifestation of the ongoing conflict between lesbian feminist criticism and nonlesbian and feminist criticism. In this case, Shari Benstock's insensitivity to the group of lesbians she considers effectively alienates those lesbian and alert nonlesbian readers who recognize lesbophobia even if accompanied by praise of a certain kind of lesbian. Doughty's remarks also suggest directly that Benstock's failings in this regard are common in feminist criticism.

Regrettably the nonlesbian feminist reviewers of *Women of the Left Bank* tend to confirm Doughty's implication that feminist and nonlesbian criticism fails to address the concerns of lesbian readers. Prominent feminist nonlesbian Nina Baym, writing in *American Literature,* for example, effusively applauds Benstock's "magnificent study" and exclaims:

Superbly crafted, at once painstaking and daring, this book will make it impossible to consider Modernism henceforth apart from the important and problematic work of such American women as Gertrude Stein, H. D., Mina Loy, and Djuna Barnes as well as the various contributions of Sylvia Beach, Natalie Barney and others. (473)

After approximately four pages of this kind of praise, Baym concludes, "The book is an inspiration, setting a standard for literary history and feminist criticism that will be difficult to surpass" (475). That Nina Baym fails to betray any hint of Benstock's lesbophobia in the book leads one to conclude that Baym either doesn't see it (a disappointment in itself) or that she shares it.

Harriet S. Chessman, however, writing in *Tulsa Studies in Women's Literature,* seems to respond directly to Frances Doughty's concerns when she affirms with almost partisan specificity that:

In particular she [Benstock] treats with boldness and sensitivity the issue of lesbianism, taking care to situate her interpretation of different lesbian modes within historically shifting cultural understandings (or misunderstandings) of homosexuality in the first half of the twentieth century. She offers valuable analyses of the intersections between different forms of lesbian experience. . . . (347–48)

I suggest that these four reviews illustrate rather schematically the conflict between lesbian feminist criticism and nonlesbian feminist criticism.

The positioning of each pair of critics gives credence to Susan Krieger's assertion that lesbians have "an important sensitivity to offer" (108), and seems to affirm the concomitant charge that nonlesbian feminists are ignoring the fruits of this sensitivity. That our attitudes need not be based solely on direct experience is demonstrated by examples of distinguished, perceptive, and respectful critical treatment of lesbian lives and work by nonlesbian feminist scholars. Similarly, of course, lesbian feminists are as diverse as any other group and need not have any particular sensitivity to anything.

Nevertheless, what lesbians have in common is being the targets of lesbophobia, a prejudice which, as we know, crosses class and race lines and national boundaries. What U.S. feminists who identify themselves as lesbian are likely to have in common is some kind of political analysis of lesbophobia. I submit that had Shari Benstock shared her work with even a small range of thoughtful and candid lesbian feminist critics, she would have been alerted to her visible problem with "butches" in the book. But my strong suspicion is that Shari Benstock did not consult many lesbians when she was writing *Women of the Left Bank*. And, quite frankly, the arrogance of that oversight angers me.

Until feminists who are not lesbians express a clear willingness to work to eradicate lesbophobic patterns and stereotypes in their own work as well as in the work of others, their criticism will foster the kind of isolation, exclusion, and distortion that violates the fundamental premises on which nonlesbian and lesbian feminism rests. Nonlesbian feminists must be particularly rigorous in identifying and resisting heterosexist notions in themselves because, as Shari Benstock shows in *Women of the Left Bank*, reading all the books is not enough.

NOTES

A version of this paper was delivered at the annual meeting of the Modern Language Association in December 1988. While many people helped me from conception to completion of this article, I would like to thank, in particular, Elaine Marks, Jane Vanderbosch, Patricia O'Hara, and Ann Pooler for generously sharing comments and criticisms.

1 My thanks to Ellen Berry for this last insight.
2 Gillian Hanscombe and Virginia L. Smyers make this assertion in *Writing for Their Lives* (Boston: Northeastern, 1987).
3 Clearly the term *mannish* as it links autonomous women and men is entirely inappropriate. Similarly, the use of this adjective to describe anything about a woman is, of course, derogatory.

3

Marilyn R. Farwell

Toward a Definition of the Lesbian
Literary Imagination

In a review of Adrienne Rich's *Diving into the Wreck,* Margaret Atwood claims that "it is not enough to state the truth; it must be imaged, imagined."[1] Contemporary women writers have waged a war of images in order to define an autonomous female imagination, and in the process they have questioned traditional literary images and offered radical re-evaluations of the creative act. Women writers have chosen images and metaphors that have ranged from demon and sickness – images that evince the conflict and turmoil surrounding the woman's effort to create – to mother and androgyne – images designed to affirm and empower the creative woman. Some writers, such as Adrienne Rich and Monique Wittig, have recently proposed lesbian as the latest metaphor for female creativity.[2] Although no little controversy surrounds a female creativity vested in lesbian sexuality, feminist theorists from different and sometimes opposing philosophical traditions have suggested and developed this metaphor as a positive, utopian image of woman's creativity.

Traditionally and fundamentally, Western metaphors for creativity present images – lover, androgyne, or mother – that exclude lesbian sexuality by privileging heterosexuality in assuming an analogy between creative production and reproduction. *Lesbian* is one of the few words in our language, if not the only one, that privileges female sexuality. For a cultural tradition that identifies sexual energy with creativity, then, lesbian as a metaphor is crucial to the redefinition of female autonomy and creativity, and although contemporary definitions of *lesbian* at times seem at odds, feminist theorists have begun to evolve a complex, problematic, and yet flexible image that both deconstructs the heterosexual pattern for creativity and creates a space for redefining the relationship of the woman writer to other women writers, to readers, and to the text.

Although contemporary feminist writers are not the first to connect lesbian with creativity – for example, Virginia Woolf, in a letter to Ethel Smyth, writes, "Women alone stir my imagination" – current feminist theory forges parameters and introduces problems not central to the earlier uses of the idea.[3] In the most well-known metaphoric use of *lesbian,* Rich claims that the woman who is self-defined, the lesbian, differs from the female who is constructed by the patriarchy, the "dutiful daughter." She ascribes creativity to this reified lesbian only: "It is the lesbian in us who is creative, for the dutiful daughter of the fathers in us is only a hack."[4] The controversy that ensued over Rich's definition and over other generalized, less sexually dependent definitions from writers such as Lillian Faderman, Blanche Wiesen Cook, and Bertha Harris involved many of the major issues of contemporary feminism.[5] Lesbian as metaphor, it was argued, ignored specificity, subsuming racial and historical differences among women; or, in our contemporary philosophical vocabulary, *lesbian* writ large essentialized and ahistoricized lesbian and female existence. On this basis, some theorists criticized Rich's later proposal of the phrase "lesbian continuum," which she described as the "primary intensity between and among women" existing at various stages in women's lives and at various times throughout history.[6] A number of literary critics also objected to a generalized metaphoric definition: Bonnie Zimmerman, for instance, called it reductionist; Gloria Bowles argued that the term was too general; and Catharine R. Stimpson derided it as "a fancily labelled metaphor."[7] In the early debate, straight women feared that naming female creativity *lesbian* meant that only lesbians could be creative. In one telling example, a prominent woman poet, upon hearing a paper on Rich's definition of lesbian, objected to the connection between lesbian and creativity because she "liked men." Alicia Ostriker simply termed it the "Lesbian Imperative."[8] But lesbians also objected out of the fear that any metaphoric definition of the word would negate the uniqueness of lesbian existence in which women relate to women sexually and form communities around this choice. Not acknowledging sexuality as the core of the definition of lesbian was, for some lesbians, missing the point. One lesbian, in response to Rich's definition of the "lesbian in us," said that if the word *lesbian* was going to be used in such a general way, she wanted another term for women who physically love other women.[9] As if to seal the coffin of a dangerous idea, Elaine Showalter recently claimed the end of an era: "By the 1980s, the lesbian aesthetic had differentiated itself from the female aesthetic . . . and the figure of the mother replaced that of the Amazon for theorists of the female aesthetic."[10]

Despite these objections, the development and exploration of this idea have continued in the pages of contemporary feminist theory, fiction, poetry, and criticism, with writers like Judy Grahn, Monique Wittig, and Alice Walker expanding and deepening the metaphoric meaning, agreeing and disagreeing over the definition of *lesbian*, and, in the attempt to refine the metaphor, addressing some of the main objections to the term.[11] In fact, Bonnie Zimmerman, in her comprehensive essay on lesbian criticism, claims that definition is now the primary concern of lesbian feminist criticism.[12] The parameters of this debate can be found in differences among feminist theorists, particularly in the debates between those who wish to name a new feminist reality and those who insist on the centrality of deconstructing the old patriarchal reality. Those feminists influenced by French theories of language argue that only opposition is possible within a language determined by a structure in which male is the subject and the center, female is the other and the marginal. Thus, Rachel Blau DuPlessis, citing and echoing Margaret Homan's earlier objection to Adrienne Rich's essentializing, claims that Rich's use of *lesbian* is effective only when "oppositional."[13] American black feminist critic Barbara Smith also sees the use of lesbian as oppositional when she calls Toni Morrison's novel *Sula* lesbian, not because of any lesbian characters but because of a political perspective critical of heterosexual institutions.[14] Monique Wittig has most fully developed the definition of the lesbian as "not-woman," economically, politically, or ideologically.[15] On the other side stand those writers – primarily American radical feminists – who affirm the need for women to rename ourselves, to define what is essential to being female. In this context the metaphoric lesbian becomes what Rich calls the creative element in all women or what Judy Grahn declares is "by extension, every woman."[16] Adrienne Rich most fully represents this philosophical position in her prose writings of the late 1970s, when she ascribed to words like *androgyne, mother,* and, finally, *lesbian* the power to rename and therefore reclaim female experience.

Both theories of lesbian as metaphor accept as vital the notion that *lesbian* is a word sufficient and necessary to describe the autonomous and creative woman. Thus both approaches can be placed in the long history of Western metaphors that connect sexual energy to imaginative creativity. In this context the problems and possibilities for the metaphoric meaning of *lesbian* can best be described in a phrase that Adrienne Rich uses to denote truth: "increasing complexity."[17]

The Western tradition offers two important sexual, and distinctly heterosexual, images of creativity – lover and androgyne – which women writers at various times have attempted to appropriate, usually unsuccessfully, for their own use. In these two metaphors, male sexuality is privileged as the source of reproduction; the female functions as the other to male subjectivity and as the margin to the male center. She is only a means to an end, for in this union of opposites woman becomes the means to man's ecstatic transcendence of the material and contingent world, a transcendence that is rooted in the male orgasm and metaphorically replicated in his poetic inspiration. Male sexuality, then, is central to the creative process because it is the only sexuality acknowledged in the heterosexual paradigm. In the Western images of androgyne and lover, then, the metaphoric union of male and female qualities – of soul and body, intellect and emotion, idea and matter – requires the absorption by the male of the female and the qualities that she represents.

Men have long assumed that their sex alone could create. Aristotle set the stage for centuries of biological and eventually symbolic theory which credits the male alone with the powers of reproduction by arguing that the semen contains the principle of motion, the potentiality as well as the actuality of the soul. The female contribution is relegated to inert matter.[18] This identification of maleness with the powers of creativity mirrors the theology that has dominated Western culture: a male god who creates the world through his own powers. Male poets and theorists have claimed even this for themselves. For Renaissance theorist J. C. Scaliger, the poet "transforms himself almost into a second deity," an idea also taken up by the better-known Renaissance critic, Sir Philip Sidney.[19] For the central Romantic theorist, S. T. Coleridge, imagination became the "repetition in the finite mind of the eternal act of creation in the infinite *I am*."[20] Creativity, reproduction, and god are collapsed into a single expression of man's identity.

Virginia Woolf was not the first to suggest that androgyny as a balance of gender opposites, a kind of psychological intercourse, best describes the fertile imagination. With a nod to Coleridge, Woolf sketches the powers that form the "fully fertilised" soul: "If one is a man, still the woman part of the brain must have effect; and a woman also must have intercourse with the man in her."[21] Woolf's use of the word "intercourse" in reference to woman's internal relation with her "male" side suggests an ambivalence about androgyny indicative of contemporary feminist debates.[22] In the historical paradigm, one that influenced much philosophical and theological thinking from Plato to Carl Jung, androgyny is a combination of male and female qualities that devalues the female. The female most often represents those qualities that need to be controlled – emotion, darkness, desire, intuition – and the result is a paradigm that focuses on male control of the dangerous side of human nature. Gerrard Winstanley, a seventeenth-century radical, defines the value system inherent in this juxtaposition of male and female principles when he describes the original fall from androgynous perfection as a time when "man" was "led by the powers of the curse in flesh, which is the *Feminine* part; not by the power of the righteous Spirit which is Christ, the *Masculine* power."[23] Carl Jung's notion of androgynous behavior is the male who, in touch with his anima, opens up to his creative side, or a female who, in touch with her animus, becomes an opinionated woman.[24] Androgyny brings creativity to men, but its benefits for women are less clear. Sally B. Allen and Joanna Hubbs have noted that the androgynous union of male and female in a seventeenth-century alchemical theory was "achieved by denying the independent status of the feminine and by containing and arrogating her creative powers."[25] By using a sexual metaphor that implies transcendence of dualism and the concomitant transcendence of the female, androgyny describes an imagination located in male subjectivity and sexuality, an imagination that is as a result free from gender and presumably from other contingencies – history, class, and race. This metaphor positions the imagination as an essence that is bound by nothing in material existence. It claims for the Western man the exclusive centrality of his consciousness. This realization led writers like Adrienne Rich to reject androgyny as a model for female wholeness, for as Rich concludes, "The very structure of the word replicates the sexual dichotomy and the priority of *andros* (male) over *gyne* (female)."[26]

The notion of male centrality also pervades the metaphor of the poet as lover. This image, like that of the androgyne, has historically been associated with the poet's muse. In Mary K. DeShazer's analysis of the concept of the muse in Western literature, she identifies three types of muses: the sexual, the spiritual, and the natural, each linking the poet to a primary force. In each case, DeShazer maintains, "the active male engenders his poetry upon the body of a passive female muse."[27] In the courtly and Petrarchan love poems of the Middle Ages and Renaissance that founded this tradition, the poet/lover is almost always identified as male. He is active and creative; he is the one who speaks. The female, the beloved, is acted upon, her usual response to the ardent declarations of her lover being "no." This answer is not an expression of her own sexual choice, but, rather, it is an expression of woman's symbolic function vis-à-vis men: to help the poet transcend the lower world of change and physicality by reminding him that the real object of his sexual passion is his own creativity. Frederick Goldin, in an aptly titled book on courtly love, *The Mirror of Narcissus,* describes the lady of these poets as "the localization of the ideal," the mirror by which the poet learns to know and love heavenly perfection.[28] Feminist critics see the image of woman as mirror for male imagination as more self-serving than does Goldin.[29] The woman remains a means by which the male completes his quest, not a lover with her own sexual/spiritual needs. In many of these poems the pains of the lover are articulated in great detail, but little is said about the lady. In Petrarchan poetry the lover is a ship tossed at sea, a heart wounded by an arrow, an actor on a stage; the lady is at best described in idealistic physical detail and at worst as the cause of all of the poet's pain. In a standard example, the sixteenth-century poet Thomas Wyatt describes the lover's turmoil: "I find no peace, and all my war is done. / I fear and hope, I burn, and freeze like ice." The poem continues in this vein for thirteen of its fourteen lines, leaving the last line for the beloved: "And my delight is causer of this strife."[30]

The connection of sexuality with imaginative creativity is paramount to this tradition. The muse of these poems, partly because she refuses physical sex, inspires the poet to write. It is here that the heterosexual paradigm is most obvious, for in communing on a symbolic sexual level with the absent, objectified "other," the poet must absorb the obviously female creative function of reproduction. In order to complete the metaphor, he not only expends his seed on an object, but he also bears the fruit: in other words he has a self-sufficient power to create. This tradition can still be found in modern writers, most obviously in Robert Graves's *The White Goddess*.[31] The contemporary male poet can invoke the muse – whether a real woman or a mythical figure – and thereby claim a creativity based on a notion of heterosexual coupling as a catalyst for *his* offspring. However, when a writer like May Sarton attempts to adopt the poet-as-lover imagery to describe a woman's creativity, as she did in *Mrs. Stevens Hears the Mermaids Singing*, she is forced into the same center/margin linguistic rules – the male as creator, the female as inspirer. Sarton's key statement on the woman writer is thus disappointing: "The crucial question seems to me to be this: what is the *source* of creativity in the woman who wants to be an artist? After all, admit it, a woman is meant to create children not works of art – that's what she has been engined to do, so to speak. A man with a talent does what is expected of him, makes his way. . . . It's the natural order of things that he construct objects outside himself and his family. The woman who does so is aberrant."[32] In this symbolic world, woman, who does not have a sexuality beyond reproduction and therefore does not have creative energy except in relation to man, cannot name her creativity with impunity.

Another common patriarchal metaphor for imaginative creativity is mother, a seemingly ironic metaphor in light of the above images that claim male sexuality as central to creativity. Yet mother is related to the above metaphors because in androgyne and lover the male who creates by himself, in effect, becomes a mother by absorbing the female power to create. In this confusion and appropriation of all gender roles, the androgyne and lover become pregnant and deliver their creative product through the impregnating inspiration of the female other. Mother, then, is related to these two heterosexual metaphors, for although it lacks the connection between ecstatic love and inspiration, it does follow the heterosexual model that associates reproduction with imaginative production. At the same time, it is essential for understanding the development of lesbian as a metaphor. Men have often found motherhood and pregnancy viable transcriptions of imaginative creativity, and women have found these images more congenial, on the surface, than other sexual images for creation. Tillie Olsen, commenting on Balzac's appropriation of pregnancy and motherhood as a description of his creative activity, agrees at first that "in intelligent passionate motherhood there are similarities, and in more than the toil and patience," for, she continues, motherhood, as does art, demands one's "total capacities."[33] Nonetheless, the fact is that this image, like lover and androgyne, has more often excluded rather than included women; for the very power to bear children has been an argument against women's ability to create books, as if physical labor precludes mental muscle. The male fascination with this metaphor is merely an extension of the absorption of the female that takes place in the images of androgyne and lover.

Women writers have exhibited a strong and ambivalent relationship to the image of the mother as one who both creates – births – and nurtures an imaginative product. Olsen ultimately finds the image absurd because, having experienced motherhood, she does not romanticize it; in fact, in the end, she sees otherhood as the antithesis of imagination.[34] Monique Wittig, as we shall see, refuses any idealization of mother because it is motherhood that domesticated the energies of the "lesbian peoples."[35] Others have found the image more compatible: Domna Stanton claims that French feminists Hélène Cixous, Luce Irigaray, and Julia Kristeva currently use the image of the mother to encapsulate the ideal female.[36] Two important American radical feminists, however, have used as a stepping-stone to their theories of lesbian the image of mother. Early in her feminist theorizing, Adrienne Rich suggests that a connecting rather than a separating of physical and imaginative creativity could "tell us, among many other things, more about the physical capacity for gestation and nourishment of infants and how it relates to psychological gestation and nurture as an intellectual and creative force."[37] Audre Lorde also forges a maternal definition of creativity when she answers Adrienne Rich's interview question, "who is the poet?" Lorde replies, "The Black mother who is the poet exists in every one of us."[38] The argument that valorizes and essentializes this natural female function was prominent in American radical feminist thought of the 1970s because the image seemed to claim for women their own power in birth, to declare its connection to the power of nature to reproduce itself, and to insist on taking back women's fecundity.

This image has become less palatable for many radical feminists because, within the context of the present symbolic system, to claim the female power to give birth is to acquiesce to assumptions that have traditionally colonized women: all women must become mothers inseminated by men to bear sons. An idealization of the mother, the reification of physical birth and gestation, was quickly dropped by most American radical feminists, as they began to develop a different idea of the mother as a stepping-stone to the less co-opted image of lesbian. In their definition of lesbian, mother is divested of male control and defined not primarily by the act of giving birth but by her relationship to the daughter. The lesbian is the woman who returns to the girl's original love for a woman, her mother, the fulfillment of which Freud denied the girl – although not the boy – but which the lesbian affirms as possible.

Lesbian as a metaphor for female creativity is unlike heterosexual images because it refuses the transcendence and reproduction model that informs the heterosexual connection between sexuality and creativity. At the same time it remains within the tradition that highlights sexuality as the core of creativity, but because it privileges a female sexuality that does not need or want male energy, it radically revises the symbolic order. For a woman to claim a sexuality and therefore a subjectivity of her own, outside of male influence or control, defies the symbology of the Western tradition. As a metaphor for creativity, lesbian also refuses many of the elements essential to the connection between heterosexuality and creativity: dualism, transcendence, ecstasy, reproduction, and a product. Instead it emphasizes the autonomy of the creative self, the community of readers and writers, and the diffuse physicality of the creative act and of the text itself. The shift in emphasis is crucial.

As a metaphor, lesbian, like the other metaphors, trades on both similarities and differences between tenor and vehicle. As a metaphor, lesbian must be held separate from actual women who form relationships and communities outside of and in resistance to the patriarchy; at the same time, it depends on abstractions from these experiences, sometimes on idealizations of these experiences. In abstracting from the literal experience, the metaphor gains a wider range of meaning but loses specificity and, of course, loses some connection with its source – lesbians. A woman who is a lesbian, then, may not necessarily be a metaphoric lesbian, as Mary Daly says when she dissociates female homosexuals who give "their allegiance to men and male myths" from women who have "rejected false loyalties to men on all levels."[39] From this perspective Adrienne Rich claims that "even before I wholly knew I was a lesbian, it was the lesbian in me who pursued that elusive configuration. . . . It is the lesbian in us who drives us to feel imaginatively, render in language, grasp, the full connection between woman and woman."[40] What is called lesbian does not depend on women loving women genitally but, rather, on the presence and attention of women to other women that is analogous to the act of loving sexually another like oneself. In fact, words like *pres-*

ence, attention, and *sight* are used more often to describe this metaphoric lesbian. While this process of abstraction has indeed been the source of much critical debate, my argument is that the word does not lose its power merely because it abstracts from lesbian experience. Instead, it functions on the symbolic level analogously to the human being who defines herself sexually as a lesbian: it stands as a disruption of the Western tradition that portrays the female and her imagination as marginal.

In her writings of the late 1970s, Rich describes the lesbian as that core of self-knowledge, power, and creativity that is potentially in all women. For many reasons, critics have shied away from a full description of Rich's development of this idea,[41] and Rich herself now disagrees with this early radical feminist formula for female identity because it does not encompass the "simultaneity of oppressions" women encounter.[42] Yet her exploration of the topic in the late 1970s remains central to any discussion of it. For Rich, the lesbian is she who, in defiance of male linguistic and social hegemony, separates herself from male constructions – Rich's "dutiful daughter" – and discovers in herself the truly unfettered woman. Lesbian, she states, "was nothing so simple and dismissible as the fact that two women might go to bed together. It was a sense of desiring oneself; above all, of choosing oneself."[43] For the poet, this choice of self opens the window on a revised notion of creativity. In her insightful essay on the metaphoric lesbian, Mary J. Carruthers groups Rich with other poets – Audre Lorde, Judy Grahn, and Olga Broumas – who remythologize lesbian as a way of "seeing the poet in the woman, not as alien or monstrous, but as an aspect of her womanhood."[44]

But Rich's distinction between physical sex and self-affirmation does not eliminate sexuality from the metaphor. Sexuality becomes self-knowledge and power because it is redefined as a diffuse and omnipresent energy, not as orgasmic sexuality associated with transcendence. Audre Lorde defines the erotic in this largest possible sense: "When I speak of the erotic, then, I speak of its as an assertion of the lifeforce of women; of that creative energy empowered, the knowledge and use of which we are now reclaiming in our language, our history, our dancing, our loving, our work, our lives."[45] Rich alludes to this statement in her discussion of the "lesbian continuum" when she defines the lesbian as not only she who says "no" to the patriarchy but also she who discovers the "erotic in female terms," the erotic as a diffuse and omnipresent energy "unconfined to any single part of the body or solely to the body itself."[46] The nature of this energy is often described in terms of women's attention to one another, their presence to one another, their sight of one another in a world where women's attention and presence are compelled, sometimes by force, to focus on men. In this awareness of self and the attention to another like the self, eroticism flourishes, as feminist philosopher Marilyn

Frye notes: "When one's attention is on something, one is present in a particular way to that thing. This presence is, among other things, an element of erotic presence."[47] It is this omnipresent energy, this attention to another rather than an orgiastic experience of transcendence that explains the metaphoric sexuality of the female creative act.

Rich also describes the *"primary presence of women to ourselves and each other"* as the "crucible of a new language."[48] The attention to ourselves demands a new language because, as Luce Irigaray says in "When Our Lips Speak Together," "If we keep on speaking the same language together, we're going to reproduce the same history. . . . If we keep on speaking sameness, if we speak to each other as men have been doing for centuries, as we have been taught to speak, we'll miss each other, fail ourselves."[49] Rich, too, sees the necessity for a new language, a common language, which can accommodate women who speak to one another, a language where women are the authors/speakers, readers/auditors, and subjects. In this act of attention, women become both the lover and the beloved, subject and object, and the resulting fecundity does not focus on a product owned by the author but on a network of relationships among author, reader, text, and even literary foremothers.

Yet the autonomous self who chooses her lesbian potential is paradoxically defined through relationship. No contradiction exists between an autonomous self and a self in relationship, no contradiction between creativity as an autonomous and as a communal act. Not dependent on a sexuality of transcendence, which demands the "other" for its ascent, this metaphor focuses on the communication within a community of subjects. The imagination described by such a metaphor is not universal or disembodied, not isolated or egotistical, but, rather, part of a community and of the contingent world.

The paradigmatic relationship of this community is the mother-daughter relationship, the return of the woman to her original love. Mother as an image of female creativity is subsumed by the larger image of the lesbian, the one whose creativity springs from her primary attention to women. Rich has made much of the story of Demeter and Persephone, of the mother finding the daughter and of the Earth's fertile growth that follows.[50] This shared subjectivity comes from what Rich calls the original homesickness: *"This is what she was to me, and this / is how I can love myself – I as only a woman can love me. / Homesick for myself, for her."*[51] Through this notion of community, Rich destroys the dualism that underscores heterosexual images of creativity, although it may be argued that the refusal of dualism is superficial because Rich still allows for female uniqueness in traditional terms. Unlike Wittig, who calls for an end to gender, Rich remains inside the historically accepted definitions of male and female. Her radical potential appears in her attempt – a successful one, I believe – to wrest the female from male control and position the woman at the center of her discourse.

One of Adrienne Rich's most unusual essays, "Women and Honor: Some Notes on Lying," illustrates many of these points with audacity and vision. This key text rarely mentions the word *lesbian* but does explore the meaning of women's relationships with one another and invites translation to the metaphoric realm. Here, where her prose strategy, usually highly rhetorical, is poetic, Rich measures the erotic charge between women by their trust of one another. In the patriarchal world, woman's honor is acknowledged only by her sexual loyalty to men; in a brave new world of relationships among women, a new code of honor based on truth and trust can begin to unfold. Trust is the primary way of being attentive to one another, and, on this trust, truth is based. Trust, she implies, is another way of making love, a way of allowing the full freedom of imagination and of sexuality. Because truth itself is based on trust and not on mere facts, it is created between two people as they open to one another. This point leads Rich to a curious epistemological place, one in which the universe is created on the trust two people share, including the universe created when the beloved declares "It is seventy degrees outside and the sun is shining."[52] Both trust and truth become the foundation of the female creative imagination: "The unconscious wants truth, as the body does. The complexity and fecundity of dreams come from the complexity and fecundity of the unconscious struggling to fulfill that desire. The complexity and fecundity of poetry come from the same struggle."[53] Because women have been alienated from their bodies and their own sexuality, they have also been alienated from their own creativity. A bond with another woman puts each in touch with her own body and her imagination because that bond opens each to the unconscious. Ultimately, the connection is with the void, the power understood by the matriarchal religions that allowed "Out of death, rebirth; out of nothing, something."[54] Thus the erotic energy of two women becomes the source of creative energy because it puts each in touch with the profound creativity of the universe. It is a creativity not described in terms of ecstasy or inspiration but in terms of a human bond.

Monique Wittig, philosophically quite separate from Adrienne Rich, has also evolved a definition of *lesbian* in which the word assumes a broader meaning than two women making love. In the space Wittig calls lesbian, any female can reject the socially defined category of woman. Significantly, lesbian can also be a metaphor for the woman writer, as Hélène Vivienne Wenzel has noted of the narrator in Wittig's last work of fiction: "The lover *j/e* in *Le corps lesbien* is also the writer whose violent lovemaking both as subject and as object with *tu* is a metaphor for the craft of the writer."[55] In this space of subjectivity that the lesbian occupies, textuality and sexuality are closely intertwined.

As a socialist feminist, Wittig does not accept theories of innate differences between woman and man or of a unique female sexuality and creativity. The lesbian is one who is beyond all gender, who is not woman, essentially the one who occupies a space from which the marginal can claim subjectivity. In her critique of contemporary French feminists' psychoanalytic theories of women and writing, Ann Rosalind Jones notes Wittig's suspicions "both of the oppositional thinking that defines woman in terms of man and of the mythical-idealist strain in certain formulations of *féminité*."[56] The source of oppression is gender itself, what Wittig calls artificial categories of man and woman that "conceal the fact that social differences always belong to an economic, political, ideological order."[57] *Lesbian* is the only word she knows that obliterates gender, the only concept in which women are not dependent on men economically, politically, socially, or emotionally. Although theoretically at odds, both Wittig and Rich differentiate the lesbian from the woman who is constructed by patriarchal codes. What lesbian as a metaphor becomes for Rich is a capacious room walled from patriarchal constraints but unlimited inside; for Wittig the space is larger, what she has called, echoing Pascal, the circle "whose center is everywhere and whose circumference is nowhere."[58]

From this place, Wittig notes, the marginal subject refuses dualism and gains an "axis of categorization from which to universalize."[59] Rich eschews a claim to the universal with its attendant implications of noncorporeality; Wittig, however, insists on the necessity of a universal point of view without losing the corporeal, for without a point from which to universalize, she explains, one exists as a contingent being, an ontological impossibility. Men are given such absolute existence because, in effect, they are already genderless; only women must exist under the sword of gender. She is marked; he is unmarked. This dualistic structure is "based on the primacy of difference" and the "thought of domination."[60] Like Rich, Wittig refuses this dualism, although Wittig eliminates it entirely and Rich dismisses one side of it, the male. Thus, in her radical fiction, *The Lesbian Body*, Wittig startles us with her goal to "lesbianize the symbols, lesbianize the gods and goddesses, lesbianize men and women."[61] Ulysses, for example, becomes Ulyssea, Achilles and Patrocles become Achillea and Patroclea. In her groundbreaking essay on this work, Namascar Shaktini rightly notes that Wittig's method of displacement is to put the subject "outside of the presence/absence and center/margin dichotomies."[62] Wittig allows the reader no recognizable point of view, nor does she give any specific identity to the lovers. They are interchangeable. Wittig accomplishes most of this shift through her use of pronouns, which she considers the center of subjectivity in language: the *elles* in *Les Guérillères* and the *j/e* of *The Lesbian Body*. These pronouns give to the marginal and other a centrality and universality, just as she argues that Djuna Barnes and Proust succeed because they posit a homosexual subject as a point from which to universalize.[63]

But this insistence on a claim to the universal does not avoid the necessity for the concrete, the physical, the particular, or the sexual. Wittig assumes both the materiality of the body and of the text. While she insists that a text, to be successful, must be universal, or it will lose "its polysemy" and become "univocal," she also claims that the marginal text must also assume a particular point of view.[64] The materiality of the body/text allows Wittig to include sexuality in her definition of lesbian as metaphor, but this sexuality is not powerful because of the woman's innate sexual uniqueness. Rather, the power of lesbian sexuality is determined by its position outside of any category; it is, as Elaine Marks states, "undomesticated."[65] The centrality of sexuality can best be seen in some of Wittig's fiction, especially in *The Lesbian Body*, a series of poems that focuses on lesbian lovers whose eroticism is neither transcendent nor within the traditional images of Western eroticism. It is a violent, disruptive, tender, grotesque sexuality, and, like the sexuality described by Adrienne Rich, it is also diffuse and omnipresent.

Outside of any categories, Wittig's lovers release creative as well as sexual energy. The text, too, is a sensual body that the lover caresses and violently puts together. As Marks states: "The power of the word and the pleasures of the female body are intimately related. Love-making is the primary source of inspiration. It opens and defines a world whose existence had been suspected but never so explicitly stated."[66] The imagination posited by this new eroticism leads the speaker to burst the bonds of recognizable sexual imagery and forge a textuality/sexuality of her own, with its own reality and language. To be outside the dichotomies, undomesticated and uncategorized, means, then, to create new images, new languages, and a new "axis of categorization."

Wittig could not be expected to rhapsodize about a tender relationship of subjects based on the archetypal mother-daughter bond. In fact, for Wittig, the mother is everything that *is* the socially constructed woman; she is the domesticated woman. In her futurist dictionary (written with Sande Zeig), Wittig opposes the amazon to the mother, the betrayer of free women: "Then came a time when some daughters, and some mothers did not like wandering anymore in the terrestrial garden. They began to stay in the cities and most often they watched their abdomens grow. This activity brought them, it is said, great satisfaction. Things went so far in this direction that they refused to have any other interests. . . . The first generation of static mothers who refused to leave their cities, began. From then on, they called the others 'eternal, immature daughters, amazons.'"[67] As in *Les Guérillères*, this lesbian community is not constituted by similar but by uncategorized females, females who are not defined by any ontological term, least of all by mother. The community is, then, a collection of these undomesticated women, not an ontological entity.

The imaginative process that is circumscribed by lesbian is for Rich and Wittig a shattering of old images and language, a space in which the woman writer can both oppose patriarchal categories and begin to define a new concept of reality. By removing the male from the audience, text, and authorial stance, Rich, like Wittig, moves the woman writer from the margins to the center of her own language. Rich does not ask or care for Wittig's universality but relies on the text's ability to communicate to and draw from the "lesbian continuum," a continuum that must include the tradition of women writers as well as contemporary readers. In her latest book of poetry, for example, Rich asks for this admittedly Romantic aesthetic relationship: "I wasn't looking for a muse / only a reader by whom I could not be mistaken."[68] Her emphasis is on the poet-reader connection, the lesbian community that forges its own identity outside the patriarchy and therefore discovers its own truth. Rich is willing to let her text be univocal in Wittig's sense. Wittig is more concerned with the position of the subject in the linguistic order, with pronouns in particular, and with the linguistic space in which the lesbian can claim universality. But for both, the word *lesbian* provides a key term for the woman writer to position herself anew in an alien language.

I am not arguing that these two approaches to the metaphoric lesbian are essentially the same or that they can be resolved in some Hegelian synthesis. I am arguing that lesbian as metaphor is one of the most vital concepts in feminist critical theory today and deserves more and not less attention. I am also arguing that, while these two definitions of lesbian depend on different and, at times, radically opposed philosophies of language, they also have important elements in common, elements that deconstruct Western sexual metaphors for creativity and point to the possibility of female autonomy. This approach, I hope, will also address some of the important objections to lesbian as a metaphor for female creativity. To argue, for instance, that this metaphor eschews sexuality is to limit sexuality primarily to genital sexuality; sexuality, I would argue, is the core of the metaphor. Yet to state that it abstracts and generalizes is, of course, true because any metaphor must; but even as a metaphor, lesbian is a constant linguistic and conceptual challenge to the patriarchy. Unlike, for instance, the image of mother, which not only fixes women in a patriarchal category but also can and has been appropriated by men, lesbian as an image is too threatening to be blithely absorbed by the male artist.

As a metaphor for creativity, "lesbian" expands our concept of the author's and the reader's relationships to the text. They both become a relation of exchanged honesty and trust; and the writing of the text becomes an act that affirms self in community with others. As a broader literary symbol of women's lives, the metaphor can revise our reading of many texts, making, for instance, the lesbians in novels such as *The Color Purple* and *The Women of Brewster Place* symbols of as well as catalysts for the existence of autonomous women's communities.[69] Thus, while the recent theoretical history of this image offers problems and controversy, the creative strengths of lesbian as metaphor can significantly enrich and complicate our culture's symbolic representation of women.

NOTES

I wish to thank the University of Oregon's Center for the Study of Women in Society for its generous support. The opinions expressed in this paper are those of the author and not necessarily those of the Center. I wish also to thank the referees for *Signs* for their helpful comments and critiques.

1 Margaret Atwood, "Review of *Diving into the Wreck*," in *Reading Adrienne Rich: Reviews and Re-Visions, 1951–81*, ed. Jane Roberta Cooper (Ann Arbor, University of Michigan Press, 1984), 238–41, esp. 241.

2 Adrienne Rich, "It Is the Lesbian in Us . . .," in her *On Lies, Secrets, and Silence: Selected Prose, 1966–1978* (New York: Norton, 1979a), 199–202, esp. 201; and Monique Wittig, *The Lesbian Body*, trans. David Le Vay (New York: Avon, 1975).

3 Virginia Woolf, *The Letters of Virginia Woolf*, vol. 4, 1929–31, ed. Nigel Nicolson and Joanne Trautman (New York: Harcourt Brace Jovanovich, 1978), 203.

4 Rich, "It Is the Lesbian in Us . . .," 201.

5 Lillian Faderman, *Surpassing the Love of Men: Romantic Friendship and Love between Women from the Renaissance to the Present* (New York: Morrow, 1981); Blanche Wiesen Cook, "Support Networks and Political Activism: Lillian Wald, Crystal Eastman, Emma Goldman," *Chrysalis: A Magazine of Women's Culture* 3 (Spring 1977): 43–60; and Bertha Harris, "Lesbians and Literature" (paper presented at the Modern Language Association Convention, New York City, 1976), cited in Barbara Smith, "Toward a Black Feminist Criticism," *Women's Studies International Quarterly* 2, no. 2 (1979): 183–94, esp. 188.

6 Adrienne Rich, "Compulsory Heterosexuality and Lesbian Existence," *Signs: Journal of Women in Culture and Society* 5, no. 4 (Summer 1980): 631–60, esp. 648. For the controversy, see Ann Ferguson, Jacqueline N. Zita, and Kathryn Pyne Addelson, "On 'Compulsory Heterosexuality and Lesbian Existence': Defining the Issues," *Signs* 7, no. 1 (Autumn 1981): 158–99.

7 Bonnie Zimmerman, "What Has Never Been: An Overview of Lesbian Feminist Criticism," in *Making a Difference: Feminist Literary Criticism*, ed. Gayle Greene and Coppelia Kahn (London and New York: Methuen, 1985), 177–210, esp. 184; Gloria Bowles, "Adrienne Rich as Feminist Theorist," in Cooper, ed.,

319–28, esp. 322; and Catharine R. Stimpson, "Adrienne Rich and Lesbian/Feminist Poetry," *Parnassus* 12, no. 2/13, no. 1 (Spring/Summer/Fall/Winter 1985): 249–68, esp. 255.

8 Alicia Ostriker, *Writing Like a Woman* (Ann Arbor: University of Michigan Press, 1983), 121.

9 Summarized in Rich, "It Is the Lesbian in Us . . .," 202.

10 Elaine Showalter, "Introduction: The Feminist Critical Revolution," in *The New Feminist Criticism: Essays on Women, Literature, and Theory*, ed. Elaine Showalter (New York: Random House, 1985), 3–17, esp. 7.

11 See Judy Grahn, *The Highest Apple: Sappho and the Lesbian Poetic Tradition* (San Francisco: Spinsters Ink, 1985); Monique Wittig, *The Lesbian Body* (n. 2 above); and Alice Walker, *The Color Purple* (New York and London: Harcourt Brace Jovanovich, 1982). See also the significant discussions by Mary J. Carruthers, "The Re-Vision of the Muse: Adrienne Rich, Audre Lorde, Judy Grahn, Olga Broumas," *Hudson Review* 36 (Summer 1983): 293–327; and Susan Gubar, "Sapphistries," *Signs* 10, no. 1 (Autumn 1984): 43–62.

12 Zimmerman, 183.

13 Rachel Blau DuPlessis, *Writing beyond the Ending: Narrative Strategies of Twentieth-Century Women Writers* (Bloomington: Indiana University Press, 1985), 135, 139. See also Margaret Homans, *Women Writers and Poetic Identity: Dorothy Wordsworth, Emily Brontë, and Emily Dickinson* (Princeton, N.J.: Princeton University Press, 1980).

14 Smith (n. 5 above), 189.

15 Monique Wittig, "One Is Not Born a Woman," in *Feminist Frameworks: Alternative Theoretical Accounts of Relations between Women and Men*, ed. Alison M. Jaggar and Paula S. Rothenberg (New York: McGraw-Hill, 1984), 148–52, esp. 150.

16 Grahn, 40.

17 Adrienne Rich, "Women and Honor: Some Notes on Lying," in *On Lies, Secrets, and Silence* (n. 2 above), 185–94, esp. 187.

18 Aristotle, "De Generatione Animalium," in *The Works of Aristotle Translated into English*, ed. J. A. Smith and W. D. Ross (Oxford: Clarendon Press, 1912), 5:729a.

19 Julius Caesar Scaliger, "Poetics," in *Critical Theory since Plato*, ed. Hazard Adams (New York: Harcourt Brace Jovanovich, 1971), 137–43, esp. 139; Sir Philip Sidney, "An Apology for Poetry," in Adams, ed., 155–77, esp. 157.

20 Samuel Taylor Coleridge, *Biographia Literaria*, ed. J. C. Metcalf (New York: Macmillan, 1926), 189–90. The best discussion of the identification of the male with literary authority can be found in Sandra Gilbert and Susan Gubar, *The Madwoman in the Attic: The Woman Writer and the Nineteenth-Century Literary Imagination* (New Haven, Conn.: Yale University Press, 1979a).

21 Virginia Woolf, *A Room of One's Own* (1929; reprint, New York: Harcourt, Brace & World, 1957), 102.

22 "Special Issue: The Androgyny Papers," *Women's Studies* 2, no. 2 (1974); Adrienne Rich, "Diving into the Wreck," in her *Diving into the Wreck: Poems 1971–72* (New York: Norton, 1973), 56, and *Of Woman Born: Motherhood as Experience and Institution* (New York: Norton, 1976), 83; Mary Daly, *Beyond God the Father: Toward a Philosophy of Women's Liberation* (Boston: Beacon, 1973), and *Gyn/Ecology:*

The Metaethics of Radical Feminism (Boston: Beacon, 1978), 387–88. Contemporary feminist criticism has, in some instances, turned to a new and more favorable view of androgyny. For example, for a discussion of androgyny as
multiplicity in Virginia Woolf's *Orlando*, see DuPlessis (n. 13 above), 63.

23 Gerrard Winstanley, "The New Law of Righteousness," in *The Works of Gerrard
    Winstanley,* ed. George H. Sabine (Ithaca, N.Y.: Cornell University Press, 1941),
    149–244, esp. 157.

24 Carl Jung, *Two Essays on Analytical Psychology,* trans. R. F. C. Hull (New York:
    Meridian, 1956), 218.

25 Sally B. Allen and Joanna Hubbs, "Outrunning Atalanta: Feminine Destiny in
    Alchemical Transmutation," in *Signs* 6, no. 2 (Winter 1980): 210–29, esp. 215.

26 Rich, *Of Woman Born,* 77n.

27 Mary K. DeShazer, *Inspiring Women: Reimagining the Muse* (New York: Per-
    gamon, 1986), 8–10.

28 Frederick Goldin, *The Mirror of Narcissus* (Ithaca, N.Y.: Cornell University
    Press, 1967), 14.

29 Feminist critic Luce Irigaray uses the image of the mirror to argue that woman
    exists in the male symbolic economy to reflect back to man *his* identity, what
    she calls *"the same re-marking itself"* (*Speculum of the Other Woman,* trans. Gillian
    C. Gill [Ithaca, N.Y.: Cornell University Press, 1985a], 21). Virginia Woolf notes
    a similar function for women, the "looking-glasses possessing the magic and
    delicious power of reflecting the figure of man at twice its natural size" (*A
    Room of One's Own,* 35).

30 Thomas Wyatt, "Description of the Contrarious Passions in a Lover," in *The
    Renaissance in England,* ed. Hyder E. Rollins and Herschel Baker (Boston:
    Heath, 1954), 198.

31 Robert Graves, *The White Goddess: A Historical Grammar of Poetic Myth* (1948;
    reprint, New York: Farrar, Straus, & Giroux, 1973), 24.

32 May Sarton, *Mrs. Stevens Hears the Mermaids Singing* (New York: Norton, 1965),
    190.

33 Tillie Olsen, *Silences* (1978; reprint, New York: Dell, 1979), 18.

34 Ibid., 18–19.

35 Monique Wittig and Sande Zeig, *Lesbian Peoples: Material for a Dictionary,* trans.
    Monique Wittig and Sande Zeig (New York: Avon, 1979).

36 Domna C. Stanton, "Difference on Trial: A Critique of the Maternal Metaphor
    in Cixous, Irigaray, and Kristeva," in *The Poetics of Gender,* ed. Nancy K. Miller
    (New York: Columbia University Press, 1986), 157–82.

37 Adrienne Rich, "The Anti-Feminist Woman," in *On Lies, Secrets, and Silence* (n.
    2 above), 69–84, esp. 77.

38 Audre Lorde, "An Interview: Audre Lorde and Adrienne Rich," in *Sister Out-
    sider: Essays and Speeches by Audre Lorde* (Trumansburg, N.Y.: Crossing Press,
    1984b), 89–109, esp. 100.

39 Daly, *Gyn/Ecology* (n. 22 above), 26n.

40 Rich, "It Is the Lesbian in Us . . .," (n. 2 above), 200–201.

41 Some recent books minimize Rich's lesbian stance, such as Paula Bennett, *My
    Life a Loaded Gun: Female Creativity and Feminist Poetics* (Boston: Beacon, 1896);

or Deborah Pope, *A Separate Vision: Isolation in Contemporary Women's Poetry* (Baton Rouge: Louisiana State University Press, 1984).

42 Adrienne Rich, foreword in her *Blood, Bread, and Poetry: Selected Prose 1979–1985* (New York and London: Norton, 1986a), vii–xiv, esp. xii.

43 Rich, "It Is the Lesbian in Us . . .," 200.

44 Carruthers (n. 11 above), 296.

45 Audre Lorde, "Uses of the Erotic: The Erotic as Power," in *Sister Outsider*, 53–59, esp. 55.

46 Rich, "Compulsory Heterosexuality and Lesbian Existence" (n. 6 above), 650.

47 Marilyn Frye, "To See and Be Seen: The Politics of Reality," in her *The Politics of Reality: Essays in Feminist Theory* (Trumansburg, N.Y.: Crossing Press, 1983), 152–74, esp. 172.

48 Adrienne Rich, "Power and Danger: Works of a Common Woman," in "On Lies, Secrets, and Silence" (n. 2 above), 247–58, esp. 250.

49 Luce Irigaray, "When Our Lips Speak Together," in her *This Sex which is Not One*, trans. Catherine Porter with Carolyn Burke (Ithaca, N.Y.: Cornell University Press, 1985b), 205–13, esp. 205.

50 Adrienne Rich, "Caryatid: Two Columns," in *On Lies, Secrets, and Silence* (n. 2 above), 107–19, esp. 115.

51 Adrienne Rich, "Transcendental Etude," in her *The Dream of a Common Language: Poems 1974–1977* (New York: Norton, 1978), 76.

52 Rich, "Women and Honor" (n. 17 above), 192.

53 Ibid., 188.

54 Ibid., 191.

55 Hélène Vivienne Wenzel, "The Text as Body/Politics: Appreciations of Monique Wittig's Writings in Context," *Feminist Studies* 7, no. 2 (Summer 1981): 264–87, esp. 284.

56 Ann Rosalind Jones, "Writing the Body: Toward an Understanding of l'Écriture féminine," in Showalter, ed. (n. 10 above), 361–77, esp. 370.

57 Monique Wittig, "The Category of Sex," in *Feminist Issues* 2 (Fall 1982): 63–68, esp. 64.

58 Monique Wittig, "The Point of View: Universal or Particular," *Feminist Issues* 3 (Fall 1983): 63–69, esp. 65.

59 Ibid.

60 Wittig, "The Category of Sex," 65.

61 Monique Wittig, "The Mark of Gender," in *Feminist Issues* 5 (Fall 1985a): 3–12, esp. 11.

62 Namascar Shaktini, "Displacing the Phallic Subject: Wittig's Lesbian Writing," *Signs* 8, no. 1 (Autumn 1982): 29–44, esp. 39.

63 Wittig, "The Point of View," 64.

64 Ibid., 65–68.

65 Elaine Marks, "Lesbian Intertextuality," in *Homosexualities and French Literature: Cultural Contexts/Critical Texts*, ed. Elaine Marks and George Stambolian (Ithaca, N.Y.: Cornell University Press, 1979), 353–77, esp. 372.

66 Ibid., 374–75.

67 Wittig and Zeig (n. 35 above), 108–9.

68 Adrienne Rich, "Contradictions: Tracking Poems, no. 20," in her *Your Native Land, Your Life: Poems* (New York: Norton, 1986b), 102.

69 Walker (n. 11 above); and Gloria Naylor, *The Women of Brewster Place* (New York: Penguin, 1983).

PART II

Locating Our Selves in the Text:
Texts as Sources of Lesbian Sense of Self

Introduction

In *Essentially Speaking: Feminism, Nature and Difference* (1989), Fuss discussed the problems faced by Lesbian and gay male theorists and activists who have based their politics on personal identity. According to Fuss (98), current Lesbian theorists have been more reluctant than have gay male theorists to follow Foucault in developing analyses of the historical construction of sexualities – a discrepancy which is not surprising, given that Foucault himself, in failing or refusing to understand sexuality as gendered, ultimately ended by conflating all sexuality as male. (See de Lauretis in Fuss, 107, and our "Sexual Identity/Textual Politics," this volume.) Fuss (98) faults Lesbian feminist scholars for our unwillingness to examine (the concept of) Lesbian identity as a historical construct, and for continuing to base Lesbian feminist politics on the idea of a "lesbian essence." As Fuss "decode[d] the sometimes abstract and fuzzy notion of identity," she noted:

In both gay and lesbian literature, a familiar tension emerges between a view of identity as that which is always there (but has been buried under layers of cultural repression) and that which has never been socially permitted (but remains to be formed, created, or achieved). . . . This tension between the notions of "developing" an identity and "finding" an identity points to a more general confusion over the very definition of "identity" and over the precise signification of "lesbian" (98–99).

We agree with Fuss that Lesbians collectively, and even individually, speak of our identity alternately as "found" or "discovered." We do not, however, see these uses of the word *identity* as evidence of our confusion. Rather, the fact that we must "find" an identity we have always had by "developing" our awareness of it results from the real conditions under which most Lesbians exist (and have existed historically) under patriarchy.

Sexuality is presented to us as *hetero*sexuality, and some of us may behave *as* heterosexuals for a time, while others reject heterosexuality throughout our lives. Lesbian sexuality is either presented as an unacceptable alternative to "normalcy," or not presented as an alternative at all. Hence, we may *be* Lesbians without knowing what we are, or, as a philosopher might put it, we may have ontological status without an epistemo-logical framework capable of determining how we, as beings, differ from other beings. We must develop an awareness of what we are – what group we belong to, who is like us and unlike us.

As linguists, the two of us agree with Fuss that *identity* has a "fuzzy" meaning, so that its use is sometimes confusing. "Fuzzy sets" are linguis-tic phenomena, not ideological confusions. To us, as to many other lin-guists, the meanings of words are "fuzzy" because the objects or ideas to which they refer share one or more basic characteristics, but overlapping sets of other characteristics. The meaning of *dog,* for example, is fuzzy be-cause the term is a label for a fuzzy set of attributes. (We apologize for any confusion caused by our pun.) Although most dogs bark, the ability to bark is not a necessary component in the definition of *dog*. If it were, the term *dog* could not be assigned to the barkless Basenji. Or, if a drinking vessel could not be termed a *cup* unless it possessed a handle, a styrofoam cup would be designated a "styrofoam glass."

Common nouns like *dog* refer not to single entities but to sets of them; in so doing, they classify groups when speakers and writers do not wish to name all the members of the group. However, all common nouns ob-scure certain differences among members of the group in the process of grouping them. This process of subtraction, however, may be seen as facil-itating discourse, allowing one of us to envision a spaniel and the other a dachshund when the word *dog* is mentioned, while at the same time agreeing, on the face of it, to assume that no breed-specific characteristics inhere in the term itself. When it is necessary to discriminate among breeds, a slightly more specific noun, like "sporting breed," or even "cocker spaniel," can be selected. All goes well, as long as both speaker (or writer) and hearer (or reader) *know what we mean*. Moreover, the inherent fuzziness in the meaning of common nouns allows for semantic change, as when a newly invented drinking vessel comes to be called a "styrofoam cup."

Dictionary definitions of *identity* show that it, too, has a specified range of meanings. These definitions include "an instance or point of sameness of likeness," "exact likeness in nature or qualities," "the sense of self, pro-viding sameness and continuity over time. . . ," "the state or fact of re-maining the same one or ones, as under varying aspects or conditions" (*The Random House Dictionary of the English Language,* Second Edition, 1987:950). While each definition shares the underlying concept "same-ness" or "likeness," under one all dogs share an identity (the condition of being a domesticated canine; "dogginess") while under another each is clearly distinct from all others, having a unique genetic and life history. Whether or not a dog has a sense of self is empirically unproven; if a Les-bian lacks the same sense, she has a form of mental illness.

In 1980 the two of us published an anthology, *The Coming Out Stories* (the second edition, *The Original Coming Out Stories*, was published in 1989), one of a group of books consisting "exclusively or largely of Lesbian first-person narratives" (Zimmerman 1985:251). Like Fuss, Zimmerman noted that identity is central to Lesbian feminist politics, but that Lesbian identity is sometimes termed a "choice," at other times a "sexual preference" (255). Quoting Bunch, Zimmerman observed that reshaping ourselves as women required us to change the identities created by male discourse, and that the restructuring of reality that occurs in the act of creating personal narratives may be "particularly essential to the formation of lesbian identity" (255).

The Coming Out Stories, *The Lesbian Path* (Cruikshank 1980), *Nice Jewish Girls: A Lesbian Anthology* (Beck 1982), and *This Bridge Called My Back: Writings by Radical Women of Color* (Moraga and Anzaldúa 1981) are among the many anthologies and journals that contain personal narratives by Lesbians, describing the process by which each "comes out" – that is, comes to the realization that what she knows about herself and feels for other women has a label, *Lesbian*; that there are, therefore, others who share these characteristics (else no label would exist); that, by stating to herself and to others that she is a Lesbian, she can increase her sense of self-worth and can join or help to create a Lesbian community. Zimmerman (1985:258) has described how "These personal narratives chart a process of growth and development, both individual and collective, a metaphoric and mythic movement."

In "Sexual Identity/Textual Politics" (this volume, pp. 1–24) we summarized the negative, damaging "identities" historically available to Lesbians under Western patriarchy. Quite frankly, we do not perceive a contradiction between the "view of identity as that which is always there (but has been buried under layers of cultural repression) and that which has never been socially permitted (but remains to be formed, created, or achieved)" (Fuss, 98–99). Lesbians have always existed but have never been "socially permitted," and have thus had to create our selves. In reading about Lesbians in history, in reading carefully between the lines to discover where Lesbians and Lesbianism have been written out of history, in discussing our lives with each other, we have discovered that, as Lesbians, we have typically lacked adequate information to name ourselves, and that, as a consequence, have often had to create a full self-concept – an identity that connected us to others like ourselves. Frye (1980:97), reviewing *The Coming Out Stories*, stated more succinctly that the book "provides a picture of what it is to be something which there is no such thing as." After reading the anthology, one young Lesbian wrote to us that she had "been struggling with [her] lesbian identity – am I gay? am I bisexual? Is it that I love women or is it just that I hate men?" and that the book had helped her "to realize (1) that yes, I do love women and that (2) . . . being a lesbian is a positive, life-affirming thing, not a sickness" (Penelope and Wolfe 1989:2). She has certainly used the word *identity* with three senses here (that of knowing there is something "different" about her – a sense of self; that of knowing that there are others who share her love for women – a group identity; and that of being proud of her shared identity – self-esteem), but the distinctions among them are quite clear.

The following essays demonstrate two of the ways in which a Lesbian writer or reader may connect her identity to literary texts. Dreher, now an author of plays and novels, describes the writer's block she experienced three decades ago, when she began a novel whose plot seemed to move toward a Lesbian resolution: one young woman, though engaged to a physician and successful in her own career, is unhappy and frightened that others will discover her unhappiness; another woman, whom she finds fascinating, enters her life. But Dreher was unable to finish the novel, "Because in 1961 I couldn't write a lesbian novel. And because I couldn't write a *lesbian* novel, I couldn't write a novel. I never finished it" (this volume, p. 111).

Dreher, growing up largely during the 1940s and 1950s, belongs to a generation that had few positive Lesbian role models in literature, pulp novels, magazines, or films. In her personal narrative, she lists some of the places she searched unsuccessfully for herself in these fictional sources, and in the lives of the Lesbians of her generation. But the negative stereotypes she learned to associate with women "who 'did things' to other women" simply frightened her (this volume, p. 113). Meanwhile, her unfinished novel provided her with solace of a sort, a fantasy into which she could "almost" retreat:

Almost. Even in the privacy of my own writing, I couldn't quite let myself see that I was writing a lesbian novel. . . . It was a novel about being different, I told myself. About friendship. . . .

If I had let it be what it was, a lesbian novel, I would have had to be what I was, a lesbian. I still avoided the word, even though I had accepted the facts. Sort of accepted. Some of the facts. I loved women. I tried not to, but I couldn't help it. (p. 113)

Dreher suggests, as Lesbians had suggested in the personal narratives we discussed above, that she had a half-conscious sense of her identity as a Lesbian, but managed to conceal it from herself. Later, a successful playwright, she began a new novel, and discovered that she was uninterested in portraying the heterosexual characters that dominated mainstream fiction; she was and remains a Lesbian writer who wants her texts to center on women only, not on women as related to and relating to men.

Dreher views novels as expressive of reality, of the author's experience(s). As Belsey (1980), for example, observes in *Critical Practice*, this "common-sense" approach to literature has been under attack since the 1960s, when poststructuralists began to assail common sense itself, along with the concepts of author, identity, and meaning, as a theoretical construct of the nineteenth and early twentieth centuries. Dreher's account allows for text and author to exert mutual influence: an as-yet-un-self-identified Lesbian creates a not-yet-Lesbian text into which she partially escapes, and is free to create Lesbian texts and fully realize her Lesbian identity only after the women's liberation movement and the gay liberation movement have made it possible for her to accept her Lesbianism – to "find" her identity. Nonetheless, there is clearly a reality outside the literary text, an author whose identity, and whose sense of identity, shapes the text, and who is quite incapable of fully shaping it until she has assumed (allowed herself to realize and accept) her Lesbian identity.

Lesbian writers, like other writers, often write on the basis of our experience. Yet it has not always been possible to write openly of one's life as a Lesbian, as the historical gulf between the writings of Sappho and those of twentieth-century writers (such as Natalie Barney, Renée Vivien, and Radclyffe Hall) demonstrates. Lesbian texts have often been unavailable as the means of "locating ourselves." Even during this second half of this century, when Lesbian books have been more generally available, Lesbians sometimes failed to find them because we did not know how they might be classified, and, having found them, were sometimes frightened to borrow or purchase them.

However, Lesbian readers, like other readers, *look* for ourselves in texts, producing what Zimmerman calls "perverse readings" of heterosexual texts. Bennett's essay demonstrates how a perverse reading of a heterosexual text – for her, a historical play by Shakespeare! – enabled her to construct a Lesbian identity for herself.

Bennett's deconstructive analysis of sex and gender in Shakespeare's *Henry V* focuses on the destabilizing effect of cross-dressing on sex and gender. "Gender ambiguity" resulted from Elizabethan performances of Shakespeare's plays because boy actors played female roles, and because certain word plays (references by characters "disguised" as to "our sex," for example) reinforced this ambiguity. Bennett does not believe that sex and gender can be completely deconstructed: "We need [the categories of gender], both to understand ourselves, in particular our bodies, and to assert our solidarity with, and historical ties to, other beings who in every other respect (race, class, age, sexual preference, nationality, etc.) may be different from ourselves" (this volume, p. 105). However, she feels that such categories provide a field for creative play, allowing our subjectivity to interpret the world (as well as the world of the play) in terms of possibilities.

Henry V, as enacted by a cast of all-female eighth-grade students at the school Bennett attended, shaped her own identity. The female "transvestite performance" exploited the text in a way that allowed Bennett to read it differently, to realize her Lesbian identity while aligning with the "multiple ambiguities of the text":

Henry V brought me out, not only because I fell madly in love with the young woman who played the king (a girl whose nickname – through one of those fortuitous freaks of circumstance – happened to be "Kingy"), but because in the rhetorical subtext of Shakespeare's play I found a mirror for the multiple ambiguities of my own situation: a "tomboy" who had no wish to become a "woman," a Jew who felt she had been "sold" to Christians. What I wish to stress here is that my intense response to the play . . . was the direct result of my having witnessed a transvestite performance. [This performance] not only sensitized me to the play's subtextual ambiguities, but it allowed me (a woman) to identify with a male, whom a woman played, . . . (p. 197)

In other words, Bennett's perspective of the world, combined with the manner in which the play was performed, provided a specific interpretation of the "text," which in turn influenced her development. Reading, like the formation of identity (including "coming out" as a Lesbian), is an ongoing process, in which text and reader influence each other.

Farwell (pp. 66–84 above) has shown how using the Lesbian as a metaphor for creativity bursts through patriarchal boundaries and frees texts and their writers to imagine new realities. Here, Dreher and Bennett demonstrate that Lesbian identity can be located (and created) by texts; that is, that texts can be appropriated and used to move Lesbian writers and readers toward self-awareness. Dreher's sexuality apparently intrudes between her and the text she attempts to create because she is unwilling to create a book which will expose her as a Lesbian to herself. Once her sense of self, of her identity as a Lesbian, is further developed through text-external sociopolitical realities, that identity comes to inform the text she creates. Bennett's sense of self, on the other hand, seems to emerge as a result of a non-Lesbian text – but one which her already (unconsciously) Lesbian self reads perversely.

Dreher's and Bennett's autobiographical accounts demonstrate the difficulties faced by Lesbians "coming out." Fuss might well describe "coming out" as another fuzzy notion, since Lesbians use the term to signify (1) realizing that one is a Lesbian, (2) telling others that one is Lesbian, and (3) having one's first Lesbian sexual experience. Yet the apparent "tension" among these notions reflects the fact that sexuality is central to Lesbian identity, as Bennett's essay suggests, and reflects as well the assumption by heterosexuals that everyone *is* heterosexual unless otherwise identified, an assumption which conceals us *as* Lesbians from each other, even from ourselves.

Given Lesbian invisibility under patriarchy, Lesbian readers have often found it necessary to find ourselves in and through texts, even by reading non-Lesbian texts "perversely," as Bennett did. For many of us, as for Bennett and Dreher, Lesbian identity and textuality are closely intertwined. Their essays here demonstrate the power of the text to challenge or empower us as writers or readers as we move toward Lesbian identities.

4

Paula Bennett

Gender as Performance: Shakespearean Ambiguity and the Lesbian Reader

One face, one voice, one habit, and two persons – A natural perspective that is and is not.

William Shakespeare, *Twelfth Night*

Sex is not a fatality, it's a possibility for creative life.

Michel Foucault, *The History of Sexuality*

The stimulus . . . is of infinite ambiguity, and ambiguity as such . . . cannot be seen – it can only be inferred by trying different readings that fit the same configuration.

E. H. Gombrich, *Art and Illusion*

In 1864, Cassell, Petter, and Galpin published the three-volume *Cassell's Illustrated Shakespeare*, edited and annotated by Charles and Mary Cowden Clarke, with illustrations by H. C. Selous. Enriching on average every fourth page of text, these illustrations suggest that Selous, a well-known nineteenth-century lithographer, was unusually sensitive to the presence of gender ambiguity in Shakespeare's plays. Indeed, there are a significant number of illustrations in which, were it not for the differences in their clothing, it would be difficult to tell Selous's women from his men.

It is not simply that Selous depicts long-haired men and strong-faced women. In stature, body type, gesture, and ambiance, his male and female figures closely resemble each other. When clean-shaven, the men's faces are no less beautiful than those of the women. The women's faces are no less chiseled than those of the men. Where characters are of superior social status, their bodies – whether male or female – are monumental, sculpted along neoclassical lines that indifferently connote the power as well as the grace and delicacy of marble. Portrayed thus, men and women seem to stand on equal (or nearly equal) footing, their billowing garments helping to obscure – as much as to signify – the sexual differences that differences in clothing are designed to represent. In pictures where homosexuality or cross-dressing is the subject (Achilles and Patroclus in *Troilus and Cressida*, Viola in *Twelfth Night*), the two sexes seem perilously close to being one.

While Selous includes many illustrations that inscribe sexual difference, especially in lower-class characters, the final effect of his efforts is to leave the possibilities of gender open. Men may be men (beards are the indisputable insignia of masculinity, as breasts are the signature of womanhood); but, then again, they may also seem very much like women. Women may dress as women but they can, with a change of clothing, just as easily pass as men.

What then is the relation between sex – the presumptive fact of physical/biological difference – and gender, the way in which this difference is constructed, interpreted, perceived, and understood? Selous does not answer this question; but by destabilizing visual representations of what is male and what is female, his lithographs – like the dramas they illustrate – raise it. In this essay, I wish to discuss the ways in which Shakespeare's pervasive gender ambiguity – an ambiguity resulting from, but by no means confined to, the fact that he wrote for a transvestite theater – undermines closure and allows the lesbian reader to reimagine or re-vision the relationship between sex and gender in alternative ways.

While many recent Shakespeare critics have argued compellingly that Shakespeare's dramas are written from a male point of view (Bamber 1982; Jardine 1983; Kahn 1981; Greenblatt 1988; Orgel 1989), the fact that his theater was transvestite, together with the ambiguity of his figurative language and his use of cross-dressing as a dramatic device, renders the stability of this "masculine" viewpoint problematic. Read from the vantage point of gender ambiguity, the vantage point, as it were, of Selous's illustrations, Shakespeare's plays appear to balance on the precarious brink of the unknown: an unknown in which sexual difference is not a fixed and given binary division, written into nature, but is, rather, subject constantly to flux. The nature and capacity of this flux to encourage alternative and competing constructions of gender, and its relevance, therefore, to the lesbian reader, who by virtue of her desire stands outside the normative limits constituting her gender in our culture, are what I wish to explore here. However conservative or radical Shakespeare may have been on the issue of women's place (and the evidence provided by his plays is here, as in so much else, ambiguous),[1] in his concern for gender slippage, he, like many other writers of his period similarly obsessed with the implications and consequences of physical and psychological transvestism, opened the door to gender possibilities that lesbian theory is only now beginning fully to explore.[2]

In *Gender Trouble: Feminism and the Subversion of Identity,* Judith Butler offers a poststructuralist argument for the kind of subversion of sexual and
gender identity that, I believe, occurs in Shakespeare's plays. For Butler, as
for other feminist poststructuralists, the "[c]ategories of true sex, discrete
gender, and specific sexuality," which, until recently, have furnished the
stable reference points for feminist theory and politics, are themselves the
concepts that feminists must overthrow (128). In basing their thinking on
the category "woman," Butler argues, earlier feminists not only committed themselves to a false universal (obliterating the differences among
women), but, because of the term's embeddedness in the sex-gender system, their use of it has reinscribed the very binary division from whose
consequences they wish to escape, namely gender hierarchy and compulsory reproductive heterosexuality.[3]

Far from being written into nature, Butler argues, sex and gender
should be viewed as the discursive products of cultural construction. That
is, they are "regulatory fictions" (32) designed to subserve the state (male
power/phallocentric "law"), and their apparent "interiority" and "reality" is nothing but an illusion produced by our internalization of what is,
in fact, a highly politicized and public discourse. "The displacement of a
political and discursive origin of gender identity onto a psychological
'core,'" she writes, "precludes an analysis of the political constitution of
the gendered subject and of its fabricated notions about the ineffable interiority of its sex or its true identity" (136). Once revealed for the performative illusions they are, sex and gender can be seen to have no ontological
status. They are dramas without which "there would be no gender at all"
(140), "deeds" without "doers" (25), "realities" constituted by acts.

For reasons I will discuss at the conclusion of this essay, I consider
Butler's insistence on the absolute deconstruction of sex as well as gender,
and, in particular, her poststructuralist jettisoning of the category
"women," problematic. But her emphasis on the subversive and destabilizing potential latent in viewing the *relation* between sex and gender as
performative (rather than as the expression of some inner being or ineffable psychological core) is richly suggestive. And nowhere are the consequences of viewing gender as performance more powerfully and lavishly
enacted than in the works of that ultimate master of performative
illusions, Shakespeare, author of five plays in which "women" masquerade as men and thirty-six in which men were originally intended to look,
act, and "be" women.[4]

As Butler observes, the destabilization of gender and sex that
poststructuralists seek to achieve through the analysis of gender's discursive origins, transvestite drama ("drag") accomplishes automatically by
virtue of cross-dressing (136–38). Because it involves one sex playing the

other, transvestism cuts gender off from its presumed origins in biological difference and turns it into performance. Like clothing, gender can be slipped on and off. It is not the necessary emanation of some mysterious inner core, but an appearance that bears a shifting and artificial relationship to the sex beneath. *Sex, itself,* that is, the biological source and originating ground of gender, *is unknowable since its nature can never be established apart from the socially constructed "apparel" in which we clothe, or interpret, it. "In imitating gender,"* Butler writes, *"drag implicitly reveals the imitative structure of gender itself – as well as its contingency"* (137). Put another way, drag makes manifest what notions of an "ineffable" gender core disguise – that femininity and masculinity are both forms of masquerade.[5]

In order to establish the potentially destabilizing effect that cross-dressing can have on our reading of gender ambiguity in Shakespeare, the best place for me to begin is with my own introduction to his plays. This occurred in 1949 when the eighth-grade class in the all-girls school I attended put on a production of *King Henry V.* A seventh grader, I had just turned twelve and was profoundly alienated from my peers and from my family. One of three Jewish children enrolled on an experimental basis in a school catering exclusively to Boston's Brahmin class, I was an actor in a social drama over which I had no control and in which I had no desire to participate. Worse, I had no wish to become the kind of society-oriented young woman the school was designed to produce and which my mother dearly wanted me to be: a young woman who "came out" socially at age seventeen. Bitter and angry at the way in which I felt I was being used, and all too sensitive to the degree to which my gender made me subject to manipulation, I had withdrawn entirely into myself. *Henry V* brought me out, not only because I fell wildly in love with the young woman who played the king (a girl whose nickname – through one of those fortuitous freaks of circumstance – happened to be "Kingy"), but because in the rhetorical subtext of Shakespeare's play, I found a mirror for my own situation: a "tomboy" who had no wish to be made into a "woman,"[6] a Jew who felt she had been "sold" to Christians. What I wish to stress here is that my intense response to the play (it obsessed me for years afterward) was the direct result of my having witnessed a transvestite performance. Seeing "Kingy" play the king not only sensitized me to the play's subtextual ambiguities, but it allowed me (a woman) to identify with a male whom a woman played, and who, in the subtext of the play, plays a woman. For years thereafter, King Henry – especially in his adolescent embodiment as the wayward Prince Hal – was my ideal role model. And Shakespeare, whose pervasive gender ambiguity I quickly discovered thanks to the Cassell's illustrated edition my family owned, formed the bulk of my education. School itself was something I wrote off.

On the surface, no Shakespearean drama seems less promising for a feminist poststructuralist analysis than *Henry V.* In it Shakespeare seems unabashedly to celebrate the ultimate masculine type, the king as conqueror. But, possibly to maintain our sympathy for a hero whose principal claim to fame, aside from his class privilege, is his unjustified invasion of another country, Shakespeare has Henry employ a discourse of humiliation, enslavement, and loss at crucial junctures in the play, a discourse that is peculiarly at odds with the upward thrust of the play's action (and Henry's career). It was to this discourse, not to the superpatriotic and masculinist, war-mongering, king-worshiping, values of the play, that I connected in 1949.

The discourse is first announced in the scene in which Henry reveals to three erstwhile companions, Cambridge, Grey, and his former "bedfellow," Scroop, his knowledge that they have "sold" him to the enemy. (Kenneth Branagh has exploited this scene's homosexual potential with stunning force in his recent film version of the play.) After expatiating at length on his grief and outrage at their attempt to "practice" on him, Henry declares:

You have conspired against our royal person,
Joined with an enemy proclaimed, and from his coffers
Received the golden earnest of our death;
Wherein you would have sold your king to slaughter
His princes and his peers to servitude,
His subjects to oppression and contempt,
And his whole kingdom into desolation (2.2.167–73)

The key words here are: *sold, servitude, oppression, contempt,* and *desolation.* As I saw it, my situation exactly. Henry might be king but he was also a (wo)man, capable of being sold – like any other object of exchange – in the traffic conducted between men. Far from being an unequivocal plus, his kingship (his "royal person") was an ironic symbol of itself: a sign not of his power but of his fittingness for sacrifice. Had not my mother told me that the liabilities of the role I was playing as one of the school's first Jewish students were "the cross I would have to carry"?

Henry depicts himself and, in particular, his body, as an object of sacrifice again and again in the play. It is not simply that the subjects' "lives . . . souls . . . debts . . . wives . . . children, and . . . sins, lay on the king," or that he must, as Henry says, "bear all" (4.1.216–18). Like a woman's, his body is the site where this "all" is borne. The sleep that is withheld, the nakedness that feels the cold like any other man, the bones that may be ransomed: these are what the king offers up as proof of his kingly/sacrificial (and, of course, Christ-like) status. Although I was oblivious to it at the time, the degree of authorial manipulation on Shakespeare's part is simply staggering. It is finally the conquering Henry – not the conquered French – with whom we sympathize, for he is, so the subtext tells us, manifestly, the one who suffers:

Go therefore tell thy master here I am;
My ransom is this frail and worthless trunk;
My army but a weak and sickly guard;
Yet, God before, tell him we will come on
Though France himself and such another neighbor
Stand in our way. (3.6.148–53)

To oppression and servitude, add frailty, worthlessness, weakness, and sickliness. Also, and most strikingly, however, add the ambiguously constructed passive position: "Tell thy master here I am," contradicted so quickly by, "we will come on / Though France himself . . . / Stand in our way." Both raped ("My army but a weak and sickly guard") and rapist ("we will come on," etc.), Henry reconfigures his aggression as his legitimate defense against being sacked himself – to a girl-child in my situation, a not-unappealing reversal of roles. To hear Henry tell it, he was the one getting the worst of it in France and the stand he makes, therefore, entirely justified, even though this "stand" was, in fact, invasion.

I pray thee bear my former answer back:
Bid them achieve me, and then sell my bones.
Good God! why should they mock poor fellows thus?
. . . Herald, save thy labor;
Come though no more for ransom, gentle herald.
They shall have none, I swear, but these my joints;
Which if they have as I will leave 'em them,
Shall yield them little. . . . (4.3.90–92, 121–25)

Here is Henry, King of England, presumably a wealthy and powerful man, a man standing, as it were, at the very pinnacle of the male hierarchy, yet what does he offer? Only his "frail and worthless trunk," his "bones" and "joints." It is these, he claims, his enemies will "sell" if they defeat him. The language is potent, but it is not the language of maleness and kingship. It is the language of femaleness and slavery; and it makes of Shakespeare's Henry V a very ambiguous character indeed, one who appears to hover between conquerer and conquered, between passive and aggressive, between king and slave, between female and male, between (dare I say it?) bottom and top,[7] rhetorically at any rate, partaking of both, unequivocally neither. A butch-femme[8] relationship in himself, Henry, to use a figure taken by Gombrich from Wittgenstein (and already applied to the play for other reasons by Norman Rabkin), is a true "rabbit-duck" – a trick image that can be read in two opposite ways, depending on the perspective from which one chooses to view it (Gombrich 1961:5–6; Rabkin 1981:33–62). And it was this rabbit-duckness that forcibly imprinted itself upon me as I watched "Kingy" play the king. (At home, after the performance, I looked up the just-cited passages in the family Shakespeare, the Cassell's edition, and read them over and over to myself, totally unaware at the time of the deeper reasons for my doing so.)[9]

Thinking back now over my early-adolescent "deconstruction" of *King Henry V,* I am convinced that the fact that I (a woman highly sensitized to my own status as victim) saw a woman play Henry's part made it possible for me to hear the play the way I did. As King Henry, "Kingy" both was and was not herself. Before my eyes – which were admittedly, peculiarly ready to infer this ambiguity – she played two persons who were one: a female who was male, a male who was a female.[10] I can remember as if it were yesterday – the tremendous sense of exhilaration I felt on learning such a possibility could be. I left the school auditorium in a trance, in love with "Kingy," Shakespeare, and King Henry all at once. While my response to the eighth-grade production did nothing to solve my social and family situation (I flunked out of school two years later and left home for good), it gave me a reading of Shakespeare and of the possible relationship between sex and gender that were in large part responsible for my survival over the difficult years ahead. In metaphorically cross-dressing his king as a slave and his man as a woman, Shakespeare, however licit or illicit his own dramatic intentions, made it possible for me to think of myself in ways outside the regulatory fictions of gender. The transvestite performance affirmed what Shakespeare's language subtextually declared: a woman could also be a man, a man a woman. Sex was not the indisputable site upon which fixed laws governing behavior and desire were indelibly inscribed; I did not have to "be" the woman my mother, and society, wanted me to be. As with Henry, the bottom could also, and simultaneously, be the top. It all depended upon one's point of view.

When a man plays a woman or a woman a man, the apparently natural and prediscursive links between sex and gender are disrupted, bringing into question not only the roles we play, but the desires we feel. With Butler, we may then ask, what purposes do these roles serve, and why do we love/need/desire the way we do? From that infinite spectrum of possible human behaviors, are there other selections we could have made, other objects, persons, or ways of being we could have chosen? In short, why have we interpreted or constructed our gender and our sexuality the way we have?

Rooted in transvestite performance and permeated with the language of figurative cross-dressing, Shakespeare's dramas lead us to interrogate normative assumptions respecting sex, gender, and desire in this way (Dusinberre 1975; Howard 1988; Novy 1984; Rackin 1987). And it is here, therefore, not in his treatment of women *qua* woman (if, indeed, he held such an essentialist notion) that his great value for the lesbian reader lies – in his opening up these basic issues to question. Unlike many feminist critics, that is, I am less concerned with Shakespeare's misogyny, for which, again, the evidence is ambiguous, than I am with what he has to say about the ambiguity of gender itself.

Given that all Shakespeare's women were played by boys, this ambiguity is, ironically, never more present than when his cross-dressed "heroines" insist upon their innately female identity: Rosalind's famous, "Dost thou think, though I am caparison'd like a man, I have a doublet and hose in my disposition?" (*As You Like It*, 3.2.194–96), for the "Rosalind" who speaks these lines, and who moves so agilely back and forth between the two genders, does indeed *have* a doublet and hose in his disposition – along with the capacity to act convincingly in full female regalia – so convincingly that male members of his audience were, notoriously, aroused (Orgel 1989:16–17). As Jardine (1983) and Orgel have separately argued, this is precisely why the antitheatrical critics in Shakespeare's day found cross-dressing so threatening and repellant. To quote Shakespeare's most self-consciously female character, Cleopatra, cross-dressing taught boys to assume "th' posture of a whore" (*Antony and Cleopatra*, 5.2.221), to, in one authority's words, "'counterfeit her actions, her wanton kisse, her impudent face, her wicked speeches and entisements,'" enticements both the boy and audience members might act on later (as quoted by Jardine, 17; see also Levine, 125, 134–35).

But what, then, is the relation between this young actor's biological sex and his different genders, genders which, like his desires, perhaps, he put on and off with his clothes? After he was restored to male garb, was the farthingale then removed from his disposition? The antitheatrical writers worried that it would not be, that, once performed, the woman could not be removed from the boy. To judge by his character descriptions of positive male figures at crucial moments, Shakespeare thought this might not be such a bad thing, that there were occasions when it would be just as well if grown men had access to the woman – or, better, to the female-gendered qualities – inside them:

Orlando on Orlando:

Then but forbear your food a little while.
Whiles, like a doe, I go to find my fawn
And give it food. (*AYLI*, 2.7.127–29)

Gertrude on Hamlet:

Anon, as patient as the female dove
When that her golden couplets are disclosed,
His silence will sit drooping. (*Hamlet*, 5.1.273–75)

Edgar on Edgar:

A most poor man, made tame to fortune's blows,
Who, by the art of known and feeling sorrows,
Am pregnant to good pity. (*King Lear*, 4.6.217–219)

However much the use of figures drawn from the maternal female body – the nursing doe, the nesting dove, the pregnant woman – seem to stereotype femininity, these images also, *in their very physicality,* render the gender of Shakespeare's male characters permanently problematic. Far from being monolithic in its phallicism, the masculinity of these characters appears to be a charade, or better, a shifting surface in which the female within them is asked, in effect, to redeem the male. For Shakespeare, the author of over a hundred sonnets that claim to be directed to a beloved young man, this could even be true (all other things being equal) of one man's love for another:[11]

Antonio on Sebastian:

. . . to his image, which methought did promise
Most venerable worth, did I devotion. (*Twelfth Night*, 3.4.342–43)

But if this is so, then was gender for Shakespeare a state of being congruent with and determined by biological sex, or was sex itself a site for play, a place where the many different guises of gender could be assumed, and their alternatives, possibilities, and desires tested? I believe that it was the latter and that the resulting gender ambiguity radically undermines, therefore, his plays' commitment to the patriarchal values they presumably encode – in, I might add, precisely the way antitransvestite writers feared such play with gender-crossing would.

To return, for instance, to my initial and singularly unlikely example, *King Henry V,* while it is true that Shakespeare appears to use gender ambiguity in this play only at those points when he wishes to palliate Henry's aggression, the king's presentation of himself as a surrogate female (that is, a sacrificial object) cannot help but put his masculinity and his kingship in a very peculiar light. For this man is as much a victim as a possessor of his crown, a crown that feminizes him even as it asserts his putatively supreme masculine prowess. If, as Norman Rabkin asserts, masculinist military values are contested in *King Henry V* (34, 49–58, 59–60), so, I would argue, and far more surprisingly, is the masculinist value the play ascribes to being king. On the level of subtext, at any rate, this most "manly" of Shakespeare's historical monarchs also plays what Jardine calls "the woman's part" (12–13).

What is true subtextually of *King Henry V* is true on the level of text in plays such as *Romeo and Juliet, Hamlet, King Lear, Antony and Cleopatra*, and *Coriolanus*. In these plays, the tension between the different constructions of gender and the values that these constructions encode is thematized in terms of the male protagonists' successful or unsuccessful struggle with their own "feminine" possibilities (Novy, 100). Whether or not one reads these plays as, finally, affirming patriarchal values (I do not), the limitations, anxieties, and terrors of an undilutedly masculinist viewpoint are the substance from which they are made. As Linda Bamber (1982) observes, in Shakespeare the masculine self is defined – or perhaps better, explored – through reference to the Other (5 and passim). And it is the presence of the Other's qualities within the male self that lies at the heart of Shakespeare's depiction of masculinity in such plays: the hero's besetting fear of his "effeminacy" and at the same time his questioning of the male-gendered values and behaviors to which he is expected, and to which he desperately wishes, to adhere (Bamber, 118; Kahn, 44–46, Novy, 164). Romeo's, Hamlet's, or Lear's presumptive sex may be male but, as they themselves recognize, their performance (their words, acts and "deeds," their goals, destinies, and desires) is not so simply described.

What is true of Shakespeare's male leads is true of a surprising number of his primary female characters as well: Margaret, Portia, Rosalind, Viola, Lady Macbeth, Volumnia, to name only some of the more obvious choices. Although these women are, as Bamber asserts, seen from a male perspective (4–6), and although even the most rebellious among them are absorbed back into the patriarchal structure by the end of their respective plays (Bamber, 32, 41; Woodbridge, 154–56), their gender itself is presented as ambiguous – an unstable and destabilizing mixture of female and male-identified traits. Leaving aside the fact that their parts were originally created for boys, these women too – as individuals – appear to have doublets and hose as well as farthingales in their dispositions. Indeed, it is precisely their potential to cross over in gender terms that – for good or ill – makes them active agents (if not psychological foci) in the plays in which they appear.

For such characters, female and male, the imposition of truly "patriarchal" gender norms (those, for example, cited by the antitransvestite writers when quoting the Bible against cross-dressing) would be tantamount to the imposition of a sterile and disempowering order upon flux – a potentially tragic limiting of the capacity to play. Following Winnicott

(1985), this is, I would suggest, precisely what happens in *Hamlet*.[12] Here the imposition of the father's desire – his law – leads ultimately to the son's fatal decision to split off his "female" self in order to "act" the man (98–99) – to kill and be killed – just as it is obedience to the father's law that puts the all-too-docile and conventionally feminine Ophelia on the downward path to destruction. Whether in male or female, it is precisely this kind of ultimately destructive internal splitting – this rejection of other possibilities – that Shakespeare's plays, in their very gender ambiguity, interrogate, subvert, and resist, encouraging us to question and resist such splitting also.

Was Shakespeare four hundred years ahead of his time? On the contrary, it was precisely because he was a man of his time that he, like other writers of his period, could bring to his depiction of the relationship between sex and gender and to his thinking about gender roles, the kind of plasticity I have described here. Indeed, Linda Woodbridge (1984) has argued persuasively that, at least where women's cross-dressing is concerned, Shakespeare was not as advanced in his attitude about gender possibilities as some of his peers, Fletcher and Heywood, for example (156–59).

But to understand how Renaissance writers could be so alert to ambiguities we ourselves are only beginning to theorize, a brief digression into the history of medicine is necessary. As a number of critics have observed, many Renaissance writers seemed to have held a "one-sex model" of sexual difference in which women were viewed, in effect, as lesser or "incomplete" men (Greenblatt, 73–86; Orgel, 13–17). Using this model, Thomas Laqueur (1990) has argued that the absolute anatomical division between the sexes that is the basis for the modern sex-gender system is a relatively recent development in European thought.[13] As he demonstrates, until the end of the eighteenth century, Western medicine did not describe women's reproductive system on its own terms but, literally, through the application of analogies drawn from the male sexual apparatus (chapter 2). Thus, a woman's vagina was identified (and drawn) as an internal penis, her ovaries were labeled female testicles, and her orgasm was thought as necessary as that of her male partner's to fertilization. (The heat generated by orgasm caused the opening of the cervix to dilate, permitting her "seed" to join with his.)

Despite the Renaissance's elaborate and heavily entrenched discourses of gender, and even sexual, difference, difference that was written into metaphysics as well as into social and legal codes, the lines demarcating *actual biological sexual differences* were not, therefore, that clearly drawn, especially in respect to the immature human body – boys and women often being grouped together. And this fuzziness, which surfaces again and again in Renaissance texts as a fascination with hermaphroditism (a fascination our own age, for similar reasons, shares), affected Renaissance thinking on gender possibilities as well. Put simply, social and behavioral differences between men and women – the regulatory fictions of gender – could not be firmly grounded in biology since biology (sex) itself drew uncertain and, in some cases, quite plastic lines. As Orgel and others have argued, this is precisely why the antitheatrical writers protested so vehemently against cross-dressing. If men and women did not dress appropriately, then what was to prevent them from becoming what they dressed? Gender was performance, indeed.[14]

This is, of course, the point. As Butler argues through her brilliant deconstruction of sex at a chromosomal level, where biological difference becomes ambiguous, gender falls with it. If we construct one, and the evidence supplied by Laqueur as well as by Butler amply demonstrates that we do, then we construct the other. Both gender and sex are normalizing fictions, the products of discourse, the end results of social construction. Without them, both behavior and desire would be free to fall where they may – theoretically at least.

But if this is true, then is it really necessary, as Butler and other lesbian poststructuralist theorists have argued, that we, as lesbians, should abandon the fictions of sex and gender altogether and cease to refer to or think of ourselves as women? It seems to me that the evidence of Shakespeare's plays points in an alternative and less wrenching direction, one made possible, ironically, by the very kind of deconstruction of the relationship between sex and gender that occurs in Butler's text.

The fact is that the highly restrictive, biologically based, and hierarchically organized sex-gender system that Butler describes and which poststructuralists are determined to subvert, a sex-gender system that unquestionably does seek to regulate desire in the interest of compulsory reproductive heterosexuality, is also the invention of the last two hundred years of European thought. It is not the product of some mythical incest taboo (Butler, 140), nor is it written indelibly into language or into the process of sexual differentiation.[15] And if this is true, then without prejudice to lesbians, we can re-construct as well as deconstruct the old sex-gender system, as Shakespeare's plays in effect show, merely by offering an alternative to it.

The categories of gender are, in Joan Scott's phrasing, "means of organizing cultural understanding of sexual difference" (1988:46) and we need them, both to understand ourselves, in particular our bodies, and to assert our solidarity with, and historical ties to, other beings who in every other respect (race, class, age, sexual preference, nationality, etc.) may be different from ourselves. We need these categories partly because we live in a society – and in a world – which, whether we want it to or not, makes sexual difference significant, and partly because, from the point of view of "flesh," "women" is what we are – whatever that "are" means, however it is constructed.

But saying that we belong to the category "women" does not mean we have trapped ourselves inside a term or inside of previous cultural understandings of what that term signifies. Sex, as Foucault says, need not be a fatality; it can also be a possibility for creative life (as quoted by Weeks 1987:49); a gendered site, as in transvestite drama, for play; and a means, as Gombrich notes of categories in general, by which to test, model, and re-vision the ambiguous messages that our environment – including our own bodies – sends us (Gombrich, 298). The category "women" ("woman" is another and far more problematic matter) will be as restrictive or as liberating, as exclusive or as inclusive, as normative or as provisional, as we choose to make it. It is, I would suggest, only in the minds of those who can never see rabbits because they are determined to see ducks (or vice versa) that the "regulatory fictions of sex and gender" (Butler, 32) and the fabrications of a phallocentric perspective must always be one and the same.[16]

NOTES

I want to thank Marianne Novy and Jonathan Goldberg for their highly insightful comments on a preliminary draft of this essay and Vernon Rosario for making the issues at stake in the history of medicine a little more clear to me. My errors are my own.

1 Feminist criticism of Shakespeare has tended to center on this issue, but opinions on the depth and degree of perniciousness of Shakespeare's male supremacism vary widely. See, passim, Dash (1981), Dusinberre (1975), Jardine (1983), McLuskie (1985), Neely (1985), Novy (1984), Woodbridge (1984), and the "Introduction" to Lenz, Greene, and Neely (1983). My own opinion is that he was moderately liberal, but, as I argue later, by no means ahead of his time. Woodbridge's comparisons of his treatment of women with those of other dramatists of the period is, perhaps, the most enlightening approach (152–81).

2 In effect, this essay addresses the impact poststructuralist critiques of gender have had on recent lesbian theory, as that theory is developed in articles by Case (1988/89), Davy (1989), de Lauretis (1990), Dolan (1989), Meese (1990), and Wittig (1981). Gilbert and Gubar outline the broader issues at stake in *No Man's Land* (1989), volume 2, chapter 8, "Cross-Dressing and Re-Dressing: Transvestism as Metaphor" (see, in particular, 362–72).

3 This critique of the feminist reinscription of the sex-gender system finds its origins in Gayle Rubin's highly influential essay "The Traffic in Women: Notes on the 'Political Economy' of Sex" (1975). In this essay Rubin provides a "preliminary definition" of the sex-gender system as "the set of arrangements by which a society transforms biological sexuality into products of human activity, and

in which these transformed sexual needs are satisfied" (in Reiter 1975:159). Rubin herself has since recanted the necessary bond which this essay establishes between the sex-gender system and compulsory reproductive heterosexuality. See "Thinking Sex" in Vance (1989:307).

4 Jardine (1983) observes that the widely held assumption that Elizabethan audiences "disregarded" the fact that women's roles were played by men is, simply, wrong. "Conventional or not," she writes, "the taking of female parts by boy players actually occasioned a good deal of contemporary comment, and created considerable moral uneasiness, even amongst those who patronized and supported the theatres" (9). Her point of view has been elaborated and substantiated by Woodbridge (1984), Novy (1984), Levine (1986), Rackin (1987), Howard (1988), Greenblatt (1988), and Orgel (1989).

Finally, it is also worth observing, as Novy notes (personal communication), that antitheatricalists also objected to across-class cross-dressing in the theater. As in *Henry V*, where a "commoner" "plays" a "king," fixed notions of kingship are also subverted. Kingship – as indeed Henry is all too aware – is also "performance."

5 The concept of femininity as masquerade was first advanced by Joan Riviere in her 1929 essay "Womanliness as a Masquerade" and popularized (if one may use such a word) by Lacan in his 1958 article "The Meaning of the Phallus." In an unpublished paper, "Masculinity as Multiple Masquerade: the 'Mature' Stallone and the Stallone Clone" (1990), Christine Holmlund observes that "the failure to study masculinity in terms of masquerade and spectacle has serious consequences . . . 1) masculinity remains the untouched and untouchable ground against which femininity figures as the repressed and/or the unspoken; 2) the differences between masculine and feminine masquerade and their various connections to power, and to resistance, go unexamined; 3) the compulsory heterosexuality organizing masculinity and femininity as complementary if unequal opposites is left unchallenged; and 4) other matrices of masquerade (race, class, age, and nationality) are often bypassed altogether" (2). Although Butler does not critique Riviere's thesis from this perspective, I believe Holmlund's argument is coherent with her approach (see Butler 50–54).

6 Marjorie Garber (1989) observes that in our culture we generally speak of experiences that "make" a man, whereas women's maturation is constructed in terms of "becoming" (138). As in my case, however, girls who resist conventional constructions of womanhood may well feel female identity is something manufactured; that is, not the outcome of a natural process. This would give the lesbian a slant that would inevitably push her toward viewing gender as performance.

7 I am using *bottom* and *top* here in the "global" sense given to them by Newton and Walton in "The Misunderstanding: Toward a More Precise Sexual Vocabulary" (1989). That is, King Henry manages to contain within himself two opposite (yet, presumably, complementary) erotic "roles," or modalities, one of which "conducts and orchestrates the episode" and one of which "responds, acts out, makes visible or interprets . . ." (in Vance, 246). As Newton and Walton observe, these roles transcend both sexual preference and gender – as, I believe, do the rest of the qualities which precede them on this list, at least *in potentia*.

8 In "Towards a Butch-Femme Aesthetic," Sue-Ellen Case (1988/89) draws on de
   Lauretis's concept of the "feminine subject" as "one who is 'at the same time
   inside and outside the ideology of gender, and conscious of being so, conscious
   of that pull, that division, that doubled vision,'" to recuperate lesbian butch-
   femme relationships as a single (though double) "subject position" in which
   the partners "do not impale themselves on the poles of sexual difference or
   metaphysical values" but flirt with them instead (56). Like Newton and
   Walton's explication of *top* and *bottom*, Case's butch-femme is an attempt to
   find a way to deconstruct sexual polarization while still maintaining the erotic
   excitement of difference. "Kingy" playing the king did much the same thing
   for me. Hence my admittedly idiosyncratic reading of Henry's peculiarly
   "doubled vision."

9 The only feeling I remember is one of intense shame that these bizarre passages
   fascinated me so. Needless to say they were tied into my sexual fantasy life, but
   that is another story.
      It might be worth noting, however, that Shakespeare reinforces Henry's sub-
   textual discourse both in the French fantasies of bringing him "in a captive
   chariot into Rouen" (3.5.53) and by the Chorus's description of him on the
   night before the battle of Agincourt as "modest" in his "smile" and "sweet" in
   "his majesty" (4. Cho. 33 and 40). There are, in fact, a slew of minor references
   of this type, all of which, I think, I picked up on.

10 As a twelve-year-old resistant to my gender and inchoate in my sexuality, I
   imaginatively indulged in crossing gender in watching "Kingy's" performance
   and it is within this context that I first experienced lesbian desire. It was, to use
   Eve Sedgwick's term, the "liminal" in her that determined and clarified my
   own sexual orientation (1989:64–65), and it is this liminality that Shakespeare
   plays on – what Orgel sees as the "metamorphic" ease with which one sex can
   "become" the other (16).

11 The data on British Renaissance attitudes toward homosexual behavior (categorized with other forms of illicit sexual behavior under the rubric "sodomy")
   is highly contradictory. Theoretically, sodomy was a crime against nature, outlawed by the Bible, but there appears to have been widespread social tolerance
   for homosexual practices, and many well-known authors, Shakespeare among
   them, wrote freely of what we would today label homosexual desire. See Bray
   (1982:7–80) and Orgel (1989:22–26).

12 Winnicott comments, "If the play is looked at in this way it seems possible to
   use Hamlet's altered attitude to Ophelia and his cruelty to her as a picture of
   his ruthless rejection of his own female element, now split off and handed over
   to her . . ." (98). Although I have no wish to make excuses for Hamlet's misogyny, this is as good an explanation of how misogyny evolves in relation to social constructions of gender as any I know.

13 Park and Nye have brilliantly contested Laqueur's use of a "one-sex model" in
   their review of *Making Sex* in *The New Republic*, arguing that, when looked at
   closely, the evidence supporting this thesis "blurs into a haze of contradictions" (1991:54). Not only does it require taking the Renaissance's use of analogies as statements of literal identity (i.e., the vagina *is* the female penis); but,

they observe, it ignores alternative Aristotelian arguments for absolute sexual difference between female and male, arguments upon which many Renaissance authorities also drew.

As a layperson, I cannot adjudicate between these rival interpretations of what, in truth, is a massive and highly contradictory body of information, information that also varies in its emphases and direction from country to country, period to period, and authority to authority. What matters from my point of view is that the possibility for ambiguity was there and that many lay writers, Shakespeare among them, exploited it. Put another way, I believe that in disputing Laqueur, Park and Nye may fall into the same trap of making their argument too absolute. A concept of sexual difference existed, but so did a good deal of confusion about how exactly this difference worked and how absolute it really was. Renaissance reliance on analogical thinking compounded the possibilities for confusion – and makes it virtually impossible for us to know exactly what they believed.

14 In reference to the antitheatricalists' position, Levine writes, "Doing is constitutive. By imitating certain actions, one becomes the thing one is imitating. . . . It is not that the actor himself has the power to shape identity, but that the part is actually constitutive and shapes the man who plays it" (1986:125). Levine makes these statements in the context of her argument that the antitheatrical writers had no notion of a "fixed [gendered] self." I follow Orgel in rooting this anxiety in the ambiguities of Renaissance anatomy as well (16–17).

15 As Rubin warns, in employing concepts fundamental to male theorists such as Levi-Strauss and Freud, feminists, including herself, run "the danger . . . that the sexism in the tradition of which they are a part [will be] dragged in with each borrowing." "'We cannot,'" she adds, quoting Derrida, "'utter a single destructive proposition which has not already slipped into the form, the logic, and the implicit postulations of precisely what it seeks to contest'" (in Reiter, 200).

16 I realize that this position appears to perpetuate a binary system; but, from my point of view, it subverts it at the same time, in a constant process of doing and undoing. That is, it establishes the categories "men" and "women" as permanently unstable and fluid sites of gendered opposition while still allowing us to speak of women's social (and sexual) experience, apart from men. A true poststructuralist position substitutes indeterminacy for difference, and, I believe, makes it impossible to speak of women's experience in any meaningful way as distinct from men's. Hence Wittig's – most ironically entitled – article, "Homo Sum" (1990).

5

Sarah Dreher

Waiting for Stonewall

The year was 1969.

The women's movement was picking up steam. NOW was picking up members. Consciousness-raising groups were springing up all over the country.

I was a clinical psychologist in private practice.

And I was in the closet.

I joined a counseling collective, really a support group, of local feminist therapists. For the first time in my life, it was all right for adult women to sit together in a room, no men allowed, and talk about being women. For the first time in my life, it was all right for women to *like* each other.

One night, some area lesbian activists came to our meeting to conduct a workshop. As part of an exercise, they instructed us to divide into two groups – lesbians on one side of the room, "straight" women on the other. A moment of panic. I looked around. Everyone else was going to her place. Any minute now, I would be very conspicuous, standing in the middle of the floor with my face the color of chalk and my heart pounding out of my chest. I thought about fainting, but didn't know how. I thought about lying, but guilt stopped me.

Time was passing. The center of the room was clearing.

I took a deep breath, and went to join my sisters.

After more than thirty years of fear and hiding, more than thirty years of loneliness and self-hatred, I walked from one side of a room to another and changed my life.

I started my first novel back in 1961, when I was a doctoral student in clinical psychology. When I stopped working on it, in 1969, I had written about one hundred pages. It's an odd bit of writing. The language is grammatically precise, but stiff, with a detached quality. At times it seems to circle around without quite getting to the point. The main character, Lauren, is a woman in her mid-twenties, a "reader" for a semipopular national magazine, on the verge of promotion. She's engaged to a young physician. Successful by all conventional standards, she should be happy by all conventional standards. But she's bored, depressed, and obsessed with doing and being what the people around her expect of her. She has headaches, and long telephone conversations with her mother that leave her shaking with rage, though she always ends up doing what her mother wants. Sometimes she drinks too much. She's afraid other people will guess the unhappiness in her secret, inner soul. But her greatest fear is of finding out her own secrets.

Into the picture comes another woman, Fran, who is "different." Fran is comfortable with herself and with her world – though by Lauren's internalized yardstick it's a small, simple, and not terribly glamorous world. Lauren is fascinated and frightened by her. Being around Fran makes her feel confused and unsettled. Being away from her makes her all too aware of her own loneliness.

The makings of a lesbian novel, of course. But this didn't turn out to be a lesbian novel. It didn't turn out to be anything at all. Because in 1961 I couldn't write a lesbian novel. And because I couldn't write a *lesbian* novel, I couldn't write a novel. I never finished it.

I was born, an only child, late in the Great Depression, and grew up during World War II and the postwar suburban homophobia of the 1950s. I was sent to boarding school, where the first official orientation message we were given was to look out for and report girls who got "too close" to other girls. I went to Wellesley College, a place I cherished, but where the punishment for lesbianism (real or suspected) was immediate, middle-of-the-night expulsion. Somewhere between puberty and my Ph.D., I fearfully acknowledged to myself that what I had feared all along was true – there was something very wrong with me. It wasn't a stage that I'd grow out of, or a phase that would pass. No White Knight would come along to sweep me off my feet and save me from a fate worse than death – though some had tried, poor things. No, I'd go on indefinitely, falling in love with my friends, choking back my feelings, pretending to be excited for them when they went on dates or met the boys of their dreams. I'd go on being a friend because I loved my friends – even if I loved them "too much." But ultimately I knew they'd leave me, their attention captured by husbands and children. I knew there'd always be a shameful secret creating a wall between my friends and me. And I knew, in the long run, I'd always be alone.

I didn't share my suspicions about myself with my friends in those days. I'm sure there were some I could have trusted. Some have told me in later years that they knew I was probably a lesbian, and were hurt I hadn't confided in them. But I couldn't, back then. I couldn't take the chance of seeing their eyes go flat, of hearing their voices turn to terrible politeness. Their friendships, even based on less than the truth, were too important to me.

My mother had landscaped our yard with my wedding in mind – a garden wedding, the roses in bloom, bridesmaids in long flowing gowns and elbow-length sleeves carrying baskets of flowers. I knew I'd never make her dream come true. Later, when my lesbianism and her refusal to accept me turned our mutual love to bitterness, it didn't matter so much. But in my younger years, when I was still my mother's daughter, it hurt me terribly to disappoint her.

I hated myself. I can't say I prayed every night to wake up normal, to miraculously be "straight." I looked around at the people who were normal, at the lives they were living, the things they wanted, their values, and wondered why they were happy with that. If I became like the people around me, I would have to stop being me. I couldn't imagine it. Instead, I prayed to find a place in which I could be who I was and not be alone. I never thought about asking the world to change, because I never believed it would.

What I did think about was suicide. I thought about it daily, and seriously.

There were few role models for people like me. I searched for myself: in movies – the rare movies there were about us, movies like *The Killing of Sister George* (lesbians are predatory and unfaithful and make their lovers eat cigars); *The Fox* (lesbians are whiny and pitiful, or are waiting to be saved by some man who comes along and kills their lovers so they can live happily ever after with a *real* man); *The Children's Hour* (lesbians ruin their loved ones' lives and hang themselves, but at least Shirley MacLaine was attractive) – in books like *The Well of Loneliness* (hardly uplifting) or Shirley Jackson's *Hangsaman* (ambiguous) – in pulp magazines and titillation trash. We were portrayed – when we were portrayed at all – in the worst stereotypes, or so carefully disguised we were only visible by reading between the lines. (I couldn't take much comfort in that. When you read between the lines, you're never sure whether you're reading between, or reading into. And, besides, she always marries the guy in the end.) They gave me moments. Moments when my life was, fleetingly, a little less lonely. But they also showed, all too vividly, what the world thought of people like me.

There were other lesbians of my generation, of course, the ones who were braver than I. They dared to live openly, to declare their truth no matter what "society" might say or do. I couldn't imagine myself in that kind of life, not the way I'd been brought up. Not knowing the things I'd been taught about that life – the role-playing, the bars, the danger. They were the ones my classmates whispered and giggled about behind their hands (while I pretended to whisper and giggle, too, and tortured myself with shame and anxiety and guilt). They were the women I'd been raised to fear. "Those women." Women who "did things" to other women. Even if I'd been able to overcome my early conditioning, I didn't have the courage to embrace that life.

About all I had the courage to do was live. Just live. One day at a time. Making the decision to live each morning, questioning it in the emptiness of each night. I plodded along, finished college, fell hopelessly in love on a yearly basis, hated myself, went to graduate school, and started my novel.

That novel got me through a lot of lonely days and desperate nights. Fran and Lauren were my friends. I could love Lauren, and love the frightened woman in myself. I could love Fran, and express – if only a little – the love I desperately wanted to give to some woman, someday. And I could feel safe. If only for a little while, if only in fantasy, I could be myself.

Almost. Even in the privacy of my own writing, I couldn't quite let myself see that I was writing a lesbian novel. I tiptoed around it. Fran and Lauren never use the word "love." They seldom touch – and when they do, Lauren deliberately feels nothing. It was a novel about being different, I told myself. About friendship. About unconventionality. About being true to one's nature. I titled it *A Different Drummer*. It was *not*, I insisted, about lesbianism.

If I had let it be what it was, a lesbian novel, I would have had to be what I was, a lesbian. I still avoided the word, even though I had accepted the facts. Sort of accepted. Some of the facts. I loved women. I tried not to, but I couldn't help it. I loved them in ways they didn't love each other, and certainly didn't love me. But I wasn't . . . couldn't. . . . So the novel wasn't about "that." It was just . . . what it was. Fran and Lauren went on dancing around their truth, and I went on dancing around mine.

But, even though it wasn't really about "that," I kept it to myself. Because I sensed there was no way in the world anyone was going to read that novel and not suspect the truth. And if someone suspected the truth, and said it to me out loud, I'd have to know the truth, too. (A college classmate *had* said it, once, and had shattered my life. It had taken me years to convince myself she was wrong. After all, I hadn't *done* anything. It was a mistake, she was jealous. It wasn't true. Really, it wasn't. I was just different. . . .)

I wasn't ready to take chances in 1961. In 1961 I was still having those daily life-or-death discussions with myself.

Lauren didn't have those discussions with herself. She went on doing what she was supposed to do, hiding and lying and being unhappy and wondering when the whole house of cards was going to fall down around her.

One evening it did.

I made a decision for myself. It was a rainy, late-winter, cold, depressing Midwestern night. My roommates were out on dates. I sat in the dark with melting slush and ice running down the window panes and decided to live or die once and for all. I was sick of my wishy-washy, ridiculous, time-wasting ambivalence. If I wanted to die, I should do it. If I wanted to live, get on with it. I decided to live. It wasn't happily-ever-after, but it was living.

Lauren went the other way. After one particularly brutal argument with her mother (which she lost, as usual), she was consumed with frustration and self-hatred. She wanted to run to Fran, but held back. She knew there was something she was about to know, something she didn't want to know, and reached for the bottle of sleeping pills her fiancé had given her. Dying was preferable to knowing the truth.

I had decided to live, but that didn't mean I was ready to come out. That happened in a series of small steps. Falling in love with a woman who wasn't afraid – well, not *too* afraid – to fall in love with me. Moving out of the Midwest – a life-affirming act in those days. (Indiana, where I was in graduate school, had, in 1964, just become one of the few states to vote for Barry "In Your Heart You Know He's Right – Far Right" Goldwater.) Settling in Amherst, Massachusetts, where – unknown to me – a lesbian community was about to be born.

I didn't come out in 1964, either. Not with a new career, in a new town. Not even with the support of a lover. I knew what could happen. After all, it had happened to me in college, when that jealous classmate had accused a friend and me of being lovers. We had nearly been expelled, and had been allowed to stay only because we promised to mend our ways and not speak to one another again. There was no way I could risk what I had now – a job, a home, some opportunity for happiness.

Fran found Lauren in the middle of her suicide attempt and saved her. I went on working on the novel. Lauren faced the fact that she didn't fit into the life that had been chosen for her. She didn't face the fact that she was a lesbian.

I had faced it for myself by then, but I wasn't comfortable with it. I had a lover, but I was afraid. All the time. We both were. We went camping. We played house. We had a dog and a garden. We called our living arrangement a "Boston marriage," after that early New England phenomenon of a household shared by two spinsters. Once in a while we made love. I tried not to think about what it meant.

Something in me wanted me to come out. Something in me screamed, "Look at me, recognize me, see me. Don't make me hide. Don't *let* me hide." That same something made me want to share my novel. But there was always the fear, and fear is very good at finding evidence for its validity.

With considerable trepidation, I showed a friend a story I'd written. It was about sisters (how many times have we used sisters as a metaphor for lovers?). When she returned it, she said only, "Well, it was very . . . emotional." Her eyes were flat, her voice polite. She never invited me to her house again. She never accepted another invitation to mine.

How did she know? Maybe it was the passion of the major character. Her desire to take care of her sister. Her devastation when her sister rejects her. All my life, it seemed, people had equated deep feeling with "strangeness" – especially when that feeling was aroused between women. Maybe, if that short story character had been devastated by a boyfriend's rejection, my friend wouldn't have become too busy to see me.

I was stuck. I knew why she had cut off our relationship. I knew what she had seen in that story. Things I saw, too, and didn't want to see . . . the self-disclosure that came through my writing.

I put the novel away.

What I didn't know, back in the mid-sixties, was that the world was about to shift in ways I couldn't have predicted.

The women's movement. The gay rights movement. Radical feminists. Stonewall.

Everything changed for us in those days. Our identities were no longer defined by homophobic families, sensationalist media, and Freudian psychiatrists. As women, we began to explore how we had been separated by the patriarchy and taught to distrust one another. We cherished one another's lives and thoughts and creative outpourings as valuable. Women who loved women were looked at with respect instead of scorn. Heterosexual women looked to us to teach them what they'd never been allowed to learn – how to love and care for other women.

Suddenly I didn't need the novel any more. For now, it was enough to be living in that brave, shining, frightening, exhilarating new world. A world of women.

When I did go back to writing, five years later, I started with plays. A group of us had formed a women's theater company and were looking for material to perform. I collaborated on a couple of comedies, then realized there were things I wanted to say that weren't particularly amusing or light. Playing for laughs had been fun, but it began to feel dishonest. Life could be ridiculous, but it could be deadly serious, too. I wanted to name the pain and target the people and conditions that caused the pain. I wanted to write about the things that moved me.

Once I started, the words tumbled out. Plays about my mother, my father, unkind lovers, bigotry, tributes to people who had touched my life with tenderness. Plays about the things that divide us, and the healing power of love. Some of the first drafts were awkward – dialogue had always been my weakest point. Some of the speeches were stiff. But it was the stiffness of inexperience, not the stiffness of hiding.

I was still a little bit afraid. My work wasn't strictly autobiographical, but the feelings the characters expressed were my feelings. The circumstances were similar. My greatest nightmare was that my play/my life would be up there for all the world to see, and the eyes of every woman in the audience would go flat.

The actors liked what we were doing, but we were a handful of women, operating in a closed, protective, and very concentrated environment. Perfectly capable of developing *folie en masse*. The actors would recover from their temporary psychosis and go back to the real world. And then I'd truly be alone again.

An amazing thing happened. The audience responded to what I wrote. Not just because it made them laugh, but because it touched them. They looked at the scenes from my life, and felt what I'd felt. They told me I wasn't crazy. Once, back in graduate school, I had scribbled in the margin of a notebook one of those thoughts that come to us out of nowhere and depart like lightning, leaving behind a comet's tail that quickly fades. "If we go deeply enough into the personal," I had written, "we strike the Universal." An interesting thought, back then. That's all it was, an interesting thought, a hope. But now . . . I was beginning to think I wasn't so peculiar after all.

I began to feel more confident. I decided to try a novel again. Plays and novels are very different things. A play is a collaborative effort – playwright, cast, director, production staff, and audience working together to create the final product. That's what makes it exciting, and ever-changing. But for the playwright it demands the ability to let go. To let go of what the characters will look and sound like. To let go of the setting, the mood, even the interpretation of the words. Trying to control all of these elements is foolish, and makes the entire project a living hell for everyone. I don't think we're on this planet to create living hells.

There were things about prose writing that I missed. Descriptions. Internal dialogue. The opportunity to soar with language, beyond the familiar spoken vernacular. The freedom to move characters around without worrying about how they were going to get from the living room to the department store in ten seconds (with a costume change). And having it all come out just the way I saw it in my mind.

So, while I was working on my plays, I went ahead with a novel. Not my old friend; I wasn't interested in "coming out" novels then. I was having too good a time to touch that old pain. Stoner McTavish had been rattling around in my head for years, and the time seemed right to start. But first I had to make a decision about the audience I would write for.

If I was interested in wide distribution (I didn't see myself as a writer yet, but it didn't hurt to think like one), lots of copies printed and sold, the logical step was to aim for the mainstream. That would mean playing down the "lesbian" aspects of the novel, and concentrating on the action. In fact, looking at the usual elements in mainstream writing, it probably meant: having my major female character – or at least one of the more major female characters – be attracted to a man; elevating a male character to a central or near-central position (boys aren't interested in paying money for books that aren't about them); having the central character *aware of* if not actually concerned about her impact on a major male character. And, if I wanted to guarantee salability, male-female romantic or sexual tension.

Right away I lost interest. Right away I suspected I was destined to be a lesbian writer.

I can't/don't want to write the things the "straight" world likes to read. I'm not interested in writing about men – not as heroes, not as victims, not as persons to be empathized with and understood, not as persons to be placated, not as persons whose approval must be sought. They don't interest me. I *want* to understand women – even villains – because I love women.

Even if I *could* make up heterosexual stories with heterosexual major characters, there was the problem of language. There's something about the words we use and the way we use them that flags our writing as "lesbian." Maybe the difference is the level of honesty and directness. We have to do certain things we may prefer not to do, in order to placate the Patriarchal Powers That Be. We do them because it's a matter of survival. But, unlike heterosexual women who look to men to satisfy needs for approval and self-esteem, we don't have to present ourselves in ways men would find attractive. The Critic that sits on our shoulders is a lesbian, not a man. It's a lesbian – a woman like ourselves – we're trying to please. Not a Being with a psychology and an agenda different from our own. So we can use qualities of language that men don't necessarily like in a woman – qualities such as directness and assertiveness. We don't have to be coy, or keep our feelings hidden, or wrap them in acceptable wrapping. Or gloss them over to ourselves. Lesbian writing seems to me to speak in a more forthright way about emotions and goals than does heterosexual women's writing. To please a heterosexual audience, I'd have to learn to use words like a heterosexual woman.

I've never been good with foreign languages.

It didn't look encouraging.

Still, out of curiosity, I wrote letters of inquiry to more than forty publishers of hardcover and paperback novels, describing the book I had planned, asking if they would be interested in seeing a draft or a sample chapter. I enclosed the requisite SASE.

Not one of the forty responded. Not to show interest, or to tell me it was the dumbest idea they'd ever heard. Nothing. I didn't exist.

Which just goes to show you.

Okay, so now I knew something. The world wasn't going to swerve off its axis over a female travel agent who risks life and limb to rescue the woman of her dreams from the clutches of an evil, but handsome, man. But I could still write it, even if it was only for my own pleasure and the entertainment of my friends. At least I could write about the things I cared about.

I did. Once I had released myself from the necessity of pleasing an audience I didn't understand and couldn't empathize with, the writing came easily and joyfully. So joyfully, in fact, that I was glad to be a misfit.

My life partner gave me a book listing women's publishing houses. Among others was a small company in New Hampshire, interested in New England writers. New Victoria and I found each other.

So here I am, a lesbian writer. A lesbian who writes for and about lesbians. What does that mean?

Just as a black woman who writes brings a black perspective to her work, as a Jewish woman brings a Jewish perspective, I bring a lesbian perspective. Being a lesbian determines who I am, what I do, and how I view the world (and how the world views me, of course). In part, this means I can trust my instincts as to what will and won't "work." If a turn of plot or feeling excites me, I can trust that it'll probably excite my readers. I feel an attachment to my readers. They're friends who speak my language. They're not going to look at me with those flat eyes and polite smiles. In a world which, for me, has come to be full of miracles, that may be the greatest miracle of all.

On the other hand, I know that the "straight" world isn't going to care one iota for what I have to say. There are exceptions, of course. There are always exceptions. But they're not in or of my world. I don't have to try to please them. I don't have to try to empathize with them. We have some things in common, and we can reach across those to touch. But there's only so far we can go together.

During the women's movement, I was close to many of the members of my counseling collective. In our meetings, we talked about the things that were mutually important to us. For one evening a week, we were sisters and friends, and sexual preference didn't matter. Some of us were friends outside the group. We spent time together and hung around one another's kitchens. But they felt out of place in gatherings of my friends, and I certainly felt out of place at their parties. We cared deeply about one another, and tried to be kind and considerate. I still have heterosexual woman friends whom I love and trust deeply, who are my sisters. We cherish our similarities, and respect our differences. But we don't go to each other's New Year's Eve parties.

That's how it has been with my writing, too. There are "straight" women who like my plays and books. They like Stoner and Gwen. But they don't want to *be* Stoner and Gwen. (If they do, they might want to take a second look at that.)

A *lesbian* writer. The words astound and delight me. But even the brightest suns cast shadows. While I may be exhilarated and amazed, there are demons I have to fight.

The most difficult is the tray load of prejudices we, as writers, have picked up in the cafeteria of life and still carry around, all directed toward trivializing us and our work. The world may read voraciously, spend millions of dollars on movies and plays and TV shows – all products created by writers. But the act, the profession of writing is still seen as a trivial pursuit. Not a "real job." And I write fiction. Not Literature, fiction. (I used to think about writing Literature, until I realized I'd never write anything if I set Literature as my goal. So I write fiction, and if Literature happens along the way, well, that's fine.) But the Collective Consciousness (you remember them, the "They" in "What will They say?" and "They won't like it if you do that") places a greater value on Literature. They may not read it, but They put it higher on the ladder of prestige. In some people's eyes, what I do isn't that important. Sometimes They play with my mind and trick me into losing respect for my work.

Writing is frightening. It's frightening because you always have that sneaking suspicion that your last book really was your last book. Your brain turns to dried leaves, and nothing comes. It's frightening because you pleased your audience last time, and you don't want to disappoint them now. It's frightening because people may hate what you write, and what you write is from the deepest places in your heart. Not only the fear of rejection, but the desire to please, can get in the way of writing. If a woman tells me she likes a particular aspect of a book or play – a certain character, a message, a level of feeling or spirit, I find myself wanting to repeat it. It may not be appropriate for the current project, but I usually can't stop myself from putting it in, and then it doesn't fit and I have to take it out. I want to know I've given pleasure, but I have to be careful.

Then there's the fact that I'm a woman. As entertainment, women's lives and thoughts are regarded as "uninteresting" to the "wider" (translation: male) audience. There are movies, and there are "women's" movies. Nobody talks about "men's" movies. There are "three-handkerchief movies." Nobody mentions the male equivalent ("three-belch movies"?). Even scripts written by men about women are perceived as somehow not about "important" things.

Add to this being a lesbian. The "straight" world doesn't want to hear what lesbians have to say. Lesbians are only going through a stage, or from outer space, or trying to get back at their parents, or sexually dysfunctional, etc., etc. In other words, Nothing-Buts, Non-Persons. What Non-Persons have to say can't possibly interest Real People.

The fear of being trivialized and rejected are horrors not limited to writers. We lesbians all suffer from them in one way or another. The trivialization might be "when are you going to grow up (and marry a man and have children)? / Get a *real* job? / Start dressing like a *real* woman?" Become a *real* person instead of a pretend person? It might be the holiday dinners that we're expected to attend, but where we must *never* mention *it* or bring *her,* where we must pretend to be "normal," where no one ever asks about *our* lives, where we're welcome as long as we present a blank screen onto which our families can project their Ozzie and Harriet visions of life.

We all know about rejection. I often wonder if that fear is greater for lesbians. We've been closed out so often, by the people we've cared about the most – families, close friends, people we've loved who've been repulsed by that love. Being rejected for love is probably the most painful of all.

Like most people, I want to be liked. To be liked, you have to take a chance. To let the world see who you are. Oh, you can create a pleasant face that has nothing to do with who you are inside, and you can become the most sought-after person in your community. But if it isn't you, how much is all that adulation really worth? The only real cure for loneliness is to be known deeply. And to be known, you have to let others know who you are. My way of doing that is to put my imaginings down on paper. It's like stripping down beyond my clothes, beyond my skin, down to basic nakedness and vulnerability. Terrifying.

Age and life haven't changed the fact that I'm a shy person. And self-conscious. It usually takes me a year or more to get around to reading one of my books after it's published, because I'm afraid I'm going to be embarrassed by what I read. And there were all those years of self-hatred and fear, and living in a society that hated what I was, for no other reason than that I was what I was. I don't know if we ever completely recover from that kind of hurt. I know I haven't. We can get past it, and go on living our lives and not let it take anything more from us than it already has. But I think there are things we always remain sensitive to, and the best we can do is separate the old from the new and keep our anxieties tucked away for the 3:00 A.M. horrors.

Up there near the top of my personal list of 3:00 A.M. horrors is what the existentialists call nonbeing. Not a negative response to what I write, but a *lack* of response. People may not like what I write, and that can hurt. But when it's so far from anything they can relate to that they don't even have a feeling about it – that's nonbeing. That means I don't belong here. And that takes me back to how things were and how I felt Before.

Then, just when things are looking their darkest, a letter will arrive. A letter from a woman I never met telling me my book made her laugh, or comforted her on a difficult trip to her family, or made her feel good about who she is. I remember that the people I write for, and *want* to write for, are my friends, my sisters, lesbians.

I want to write about things that reflect us back to ourselves and make us real. Most of what we read and see has so little to do with us. We've learned to take what we can from it, to suspend our lesbianism so we can enjoy the movie or the book or the TV show. Because I'm a lesbian, I can look at the world through lesbian eyes, take it in and put words to it and give it back for others to connect with. I can write those little warm moments that touch other lesbians' hearts. I know what makes us angry, or glad, or sentimental. I know what makes us feel alone. For much of my life I couldn't reach out. Now I can, and it's a pleasure and a privilege.

It's also a responsibility. Words can hurt, and they can heal. In my younger years, I read books that contained lesbian characters who made me despise my lesbianism. I want the lesbian women who read my books to love themselves for who they are, not to be humiliated. Certainly, lesbians sometimes behave in ignoble ways. We can be cruel and thoughtless and selfish and vindictive and ridiculous and hard. But it's because we're human, not because we're lesbians.

I often find myself thinking about Then and Now, putting them side by side and trying to make sense of what's happened during the course of my life. I shift back in time to when I was twenty, and think of the things I wanted then. I wanted to have friends who felt and thought the way I did. I wanted someone to share my life. I wanted not to hate myself. I wanted to write books that would please and move and comfort. I never thought any of those dreams would come true.

It probably wouldn't have happened if we hadn't gone through the anger, frustration, upheaval, joy of the women's and gay rights movements. If there is truth to the idea that we choose the time and place of our entry into life, then I must have chosen to witness the Before and After of lesbian liberation. It's important to me to be a witness to that change, and to be sure we never forget where we were – so we can never be put there again. Lauren and Fran are products of the Before times. I cherish what they are – their sad struggle, even their foolishness. They remind me of where we started and how far we've come.

Often, as I'm writing, I think about the young woman I was, and I try to write what would have pleased her and given her courage. It's loneliness I want to touch. When I picture my "typical reader" (as if there could be such a person), it's always the me that used to be – a young lesbian in a strange, cold world. Alone and afraid.

I write for the solitary lesbians who lie awake in the dark, hearing the emptiness of the night, wanting to believe in themselves. The ones who look for a spark of hope that there's someplace, somewhere that they can live at peace. Someone who can love them. Someone who isn't afraid of their love. I think they're still out there. And I think they're still inside us, despite the progress of the past twenty years. I think sometimes we still hurt for the people we used to be.

For those of us who still live in that world, and for those of us who remember, someday I'll finish *A Different Drummer*.

PART III

Applied Literary Criticism:
Lesbian Feminist (Re)Visions of the Canon

Introduction

In 1985 Gayle Greene and Coppelia Kahn published *Making a Difference: Feminist Literary Criticism*, an anthology whose title asserted that feminist literary criticism had the power to change critical practice, and perhaps mainstream culture as well. Just what kind of "difference" feminist criticism *was* making after all, Greene and Kahn left the reader to determine. In their opening chapter, Greene and Kahn were more explicit, couching their discussion of literary criticism within the broader context of feminist scholarship, which seeks to expose the male bias in disciplines and to present a female perspective.

Because it deconstructs what Greene and Kahn called the "social construction of gender," feminist scholarship has revolutionary potential (2). While it derives from feminist politics, feminist scholarship also "participates in the larger efforts of feminism to liberate women from the structures that have marginalized them; and as such it seeks not only to reinterpret, but to change the world" (2).

When a Lesbian feminist reads the phrase "the structures that have marginalized them," she thinks immediately of institutionalized heterosexualism, marriage, and institutionalized motherhood, and imagines her views will be included in the volume. However, as is typical of anthologies of feminist criticism, the Lesbian feminist perspective is central only in the lone essay by Lesbian feminist Bonnie Zimmerman, "What Has Never Been" (this volume, pp. 33–54).

Indeed, the remainder of Greene and Kahn's introductory chapter, "Feminist Scholarship," addressed the directions they prescribed for postmodern feminist criticism. They assigned to "radical feminists" the hypothesis that gender "is grounded in male attempts to control female sexuality," conceding that "it is generally true that gender is constructed in patriarchy to serve the interests of male supremacy" (3). By using this syntactic construction, in which location has been substituted for agency, Greene and Kahn avoided assigning responsibility for constructing gender to either sex; gender is simply constructed "in patriarchy." Because gender had merely "been" constructed "in" patriarchy, Greene and Kahn considered it possible to dismantle the notion of gender through structuralist and poststructuralist criticism, undoing an epistemology based on binary oppositions. (Presumably, the deconstruction of gender would in turn undo the effects of patriarchal control of sexuality – and perhaps even overturn male supremacy – an outcome that Greene and Kahn wisely avoided predicting.) By the end of the chapter, it is French feminist criticism, with its reliance on Derrida and Lacan, which is said to pose the radical challenge:

If Anglo-American feminist criticism has drawn back from the more far-reaching implications of its positions, French feminist criticism, which participates in Derridian deconstruction and Lacanian psychoanalysis, has presented a radical challenge to humanist-empiricist assumptions. The most radical feminist literary criticism has been informed by structuralist and post-structuralist French thought. . . . Since, as Derrida has demonstrated, thinking in terms of binary opposition always implies the subordination of the second element to the first, to reverse the order of the pairing – which an alternative literary canon based on redefined values does – can only reduplicate the initial system. . . . (25–26)

In the space of this essay, Greene and Kahn abandoned political radicalism in favor of "radical" criticism – criticism based upon structuralist and poststructuralist thought.

Meanwhile, having overlooked the role males have in constructing the hierarchical oppositions that exist within patriarchy, Greene and Kahn evidently accepted as trivially obvious the truth of Derrida's contention that binary oppositions must by their very nature be hierarchical. Perhaps, however, this "truth" is obvious only if human beings – men and women, for example – are the entities placed in opposition. Where, for instance, is the hierarchy in opposing round figures to figures with straight sides? Ungulates to nonungulates? Perhaps Derrida and his followers are incapable of moving their intellectual locus outside the world created by a patriarchal epistemology, one in which the equations set up by patriarchal binary opposition guarantee a "sovereign position" to "man" (25). The possibility that reversing the order of the "pairing" might also privilege women is likewise overlooked. Never mind, though – feminist deconstructionists follow Derrida, in refusing to recognize authors of texts or political institutions, and, in fact, in declining to recognize an external reality prior to the "signifying text." Here, two of them ended uneasily with the admission that "deconstruction may lead to a scepticism which is used to justify the evasion of political positions" (26).

Derridian analysis, according to Greene and Kahn, points up the pitfall inherent in Elaine Showalter's (1979) "gynocriticism," an attempt to establish a continuous tradition of women writers and to determine what, if anything, is unique about women's writing. Their charge, that such attempts are reductive and counterproductive, assigns recent Lesbian feminist attempts to reconstruct our own literary past to an intermediate (immature?) stage of feminist literary criticism:

Feminist criticism should avoid "the women's literature ghetto – separate, apparently autonomous, and far from equal"; and while not abandoning our new-found female tradition . . . return to confrontation with "the" canon, examining it as a source of ideas, themes, motifs, and myths about the two sexes. . . . The value of gynocriticism may be . . . as an intermediate stage on the way toward a more comprehensive literary criticism which considers both male and female traditions in their interactions, avoiding the "model of oppression." . . .

Such a criticism would question "not whether a literary work has been written by a woman and reflects her experience of life, or how it compares to other works by women," but the way the text works as a signifying process which inscribes ideology. . . . (24–25)

In this passage, Greene and Kahn advised feminist critics to avoid both gynocriticism and criticism based on "models of oppression" in order to "confront the canon" once again, this time by examining texts. As is typical of much deconstructive criticism, they assigned agency to the "text," which "works as a signifying process"; the process, not (male) human agents, "inscribes ideology."

Just how a textual analysis would bring an end to men's oppression of women is not clear, since deconstruction detaches texts from the writers who created them. That the canon is the result of male authority, consists largely of texts produced by men, and so inscribes *male* ideology, is overlooked by deconstructive methodology. If Lesbian feminist and non-Lesbian feminist critics restrict themselves to exploring "texts" and "signifying processes" in the abstract, ignoring the role played by men in creating patriarchal ideologies "inscribed *in*" texts, we will allow ourselves to be deflected from feminist social and political goals. We will perceive power as inhering in texts alone, and ignore the real (material) power exercised by men over women in patriarchy. Small wonder that the deconstructive agenda has found such widespread acceptance in academic circles.

Moreover, there is a danger inherent in choosing to avoid a Lesbian literary "ghetto." Absorption into the more comprehensive (mainstream) literary tradition carries with it the risk of erasure through assimilation. John D'Emilio, in his history of the American "homosexual minority" (1983:136–37), has cited Barbara Grier's assertion that Lesbian fiction was assimilated into the mainstream American literature during the 1960s, accepting unquestioningly her observations.

Grier's survey of contemporary novels from the late 1950s uncovered the beginnings of a slow but steady increase in the number of books with lesbianism as a major theme. By 1966 the situation had so changed that Grier announced the demise of lesbian fiction per se. "There is no such thing as a separate Lesbian literature," she wrote. Gay women, she claimed, so populated the pages of contemporary fiction, their existence so "taken-for-granted" as an aspect of social life, that a "complete integration" of lesbianism into the mainstream had been achieved.

In fact, as we have discussed earlier, Lesbians were still largely absent from mainstream literature in the 1960s. Moreover, the few Lesbian characters who did appear were treated as members of a subculture, an oppressed minority, not as creators of a positive, alternative culture. Perhaps Grier's founding of Naiad Press in 1973 was a tacit retraction of her earlier claim.

Nonetheless, we would not deny that deconstruction can be a useful tool for Lesbian readers and critics. Since deconstruction frees a text from the constraints of a single reading, it challenges the Lesbian feminist to seek herself in a text not obviously Lesbian, for its meanings are plural and contradictory, continually in process. Such criticism "seeks out 'the lack in the work, what it is unable to say'"; it provides opportunities for "naming our selves, uncovering the hidden, making ourselves present . . . [to] begin to define a reality which resonates to *us*, which affirms *our* being" (Greene and Kahn, 26, citing Adrienne Rich, 1979b:245). If deconstructive criticism is capable of attacking patriarchal ideology, of changing "the tradition that has silenced and marginalized us [women]" (26), the news is doubly welcome to Lesbians, who have been relegated to the thin edges of the margins accorded to women, so effectively silenced by patriarchy that we are virtually at a loss in our efforts to establish a continuous tradition that extends beyond the nineteenth century.

Bonnie Zimmerman ("Perverse Reading: The Lesbian Appropriation of Literature," this volume, pp. 135–149), in fact, suggests that we extend reader-response theory to a "perverse" reading of "heterotexts," a strategy that deconstructs their meanings:

I would go even farther [than Judith Fetterley suggested in *The Resisting Reader* (1978)] and suggest that lesbian-feminist readers resist "heterotexts" by privately rewriting and thus appropriating them as lesbian texts. There is a certain point in a plot or character development – the "what if" moment – when a lesbian reader refuses to assent anymore to the heterosexual imperative; a point in the narrative labyrinth where she simply cuts a hole and follows her own path.

Zimmerman contends that perverse readers detect clues already present in texts, whether consciously placed there by the author or not. The Lesbian reader is able to exploit such possibilities because she has learned to read similar clues in life. (In this anthology, both Paula Bennett's essay and Toni McNaron's provide examples of perverse readings.)

Unlike Greene and Kahn, Zimmerman is unwilling to concede that "'the world is the product of interpretation' alone; the world is also the product of human activity" (p. 147), and the position from which we attempt to change the world is crucial. She suggests that a Lesbian reading of a literary text at once "makes the text more personally meaningful to lesbian readers" (p. 142) and exposes the heterosexual biases underlying anti-Lesbian stereotypes. The revolutionary potential in "perverse reading" lies in eliminating Lesbian invisibility and shattering male and male-centered illusions by offering an alternative perspective.

As was discussed in our introduction to this anthology, "Sexual Identity/Textual Politics," until the late nineteenth century, when Lesbianism was pathologized, Lesbians *qua* Lesbians were virtually invisible. Whether or not women identified themselves as lovers of other women emotionally and behaviorally, historians, biographers, and critics did not identify them as Lesbians. Now we (Lesbians) have begun to research our own pasts, seeking documentation that will verify our earlier existence. Because of this discrepancy between what may be seen as Lesbian prehistory and Lesbian recorded history, we have arranged the essays in this section roughly chronologically, according to the dates when the texts analyzed were produced.

In the essays that follow Zimmerman's, Swanson and Fetterley offer "perverse readings" of texts not explicitly Lesbian, while other critics analyze texts within the evolving Lesbian canon. Those texts not (known to be) written by Lesbians are deconstructed so as to expose their liberating potential for Lesbians: themes, plots, and characterizations are interpreted in terms of their ability to challenge institutionalized heterosexuality – the patriarchal view that locates women only in terms of their relationships with men. In identifying or constructing the Lesbian subtexts of works by non-Lesbian authors, Swanson enlarges the range of works accessible to a Lesbian perspective. Fetterley discusses a novel by a Lesbian author which, although it omits explicit Lesbianism, may have helped the writer to establish her own identity as a Lesbian. Allen, Rosenfeld, Stenson, Crowder, Kawada, and Carlston provide analyses of works written by (presumably) Lesbian authors (although it might be better to approach Djuna Barnes as a bisexual).

In *Writing beyond the Ending: Narrative Strategies of Twentieth-Century Women Writers* (1985), Rachel Blau DuPlessis suggested that women writers in this century have employed a variety of narrative strategies in order to subvert the traditional ending of romance plots: heterosexual marriage. Their strategies included alternative family structures and emotional ties between women. Swanson writes of eighteenth- and nineteenth-century middle-class British women novelists who attempted "to replace the romantic heterosexual plot with new stories that challenge compulsory heterosexuality" (this volume, p. 152), and thus created novels in which the conventional heterosexual romance plot is disrupted and temporarily decentered by romantic friendships and passionate relationships among women. Drawing upon Rich's (1980) definition of compulsory heterosexuality – enforced and reinforced by social, economic, and psychological structures – as well as her notion of the Lesbian continuum (see Zimmerman's "What Has Never Been," this volume, pp. 33–54), Swanson posits a location along the Lesbian continuum for those women novelists whose female characters resist male domination and heterosexuality.

Although explicit Lesbian sexuality is lacking in the book, as might be expected in a text produced in the United States during the late nineteenth century, Fetterley reads Sarah Orne Jewett's *Deephaven* as a Lesbian text. Noting that Jewett's novel was published during the year she met Annie Adams Fields, who was to become her life companion for thirty-five years, Fetterley reads *Deephaven* as an expression of the narrator's sexual desire for another woman and "the anxieties as well as the pleasures attendant upon that desire" (this volume, p. 166). She further argues that Jewett, in "writing out the relationship between Helen and Kate" (p. 166), may have made her own relationship with Fields possible: "*Deephaven* may have facilitated Jewett's life choice by allowing her first to imagine it in fiction" (p. 165). Fetterley's analysis, like Dreher's (this volume, pp. 110–122), considers the creation of relationships between women in a fictional text to be intertwined with the developing Lesbian identity of the woman who creates the text.

Allen's essay on Barnes, author of *Nightwood*, demonstrates how that celebrated novel, as well as Barnes's "little girl" stories, call into question the categories "male" and "female." Barnes, who declared that she was not a Lesbian but "just" loved Thelma Wood, created narratives in which a sexuality founded on likeness (rather than difference) often reflects the dynamics of power that occasionally erupts into violence. In her interpretation of Barnes, Allen "look[s] to shadows rather than to surfaces, and . . . read[s] in the context of feminist work on 'difference,'" (this volume, pp. 184–5), exploring concepts and issues now central in feminist theory.

Both *Nightwood* and the "little girl" stories explode the binary structure underlying Western thought from Plato forward that feminist theorists like Irigaray and Chodorow so radically question. By refusing the categories "male" and "female," by shifting terms of sexual difference, Barnes's texts become examinations of dichotomous difference. By refusing to take maleness and the phallus as the norm, by questioning the construction of gender and the nature of sexuality, they rupture the surface of convention and illuminate the world of the night. While Barnes may have denied her lesbian relationships, her texts question the dichotomous presence of sameness and difference in their presentation of lesbian sexuality. (p. 185)

Lesbianism is a theme Allen sees as developing in Barnes, emerging from the shadows to occupy center stage in *Nightwood*, in which "lesbianism and meditation on inversion preoccupy the central characters" (p. 196).

Marthe Rosenfeld's essay connects the "modernity" of Nicole Brossard's later works, *Amantes* and *Picture Theory*, to her Lesbianism, asserting that Brossard must invent a new language to express Lesbian meanings. Brossard, a contemporary Lesbian feminist writer from Québec, contrasts with Barnes in her emphatic assertion of her Lesbian identity and the transformative potential of Lesbianism:

An avant-garde composition consisting of poems and prose passages, *Amantes* deals with the lovemaking of four lesbians who are staying at the Barbizon Hotel for women and who learn to articulate their feelings as well as their thoughts by associating with their own kind. To evoke the atmosphere of this female space, Brossard experiments with form and typography. . . . Unlike traditional literature, whose texts refer for the most part to an objective reality, the words of *Amantes* create their own mental space. (p. 201)

Rosenfeld demonstrates that because Brossard chooses Lesbianism as a position from which to change language, her experimental language expresses Lesbian meanings. In the revolutionary utopian quest for a new language that will rupture patriarchal culture and insert women into history, a Lesbian epistemology makes it possible to choose and/or create the language structures capable of expressing new visions of the world.

Linnea Stenson traces the development of Lesbian identity in twentieth-century Lesbian novels, beginning with the Lesbian-as-"invert" in novels that adopted the pathological view developed by nineteenth-century sexologists, and culminating in Radclyffe Hall's *The Well of Loneliness*, published in 1928. Through the 1930s, Lesbian novelists created Lesbian characters who were isolated from each other, without communities. In the "pulp" novels of the 1950s and 1960s, Lesbian characters were shown in communities, but these communities were set in the bars.

Situating Lesbian literature within the social and political climate prevalent in mainstream culture in the United States during different periods, Stenson attributes the broader vision of Lesbian community – the "lesbian nation" – to the feminist and gay rights movements. The black civil rights movement also shifted the vision of Lesbian community, creating the environment in which explicit treatment of black Lesbian lives could flourish for the first time. Until the 1970s, Stenson notes, "explicit treatment of lesbian themes in literature from working-class communities and communities of color is scarce" (this volume, p. 209). From the publication of Shockley's *Loving Her* in 1974, the first openly Lesbian novel by an Afro-American woman, many Lesbian novels have focused on diversity among Lesbian communities. In the 1970s novels Stenson summarizes, Lesbian characters find positive self-identities and contribute actively to their communities, seen increasingly as supportive of Lesbian struggle.

As we discussed in our introduction to part 2 of this anthology, theorists like Fuss have criticized Lesbian feminist scholars for failing to adopt a constructionist view of Lesbian identity. Carlston's essay on Lorde's autobiographical *Zami: A New Spelling of My Name* (or, as Lorde termed it, her "biomythography") shows that this essentialist view may prevail even when authors otherwise describe identity as constructed and in flux.

Carlston outlines the various definitions Lorde provides for identity. Race, for example, is a socially given category embedded in language, while Lorde constructs and chooses her identity as poet. Her identity as a Lesbian, however, is "both chosen and essential, or at least essentialized in Lorde's mythology" (this volume, p. 227). Yet Lorde's emphasis on her discrete identities "allows for the possibility . . . of coalition, without neutralizing difference" and helps her to negotiate among her various identities:

Furthermore, by relativizing her identities – Audre *feels* more or less black, more or less lesbian, according to circumstances – Lorde avoids essentialism without denying the effective reality of her position at any given moment. The fluidity of her categories of identity both hierarchizes them within a specific sociohistorical context, and allows for the possibility of a rearrangement of their configuration at any time. (p. 233)

Carlston praises the complexity of Lorde's treatment of identity, which adds the notion of "positionality" to identity and coalition politics:

Offering as it does the possibility of collective political agency that yet does not suppress difference, the "politics of location" seems capable of avoiding many of the pitfalls of both radical and deconstructive feminisms, and even of providing a model of pluralistic politics to other progressive movements. . . . To the idea of coalition between individuals Lorde adds the concept of "positionality," or individual identity as an unstable construct, constantly (re)produced both by and within the social matrix, and by the subject's conscious creation of her self. (p. 226)

Lorde's positionalism allows for a view of identity as the product of both "social inter-(re)action and self-(re)creation," reconciling the apparent contradiction between identity politics (implying essentialism) on the one hand, and personal and social change through coalition(s) on the other.

Crowder's essay, "Separatism and Feminist Utopian Fiction," chronicles the emergence and virtual disappearance of feminist utopian fiction during the period 1968 through 1985. Quoting the Radicalesbians, Crowder explains the surge in Lesbian utopias on the basis of women's rage against their abuse by men: "If 'a lesbian is the rage of all women condensed to the point of explosion,' then it is not unreasonable to conclude that the rage of all women, when condensed to the point of explosion, will produce lesbian texts" (this volume, p. 238). Crowder mentions the psychological effect Lesbian utopias had upon her personally. Cognitively, she benefited from strong female role models. Emotionally, she recovered the hope that the world might be made anew, better, more beautiful (p. 238).

However, the Lesbian communities depicted in utopian fiction rest on the elimination of men, resulting either from the war women wage against men or from some unexplained plague. Wittig's *Les Guérillères* and Russ's *The Female Man* provide Lesbian separatist utopias as solutions to a culturally based male supremacy, while some later utopias "depict men as inherently violent, hierarchical, incapable of humane, or even human, relationships with women, children, the earth, or other men" (p. 242).

The rift between writers who view men as *essentially* different from women and those who see male supremacy as a *construct* mirrors similar theoretical debates within separatist theory, as evidenced by the articles in Hoagland and Penelope's *For Lesbians Only: A Separatist Anthology* (1988). Crowder sees the privileging of nature as a problem for separatist utopias, since they could be achieved only through the elimination of men, but women are assumed to be innately nonviolent. The fantastic ways in which men are removed by many authors do not provide a manifesto for concrete social and political activism, she argues, clearly perceiving the potential of Lesbian literature as a catalyst articulating strategies for real (external) social revolution.

In the next essay, Louise Kawada presents the "compelling vision" (this volume, pp. 251–62) of Lesbian comedic novels as capable of transforming both individual readers and (Lesbian?) culture. Kawada regards Brown's *Rubyfruit Jungle* as beginning to break down the dichotomized categories which Cixous, for example, identified as integral to phallocentric modes of thought:

> Cixous would break down even those deeply ingrained patterns of thought, far more subtle and elusive than any political codification. . . . moreover, Cixous and Clément are privileging a Lesbian perspective that (re)fuses ideas of otherness and superiority in a relationship. To enter into that perspective where binary divisions, hierarchies no longer have meaning is to renew oneself, become whole, and experience a sense of joy and renewal. . . . (p. 254)

Rubyfruit Jungle interrogates gender, "the constructs in our society that order and hierarchize sexual relations" (p. 257). Like the authors of some of the separatist utopias discussed by Crowder, Kawada seems largely to accept essentialist views of Lesbians and of women generally. However, the essentialist position is not a problem for Kawada. Rather, Lesbian novels like Brown's and Alther's (*Other Women*) might both "recover and extend the idea of comedy" (p. 258), and lead all of us to a radically new vision of the world based on "*jouissance,* a play-filled ebullient sense of sexuality" (p. 261).

6

Bonnie Zimmerman

Perverse Reading:
The Lesbian Appropriation of Literature

Feminist critics have demonstrated that literary texts and acts of reading are gendered, that it matters whether a writer, reader, or critic is male or female. The question addressed in this essay is, if a text has gender, does it also have sex? To put it more seriously, does the affectional preference, or sexual orientation, of a writer and more specifically of a reader or critic influence the ways in which she reads texts and criticizes them? How are "literary seeing and critical knowing" – to quote Joan Hartman and Ellen Messer-Davidow – "centered in a [lesbian] self?"[1] My assumption is that lesbianism, like heterosexuality, is a way of seeing and knowing the world. How we understand the self and the world that constitutes it – and that it constitutes – affects how we read and understand literature.

No one is born with a perspective; perspective is something we acquire as a result of living in the world. The kind of perspective we acquire is determined partly by the social meaning of certain conditions of birth, such as our gender or race. Gender, for instance, is supposed to be fixed at a very young age – perhaps as young as eighteen months. From that point on, family and society firmly impose a gendered perspective on the girl or boy, one that will mark the child's consciousness, her point of view, for her entire life, whether she accepts or rejects given gender constructs. Racial and ethnic perspectives, and possibly those of class as well (when not obscured by a social mythology of classlessness), may also be developed early in life. But the process of developing a lesbian or gay perspective is not so clear, partly because women become lesbians any time from puberty to old age. Furthermore, there is little agreement among lesbians as to whether or not one is born gay, as one is born female or black. Lesbian writers of retrospective narratives often claim to have felt themselves to *be* lesbian from birth, or age two, or certainly from puberty, and thus always to have had a lesbian perspective. Many claim that there is an "essential" lesbian vision, marked by strong attractions to another girl or woman, feelings of difference, or perhaps rejection of traditional female socialization.

But fictional and autobiographical accounts of lesbian identity formation are retrospective, products of the very perspective that they purport to explain. They tend to isolate factors that create a sense of continuity within the self, while ignoring factors that clash with current identity.[2] For example, a woman might focus on the fact that she was intimate friends with Sally at age six and fail to note that so were a dozen other girls, none of whom became lesbians. I would suggest that lesbianism is not an essential identity (whether biologically or developmentally produced) that somehow can be mined from the deep recesses of the self, but rather, a way of knowing and acting – a mode of communication between self and world. It may very well be that lesbian identity and perspectivity are fluid, overlapping with heterosexual female or gay male perspectives. Most lesbians see the world as a heterosexual for some period of their lives and develop a multiple perspectivity – a form of cultural "bilingualism" – that can reinforce the connections, rather than the oppositions, between lesbian and heterosexual feminist perspectives.

Nevertheless, at a certain point some women act upon their feelings, choose a different life path, and claim a personal and sometimes public self-definition as a lesbian. It seems to me, then, that *choice* is essential to our understanding of lesbian perspectivity, even if biological or developmental factors push some women toward making that choice. That choice may involve nothing more (nor less) than the gender of sexual partners, or it may involve a totally transformed political stance in the world. But, however it is understood by the individual, wherever she places herself on the "lesbian continuum," lesbian identity is established when the individual sees the world anew as a lesbian, more than by a sexual act or by birthright.[3] Lesbianism is not something that happens to a woman, it is something she seeks and discovers, whether in the world or in herself. At some point a woman must "come out" – that is, adopt a lesbian identity or point of view. The more self-reflective and self-conscious one is – the more one is aware of one's agency – the more defined one's lesbian perspective will be. This is the position from which I will be developing my argument. As a self-conscious lesbian, I choose, I act, I claim responsibility for how I know the world. And I think this can serve as a useful model for how I choose to know the world as (in my case) a woman and a Jew. Our ubiquitous social mythology enforces a perspective that is white, male, Christian, straight; seeing from the position of the Other (to use Simone de Beauvoir's existentialist terminology) forces me radically to restructure this pervasive ideology.

What then is a lesbian perspective? How do lesbians see, read, and know the world?[4] Many lesbian critics and philosophers agree that lesbians see, not from the center of what Marilyn Frye names "phallocratic reality," but from its edge.[5] And because lesbians see "obliquely," as Monique Wittig puts it, we note different lights and shades, different presences and absences, different emphases and omissions.[6] Frye uses the metaphor of the theater to explain what lesbians see. Reality is organized by men as a stage on which they are the principal actors and women the stagehands and backdrop. To maintain the fiction of this reality, no one must attend to any other movements but those of the main actors, men. Reality relies on not seeing the background, women. But lesbians construct an alternative reality by attending to, or focusing on, that background. In Frye's words, lesbians "are in a position to see things that cannot be seen from within the system. What lesbians see is what makes them lesbians and their seeing is why they have to be excluded [from phallocratic reality]. Lesbians are women-seers" (1983:173).

How is lesbian seeing different from male or heterosexual female seeing? Traditionally, men see women in relation to themselves as sexual objects or as domestic servants. Throughout history, men have also seen women as exemplars or archetypes, both positive and negative: Eve or Mary, witch or saint, angel in the house or unsexed woman. Thus men see women either as appendages or as a class, but not as individual and independent persons with agencies and perspectives of their own. Heterosexual women see other women in more complex ways. Some state proudly that they do not see women at all ("I prefer talking with men"; "Sex has nothing to do with my work or life"), but this stance is ingenuous. In fact, these "queen bees" do see women in the background and are uncomfortable noticing what male-centered vision obscures. They may even more assiduously maintain the male illusion of female invisibility. Another way heterosexual women see other women, according to patriarchal mythology, is as rivals. This vision results when a women watches the stage wearing the distorting lenses of androcentrism. She still sees men at the center, but takes note as well of any woman who inches closer to them than she is. Finally, a heterosexual woman may see other women within the roles and institutions established by a male-centered perspective: that is, woman as wife, as mother, as seductress, as mistress, even as independent woman (since "independent" here actually functions as a synecdoche for "independent from men or marriage"). This was the approach taken by the earliest feminist critics in texts and courses generally titled "Images of Women" (an approach still used in classrooms) and is, to my mind, a basically heterosexual approach to literary criticism.

On the other hand, lesbian and heterosexual feminists see women similarly, in that their visions both include women relating to other women.

To quote from an early lesbian feminist polemic, "The Woman-Identified Woman": "It is the primacy of women relating to women, of women creating a new consciousness of and with each other, which is at the heart of women's liberation, and the basis for the cultural revolution."[7] Lesbians brought female bonding to the center of feminist discourse, and now most feminists see women in relation to other women, often minimizing whatever male or heterosexual action is taking place on the world stage. Thus, one way I would restate Frye's definition is that lesbians are woman-relating-to-woman seers. This places at the center of a lesbian perspective women-bonding and female friendship, as in Barbara Smith's interpretation of *Sula*, Blanche Wiesen Cook's analysis of female support networks, and Lillian Faderman's study of romantic friendship.[8] These critics and historians look obliquely at phallocentric reality, placing what had been central – men and women's dependence on men – off center or indeed offstage. Our perspective shifts to what had been background, women's relationships with women, thus making reality gynocentric.

As I have stated, many if not all heterosexual feminists now see women in this lesbian way. There is considerable overlap between a lesbian and feminist vision. Patriarchs know this to be true. They insist that all feminists are lesbians ("You're taking a women's studies course? But they're all dykes over there!") and suspect that all lesbians are feminists. The key point made by Adrienne Rich in "Compulsory Heterosexuality and Lesbian Existence" is that no firm line can be drawn between lesbian experience and other female experience. But many lesbians know – or believe we know – that we see women differently than do even the most feminist of heterosexual women. What is the distinctiveness of, to paraphrase Djuna Barnes, this vision with a difference?[9]

The most immediate and self-evident (to a lesbian) answer is that lesbians include sexuality – desire and passion – as a possibility in women's relationships with each other. Lesbians not only *see* women, but desire and feel passion for them. This is certainly one part of the discord that often exists between lesbians and heterosexual women, whether feminist or not. Heterosexual women may fear that lesbians will see them as sexual objects, as men do. Indeed, many lesbians, particularly those who come out as a result of feminist awakening, avoid the use of sexual imagery in their writing as a reaction to patriarchal reification of both heterosexual women and lesbians. But this is a futile avoidance. Lesbian being-in-the-world is sexual; it is largely our sexuality that distinguishes us from other women. But not sex alone – lesbians also feel romantic and passionate about women. Thus a lesbian reader of literature will note women relating to each other, but see and emphasize the sexual, romantic, and/or passionate elements of this relation. Furthermore, a lesbian perspective focuses on the primacy and duration of the female friendship. This is why

Sula makes sense as a lesbian text, despite its pervasive heterosexuality. The friendship between Sula and Nel is primary; it is more important in their lives than any other connection, and it endures beyond death.

Finally, lesbians look beyond individual relationships to female communities that do not need or want men. Although I wish to keep women center stage in my argument, I do need to point out that much lesbian reading and writing quite explicitly excludes men (except, perhaps, as a symbol of danger) from the newly designed theater. What lesbians see is what women may always have suspected: that men are not essential to women. Of course, in actual patriarchal societies men are represented as essential for survival, even for making the world meaningful. It is therefore simply impossible for women and lesbians to avoid seeing and interacting with men in some way. But in a literary text – the lesbian utopia – writers and readers imagine possibilities that do not actually exist. Thus Marilyn Frye's comment that lesbians are "woman-*seers*" is actually a pun. Lesbians "see" women, and also have a "prophetic" knowledge or idealized vision that women could live fully and contentedly without men. In a lesbian perspective, women are both necessary and sufficient.

The creation of new possibilities and the transformation of old realities by writers and readers is central to my theory of lesbian perspectivity. Because self-conscious lesbians see the world in a particular way, we also write and read literature from a unique vantage point. I want to explore here some ways in which lesbians read or "misread" texts. In *The Resisting Reader,* Judith Fetterley argued that:

The first act of the feminist critic must be to become a resisting rather than an assenting reader and, by this refusal to assent, to begin the process of exorcising the male mind that has been implanted in us.[10]

I would go even farther and suggest that lesbian-feminist readers resist "heterotexts" by privately rewriting and thus appropriating them as lesbian texts. There is a certain point in a plot or character development – the "what if" moment – when a lesbian reader refuses to assent anymore to the heterosexual imperative; a point in the narrative labyrinth where she simply cuts a hole and follows her own path.

I am calling this reading strategy "perverse" to reclaim a word defined by the dictionary as "willfully determined not to do what is expected or desired."[11] The emphasis in this definition is on *will*, that is, again to turn to the dictionary, "the faculty of conscious and particularly of deliberate action; the power of control the mind has over its own actions." Thus a perverse reader is one highly conscious of her own agency, who takes an active role in shaping the text she reads in accordance with her perspective on the world.

Two parallel scenes from Jane Rule's story "Inland Passage" demonstrate how a text can be interpreted according to the reader's perspective.[12] This is a simple story of two mature women falling in love as they cruise the inland passage to Alaska. Fidelity first presents herself to Troy as another heterosexual woman by interpreting a scene before them:

"See those two over there?" Fidelity said, nodding to a nondescript pair of middle-aged women. "One's a lady cop. The other's her prisoner."
"How do you figure that out?"
"Saw the handcuffs. That's why they're sitting side by side." (1985:221)

After Fidelity and Troy have fallen in love and come out to each other, they see the two women again. This time Fidelity explicates the scene differently:

"I was wrong about those two over there," Fidelity said. "They sit side by side because they're lovers." "And you thought so in the first place," Troy said. Fidelity nodded. (235)

The text that Fidelity reads presents itself as a blank page: the two women are a "nondescript pair." It is Fidelity, the reader, the agent, who creates the story about them, derived not only from her point of view, but also from the point of view she wishes to make known to the world. In the first reading, Fidelity seems to read as a heterosexual; in the second, as a lesbian. But even the first time, she is reading not as a heterosexual but as a closeted lesbian. The clue is that the story she relates is one of imprisonment and bondage, an ironic reference to the heterosexual myth that lesbians capture and tie other women to them. The second reading deconstructs the first: imprisonment is revealed to be mutual love.

Fidelity is a very perceptive and creative misreader. She illustrates a feminist or lesbian feminist reading strategy that Elaine Showalter and Sharon O'Brien describe as an oscillation between figure and ground.[13] Thus we might say that a lesbian has double vision, a self-reflective point of view that attends to the text as it has been constructed by hetero- or androcentric readings (the traditional figure that becomes the ground) and as it is newly constructed by lesbian awareness (the traditional ground that is reconstituted as the figure). Further, a conscious lesbian reader – that is, a lesbian aware of her own agency, her role in constructing the meaning of a text – will attend to the way in which the figure is shaped by the ground, and the way the ground changes when the figure is noticed. If lesbians are women who attend to women attending to each other, then a lesbian will note the centrality of Sula and Nel's love and at the same time acknowledge that this love is powerfully muted by the het-

erosexual dynamics of the novel. A lesbian critic might point to the re-
demptive role of female friendship in George Eliot's novels and counterpoint the "homoerotic" climax of a novel (the meeting between Maggie
and Lucy in *The Mill on the Floss*, or between Dorothea and Rosamond in
Middlemarch) with its heterosexual climax (Maggie and Tom's death embrace, or Dorothea and Will's confession of love). A lesbian critic might
attend to Lizzie's erotic plea to her sister Laura in Rossetti's "Goblin Market" – "Eat me, drink me, love me, / Laura, make much of me" – and
"make much of" the poem as a parable of how pure love between women
overcomes impure lust between women and men. In doing so, she would
be able to explain why husbands are so conspicuously absent from the
ostensibly heterosexual ending of the poem.

Another text that has drawn the attention of lesbian critics is Kate
Chopin's *The Awakening*.[14] But, surprisingly, even they have failed to attend to the background of the novel where woman sees woman. Behind
the romantic heterosexual plot that establishes the novel's foreground lies
a shadowy lesbian story. Edna Pontellier has close friendships with two
women, Adele Ratignolle and Mlle Reisz. Each represents a road not
taken by Edna: the path of the contented wife from which she strays and
the path of the artist on which she stumbles and falls. These women are
both monitory figures and real presences in the novel, with whom Edna
forges "the subtle bond which we call sympathy, which we might as well
call love."[15] Each suggests an alternative world for Edna, in which women
might be primary for themselves and each other. With Adele Ratignolle
Edna shares one exquisite afternoon alone and unshackled on the beach,
a moment in female space or what Elaine Showalter named the "wild
zone."[16] Edna loosens her clothing (signifying both freedom and sensuality) as the hot sun, the novel's symbol of sexuality, pours over them. She
recounts her adolescence, a time of possibility before marriage and motherhood tied her to her present life. The scene ends with the entrance of
Robert, accompanied by the children the two women have momentarily
forgotten. Robert is no liberatory figure here, but one more actor in the
world of men, marriage, and motherhood that Edna is soon to flee.

The connection between Edna and Adele is exceedingly sensual; the
one between Edna and Mlle Reisz is spiritual and intellectual. Mlle Reisz's
self-definition, indifference to men and family life, and admiration for
Edna can be read as subtle suggestions of the lesbian. After the Pontelliers
return to New Orleans and Robert leaves for Mexico, Mlle Reisz becomes
Edna's mentor and confidante. But, as Robert's physical presence interrupts the communion between Edna and Adele on the beach, so his textual presence interrupts the communication between Edna and Mlle
Reisz. Their meetings revolve around his letters, and, while Mlle Reisz

soothes (and seduces) Edna with her music, Edna drifts back into fatal fantasies of heterosexual romance.

Such a lesbian reading of *The Awakening* has a number of consequences. One is simply that it makes the text more personally meaningful to lesbian readers. As one of my students responded when asked if she thought she read differently as a lesbian, "Of course. Remember that scene in *The Awakening?* That's *my* scene!" Furthermore, by drawing attention to the lesbian figure in the ground, we are able to see new complexity in women's past and contemporary lives. Lesbian historians have established that many women did choose women over men in the late nineteenth century. What forces prevented Edna from doing so? How would her life have been different if she had? How would our lives be different were we able to wander or reside in the wild zone? And, finally, in a lesbian reading, *The Awakening* appears not so much as a pathetic or heroic tale, but rather as an ironic tragedy. Edna is a tragic heroine; her flaw is her inability to detach herself from men and male definitions of love and romance. Kate Chopin, however, distances herself from her heroine by portraying one way out of her muddle: the friendship and even the erotic companionship of other women.

Perverse reading reveals subtexts of female friendship previously unrevealed; it also leads to the rewriting of cultural stereotypes and literary conventions by reversing the values attached to the idea of lesbianism. In *Desert of the Heart,* for example, Jane Rule revised such negative conventions as the "mark of Cain," the "narcissistic mirror," and the "life against nature" that were used to establish a deviance model of lesbianism.[17] In this, Rule anticipated the lesbian feminist movement that emerged in the early 1970s and revised the old text that society had written for lesbians. That text was so riddled with errors that it was not even fit for editing, so lesbian readers, of life and literature, claimed the right to have a literature infused with positive symbolism.

A new generation of authors, many of them writing for the first time, provided positive, validating images steeped in the emerging mythology of lesbian feminism. Molly Bolt replaced Stephen Gordon as the quintessential lesbian hero; Patience and Sarah idylled in the green world undisturbed by any intrusive corn god; the hill women of the Wanderground infused the old amazonian myth with new power and sensuality.[18] Furthermore, empowered by lesbian feminist consciousness, readers are able to expose the patriarchal and heterosexual biases behind the old destructive stereotypes, strip them of their negativity, and even transform them into images of power and promise. The lesbian vampire becomes a Lilith figure who is our ancestral sister. The man-hating dyke arrogantly states her reasons for coming to such a position. The mark of Cain is worn proudly as a talisman against patriarchal evil. The existence that patriarchy labels as a sin or perversion, the lesbian, from her vantage point, sees as a logical strategy for survival.

What is also necessary for the survival of the lesbian resisting reader is an imaginative mind that can invent lesbian plots even if they are not exactly there. My theory of perverse reading was developed from just such a spinning of a new plot from an author's actual text. Let me give one example of this reading strategy taken from popular culture. During the 1984 television season, the writers of "Dallas" introduced a new character, Jamie Ewing, who first appeared as a tough, no-nonsense tomboy. A strong friendship developed between her and Suellen Ewing, herself rebelling against the infidelity of her notorious husband, J.R. As a lesbian reader/viewer, I immediately noticed that the scenes between Jamie and Suellen almost always took place in the bedroom, suggesting both lesbian sensuality and that female space in which Edna and Adele idylled in *The Awakening*. The triangle created by the three characters finally was broken up in a remarkable confrontation during which Jamie challenged J.R.'s control of Suellen. The powerful iconography of the scene contrasted an isolated J.R. with the two closely bonded women.

At that moment, the lesbian viewer could move in two directions. She could follow the writer's lead toward the conventional heterosexual (and sexist) resolution: J.R. breaks up the two women, precipitating Suellen's decline into alcohol dependency (for the second or third time in the series' history), and Jamie's transformation into a spiteful, clinging feminine stereotype. Or the lesbian viewer could write her own plot – the one that is never seen on prime-time television – in which Suellen and Jamie thumb their noses at J.R. and the entire Ewing clan, and walk off the set together. Like Carolyn in Lisa Alther's *Other Women*, I put myself and my point of view in the text:

> As she sipped her coffee, she watched a movie about two career girls on the make in New York City. She realized she'd seen it before. The good-looking one got Jimmy Stewart and the other one got promoted to editor. If only once the girls would get each other. But probably that was asking too much of Twentieth Century Fox.[19]

That may be too much to ask, but lesbians must ask just the same. As one of my students put it, we're constantly frustrated at what's not there (as well as at what is *endlessly* there). The world lesbians live in consists of women with short hair and jeans, or long hair and pearls, who are lesbians. Daughters come out and do or do not break their mothers' hearts. Married women get fed up with men or simply fall in love with their next-door neighbors. Some women who get breast cancer, or write gothic novels, or go underground, or get tenured are lesbians. But, except for the submerged genre of lesbian fiction that seldom can be found outside feminist bookstores, our literature and mass media rarely express a lesbian point of view. Even in mainstream feminist literature, life is unremittingly and often uncritically heterosexual. When it is not, as in novels like Doris Grumbach's *Chamber Music* or Alice Walker's *The Color Purple*, the lesbian reader experiences a moment of almost sublime surprise and satisfaction. More often, however, we feel betrayed. To continue reading at all, we must somehow see and know literature differently, imagining possibilities otherwise ignored and suppressed. In this way we appropriate it for our own needs and incorporate it into our own worldview.

In short, lesbians come to literature with different emotions and experiences. For us, the feminist ideal is not necessarily an equal partnership between a previously domineering husband and a dominated wife – the staple feminist plot. Adolescent crushes on best friends or older women are not phases to outgrow. Two adult women falling in love is not another obligatory lesbian interlude. A lesbian character getting her head sliced off is neither amusing nor ironic. We have a different perspective, certainly on everything involving sexuality, gender identity, and human relations. One woman's happy ending may be another's disappointment. And one woman's embarrassment may be another's reward.

Let me emphasize that the lesbian resisting reader, reading perversely, is not merely demanding a plot or character study that the writer has not chosen to create. She is picking up on hints and possibilities that the author, consciously or not, has strewn in the text. A text that manifests certain symbolic elements – perhaps the absence of men, of women's attention to men, or of marked femininity; perhaps the presence of female bonding, or of strong and independent female characters – may trigger the act of lesbian reading. The reader is simply bringing to the text an understanding of the world as *she* has learned to read and thus to know it.

Lesbians (like most members of stigmatized groups) learn very quickly to "read" life. The very nature of lesbianism – a minority status that can be identified by few if any visible signs – requires that lesbians become skilled readers of external appearance and behavior. Judy Grahn's short story "Boys at the Rodeo" is an excellent illustration of this ability.[20] As the narrator watches the competition for rodeo queen, she notices that the "last loser sits well on a scrubby little pony and lives with her aunt and uncle. I pick her for the dyke even though it is speculation without clues. I can't help it, it's a pleasant habit" (1981:12). Later she observes other participants in the rodeo: "One small girl is not disheartened by the years of bad training, the ridiculous cross-field run, the laughing superior man on his horse, or the shape shifting goat. She downs it in a beautiful flying tackle. This makes me whisper, as usual, 'that's the dyke'" (13). As Grahn's phrase "speculation without clues" suggests, lesbians are like cryptographers or detectives – or literary critics – for all life presents itself to lesbians as a coded text in need of deciphering and explication.

But there is a significant difference between such active explication as a "common reader" (to use Virginia Woolf's term) and traditional literary criticism. That difference provides insight into the impact of professional training on literary reading and into the way in which academics construct knowledge. In my explication of Jane Rule's story, for example, I functioned as a trained literary critic bringing her personal perspective to an interpretation of an unambiguously lesbian text. But this training more often causes conflicts as I read "perversely" texts that are ostensibly heterosexual or ambiguously sexual. I have been taught to have such respect for, or fear of, the written text, that when I compensate for the paucity of lesbian literature – for the false world projected by our culture – by spinning a different story out of the author's material, I consider such behavior to be irresponsible. I suspect myself of indulging in wish fulfillment. In other words, my literary training eliminates my individuality, my perspective, from my reading. As a common reader of life and literature, I feel responsible to myself and to a community of lesbian readers. But as a trained critic, I am uncomfortably aware of my membership in a literary community that finds my perspective "narrow" or "distorting." Like Grahn's narrator, I worry that I am speculating without clues, that, "as usual," I am seeing what is not there. The very social context (heterosexualism) that my reading intends to challenge becomes a constraint upon the possibility of such a reading.[21]

The only way out of this circular prison, I believe, is to untrain the critical self, not by abandoning the techniques of criticism, but by abandoning the impersonal attitude that critical training cultivates. This means reading audaciously and often "naively" – that is, as one reads privately but fears to do publicly. By doing so, lesbian critics have provided fresh and radical interpretations of literary texts, traditions, and even values. As Melanie Kaye puts it, "What does it mean when people can envision only two possible ends to any story [i.e., marriage or death]?"[22] The self-conscious lesbian reader sees or imagines other possible endings that expand opportunities not only for writers of texts but also for women actively creating their lives. Thus, lesbian critical readings are not only possible but necessary to revitalize the conventions we find stale and meaningless.

This discussion of how a lesbian perspective shapes reading and knowing leads me to thoughts about a feminist theory of perspectivity. White heterosexual men define their perspective on the world as objective truth and thus discount women, people of color, and homosexuals as deviant perceivers. Feminists, as well as other theorists, have insisted, with some modest success, that "truth" be redefined to account for the values and visions of those considered "other" in the Western worldview. Who will determine the values assigned to competing perspectives? To adapt questions raised by Jane Tompkins concerning the relationship between discourse and power: "What makes one set of perceptual strategies or literary conventions win out over another? If the world is the product of interpretation, then who or what determines which interpretive system will prevail?"[23] I guess that the determiners of truth will be those with the power of definition. Currently, in the academy, this power lies in the hands of those who edit texts and journals, hire and fire junior faculty, approve or reject dissertation topics, disperse grants, and so on. These hands still belong, for the most part, to the very white men who have established their perspective as objective truth.

But women's studies have had an impact on the academy. Increasingly women are being absorbed into the decision-making body, and some of them articulate a feminist notion of literary value and meaning. Given the fact that people with power will prefer to incorporate newcomers as similar to themselves as possible, it is hardly to be expected that, now or in the long run, these new powermongers will be lesbians, women of color, or women outside academia. It is therefore possible that feminist inquiry itself will maintain the competitive marketplace of ideas. We have often battled between a radical feminist perspective and a socialist feminist perspective, or between separatist and integrationist strategies. Of particular relevance to my argument are the struggles between lesbians and heterosexuals. Lesbians insist that heterosexuality is the result of brainwashing and not at all a feminist option. Heterosexuals devoutly wish lesbians would stop making trouble and return to the bedroom where they belong. The history of the women's movement suggests that feminists are vulnerable to the same tendency that we urge the academy to abandon – the tendency to impose a dominant perspective.

Nevertheless, many feminists have proven to be sensitive to the moral persuasion of people who articulate perspectives different from those of individuals in the mainstream (or the feminist tributary) of literary criticism. Feminist critics understand that criticism must incorporate actively the visions and insights of lesbians, women of color, and working-class women. And lesbians (for example) need to encourage replacing the competitive model of academic inquiry with a communicative model based on empathic understanding and respect for diversity.

The model of inquiry proposed by this essay could be one alternative to the quasi-military model alluded to in Tompkins's question quoted above. Ours is a model that should appeal to literary critics who understand that no single interpretation of a text is complete without reference to many others. Conflicts and differences will always occur among varying interpretations. Far from agonizing over these differences, literary critics revel in them (albeit quite nastily at times). In fact, our careers depend upon our ability to come up with new interpretations of old texts. Literature can best be understood and appreciated through interactions among differing interpretations. Perhaps this is why lesbians and other "deviant" perceivers have had an increasing influence on literary study.

Does this mean that all perspectives are equally tolerable, valid, and valuable? Certainly not. All perspectives result from the same set of factors, primarily a person's social and cultural situation (her sex, race, class, sexuality, and so on) and personal history. What distinguishes the validity of one perspective from another is how self-reflective it is and how open it is to admitting the validity of other perspectives. There is nothing wrong with seeing and knowing the world as a heterosexual, but there is a good deal wrong with seeing and knowing it as a heterosexualist. The heterosexual perceiver would be aware of how her perspective is shaped by her particular situation, and she would seek out and welcome lesbian perspectives that resonate with her own. The heterosexualist perceiver, on the other hand, might not even be aware of other agents or her own agency, and thus would posit her perspective as the natural or universal vision of the world. Furthermore, once aware of lesbian perspectives, she might cling to her culturally dominant and privileged position and dismiss them as irrelevant.

I believe that feminist inquiry must continue to trust that such narrowmindedness is the product of ignorance, not malice, and that, as lesbian scholars articulate both a lesbian perspective and a critique of the heterosexualist perspective, most unreflective thinkers will change and adjust their own vision of the world. The only perspective that has no place in feminist inquiry is the one born of prejudice and maintained in anger or fear. Furthermore, perspective or point of view is only part of the project feminist scholars are undertaking. I cannot agree that "the world is the product of interpretation" alone; the world is also the product of human activity. *Point of view* – how we as concrete historical agents understand the world – must become *standpoint* – the position from which we try to change the world. At this time, the similarities among various feminist perspectives – radical, socialist, lesbian, heterosexual, black, white – may be more crucial than their differences. When it comes to acting in the world, even when the world is nothing more than the academy, it is often to our advantage, indeed our survival, to act from one standpoint.

I have been searching for a concluding metaphor to express my vision of feminist and lesbian feminist inquiry. Perhaps this inquiry is like a mosaic of contrasting yet harmonizing viewpoints, or a kaleidoscope continually transforming patterns as it is twirled. But the metaphor I like best is one that I often use in literature classes. The encyclopedia my family owned when I was a child had a marvelous section on human anatomy. Each system of the body was drawn on transparencies laid one on top of the next. Each system could be viewed separately with complete attention to its use and meaning in the human body. But viewed together, one through the other, the transparencies created a three-dimensional image of the body as a whole. Our perspectives – of class, race, sexuality, political persuasion – are not discrete entities that, to use yet another metaphor, can be mixed and matched like Villager separates. Perspectivity, rather, involves the continual layering and deepening of visions in communication, not in competition, with each other.

NOTES

1 Joan Hartman and Ellen Messer-Davidow, "Learning to See: Feminist Perspectives in Literary Study," paper presented in the session on "Critical Issues in Feminist Inquiry: Agency and Perspective," National Women's Studies Association Convention, June 1984.

2 See Bonnie Zimmerman, "The Politics of Transliteration: Lesbian Personal Narratives," *Signs* 9, no. 4 (Summer 1984), 667–68; and Marilyn Frye, review of *The Coming Out Stories*, ed. Julia Penelope Stanley and Susan J. Wolfe, *Sinister Wisdom* 14, Summer (1980), 97–98.

3 The phrase "lesbian continuum" was coined by Adrienne Rich in "Compulsory Heterosexuality and Lesbian Existence," *Signs* 5, no. 4 (Summer 1980), 631–60. Rich uses it to indicate the congruence between female friendship and lesbian love. I am using it to suggest the variety of self-concepts among lesbians.

4 The terms "see," "vision," "point of view," and "perspective" may be construed as ableist. However, they are used so extensively in Western thought that my argument cannot be developed without them. I would suggest that these words always be understood to be *metaphors,* not signs of a particular physiological ability.

5 Marilyn Frye, *The Politics of Reality: Essays in Feminist Theory* (Trumansburg, N.Y.: The Crossing Press, 1983), 162.

6 Monique Wittig, "The Point of View: Universal or Particular?," *Feminist Issues* 3, no. 2 (Fall 1983), 65.

7 Radicalesbians, "The Woman-Identified Woman," reprinted in *Liberation Now!*, ed. Deborah Babcox and Madeline Belkin (New York: Dell Publishing Co., 1971), 292.

8 Barbara Smith, "Toward a Black Feminist Criticism," *Conditions: Two* (October 1977), 25–44; Blanche Wiesen Cook, "Female Support Networks in the Nineteenth Century," *Chrysalis* 3 (Autumn 1977), 43–61; Lillian Faderman, *Surpassing the Love of Men* (New York: William Morrow, 1981).

9 Djuna Barnes, *Ladies Almanack* (New York: Harper & Row, 1972), 26. What follows is a discussion of one way of thinking about lesbian seeing. There are many other ways. Monique Wittig (note 6 above), for example, suggests that a lesbian point of view requires the "suppression" of gender (64). For Bertha Harris lesbian existence and vision is that of the "unassimilable" and "outra-

geous." Harris, "*What we mean to say:* Notes Toward Defining the Nature of Lesbian Literature," *Heresies* 3 (Fall 1977), 6.

10 Judith Fetterley, *The Resisting Reader* (Bloomington: Indiana University Press, 1978), xxii.

11 All dictionary definitions are taken from *The Random House College Dictionary* (1975).

12 Jane Rule, "Inland Passage," *Inland Passage* (Tallahassee: Naiad Press, 1985), 211–36.

13 Elaine Showalter, "Feminist Criticism in the Wilderness," *Critical Inquiry* 8, no. 2 (Winter 1981), 204; Sharon O'Brien, "'The Thing Not Named': Willa Cather as a Lesbian Writer," *Signs* 9, no. 4 (Summer 1984), 597.

14 See Adrienne Rich on *The Awakening* in "Compulsory Heterosexuality," 657. Also Kathryn Pyne Addelson, "'On Compulsory Heterosexuality and Lesbian Existence': Defining the Issues," *Signs* 7, no. 1 (Autumn 1981), 195–97.

15 Kate Chopin, *The Awakening* (New York: Avon, 1972), 26.

16 Showalter, 200–201.

17 See Marilyn R. Schuster, "Strategies for Survival: The Subtle Subversion of Jane Rule," *Feminist Studies* 7, no. 3 (Fall 1981), 431–50.

18 See Rita Mae Brown, *Rubyfruit Jungle* (New York: Bantam Books, 1977); Isabel Miller, *Patience and Sarah* (New York: Fawcett Crest, 1973); Sally Miller Gearhart, *The Wanderground* (Watertown, Mass.: Persephone Press, 1979).

19 Lisa Alther, *Other Women* (New York: Alfred A. Knopf, 1984), 19.

20 Judy Grahn, "Boys at the Rodeo," *Lesbian Fiction,* ed. Elly Bulkin (Watertown, Mass.: Persephone Press, 1981), 11–16.

21 I owe the term *heterosexualist* to Sarah Lucia Hoagland in *Lesbian Ethics: Toward New Value* (Palo Alto, Calif.: Institute for Lesbian Studies, 1988).

22 Melanie Kaye, "Culture Making: Lesbian Classics," *Sinister Wisdom* 13 (Spring 1980), 25.

23 Jane P. Tompkins, "The Reader in History: The Changing Shape of Literary Response," in Tompkins, ed., *Reader-Response Criticism: From Formalism to Post-Structuralism* (Baltimore: Johns Hopkins University Press, 1980), 226.

7

Diana L. Swanson

Subverting Closure: Compulsory Heterosexuality and Compulsory Endings in Middle-Class British Women's Novels

The novel alone was young enough to be soft in her hands. . . . Yet who shall say that even now "the novel" (I give it inverted commas to mark my sense of the word's inadequacy), who shall say that even this most pliable of all forms is rightly shaped for her use?

   It seems to be her first book, I said to myself, but one must read it as if it were the last volume in a fairly long series, continuing all those other books that I have been glancing at – Lady Winchilsea's poems and Aphra Behn's plays and the novels of the four great novelists. For books continue each other, in spite of our habit of judging them separately.

Virginia Woolf, A Room of One's Own

Conventions, like clichés, have a way of surviving their own usefulness. They are then excused or defended as the idioms of living. For every-one, foreign by birth or by nature, convention is a mark of fluency. That is why, for any woman, marriage is the idiom of life.

Jane Rule, Desert of the Heart

When I first began reading novels by British women writers from the eighteenth to the early twentieth centuries, I was especially interested in how women wrote about love and friendship between women; I was in search of what Adrienne Rich describes as "a flickering, often disguised reality which came and went throughout women's books. . . . It was a sense of desiring oneself; above all, of choosing oneself; it was also a primary intensity between women" (1979:200). In 1929, in *A Room of One's Own*, Virginia Woolf describes reading an imaginary novel, *Life's Adventure*, by an imaginary new novelist, Mary Carmichael, and being shocked to discover that "Chloe liked Olivia." "Chloe liked Olivia for perhaps the first time in literature," Woolf says (86). I now know that in women's novels Chloe liked Olivia well before the twentieth century, but usually Chloe and Olivia's story was enclosed and overshadowed by Chloe and Roger's.

I discovered that I couldn't think about women's friendships in these novels without first thinking about the function of marriage. Marriage formed the continuously present background or encroaching future against which the women's friendships were played out. The courtship and marriage plot generally held center stage and provided the closure demanded by traditional narrative conventions. In other words, compulsory heterosexuality shaped the form of the novels British women could write as much as it shaped the form of the lives they could lead.

I take my definition of compulsory heterosexuality from Adrienne Rich's now classic article, "Compulsory Heterosexuality and Lesbian Existence" (1980). In this piece, Rich argues that sexual and social life for women has been institutionalized as heterosexual. She points out that while heterosexuality is presumed to be the innate, mature, inevitable orientation of women, enormous and often violent social, economic, and psychological forces direct, encourage, and compel women into living heterosexual lives. The means by which heterosexuality is enforced range from rape and incest to inequitable pay and discrimination in hiring to silence about and distortion of women's history and lesbian existence to romanticization of heterosexual relationships in music, film, and literature. *All* women are systematically denied both the right to choose their sexual and affectional lives and the knowledge and autonomy they need to make those choices. The traditional novel participates in enforcing heterosexuality by presenting "heterosexual romance . . . as the great female adventure, duty, and fulfillment" (1981:26) and denying the existence of alternative stories and the power of love between women.

Joanne S. Frye, in *Living Stories, Telling Lives* (1986), helps to clarify the connection between social and literary conventions. She points out that the "grounding of narrative in social expectation" doubles the ideological force of novelistic conventions; the novel formally links aesthetic structures and social structures (30). The literary conventions that control a heroine's career and the social conventions that control women's lives create and reinforce one another.

Carol P. Christ simply and eloquently describes the dialectical relationship between stories and lives:

Stories give shape to lives. As people grow up, reach plateaus, or face crises, they often turn to stories to show them how to take the next step. Women often live out inauthentic stories provided by a culture they did not create. The story most commonly told to young girls is the romantic story of falling in love and living happily ever after. As they grow older some women seek to replace that story with one of free and independent womanhood. (1980:1)

In this article, I tell the story of the attempts of some British middle-class women novelists to replace the romantic heterosexual plot with new stories that challenge compulsory heterosexuality.

I

COMPULSORY HETEROSEXUALITY AND THE NOVEL

Virginia Woolf implies in *A Room of One's Own* that the form of the novel, young and pliable among literary forms as it is, is still not conducive to women's expression. Feminist critics since have pointed to ways in which the form and conventions of the novel are heteropatriarchally defined, limiting the possibilities of plot and action for the heroine and the meanings and feelings expressible within "a novel." Leslie W. Rabine, in *Reading the Romantic Heroine* (1985), traces the drive towards univocality and the suppression of difference, particularly female difference, in romantic texts from *Tristan and Isolde* in the twelfth century, through romantic novels in the eighteenth and nineteenth centuries, to Harlequin Romances in the twentieth. She points to the "lack of cultural codes for feminine personal and historical development in romantic love narrative" (5) and analyzes the ways in which "the independent feminine voice [is] submitted to the totalizing masculine voice of romantic narrative" (7). In romance, argues Rabine, the central hero's quest for a unified, coherent, integral self makes the heroine a mirror to the hero, reflecting this self back to him. The woman becomes a lack, a blank, and can therefore serve as metaphor for the hero's desire.

Rachel M. Brownstein focuses on what happens when in "a novel, a 'realistic' rewriting of romance, a conscious female protagonist takes the quester's place" (1982:xxi). The heroine is both the metaphor for the "ideal of the integrated self" (xxi) and the quester after it. But the choices available to the heroine, the possible ways to accomplish this quest, are extremely limited. The choice of a marriage partner is the one self-defining choice most heroines have. The other possible conclusion to the quest is death. This is compulsory heterosexuality indeed. As Brownstein puts it, "a heroine moves toward her inevitable end, death or marriage, along lines her body generates: the domestic novel binds her over and over to the [hetero]sexual plot" (81). And again:

The main thing about the heroine is that hers is always the same old story.
The paradigmatic hero is an overreacher; the heroine of the domestic novel, the descendant of the Rose, is overdetermined. The hero moves towards a goal; the

heroine tries to be it. . . . A hero is extraordinary, exempt from the rules of society; a heroine must stick to the social code and then some. (82–83)

Nancy Miller, in her study of eighteenth-century novels centered on female protagonists, *The Heroine's Text* (1980), argues likewise that "the heroine's text is plotted within this ideologically delimited space of an either/or closure" in marriage or death (xi). She suggests that through the nineteenth century and even in the late twentieth "experience for women characters is still tied primarily to the erotic and the familial" and "female *Bildung* tends to get stuck in the bedroom" (157). Joanne S. Frye also points to the heroine's lack of options and argues that the novel inscribes and reinscribes the "'culture-text' of femininity" that renders femaleness and autonomy incompatible (1986:3). In her article "Fictional Consensus and Female Casualties" (1983), Elizabeth Ermarth shows that realism is "an aesthetic form of consensus" homologous to, having the same origins as, "other . . . forms of consensus such as the political" (3). Like institutionalized political processes, "fictional representation" has not "represented" women's experiences and viewpoints. "Realistic" narrative conventions form a rule of consensus that is for women actually a rule of force. What the "realistic" novel does represent realistically is the disenfranchisement of women from the ordering of the social world. These and other critics have in various ways shown the coerciveness of the novel form for female characters and women writers, its suppression of female experience and desire, and its intimate relationship to the misogynistic coerciveness of social institutions.

Given the way that Freudian psychoanalysis is often used to control women and enforce compulsory heterosexuality and femininity, it seems to me very significant that Freud, as Susan Katz argues in her article "Speaking Out Against the 'Talking Cure'" (1987), borrows nineteenth-century narrative conventions in order to write his case studies of women, but not of men. Specifically, he uses marriage as the ending which proves he has effected a "cure," indicating his patient's newfound mental and emotional health. This is especially disturbing in light of Freud's comment in his essay on "Femininity" (1933:119) that, after achieving so-called normal femininity through heterosexuality, marriage, and a baby, the thirty-year-old woman's life story is essentially over. As Rachel Blau DuPlessis points out in *Writing Beyond the Ending*,

the pitfalls to be avoided by a woman seeking normal femininity are very consistent with the traits of the female hero in narrative: defiance, activity, selfishness, heroic action, and identification with other women. . . . Freud poignantly realizes that the achievement of femininity had left "no path open to [a woman] for further development." (1985:35)

From a woman's perspective the comic (marriage) and tragic (death) endings are disturbingly similar.

Frye argues, however, that the novel's close links to social realities also makes it open to change:

[The novel's] dialogic capacity, its openness to contemporary reality, its inclination towards a "decentering of the ideological world" interact with its ties to popular and broad-based experience. It bears within its evolution as a popular form the protean capacity to resist cultural fixity and to reinterpret the lives of women. (1986:24–25)

I am concerned here with exploring the responses of British women writers to the formal coerciveness of the "realistic" novel and tracing the extent to which these writers find the novel open, as Frye argues, to expressing female resistance to the demands for an "either/or closure," especially for closure in marriage.

II

SUBVERTING CLOSURE: BRITISH WOMAN NOVELISTS,
1760–1930

Many novels by British women from the eighteenth, nineteenth, and early twentieth centuries paint a picture of marriage as the final confirmation of the heroine's loss of autonomy and her education into "femininity." "Femininity," in its denial of self, feeling, and strength, its demand for charm, sacrifice, and service, entails for the woman a fundamental dishonesty towards herself and others about who she is. Over and over again, in order to marry, the heroines must give up those lively qualities that have made them heroines in the first place. Legally, marriage also meant giving up control, such as they had, of their bodies and lives. In this way, the marriage ending is a kind of death.

Sorrow about the closure that demands the death of the heroine in one way or another suffuses many middle-class British women's novels. Many of them treat marriage in contradictory ways, using it as a resolution and supposedly happy ending while at the same time undercutting and questioning that "happy ending." Others refuse to write the marriage ending at all. Often, a tension between the necessity of marriage and a desire for the pleasure and mutual support of friendship between women runs through these novels and provides a way for the novelist to subvert the marriage ending.

Through the use of her controversial term "lesbian continuum," Rich attempts to indicate that the whole range of women's passionate relationships with women, sexual and otherwise, has been discounted, undermined, prevented, and made invisible because all these relationships embody the potential for "the sharing of a rich inner life, the bonding against male tyranny, the giving and receiving of practical and political support" (1981:21). Janice Raymond has coined the terms "hetero-relations" and "hetero-reality" to indicate that not only do we live in a heterosexist society, "we live in a hetero-relational society where most of women's personal, social, political, professional, and economic relations are defined by the ideology that woman is for man" (1986:11). Women together constitute the threat that, by sharing perceptions, energy, time, and love, we will demystify and act to change the personal/political arrangements of our lives. While it is inaccurate and ahistorical to call the passionate relationships and romantic friendships of women before the twentieth century "lesbian" in the way we understand the term now, I believe it is important to recognize and seek to understand the political significance of those relationships and the continuities between them and woman-identified and lesbian existence today. The presence of female friends works in many eighteenth- and nineteenth-century novels as a force subversive of the compulsory heterosexuality inherent in the novel's controlling conventions and formal closure.

Cecilia (1782) by Fanny Burney provides a prime example of how social rules and conventions culminating in marriage diminish and control women and separate them from each other. Burney creates a wild world, out of control. In its vulnerability to chaos, it is the world seen from a woman's perspective. Cecilia is an upper-middle-class woman with greater prospects for independence than most women in her time. She inherits a large fortune from her uncle with the stipulation that the man who marries her must take her name and give up his own, a reversal that points up the injustice of the law requiring the woman to give up her identity at marriage. Cecilia intends to live independently in a house of her own once she comes of age and into control of her money. Instead, she endures a long series of mishaps and emotional tortures largely through the manipulation and neglect of her male guardians, falls in love, gives up her name and therefore her fortune and independence to marry Mortimer Delville, and suffers a period of insanity before she finally finds some peace. The long plot is intricate and involved and makes clear Cecilia's powerlessness as a woman even in small matters (with large consequences), such as ordering a carriage to stop. To the disenfranchised, with little control over the forces that order their lives, the world looks out of control, crazy. The alternative is that they themselves are crazy, and in the face of the forces ranged against her, Cecilia gives up her own perceptions and internalizes the craziness. I find myself wondering whether the "lesson" is marry *or* go mad, or marry *and* go mad, thinking that either one is appropriate, and wishing that Cecilia had the possibility to *not* marry and *get* mad.

Her painful odyssey begins when her male guardians separate her from her "aged and maternal counsellor [Mrs. Charlton], whom she loved as her mother" (2) and bring her to live in London. Denial of the possibility of devoted female friendship causes the final event which pushes Cecilia over the edge into madness. Mortimer, to whom she is now secretly married, believes that Cecilia's visits to the Belfield house are on behalf of not her friend Henrietta but Henrietta's brother, and Mortimer sets out to confront Mr. Belfield. While vainly searching the London streets for Mortimer, terrified that he and Belfield will duel, Cecilia finally succumbs to madness. During the many pages in between these two events, Cecilia often laments her lack of a female friend to help her and give her advice (see, for example, pp. 560, 811, 854). Thus, Cecilia's journey to adulthood is marked from beginning to end by forcible separation from her female friends and denial of her connections to other women. In this society, only love felt for a man is possible or even visible, and, most importantly, only love felt by a man can be effective. By the time Cecilia comes of age and into control of her inheritance, her lack of independence is firmly established.

Cecilia recovers from her insanity and lives, married, with the man she loves. Burney presents this resolution, however, not as an uncomplicated "happily ever after" but, as Judy Simons says in her introduction to the novel, as "a form of compromise" (1986:xii). Burney ends the novel with these words:

At times [Cecilia] murmured herself to be thus portionless, though an HEIRESS. Rationally, however, she surveyed the world at large, and finding that of the few who had any happiness, there were none without some misery, she checked the rising sigh of repining mortality, and, grateful with general felicity, bore partial evil with cheerfullest resignation. (919)

Yet marriage, forced upon her for survival as it is, does give Cecilia some limited control over her life. Marriage, for middle- and upper-class women, can mean, if their husbands are not complete tyrants, obtaining a small piece of the world to order and arrange in their own image, so to speak. Charlotte Lucas of *Pride and Prejudice* (1813) knows this when she decides to marry Mr. Collins; she will have a parlor, linen cupboards, and geese and ducks of her own. In *Millenium Hall* (1762) Sarah Scott creates an entire world, not just a household, ordered by women. Loosely based on her life with Lady Barbara Montagu, this utopian novel depicts a social order based not on marriage but on female friendship.[1]

The central story of *Millenium Hall* is that of Miss Mancel and Mrs. Morgan, steadfast romantic friends, who are cruelly separated by Mrs. Morgan's husband. "'Madam,'" says Mr. Morgan to his wife, "'my wife must have no other companion or friend but her husband; I shall never be averse to your seeing company, but intimates I forbid; I shall not choose to have my faults discussed between you and your friend'" (80). Behind this statement lies the knowledge that women together means potential questioning of patriarchal authority. Their affection, however, outlasts Mr. Morgan. When he dies, they use Mrs. Morgan's independent income to establish a community for women called Millenium Hall. Miss Mancel explains, "'What I understand by society is a state of mutual confidence, reciprocal services, and correspondent affections; where numbers are thus united, there will be a free communication of sentiments'" (61). The women of Millenium Hall challenge the efficacy of reason uninformed by feeling and experience, and create a society based not solely on rational economics but on respect and compassion for others (60). While giving the male narrator a tour of their estate,

Mrs. Morgan stopped us in one spot saying . . . that building (pointing to what we thought a pretty temple) which perhaps you imagine designed only for ornament or pleasure, is a very large pidgeon house, that affords a sufficient supply to our family, and many of our neighbors. That hill on your right is a warren, prodigiously stocked with rabbits, this canal, and these other pieces of water, as well as the river you saw this morning, furnish our table with a great profusion of fish. (59)

These women have moved beyond their domestic interiors to shape the world at large.

Before they created their own world, these women had often struggled between what Scott calls "duty" and "inclination," between what they felt they owed parents or other authorities and what they desired for themselves. They usually felt obliged or were forced to deny themselves. In Millenium Hall, these conflicts do not exist. As Maureen Heacock suggests in her article "Women's Identity and Women's Community" (1987), for these women self and society are no longer at odds because they have created their own social order.

While Scott's story clearly exposes marriage as a coercive institution which separates women from each other and their own desire, power, and authority, she does not go so far as to explicitly and openly criticize marriage as an institution. Mary Wollstonecraft takes the radical step of making a structural critique of marriage as her society instituted it. Neither of her novels ends with marriage. Wollstonecraft based her first novel, *Mary, A Fiction* (1788), in large part on her passionate friendship with Fanny Blood, with whom she lived and ran a school for some years (Godwin 1969:18, 42; Faderman 1981:138–42). In the novel, Mary's marriage occurs early under pressure from her parents. Throughout the book, Mary feels a violent revulsion against her husband and wants only to live with and nurse her ailing and passionately loved friend, Ann, who eventually dies in her arms (as did Fanny in Wollstonecraft's). The novel ends with Mary looking forward to death as an escape from marriage. "In moments of solitary sadness, a gleam of joy would dart across her mind – she thought she was hastening to that world *where there is neither marrying*, nor giving in marriage" (68, emphasis in original).

Wollstonecraft's second and unfinished novel, *The Wrongs of Woman: or, Maria* (1798), condemns marriage as a form of female slavery in which the woman is put, body and soul, under the legal control of her husband. Maria addresses (on paper) a court of law to defend her right to end her marriage because her husband has attempted to pay off a debt with her sexual favors. She argues that the law should not force a woman to remain in her husband's house when she no longer loves him, and that the duties of conjugal obedience and fidelity should be reciprocal. Maria writes that "a false morality is even established, which makes all the virtue of women consist in chastity, submission, and forgiveness" (196–197). The judge's response is, "'What virtuous woman thought of her feelings?'" (199). Wollstonecraft here challenges "femininity" itself as false and degrading, as denying women the right to their own feelings and integrity. The prison/insane asylum to which Maria's husband commits her makes a fitting symbol for conventional marriage as Wollstonecraft sees it.

While *Mary* ended in despair, in *Maria* Wollstonecraft may have been working toward a more positive resolution. Maria finds that Darnford, who seemed to her a romantic savior while she was in prison, proves to be false. The last fragment of the novel describes Maria attempting suicide but being saved by Jemima, her other friend from prison, who has found Maria's lost daughter. It is Jemima who has the keys not only to the literal prison, but to the prison of romantically mystified and coercive heterosexual relations as well. Janet Todd (1980b) reads *Maria* as the story of Maria's choice between sentiment, romance, and Darnford, and self-knowledge, friendship, and Jemima. She suggests that the concluding fragment implies that Maria finds true support from Jemima and that they will form a home together jointly to mother Maria's daughter (208–26).

Frances Trollope, in her novel *Fashionable Life* (1856), does create such a female partnership. While Scott escapes the conventional marriage ending through creating a utopia, a no-place where she could imagine the unimaginable occurring, Paris as a *foreign* place allows Trollope to envision a radical alternative. In the novel, the heroine, Clara Holmwood, is again an heiress. After being rejected by Lord Henry Hamilton, to whom she had proposed marriage (a radical act in itself), Clara moves to Paris where she creates a partnership and a home with Lady Amelia Wharton and her daughter, Anne. Trollope spends most of the novel portraying what she calls "their union" or "female co-partnership" as a harmonious and equal relationship. Yet, in the last fourth of the book, this partnership is suddenly dissolved: Clara is defrauded of her fortune; she, Lady Amelia, and Anne return to England; Lord Henry proposes marriage, and Clara accepts. In the context of the novel, the switch in focus from Clara and Amelia to Clara and Henry is abrupt, surprising, and disconcerting. This kind of incongruity and awkwardness points to the enormous pressure women writers felt to resolve their heroines' stories in marriage whether or not it made sense within the particular story they were telling.

Charlotte Brontë, in *Shirley* (1849), also imagines female union and power; in this historical novel, however, nineteenth-century capitalist patriarchy effectively destroys that vision. Rooting her story firmly in historical facts and dates, Brontë cannot extricate her heroines from patriarchally structured marriages.

The novel's two heroines are Shirley Keeldar and Caroline Helstone, who become devoted friends. Their relationship is even suggestive of a butch-femme romance. When Shirley first meets Caroline she gives her a bouquet of flowers and stands over her "in the attitude and with something of the aspect of a grave but gallant little cavalier" (212). During this first meeting, Shirley begins her playful verbal cross-dressing, saying "'Shirley Keeldar, Esquire, ought to be my style and title. They gave me a man's name; I hold a man's position . . . really I feel quite gentlemanlike'" (213). The next chapter, titled "Shirley and Caroline," begins with Shirley wondering to herself who she would pick as the lady of the manor if she really were Shirley Keeldar, Esquire. The chapter goes on to describe Shirley and Caroline coming to know each other and discovering the harmony of their personalities. They describe this harmony as what they look for in a husband (224). Shirley says that if she became convinced that all men were "necessarily and universally different from us," she would never marry (223). In other words, the perfect husband would be like a woman, and the perfect marriage would be as harmonious as their friendship. Given the choice, Shirley Keeldar, Esquire, would choose Caroline as the lady of the manor.

During one of their walks together, Shirley tells Caroline a beautiful myth about Eve as a strong and glorious mother of creation. Standing with Caroline on a hill overlooking the parish church, Shirley introduces her story, saying, "'Cary, we are alone: we may speak what we think'" (314). When Caroline says they should go into the church, Shirley replies "'I will stay out here with my mother Eve, in these days called Nature. I love her – undying, mighty being!'" (316). Shirley refuses to enter the patriarchal church where women are seen and not heard. We do not see her in church again until her wedding day, soon after which we learn that Nature dies out of the Hollow.

On another walk, Shirley and Caroline plan an excursion to Nunn-wood, to visit the ruins of an old nunnery which lies at the heart of the wood. They agree that they will go alone; with men there they would for-get Nature, their great mother Eve, and would lose the happiness she could give. Shirley and Caroline never take this excursion, which is both a journey back in historical time to the site of a women's community and back in mythological time to their source of woman-strength, mother Eve.

Instead, Shirley, described as Eve's daughter and a "leopardess," is "fettered," "conquered," "bound," "vanquished," "restricted," and "chained" by Louis Moore, "Adam's son" and her "keeper" (578, 592, 433, 579). And Caroline marries Robert Moore although she hates his plan to develop the textile mill and "'change our blue hill-country air into the Stilbro' smoke atmosphere'" (598). The narrator announces their mar-riages in the manner of a newspaper. Shirley and Caroline's names are printed without surnames, a comedown from Shirley's playful yet proud "Shirley Keeldar, Esquire," and surrounded by the full names and titles of their male relatives and husbands, a verbal enactment of the way they are confined by male relatives and male institutions. We last see Shirley and Caroline standing by while their husbands dedicate the new textile mill. Then the narrator looks back with wistfulness to the day when the last "fairish" was seen in the Hollow. The myth of womanly power, embodied in Eve as Nature, gives way to capitalist progress. The green hollow with its brook becomes a place of paved roads and smoke and cinders from the new mill. Marriage is figured here as the Fall and the expulsion from the Garden. This novel works in the opposite direction from *Millenium Hall,* in which the women survive marriage to create a fruitful garden, to usher in "the Millenium" without the need for the second coming of Christ. Shirley and Caroline's green and peaceful premarriage world of friend-ship has given way to the economic realities of the patriarchal world where they act only as the wives of the "captains of industry." In this world, women have power only in myths and fairy tales. Sandra Gilbert and Susan Gubar (1979a) suggest that Brontë purposely calls attention to the contrived conventionality of the traditional happy ending (397). In-deed, Brontë gives us a deluge of marriages at the end of *Shirley,* those of Sweeting, Donne, Caroline, and Shirley, overdoing a "good" thing in order to call it into question.

In the early twentieth century, formal experimentation as well as some gradual changes in cultural values and socioeconomic conditions opened up new possibilities for breaking out of conventions. It is interesting to note that Virginia Woolf's first novel ends in the heroine's death, her sec-ond in marriage, while *Mrs. Dalloway* (1925) ends with Clarissa simply walking into the room and transfixing her friends with her living pres-ence. Woolf worked her way out of closure to a new freedom. Setting twentieth-century writers such as Woolf against the background I have been delineating provides an alternative way to interpret their formal experimentation. The formal and stylistic innovations of these early twentieth-century women writers had, at least in part, a different impetus than those of the male modernists: a desire to challenge and change social and literary conventions that restrict women.[2] For example, in *Mary Olivier: A Life* ([1919] 1980), May Sinclair explores a writer's emotional and intellectual development and her need for practical and psychological independence through the limited/unlimited point of view of Mary's consciousness as she lives from infancy to middle age. While the choice still seems to be between marriage or self-identification, Mary chooses living for herself in spite of her love for Richard, a fellow writer. She has grown beyond self-sacrifice to live "her secure, shining life" as an independent woman and writer (374).

Sydney Warren's refusal of marriage in Elizabeth Bowen's novel *The Hotel* (1927) also signals a gain in maturity and self-knowledge. Bowen frames the novel with a story of Miss Pym and Miss Fitzgerald, devoted friends. The first scene shows them quarreling and the last shows their reconciliation hand in hand. The possibility of female friendship as an alternative to the marriage ending is here set forth explicitly on the page. In between this story of Pym and Fitzgerald, Sydney Warren, in love with Mrs. Kerr, contemplates marriage to the Reverend James Milton as a reaction to Mrs. Kerr's rejection. Bowen describes Sydney as caught in a patriarchal plot, deadened into a fictional heroine. "She stood between Tessa and Mrs. Kerr as inanimate and objective as a young girl in a story told by a man, incapable of a thought or a feeling that was not attributed to her, with no personality of her own outside their . . . projections upon her" (280). Sydney regains her sense of self, however, in time to call off her engagement. Milton's name underlines the sense that Sydney has escaped a patriarchal literary plot.

The whole novel calls into question the possibility of lasting heterosexual union. A female friendship encircles the book, while heterosexual relationships seem to be dispersive, not unifying. Sydney sits in the hotel dining room watching wives and husbands come into dinner separately, with little to say to each other. "It seemed odder than ever to Sydney, eyeing these couples, that men and women should be expected to pair off for life. During intervals between the courses women reft from intimate conversations looked across at each other's tables yearningly" (25). The most cohesive group in the novel is the circle of matrons who have established the drawing room as their territory. These women, who criticize Sydney's relationship with Mrs. Kerr as "unhealthy," nevertheless discuss with each other how they come to hotels for the winter in order to meet and be with other women; they all agree that "'the best type of man is no companion'"

(90). Mr. Lee-Mittison's picnic is a paradigm of the heterosexual society of the hotel. The whole party marches off together from the hotel up into the hills, but after lunch they disperse aimlessly and somehow never reunite but straggle back by twos and threes. The particular event that touches off the dispersion is the uninvited arrival of Victor, who lures Veronica away. Seeing the two of them kiss in the distance sends a shock wave through the group from which it never recovers. In this novel, heterosexuality seems not to be an effective basis for a cohesive society. The only people who seem truly to communicate are Miss Fitzgerald and Miss Pym, who "drew in each other's ideas and gave out their own by a gentle process, almost like breathing" (8), and the group of matrons who gather every day in the hotel drawing room.

On the other hand, in Radclyffe Hall's *The Well of Loneliness* (1928), heterosexuality is solid and unassailable while love between women is fragile and vulnerable. This difference arises because Hall writes about explicitly sexual relationships, Bowen homosocial ones, and because Hall's goal was to win sympathy for homosexuals from mainstream society. The novel ends with a marriage that is death to her protagonist, Stephen Gordon, a crucifixion of her love for the sake of her beloved. Hall has created a vantage point that makes the traditional comic ending clearly tragic. The novel fulfills the traditional requirement to end with an engagement to be married but allows the heroine to escape that marriage, at the same time making the marriage synonymous with Stephen's spiritual death. Yet it is also a marriage that Stephen herself arranges between two people each of whom she has rejected. Not a passive heroine waiting to be claimed or rejected, Stephen places herself in a centrally powerful position by this act, writing the life plots of Mary and Martin, as well as her own. While Mary walks away with Martin, as Stephen had planned for her to do, the anguished voices of Stephen's fellow "inverts" "possessed her. Her barren womb became fruitful" and all their voices become one with hers (457). Thus, this ending is also a rebirth (resurrection) and a "childbirth." Stephen is giving birth both to herself and to her next book. She can and will no longer remain silent about a central part of her identity. As Adolph Blanc told Stephen earlier, she must tell the world of "the suffering of millions" (390). The end of the novel becomes its birth; she will write *The Well of Loneliness*. Stephen's career is just beginning, rather than ending.

The struggles with the necessity and necessities of the marriage ending that I have been describing form a connecting thread through middle-class British women's novels from the eighteenth to the early twentieth century, a history of women writers working their way out of or around the deathly closure demanded by the novel form itself. As Rich insists, there have always and everywhere been women who resisted male dominance and compulsory heterosexuality. I would add that women have always told subversive stories, directly or indirectly, sometimes in muted or coded voices, but there for us to search out and learn to interpret. If we shift the focus of our interpretive attention, following Janet Todd's suggestion that "although the action of the novel usually takes place in the heterosexual plot, its sentiment may be centered in female friendship" (1980:2); if we attend to subtexts and subplots; if we search out lesser-known books and writers, we find evidence of an empowering female tradition of resistance. Women novelists, despite the pressure to keep within patriarchal conventions, have spoken profoundly to other women, criticizing the institution of compulsory heterosexuality, expressing deep emotions between women, and creating new stories and visions of community for women.

Rich calls for us to make visible "the history of women who – as witches, *femmes seules*, marriage resisters, spinsters, autonomous widows, and/or lesbians – have managed on varying levels" to resist hierarchical, violent social relations, including compulsory heterosexuality (1981:7). I suggest that the repeated and ongoing subversion of novelistic convention by British middle-class women writers through representations of love between women constitutes a female literary tradition of marriage resistance. What Rachel Blau DuPlessis describes as "the project of twentieth-century women writers to solve the contradiction between love and quest and to replace the alternate endings in marriage and death that are their cultural legacy from nineteenth-century life and letters by offering a different set of choices" (1985:4) is not a project originating with twentieth-century writers but is the continuation of a struggle begun by their literary foremothers. This quest is also a literary struggle against compulsory heterosexuality in the novel and in the "idioms of living."

NOTES

1 *Millenium Hall* became very popular (four editions had been printed by 1778) and represented both an ideal and a blueprint for female romantic friends such as the Ladies of Llangollen, Eleanor Butler and Sarah Ponsonby (Mavor 1973:83–86; Faderman 1981:103–6). Elizabeth Mavor points out that a number of small "lay convents" besides that of Sarah Scott and Barbara Montagu were created by female friends in the eighteenth century (86).

2 In *Writing for Their Lives: The Modernist Women,* Gillian Hanscombe and Virginia Smyers make just such an argument, demonstrating "a clear connection between literary endeavour and the shunning of conventionally heterosexual lives: a challenge to what many feminists now call 'heterosexism'" (1987:xv). They suggest that "this simultaneous breaking with both literary and social conventions . . . constitutes the radicalism of early twentieth-century women writers" (11).

8

Judith Fetterley

Reading *Deephaven* as a Lesbian Text

In 1877 Sarah Orne Jewett (1849–1906), born in South Berwick, Maine, but by virtue of family background, class privilege, and cultural interest fully conversant with literary Boston, published a book called *Deephaven*, based on a series of sketches she had previously published in *The Atlantic Monthly*, literary Boston's premier magazine. *Deephaven* tells the story of Kate Lancaster and Helen Denis, two young women (they are both twenty-four) currently living in Boston, who choose to spend a summer together in a town in Maine called Deephaven, birthplace of Kate's mother's father. They are not eloping nor are they running off together; indeed, after a few initial reservations, family members join in active support of their plan. Nor are there, with one or two possible exceptions, any overtly sexual references, certainly no explicitly sexual scenes such as we have come to expect from contemporary novels that we label "lesbian." So why do I wish to bring this text to the attention of lesbian readers and why do I wish to make it part of the recoverable history of lesbian writing?[1]

I do not wish to argue here that any nineteenth-century text dealing with the friendship of two women should be read as a lesbian text. I have read many such texts, including Jewett's own later *Country of the Pointed Firs* (1896), and I would not write this essay about such texts. My interest in presenting this reading for *Deephaven* rests on several factors. Inevitably and now, with the erosion of New Criticism's dominance over academic reading practices, acceptably, I read *Deephaven* in the light of Jewett's life. Sometime in 1877, the year she published *Deephaven*, Sarah Orne Jewett met Annie Adams Fields, then wife of James T. Fields, former editor of *The Atlantic Monthly* and a partner in the prestigious Boston publishing firm of Ticknor and Fields. When James Fields, who was several years senior to Annie, died in 1881, Jewett and Fields began a pattern of intimate and shared life that lasted until Jewett's death in 1906. They spent winters together in Fields's home on Charles Street in Boston. In the summers Jewett divided her time between visits to her family still living in South Berwick and visits to Annie's summer home in Manchester-by-the-Sea, Massachusetts. The two women traveled together, shared literary and social interests, and were each other's life companion. *Deephaven* may have facilitated Jewett's life choice by allowing her first to imagine it in fiction.

A second reason has to do with my own personal history. Reader response theory reminds us of our responsibilities to identify the role that personal history plays in any reading we offer to others. I belong to the generation of women who grew up before the women's movement or the gay rights movement made lesbianism visible. Unlike many of my generational peers, I lacked the imagination and/or the courage to discover or invent it for myself. Thus my adolescence and my young adulthood were spent longing for something I believed I could never have. My relations with the women I loved, rarely physical, occurred in the context of their desired and expected marriage, and our time together was always time out from the real time of progress toward marriage. Needless to say, during these years I experienced frequent depressions. *Deephaven* begins with a depressed narrator and tells the story of a relationship whose intimacy cannot be projected beyond a single summer. In *Deephaven* I read the story of my own adolescence and young adulthood.

I do not read every Jewett text as a lesbian text simply because Jewett formed a lifelong relationship with another woman. Nor do I read all texts as lesbian texts simply because I am a lesbian. Predisposed for the reasons expressed above to read *Deephaven* as a lesbian text, I find it responsive to such a reading. Jewett dedicates *Deephaven* "first to my father and mother, my two best friends, and also to all my other friends, whose names I say to myself lovingly, though I do not write them here" (35). If certain conventions prevented Jewett from saying the names of her friends with love in print, other conventions, the conventions of fiction, enabled her to create a narrator who could say a friend's name lovingly in print: "I shall be glad if you learn to know Kate a little in my stories," says Helen Denis, the narrator of *Deephaven*. "It is not that I am fond of her and endow her with imagined virtues and graces; no one can fail to see how unaffected she is, or not notice her thoughtfulness and generosity and her delightful fun, which never has a trace of coarseness or silliness" (54–55). And she concludes her rehearsal of her friend's virtues with the apostrophe, "dear Kate Lancaster!"

In the preface she wrote several years later for an 1893 edition of *Deephaven*, Jewett claims that her goal in writing the book had been to introduce to each other two kinds of people who were coming more and more in contact as middle-class Bostonians increasingly spent their summers in rural New England. While by no means wishing to dispute the integrity of Jewett's analysis of her intention, I would suggest that the second preface serves as a cover for the original text. Though it signals the relational nature of her text's subject and intent, the second preface nevertheless directs the reader's attention away from the relationship of loving friendship and toward the relationship of city folk and country folk. Reading the second preface as cover, however, enables us to recover the degree to which Deephaven as town serves in *Deephaven* as text as a cover for Jewett's writing out the relationship between Helen and Kate. Exploring the characters, customs, and history of Deephaven, with the intent of explaining country ways to city readers, provides an acceptable narrative frame for the text of Helen and Kate's relationship. Yet, as I hope the essay that follows will demonstrate, *Deephaven* takes its shape from the narrator's desire for Kate and expresses the anxieties as well as the pleasures attendant upon that desire.

LESBIAN ANXIETIES

Deephaven opens on a note of depression: "I had been spending the winter in Boston, and Kate Lancaster and I had been together a great deal, for we are the best of friends. It happened that the morning when this story begins I had waked up feeling sorry, and as if something dreadful were going to happen. There did not seem to be any good reason for it, so I undertook to discourage myself more by thinking that it would soon be time to leave town, and how much I should miss being with Kate and my other friends" (37). Though the narrator remains officially cheerful, hoping that "the good luck which followed will help some reader to lose fear, and to smile at such shadows if any chance to come," and later announcing that, while twenty-four is a pleasant age, "next year is sure to be pleasanter, for we do not mind growing older, since we have lost nothing that we mourn about, and are gaining so much," the mood of *Deephaven* remains depressed (37, 54). And though the narrator also claims that "to this day I have never known any explanation of that depression of my spirits," the text she writes suggests several sources for her pervasive depression (37). Helen's spirits lift when she arrives at the breakfast table and finds beside her plate not just the hoped-for letter from her father but also a "note from Kate" announcing a "plan." Since Kate's plan includes an invitation to spend the summer with her in Deephaven, readers are likely to infer that Helen's depression derives from the impending loss of Kate and is relieved by the delay of that prospect, however temporary.

Though Kate obviously loves Helen enough to select her as the special friend with whom she wishes to spend her summer, Helen is telling the story, and the story she tells is the story of her love for Kate. Indeed, the very qualities that Helen identifies as making Kate so lovable – her class and family status, her tact, her sociability – equally identify Kate as pre-eminently marriageable. Moreover, while Helen, by writing *Deephaven*, can be imagined as beginning a career that will displace marriage, no such alternative interest seems present for Kate. Thus Kate figures in the text as heterosexual, and thus *Deephaven* presents a classic lesbian experience: a lesbian woman in love with a heterosexual woman who is willing to take time off before getting married to play, but only to play, with an alternative.[2] The shadow of eventual separation hangs over Helen's summer, providing sufficient cause in itself for her pervasive depression.

Though Helen creates an image of equality through the creation of the fictive "we" that forms the primary narrative voice in *Deephaven*, there are imbalances in her relationship with Kate that also suggest a source for her depression. Kate Lancaster, not Helen Denis, has a plan. Though Kate has access to greater social and economic resources than Helen, making it easier for her to have plans, such disparity only emphasizes Helen's dependency. Helen does not present herself as capable of lifting her own depression, as able to act directly to accomplish her desire. Thus *Deephaven* constructs the lesbian partner as relatively powerless, perhaps because of the socially problematic status of her desire, perhaps because, for this reason, she can not articulate her desire even to herself and hence cannot act in relation to it.

Other differences between Helen and Kate emphasize Helen's relative lack of status and power. Though Kate's plan originates in the fact that her family is dispersing for the summer, she has a family to be dispersed; father, mother, brothers form a significant presence in the text. Moreover, Kate invites Helen to spend the summer in the home of her mother's father's parents. Kate has roots in Deephaven, and when she arrives, the people there greet her as returning royalty. In contrast, Helen presents herself as effectually an orphan. She lives with an aunt, receives an occasional letter from her father, apparently has neither mother nor siblings, and certainly no ancestral home to which she might bring her beloved. During the summer, Kate and Helen visit Miss Chauncey, a crazed and elderly woman living in an ancestral home falling down around her. At one point in the visit, Miss Chauncey claims to see in Kate a likeness to her own mother. She invites Helen and Kate to look at the portrait of her mother to confirm her claim, but when she turns to the place where the portrait used to hang, she finds only a blank space on the wall, the portrait having been sold, like all the rest of her possessions, to pay for her keep. This tragic moment of recognition and loss serves to foreground the issue of origins and descendants, of generational continuity, and to suggest that this issue constitutes another source of anxiety for Helen. Kate's generational continuity is the product and luxury of heterosexuality. The blank space on the wall of Miss Chauncey's parlor, the absence of Helen's mother in the text, serves as an emblem for the lesbian woman's difficulty with origins. Lacking a portrait of one's origin makes it difficult to establish connections, community in the present. Kate has a place in both Deephaven's past and present, but who is Helen Denis to Deephaven without Kate?

The experience with Miss Chauncey, who has regressed in her imagination to the age of Helen and Kate – one is reminded here as well of Jewett's often-quoted remark, "This is my birthday and I am always nine years old" – triggers an additional anxiety that can be connected to Helen's presumptive lesbianism. During their first few days in Deephaven, Helen and Kate rummage through the desk of Kate's grandaunt Katherine, whose recent death has left her house unoccupied and has thus provided the occasion for Kate's invitation. In the desk they discover a packet of letters from "'my dearest friend, Dolly McAllister, died September 3, 1809, aged eighteen'" (49). The narrator chooses to share with her readers the one that begins: "'My dear, delightful Kitten: I am quite overjoyed to find my father has business which will force him to go to Deephaven next week, and he kindly says if there be no more rain I may ride with him to see you. I will surely come, for if there is danger of spattering my gown, and he bids me stay at home, I shall go galloping after him and overtake him when it is too late to send me back. I have so much to tell you'" (49). While the trip to Deephaven represents for Helen and Kate a commitment to the values of a specifically reconstructed past, their very presence in grandaunt Katherine's house reading her letters from Dolly implies a vision of history as progressive. Kitten and her Dolly could not get together without their fathers' permission, assistance, and presence, and then they could only visit. Kate needs her father's permission, and obviously his financial assistance, if nothing else, but she can get to Deephaven without him and she can stay there without him for several months. Female friendship has more space in 1877 than it did in 1809.

Nevertheless Kate's plan represents an aggressive occupation of that space and as such requires from Kate a compensatory gesture. Though Kate greets Helen the morning she announces her plan "with great ceremony" and the solemnity of a kiss, both she and Helen soon revert to behavior that leads Helen to exclaim, "You would have thought we were two children" (38). And as Kate finally begins to unfold her plan, she continues to develop the regressive fiction: "'It might be dull in Deephaven for two young ladies who were fond of gay society and dependent upon excitement, I suppose; but for two little girls who were fond of each other and could play in the boats, and dig and build houses in the sea sand, and gather shells, and carry their dolls wherever they went, what could be pleasanter?'" (38) Casting herself and Helen in the role of children and describing her plan as an invitation to play makes it safe, safe because not adult or serious, and safe because only temporary.

For Helen, however, the fiction of becoming a little girl again may be problematic. Kate can create a regressive fiction to cover her aggressive assertion of her right to time because her presumptive heterosexuality implies a relation to time perceived as progressive. For Helen, since Deephaven still preserves into the present the persons, customs, and architecture of the past, it presents the terror of stopped time, of being out of time: "It seemed as if all the clocks in Deephaven, and all the people with them, had stopped years ago" (71). Helen finds her terror most powerfully embodied in the regressive fantasies of Miss Chauncey. If one doesn't marry, can one grow up? To the degree that Deephaven becomes identified for Helen with the space she occupies with Kate, the question becomes, can Helen grow up in Deephaven, can Helen grow up as a lesbian? Or is the lesbian choice a socially regressive act that takes a person out of history, out of the communal flow of generational time, and traps one permanently in the stopped time of an insane fantasy? If, as Sarah Sherman argues in *An American Persephone* (1989), the core of female identity and development lies in the recognition that the mother contains the daughter and the daughter contains the mother, and if that recognition leads, and here Sherman quotes Jung, to a woman's "'feeling that her life is spread out over generations – the first step toward the immediate experience and conviction of being outside time, which brings with it a feeling of *immortality*,'" then the question of origins and the question of one's relation to time are at root the same, and both are problematic for the lesbian woman, who must frequently find both mother and daughter outside of the biological relation (63).

Despite Helen's determined cheerfulness, then, the trip to Deephaven begins from a place of depression and anxiety. While the summer in Deephaven resolves neither her depression nor her anxieties, and while *Deephaven* is not a "here's how I did it and you can do it too" book, it does begin the work of creating alternative structures. Grandaunt Katherine's west parlor, Kate and Helen's favorite room in the house and the room in which Helen writes, contains one portrait of a young girl, who "seemed solitary and forlorn among the rest in the room, who were all middle-aged" (47). During the summer Helen and Kate grow fond of this girl and when they leave Deephaven they imagine that the portrait begs to be taken with them. Though we can read this incident as another version of Helen's question, can I grow up in Deephaven?, we can also read it as indicative of Helen's beginning to construct an alternative genealogy – the portrait is both old and young, painted a long time ago but portraying a young girl, thus potentially both mother and daughter – to fill in the blank space on her version of Miss Cauncey's wall.

DEEPHAVEN AS LESBIAN SPACE

By calling her first chapter "Kate Lancaster's Plan," Helen directs our attention at once to Kate and her plan. And what a wonderful plan it is! For Kate it means that instead of spending a summer in Newport keeping house for her Aunt Anna's visitors, she will be mistress of a household herself and have two servants to keep house for her. For Helen it means a summer with Kate and a chance to experience what it would be like to set up a household with another woman. As Kate develops her plan, her parents find it more and more pleasant, until at last her mother wishes she were going too. Kate's plan has conversionary powers, suggesting that, while she and Helen may themselves have no models, they may become a model for others.

Kate and Helen enjoy planning the practical aspects of their summer, gaining a sense of importance from, as Helen puts it, "being housekeepers in earnest," for though they must disguise their plan as play, in fact it represents a chance to experience unprecedented independence (40). Helen and Kate arrive in Deephaven at sunset, and Kate brings Helen to her home in a scene reminiscent of those in nineteenth-century novels describing the return of bride and groom from the honeymoon. Indeed, Kate's plan resembles a proposal of sorts, and the rightness of both the proposal and its acceptance seems affirmed as they enter their "new" house together: "The hall door stood wide open, and my hostess turned to me as we went in, with one of her sweet, sudden smiles. 'Won't we have a good time, Nelly?' said she. And I thought we should" (43). Why shouldn't Helen love someone capable of devising so brilliant a plan for their pleasure?

Kate takes Helen to the house of her recently deceased grandaunt Katherine Brandon, a woman who never married and had no children. Indeed, as Helen describes the house to us, she notes, "It was impossible to imagine any children in the old place; everything was for grown people." But she adds, almost immediately, "It is a house with great possibilities" (44). In its refusal to accommodate itself to children, here the signature of the heterosexual norm, grandaunt Katherine's house offers Helen and Kate an alternative, lesbian space, a space in which two young women can imagine what it would be like to live life without husbands and children. In this space Kate and Helen do not have to read the letters from a sailor lover perhaps lost at sea that they discover in grandaunt Katherine's desk, "tied with a very pale and tired-looking blue ribbon," while they can choose to read the letters from Katherine's beloved Dolly, letters that Katherine herself has evidently read over many times (49).

In Deephaven Helen and Kate become acquainted with several women of their mothers' and grandmothers' generation who, like grandaunt Katherine, have chosen not to marry. And while the figure of Miss Chauncey casts a shadow over the figures of Katherine Brandon, Honora Carew, and Rebecca Lorimer, suggesting that insanity, poverty, and isolation can result from remaining single, the words of Mrs. Patton, longtime neighbor of grandaunt Katherine and also known as the widow Jim, cast an equally long shadow over the prospect of marriage. Married to a drinking man, Mrs. Patton carries a battle scar; she has a dent in the side of her forehead from a stone bottle her drunken husband threw at her. Mrs. Patton has earned the right to her summary judgment of the experience of marriage: "'I come back here a widow and destitute, and I tell you the world looked fair to me when I left this house first to go over there. Don't you run no risks, you're better off as you be, dears'" (63). Mothers frequently pressure daughters to marry, but the "mothers" Kate and Helen find in Deephaven bring no such pressure to bear. Even Mrs. Kew, who becomes perhaps their best friend in Deephaven and who is happily married to the keeper of the Deephaven light, recognizes that her marriage is based on major compromise – "'I was raised up among the hills in Vermont, and I shall always be a real up-country woman if I live here a hundred years'" – and she never presents her decision as either normative or right (41).

Helen and Kate find other freedoms in Deephaven as well as freedom from the pressure to marry. Indeed, in her narrative Helen constructs Deephaven itself as a kind of lesbian space. It is a shock to discover Helen and Kate renting wagons to take the children of Deephaven to the circus, just as earlier it was a shock to find reference to the "barefooted boys" who hang out at the wharves, for Helen has constructed an image of Deephaven as being as childless as grandaunt Katherine. Helen also describes Deephaven as virtually without young people, persons of her own and Kate's generation. With no young men to create the prospect of impropriety or the threat of physical danger, with no peers to create a constrictively normative context, in a world made up of old men and old women, Helen and Kate are as free as the barefooted boys. Though accomplishing Kate's plan requires that she and Helen present themselves as little girls, the brilliance of Kate's plan lies in taking them to a place where they can be boys as well. In Deephaven, Kate and Helen get to hang out on the wharves and in the fish houses. They get to go cunner fishing with Captain Sands, who has heard from Tom Kew that "'they don't put on no airs, but I tell ye they can pull a boat well, and swim like fish'" (119).

They roam the outlying areas looking for wild mushrooms and interesting people; they get their clothes wet and covered with fish scales and blackberry briers; and they stay out late at night to watch the moon rise.

As young women, Helen and Kate participate in Deephaven's female culture. They receive and pay visits; they are initiated into the history of the social relations of Deephaven's first families; they learn family secrets like the story of Miss Chauncey's madness and the story of the mysterious disappearance of grandaunt Katherine's favorite brother; they share in the appreciation of old china; they come to understand the economic realities that govern the lives of these elderly women. However, since being in Deephaven allows Helen and Kate to construct themselves imaginatively as boys, in Deephaven they also participate in male culture, a space usually closed to girls. When the old men of Deephaven get together, they close ranks against Helen and Kate and will not let them listen to their conversation. But when these same men are by themselves, they behave quite differently. Danny, at work cleaning mackerel, responds with an emphatic "yes" when Helen and Kate ask if they can watch him, and from watching him they learn how to "sliver" a porgy. Captain Sands lets them rummage around in his warehouse and lets them in on the secret ways sailors have of stealing liquor from a ship's cargo. In the company of these men, Helen and Kate learn to tie knots and whittle kelp; they crack clams and cut them up for bait; they mend tackle, take the oars, fish off the wharves and in boats.

Though Deephaven is a gendered world, it offers Helen and Kate opportunities to cross gender lines. And it provides models of other women and men who have experimented with such crossing. Indeed, many of the old men who initiate Helen and Kate into some of the rituals of male culture also have characteristics that could well be described as feminine. Danny shares with Kate and Helen the story of his cat whom he saved from a group of boys trying to drown it with stones. Captain Lant, who describes himself as "condemned as unseaworthy," has in fact made a conscious decision to give up the sea and remain on land because "she" couldn't stand his absence. And Captain Sands has filled his warehouse with objects whose value could only be described as "sentimental," objects that remind him of persons or places he knew in his past. Later, on a trip into the back country, Helen and Kate meet Mrs. Bonny, who "wore a man's coat, cut off so that it made an odd short jacket, and a pair of men's boots much the worse for wear; also, some short skirts, beside two or three aprons" (135). They pay her many subsequent visits and "used to carry her offerings of tobacco, for she was a great smoker, and advised us to try it, if ever we should be troubled with nerves" (139).

Helen never indicates that she and Kate did try tobacco, but during those long walks and long nights together, who knows what they might have tried? For physical freedom, freedom to move about in the world, can lead to greater freedom of thought, and in Deephaven Helen finds as well the opportunity to rearrange her mind. Deephaven provides the occasion for trying out a perspective from which one might view the marginal as central and the central as marginal. The choice of Deephaven as a summer destination in itself enables a certain version of this experiment to occur. While Helen and Kate may have made themselves appear odd to their contemporaries by choosing to summer in Deephaven, the oddities of Deephaven provide a cover for whatever is odd in the relation between Helen and Kate and construct as well a context within which Helen and Kate can view themselves as normative.[3]

When Helen and Kate arrive in Deephaven, the first thing the people there notice is not that they are two women living together, but rather that they are young, outsiders, and modern. As Helen says, the faces in Deephaven "were not modern American faces," and she later remarks that when she and Kate "first went out we were somewhat interesting on account of our clothes, which were of later pattern than had been adopted generally in Deephaven" (73, 164). Since youth, modernity, and urbanity, however, constitute the dominant forces in American culture, by coming to Deephaven Kate and Helen have positioned themselves to represent the norm. It is only in this context that I think one can fully understand Kate and Helen's tendency to make a fetish of the old-fashioned: "As for our first Sunday at church, it must be in vain to ask you to imagine our delight when we heard the tuning of a bass viol in the gallery just before service. We pressed each other's hands most tenderly, looked up at the singers' seats, and then trusted ourselves to look at each other. It was more than we had hoped for" (71). Indeed, one could argue that it is precisely Deephaven's "difference" that enables Helen and Kate's erotic relation. For not only can one speculate that to the Deephaven natives sitting in the church Helen and Kate seem so different that no oddity in their relationship would be noticed; one can also understand that emphasizing the old-fashioned in Deephaven allows Helen, whom we know from the instance of Miss Chauncey to have a terror of being queer, to project her anxiety outward and to view Deephaven as queer rather than herself.

Projection and cover, however, have limited and even potentially negative value. But Deephaven offers Helen more powerful and interesting occasions for rearranging her mind. As if to emphasize its importance, Helen places at the center of her narrative her encounter with the "Kentucky giantess," part of the sideshow of freaks accompanying the circus Helen, Kate, and Mrs. Kew attend at nearby Denby. Helen and Kate enter the sideshow following the lead of Mrs. Kew, who has looked at the picture of the giantess outside the tent "wistfully" and "confessed that she never heard of such a thing as a woman's weighing six hundred and fifty pounds" (106). Inside Kate and Helen feel ashamed of their participation in the act of freak-watching and they go off to look at a cage of monkeys. When they come back to see if Mrs. Kew has had enough, they find her in conversation with the giantess, who turns out to be someone Mrs. Kew used to know. Kate and Helen hear Mrs. Kew declare, "'I thought your face looked natural the minute I set foot inside the door,'" and naturalizing the giantess is precisely what Mrs. Kew manages to do (106). By the time Helen and Kate leave, they know that the Kentucky giantess is not from Kentucky but from Mrs. Kew's home town in Vermont; that she weighs 350 not 650 pounds; that her name is Marilly and that her father drank himself to death after running through all his money, leaving her no way to live except off her strangely and uncontrollably increasing size; that she has a son whose wife doesn't want to take care of her and that she believes "'it would be something like if I had a daughter now'" (107). Mrs. Kew has turned a freak into a person and in so doing has called into question the category of "freak," for everybody is somebody's old acquaintance and everybody has a story to tell to someone who will listen.

Yet for Helen the transformation is incomplete, suggesting the limitations of her ability to rearrange her conceptual frameworks. She continues to refer to Marilly as the giantess and describes her finally as "that absurd, pitiful creature" (107). Normalizing the freak seems beyond anything Helen can accomplish herself or can imagine as a possibility for many others, and so Marilly remains for her a terrifying image. An incident that occurs later in the summer, however, provides an easier model for Helen to follow. Helen includes this incident in the chapter that also contains her description of the circus, and she calls the event "another show," thus linking it to the circus. She and Kate attend an evening lecture, advertised as free, on "The Elements of True Manhood." This lecture is delivered to an audience consisting entirely of old men, women, and children. To Helen and Kate the lecture is dreary and interminable, but the lecturer reads on and on, taking no notice of his audience's increasing fatigue, and at the end delivers the crowning insult of asking them to pay for his performance. In her final chapter Helen lists some of the books she and Kate read during the summer and includes in the list "Mr. Emerson's essays." It seems reasonable to assume that the figure of Emerson provides a frame for the evening lecture and that in perceiving the lecture to be a kind of circus Helen accomplishes the work of regionalizing Emerson's "universals," of identifying the apparently central to be potentially marginal. In the context set by Deephaven, the lecturer's presumptively universal subject – young white men – is redefined as local, relevant only to a particular group of people, none of whom happen to be in the audience. And in this context the lecturer himself is more of a freak than Marilly, for she is more aware of her audience than he is and she delivers more of what her audience paid for and can use than he does. If naturalizing the freak proved difficult for Helen, a transformation she could witness but not perform, realizing the freakish nature of the so-called norm is something she can do. If she cannot learn to see the odd as normal, she can learn to see the normal as odd.

THE LESBIAN RELATIONSHIP, OR, KATE AND HELEN TOGETHER AT LAST

Trying to find her way out of the bewildering realization that she must end her story, Helen comments, "I remember so many of our pleasures of which I have hardly said a word. There were our guests, of whom I have told you nothing, and of whom there was so much to say" (162). And of whom there were evidently so many. By telling us what she didn't include, Helen tells us what mattered to her about her summer. Her list of guests startles us, because throughout her narrative she has created the impression that she and Kate were alone together in Deephaven. Had she chosen to focus on their visitors she would have created a very different story. But she didn't, so while the text *Deephaven* gets its structure from the place Deephaven, Helen reminds us at the end that what matters to her is that she and Kate are in Deephaven together.

Helen's text includes many (though rarely foregrounded) references to the life she and Kate create with each other. For example, we learn that there is one room in the Brandon house with a sofa "broad enough for Kate and me to lie on together," which they do in the evenings (47). And we learn that she and Kate used Miss Brandon's old blue china and that when they ate "Kate sat at the head and I at the foot of the round table" (46). We know that they keep house together, plan meals, do the shopping, deal with the butcher, catch fish for their dinner. Helen tells us that they were sometimes gone all day on long walks and that they spent considerable time in the Deephaven burying ground trying to read the inscriptions on the gravestones. They make a thorough rummage through grandaunt Katherine's possessions; they sing and play the piano; they read together, and together they write a tragic "journal" that they hide in a drawer of grandaunt Katherine's desk for someone like themselves to find later. Indeed, if one combined all the references in *Deephaven* to Kate and Helen's life together, one would have a small but fascinating text, a text that creates an alternative space in *Deephaven*. Many of Helen's narratives contain a reference to the conversation she and Kate had afterwards about their experiences of the day. Though Helen rarely describes this "afterwards" in any detail, her references to it indicate the degree to which the experience she recounts becomes significant by virtue of the experience she does not recount. Thus to understand the value of what we are reading, we must fill in the space identified by "afterwards." In this space

Kate and Helen establish and develop their relationship: "We were together always, and alone together a great deal; and we became wonderfully well acquainted. We are such good friends that we often were silent
for a long time, when mere acquaintances would have felt compelled to
talk and try to entertain each other" (164).

In *Deephaven*, the lesbian relationship is one of harmony and accord
based on a similarity of interests, tastes, and values. It develops through
shared experience and is enabled by both talk and silence. Kate and Helen
do everything together and see everything the same way, and *Deephaven*
articulates the attraction of sameness. Yet Kate and Helen are not the same
person, and Helen loves Kate and wants to tell us so and why, though she
foregrounds this text even less frequently than the text of their "afterwards." In Boston, Helen has the key to Kate's house; and the morning
Kate announces her plan Helen goes straight to Kate, where "my latchkey
opened the Lancasters' door, and I hurried to the parlor, where I heard my
friend practising with great diligence. I went up to her, and she turned her
head and kissed me solemnly. You need not smile; we are not sentimental
girls, and are both much averse to indiscriminate kissing, though I have
not the adroit habit of shying in which Kate is proficient. It would sometimes be impolite in any one else, but she shies so affectionately" (37–38).
Kate has tact, a quality Helen associates with the manners that accompany
Kate's social class. For Helen, Kate's tact has value because "she is not polite for the sake of seeming polite, but polite for the sake of being kind" (55).
Most of the explicit comments Helen makes about Kate's charm refer to
this quality, and one can sense here both Helen's class bias and her comfort
in announcing an affection based on so conventionally feminine a quality.

Helen sees her adoration of Kate reflected in the people of Deephaven,
who respond to the indices of Kate's class status as well, and she indirectly expresses her own attraction to Kate through her accounts of their
response. On the stagecoach to Deephaven, where Helen and Kate first
meet Mrs. Kew, Kate subtly introduces the subject of her own lineage by
asking Mrs. Kew if she knows the Brandon house: "'There! I wonder I
didn't know from the beginning, but I have been a-trying all the way to
settle it who you could be'" (41). When Mrs. Patton makes her first visit
the morning after Kate and Helen arrive, she hesitates when she sees
Helen, drops "a fragment of a courtesy," and queries doubtfully, "'Miss
Kan'k'ster?'" When she sees Kate, she lights up, shakes her hand "delight-
edly" and exclaims, "'Well, I should know you were a Brandon, no matter
where I see you. You've got a real Brandon look; tall and straight, ain't
you?'" (56). Even Miss Chauncey imagines that Kate, not Helen, resembles her mother.

One incident in particular serves to associate Kate's sexual attractive-
ness with her class status and to express this element of Helen's relation to

Kate. During a visit with Mrs. Kew, Kate offers to show a group of tourists around the lighthouse, since Mrs. Kew has hurt her ankle. Following the tour, one of the girls waits until everyone else has left and then bursts out with an invitation to Kate to come to Boston next winter. She herself has a good job in a "nice" store, and she offers to get Kate a job there too and to share her own room with Kate. When she discovers her mistake in assuming that Kate is "of Deephaven" rather than "of Boston," she retreats in embarrassment and confusion, leaving Kate to declare to Helen, who has "heard it all," that this was an incident "worth having" (52). For us the incident is certainly worth having, since, like the story that emerges of the Widow Jim's devotion to grandaunt Katherine, it doubles the relationship of Helen and Kate and provides a context for reading that relationship. And while the incident establishes that working-class girls fall in love with each other just as middle- and upper-class girls do, it also suggests that erotic attraction between women occurs across class lines and may indeed be stimulated by class difference. Mrs. Patton, like the working-class girl who proposes to Kate, loves up, but so after all does Helen.

Though Helen emphasizes Kate's tact, the encounter with the shop girl suggests that Kate is also something of a tease, a quality Helen later refers to when she describes Kate as being "very clever at making unsatisfactory answers when she cared to do so" and both of them as being "often naughty enough to wait until we had been severely cross-questioned before we gave a definite account of ourselves" (132). Indeed, this naughtiness forms a delightful counter to the immense gentility of *Deephaven* and even suggests a vantage point from which to interpret Kate's plan itself. Helen indicates that during the summer she and Kate "were singularly persistent in our pursuit of a good time," and she attributes this persistence to Kate's capacity for fun (55). We find evidence throughout the text of Kate's willingness to behave in unconventional ways in order to have fun, from the start of their journey to Deephaven, when Kate throws her orange out the stagecoach window, to one of the last incidents Helen describes, when she and Kate decide to break into Miss Chauncey's house and gamely climb over the boards blocking the entrance to it. Helen's first words to us are "Kate Lancaster's Plan," and she makes us see why she would love someone with the imagination to invent such a plan, the authority to bring it off, and the naughtiness to realize its possibilities.

"THAT WAS IT – GONE!"

Kate is rich, Kate is sweet, Kate is fun, Kate must surely be beautiful, but by the end of the summer Kate is gone. Helen's narrative projects separation in both the immediate and the long-range future. Commenting in the last chapter on the Deephaven treasures they take back to Boston with them, Helen notes that "this very day you may see in Kate's room two great bunches of Deephaven's cat-o'-nine-tails" (165). And she wonders "if some day Kate Lancaster and I will go down to Deephaven for the sake of old times, and read the epitaphs in the burying ground, look out to sea, and talk quietly about the girls who were so happy there one summer long before" (165). Though both remarks assume continued contact, neither implies that the summer experiment will be repeated either in Boston or in Deephaven. Since Helen has earlier noted that she and Kate never tired of each other, the choice to live separately cannot be the result of internal difficulties but must rather be the result of "the way things are." Interestingly enough, it is Kate who "laughingly proposed one evening, as we sat talking by the fire and were particularly contented, that we should copy the Ladies of Llangollen, and remove ourselves from society and its distractions" (160). Is Kate toying with the lesbian alternative from her position of class privilege and heterosexual privilege, or is she seriously thinking of invoking her class privilege as license to deviate from the heterosexual norm, as did Lady Eleanor Butler when she eloped with Sarah Ponsonby and established a lesbian household in Llangollen? We don't know, because Helen rejects this proposal as quickly as she accepted Kate's initial plan: "'I suppose if we really belonged in Deephaven we should think it a hard fate, and not enjoy it half so much as we have this summer. Our idea of happiness would be making long visits in Boston, and we should be heartbroken when we had to come away. . . . We should have the blues dreadfully, and think that was no society here, and wonder why we had to live in such a town'" (160).

If the summer in Deephaven has given Helen the opportunity to imagine a way of life that she might permanently assume and has provided her with the opportunity to experiment with the conceptual reframing necessary to such an assumption, it has not enabled her to make the move from play to permanence, from time out to real time; it has not enabled her to develop mechanisms powerful enough to assuage her anxieties. Helen ends her narrative "in shadow," the title she gives to one of her final chapters, whose images of loss reassert her initial depression. Early in the summer Kate and Helen make the acquaintance of a poor family trying to eke out a living on a farm some ten miles outside Deephaven. Struck by the poverty and despair of the lives of the man and woman and their children, Kate and Helen speak often of them and make many plans for a return visit. They do not return, however, until late October, just before they are to leave Deephaven, and they arrive only in time to witness the man's funeral. The woman has died earlier and the man, incapable of surviving alone, has drunk himself to death. "In Shadow" describes a world in which "a strange shadow had fallen over everything," and the chapter itself casts a shadow over the conclusion of Helen's narrative (148). Helen hears one of the mourners ask, "'He's gone, ain't he?'" and she reiterates, "That was it, – *gone*" (148). She concludes the chapter with the following meditation: "I think today of that fireless, empty, forsaken house, where the winter sun shines in and creeps slowly along the floor; the bitter cold is in and around the house, and the snow has sifted in at every crack; outside it is untrodden by any living creature's footstep. The wind blows and rushes and shakes the loose window sashes in their frames, while the padlock knocks – knocks against the door" (149).

A marriage ended, a house deserted, children abandoned, winter supplanting summer – these images reflect Helen's sense of the fragility of her own happiness and adumbrate her own impending loss. Though still October, the day of the funeral "was like a November day, for the air felt cold and bleak" (148). With the coming of November, Helen and Kate must either leave Deephaven or change the terms of Kate's plan from a summer's play at being girls to an adult decision to establish a household together. Shortly before they leave Deephaven, Helen remarks to Kate, "'I think the next dwellers in this house ought to find a decided atmosphere of contentment,'" and she continues, "'Have you ever thought that it took us some time to make it your house instead of Miss Brandon's? It used to seem to me that it was still under her management, that she was its mistress; but now it belongs to you, and if I were ever to come back without you I should find you here'" (162). Though Kate and Helen have infused the Brandon house with new life and an atmosphere of contentment that Helen can imagine future inhabitants enjoying, how long in fact will the house survive their desertion? And how will Helen recover Kate if the house is gone?

These questions come into focus in the penultimate chapter, describing Helen and Kate's encounter with Miss Chauncey. Miss Chauncey's house is literally falling down around her, and her ruined house reflects her ruined mind. So deeply does Miss Chauncey identify herself with her house that, though having been persuaded to spend the winter following Kate and Helen's summer with a neighbor, she nevertheless one day "stole away from the people who took care of her, and crept in through the cellar, where she had to wade through half-frozen water, and then went upstairs, where she seated herself at a front window and called joyfully to the people who went by, asking them to come in to see her, as she had got home again" (157). Needless to say, Miss Chauncey dies soon after this event. Though Helen tries to distance herself from Miss Chauncey by labeling her "a poor creature," she does, as noted earlier, in fact identify with her. Through the image of crazy Miss Chauncey in her ruined house, Helen projects her deepest fears that she will not survive the loss of Kate and that in trying to recover Kate by returning to Deephaven she will herself become a crazy woman inhabiting a house in ruins.

Despite the fact that Helen constructs Deephaven as lesbian space and uses her summer there to experiment with the possibility of reframing the marginal as central, she finds in Deephaven terrifying images of what she might become – Miss Chauncey; Marilly; Mrs. Bonny, whose gender crossing occurs in a context of dirt and poverty from which Helen's middle-class fastidiousness recoils; even grandaunt Katherine, who never replaced the connection of a best friend dead at eighteen. Marilly, the "Kentucky giantess," out of control of her circumstances and thus vulnerable to exploitation and exhibition, in particular presents the self as freak. Deephaven provides no models that show Helen how she might live an adult life based on an intimate and permanent connection with another woman; Helen does not find a mother in Deephaven. And in Marilly's lament for the daughter she never had, we may hear Helen's lament for the absent mother, that blank space in her story like the blank space on Miss Chauncey's wall; for, like Marilly's, Helen's narrative contains no portrait of her mother. Does Helen mean to suggest that if she had a mother she would not fear becoming a freak?

IN CONCLUSION

Though Helen does not tell us a story of how she overcame her anxieties and lived happily ever after with her beloved, simply by telling us the story she reconfigures its elements. Kate has her portrait and her cat-o'-nine-tails to remind her of her summer with Helen, but Helen has the experience of writing *Deephaven*; and, having written *Deephaven*, she has created a way of recovering Kate more sure, more under her control, than the fate of the Brandon house. In writing *Deephaven*, she has additionally assumed control over the presentation of self, thus avoiding the fate of Marilly. And she has reconfigured the issue of power in her relationship with Kate, for it is she who determines how we will see Kate. Moreover, though Helen did not find a mother in Deephaven, through writing she creates herself as a "mother" for her reader-daughters, offering them a model to grow up on.

Though within *Deephaven* Deephaven itself appears as a temporary space, a space Kate and Helen can occupy only until November, Helen's text is subject to no such limitations. And what characterizes that text, what provides its ultimate distinction and shapes the way we see, is Helen's invention of the narrative "we." Though Helen clearly writes *Deephaven* herself, the narrative voice she gives us to read through is dual, communal. Only rarely does Helen write the word "I," and then most frequently she invokes it to adore Kate. Her story establishes separate identities but it records shared experience. By inventing what I call "a 'we' to see the world," Helen creates a form for her relationship with Kate more permanent than the Brandon house, and she offers this form to her readers so that in reading *Deephaven* they too may occupy lesbian space.

But for me the beauty of *Deephaven* lies in the fact that Helen does not offer her text as a preferable substitute for the experience she did not have. She offers her text as compensatory, but in so doing she keeps our focus on what needs compensation. Thus when we finish *Deephaven*, we do not forget that Kate and Helen no longer occupy the space described in or provided by the book, and we can, if we wish, grieve that loss. The years that intervened between the original publication of *Deephaven* and the second edition that served as the occasion for Jewett's preface saw the solution for Jewett of the dilemma she articulated through the figure of Helen Denis. Having established her heterosexual credentials through her marriage to James Fields and, indeed, having created with him a union so noted in the Anglo-American literary community that a second marriage would have seemed the desecration of a shrine, Annie Fields was free to form a relationship with Sarah Jewett like that which Jewett described between Kate and Helen – but which lasted for twenty-five years rather than for a single summer. While Jewett found in life what she was unable to imagine in fiction, she did not choose to recreate in fiction what she found in life. Writing in 1893, Jewett cast a somewhat dim eye on the work of her youth. She distanced herself from it by claiming to feel like the "grandmother" of its author and its heroines, whom she now compared to the heroines of Samuel Richardson's *Clarissa* (1748). Since the relationship between Clarissa Harlowe and Anna Howe occurs entirely within the confines of a heterosexual plot, their letters to each other constituting a rather heady form of "boy talk," that is, girl talk about boys, such a comparison has the effect of reframing the relationship between Helen and Kate and erasing its lesbian content.

Sarah Sherman identifies *Deephaven* as a mother text for *The Country of the Pointed Firs*, and suggests that the close reading Jewett gave *Deephaven* in preparing the preface for the 1893 edition enabled her to construct *The Country of the Pointed Firs* as a conscious revision of the earlier text and to transform more effectively its crudities into the latter's consummate artistry. While I certainly agree that *The Country of the Pointed Firs* constitutes a revision of *Deephaven*, and while I appreciate as well the artistry of the later text, as a lesbian reader I also notice something missing in the revision and am thus less likely to participate in an unqualified preference for it. *The Country of the Pointed Firs* presents a single, middle-aged narrator who returns to spend a summer in Dunnet Landing, a place she has briefly visited before, and who encounters there older women who serve her as mentors and mothers. As Sherman so extensively documents, in this text Jewett, freed by the death in 1891 of her own biological mother, resolves the relationship of mother and daughter, so problematic in *Deep-*

haven. While within this framework *The Country of the Pointed Firs* constitutes an advance over *Deephaven,* in the framework I have proposed for reading *Deephaven, The Country of the Pointed Firs* appears regressive, for it backs off from exploring how the relationship between mother and daughter might be solved by the daughter's adult relationship with a female peer. The unnamed narrator of *The Country of the Pointed Firs* resembles Helen Denis, but the later text contains no analogue for Kate and hence no analogue for the erotically charged relationship between two women who could be imagined as spending their lives together. In other words, in revising *Deephaven* as *The Country of the Pointed Firs,* Jewett erased the lesbian content of her earlier work. For those of us who have come to love Kate, we may perhaps be excused our textual preference.

NOTES

1 I wish to make a note here on my use of the term *lesbian*. As Adrienne Rich has demonstrated in "Compulsory Heterosexuality and Lesbian Existence"(1980), the pressure to label behavior heterosexual parallels and intersects with the pressure to enforce behavior that can then be so labeled. Feminists, Rich suggests, need to resist this pressure and to label increasingly large portions of women's behavior as "lesbian." I would note, as others including Rich have noted as well, that the pressure to justify their usage placed on those who use the term *lesbian* has no equivalent, even in most feminist contexts, for those who use the term *heterosexual*. This asymmetry has the effect of intimidating and silencing those who seek to carry out the work of challenging the assumption of universal heterosexuality in the past and present. In the instance of Jewett and the writing of *Deephaven,* the case for invoking the term *lesbian* seems particularly strong, since there is no evidence in her life of interest or behavior that could reasonably be labeled "heterosexual" and much that could reasonably be labeled "lesbian." I might also note that it is by no means clear that emotions and experience I now label "lesbian" are *not* similar to the emotions and experience of a woman like Jewett, since the culture I inhabit has much in common with the culture she inhabited, particularly in its construction of women and sexuality. As Lillian Faderman puts it, in discussing those women who entered into a "Boston marriage," "if their personalities could be projected to our times, it is probable that they would see themselves as 'woman-identified women,' i.e. what we would call lesbians, regardless of the level of their sexual interests" (1981:190). And finally I might note that while others, usually those who have already enjoyed its fruits, may be busy deconstructing the concept of "history," I am still in search of a usable past. The project of history is always born out of the needs of the present, and we construct or deconstruct history according to our needs. Thus while I recognize the difficulties that may attend my use of the term *lesbian* to describe *Deephaven,* I am suspicious, if not of the motives, then at least of the effects of too much attention to these difficulties. For as long as the assumption of universal hetero-

sexuality remains unchallenged by precisely such appropriations as I am here proposing, then the default label will dominate and govern interpretation. In other words, if I do not read *Deephaven* as a lesbian text, then it will be read as a heterosexual one. For an example of such a reading, see Sarah Sherman's analysis in *An American Persephone* (1989).

2 Like me, Sarah Sherman finds "the most important thing about these heroines is that there are two of them" (120). However, she quickly converts these two to one, claiming that in *Deephaven* "Jewett has split her own persona" (120). Noting the similarities between Kate's background and personality and Jewett's, she identifies Kate as Jewett's "best, idealized self" (122). While I find this observation insightful – it suggests, for example, that in *Deephaven* Jewett may have been trying to imagine herself as the object as well as the subject of desire – Sherman's reading has the effect of removing the lesbian content from the text. I, of course, wish to do just the opposite.

3 It is difficult to speak simply about Jewett's relation to possible oddity in romantic attachments between women. On the one hand, we have the evidence, so carefully summarized by Lillian Faderman, to the effect that during the nineteenth century romantic friendships between women were considered normal; indeed such attachments, since they were considered more spiritual than relations between men and women, were frequently perceived to provide a superior alternative to marriage for women. And we have the evidence from Jewett's own "Boston marriage" with Annie Fields, a relationship that, at least during Jewett's life, seems to have carried no taint of abnormalcy. On the other hand, we have the evidence presented by Josephine Donovan (1986) in her discussion of *A Country Doctor* (1884), and supported by Bonnie Zimmerman's reading (1990a) of George Eliot, to the effect that those circles in England and America who had contact with German scholarship during the decade of the 1870s would have had the opportunity to note the beginnings of the tendency, increasingly prevalent by the end of the century, to morbidify romantic relations between women. (Kate and Helen take German dictionaries with them to Deephaven, but they do not open them, and Helen finally puts them in a closet to avoid the mortification of their "silent reproach" [163].) Donovan concludes her essay by claiming that Jewett's father, Dr. Theodore Jewett, who specialized in obstetrics and the diseases of women and children, would most likely "have been aware of the sexologists' theories and that he and Sarah may have discussed them. Her own proclivities could have readily identified with this 'new type' of woman that European theorists were condemning as a pathological freak" (26). Donovan argues that Jewett rejected those theories and wrote *A Country Doctor* specifically to counteract them. Whether or not one accepts Donovan's reading of *A Country Doctor*, one could argue that a younger Jewett might not have felt so self-confident and that an early work like *Deephaven* might well contain some evidence of anxiety on the subject.

9

Carolyn J. Allen

Sexual Narrative in the Fiction
of Djuna Barnes

Djuna Barnes's status as a lesbian culture hero has shifted dramatically since the early 1970s. In 1973 Bertha Harris lovingly celebrated Barnes and her Paris Circle as models for Harris's own life as a lesbian; in 1984 Tee Corinne characterized Barnes as homophobic.[1] There is of course evidence for both positions. Barnes herself said she was not a lesbian, that she "'just loved Thelma,'"[2] and as she grew older and more isolated, she had a low tolerance for her female admirers.[3] Nevertheless, Harris is right to honor her as a representative of "practically the only available expressions of lesbian culture we have in the modern western world" since Sappho (87). Even though Barnes's denial of her lesbianism, reinforced as it was by a homophobic dominant culture and a new literature of sexology,[4] emerges in what little biographical information we now have, *Nightwood* (1936) and *Ladies Almanack* (1928) remain classics of lesbian imagination. I will argue further that three of her stories, linked by the "little girl" who narrates them, also belong to that imaginative tradition.

While *Nightwood* may be what Catharine Stimpson calls a lesbian narrative of damnation,[5] it portrays in Robin and Nora's relationship a current of lesbian sexuality that was debated in much feminist work in the 1980s. Its references to mother-child dynamics, both emotional and sexual, anticipate recent discussions in feminist psychology and theory. In less overt but equally powerful ways, Barnes's "little girl" stories have in their textual shadows this same configuration. These stories, so-called because of the original titles of two – "A Little Girl Tells a Story to a Lady" and "The Little Girl Continues" – culminate in a third that is a direct precursor to *Nightwood*, "Dusie." All three interrogate gender identity and homosexuality. In my reading of them I look to shadows rather than to surfaces, and

I read in the context of feminist work on "difference," work that provides the light necessary for the play of these shadows.

The history of feminism's "second wave" is in part a history of the shifting value placed on difference. Beginning with a realization that the stress on difference between men and women had resulted in unequal separate spheres, feminist thinkers moved first against sexual difference toward a stress on abilities and talents shared by women and men. In the seventies, the tenets of liberal feminism came under attack by radical feminists who now celebrated women as different from – and superior to – men. In the 1980s many feminists argued from a position that stresses differences among women, in recognition of the danger inherent in obliterating factors of race and class in discussions of oppression.[6]

Alongside this feminist dialogue on difference and oppression developed another on difference and repression,[7] growing primarily out of Freudian and neo-Freudian psychoanalysis and centered on the oedipal/castration crisis in the formation of sexuality. In this model, especially as it is reformulated by Lacan reading back through Levi-Strauss and Saussure, woman is Other, lack, the means by which man knows what he is. French feminist scholars have criticized Lacan's theory because it does not permit woman to have difference of her own, to occupy anything more than a negative space. Feminists revising these models focus on possibilities from investigating the preoedipal, and thus the role of the mother rather than the father. In different revisionist ways, French psychoanalysts Julia Kristeva and Luce Irigaray both make the mother prominent in their work, though both still write with the father of psychoanalysis and his son, Lacan, looming over them.[8] Others acknowledge directly that the model simply is an inadequate base for understanding the construction of the female subject. American sociologist Nancy Chodorow in her reinterpretation of object-relations theory argues further that the stress on sexual difference by male psychoanalysts demonstrates their own male need to remain as differentiated as possible from the feminine in light of the problematics of separation from the mother as first caretaker.[9]

Both *Nightwood* and the "little girl" stories explode the binary structure underlying Western thought from Plato forward that feminist theorists like Irigaray and Chodorow so radically question. By refusing the categories "male" and "female," by shifting terms of sexual difference, Barnes's texts become examinations of dichotomous difference. By refusing to take maleness and the phallus as the norm, by questioning the construction of gender and the nature of sexuality, they rupture the surface of convention and illuminate the world of the night. While Barnes may have denied her lesbian relationships, her texts question the dichotomous presence of sameness and difference in their presentation of lesbian sexuality.

Nightwood's seventh chapter, "Go Down Matthew," contains the novel's most extended discussion of gender and sexuality. Together Nora and Matthew give us a portrait of the invert, "the third sex." In that portrait we recognize the boy in the girl, the girl in the Prince, not a mixing of gendered behaviors, but the creation of a new gender, "neither one and half the other."[10] A woman loving someone of the third sex loves her as herself and her child. It is clear throughout the chapter that both these dynamics are at work in Nora's relation to Robin. Thus the Lacanian insistence on sexual difference is overturned here in favor of likeness, "she is myself" (127). Here there is no Other, there is only oneself; "on her mouth you kiss your own" (143). The lover is not only like one's self; she is one's self.

But the chapter takes up difference as well. A man lies bejeweled in a velvet-lined box staring into the mirror to contemplate his own difference. Here he sees not a recognition of himself as differentiated subject, but himself as like the figure in the mirror and unlike the rest of the world. He celebrates his nonconformity. As such he resembles Matthew, Nora, and Robin, whose sexuality is "an honorific reappropriation of sexual difference."[11] That is, in their love of the same sex, they, like the man in the box, admire their non-conformity, their sexual difference from the rest of the world. Barnes is particularly clear about this difference in *Ladies Almanack:*

This is the part about Heaven that has never been told. After the fall of Satan . . . all the Angels . . . gathered together, so close that they were not recognizable, one from the other. And not nine Months later, there was heard under the Dome of Heaven a great Crowing, and from the Midst, an Egg, as incredible as a thing forgotten, fell to the Earth, and striking, split and hatched, and from out of it stepped one saying, "Pardon me, I must be going!" And this was the first Woman born with a Difference.
    After this the Angels parted, and on the Face of each was the Mother look.[12]

The angels merge and give birth to the woman with a difference, the lesbian whose manners and mores as seen in the Natalie Barney circle are the subject of the book's fond wit.[13]

So although Robin and Nora are alike because they are both women, they are also lesbians, women with a Difference. And even in their likeness, they are different people, a differentiation marked especially by the text's casting of Nora as mother, Robin as child. Here is the second dynamic in *Nightwood*'s lesbian relationship – one's lover is not only one's self, but also one's child. Nora tells Matthew about her search for Robin: "'I haunted the cafes where Robin had lived her night-life. . . . I danced with the women, but all I knew was that others had slept with my lover and my child. For Robin is incest too; that is one of her powers'" (156).

Barnes uses the word *incest* to name a sexual and emotional dynamic in which one woman is the nurturer, the other, more childlike, the (often unwilling) recipient of this caretaking. For many readers the term, with its horrific connotations of violation, will seem an unfortunate choice. It is clear in *Nightwood,* however, that Barnes intends the familial connection so that "mother-child" becomes a trope for a network of sexual and emotional responses. Earlier in the passage Nora touches on one of these when she attributes Robin's desertion of her to her need to be separate: "'she wants to be loved and left alone, all at the same time. . . . A shadow was falling on her – mine – and it was driving her out of her wits'" (155). This explanation implies the fluidity of boundaries between self and other that some psychologists have noted both in lesbian relationships and in mother-daughter dynamics.[14] It adds to the reference about Robin as Nora's child by suggesting the kind of emotional currents at play in their relationship. This relationship is infused with an imbalance of power of mother to child that is righted when Robin the lover expresses her adult autonomy by leaving Nora to sleep with other women. At the same time the mother-child union is shot through with a measure of sexuality, since mother and child are also lovers.

As lovers they cannot conceive, so they share a doll to mark their union. Here is another turn on sameness and difference, for the doll resembles the child, yet is not alive: "The doll and the immature have something right about them, the doll because it resembles but does not contain life, and the third sex because it contains life but resembles the doll" (148). Robin is like the doll in her childlikeness, but different from it in her "containing life"; similarly, Nora is like Robin in that they are both women, but different from her as a mother from a child. Finally Matthew, Nora, and Robin are like each other in their same-sex orientation, but different from the world at large.

Neither of these currents is startlingly new in lesbian fiction; Barnes's French contemporary Colette, for example, also touched on the mother/daughter dynamics in lesbianism. Nor is either unexplored by psychoanalysis. Work done in the 1980s, however, leaves aside nineteenth-century sexology's emphasis on sickness to celebrate the same kind of ambiguities that emerge in Barnes's novel. This work directly or indirectly attacks the phallocentric insistence on sexual difference and opens the way for alternative theorizing.

Luce Irigaray's two companion essays, "Quand nos lèvaries se parlent" (1980; "When Our Lips Speak Together") and "Et l'une ne bouge pas sans l'autre" (1981; "And the One Doesn't Stir Without the Other") both rupture the Lacanian model of sexual difference and provide a text against which to read Barnes's "little girl" stories.[15] The first essay is, among other things, a dialogue between two women lovers who acknowledge their likeness ("When you say I love you . . . you also say I love myself" [70]). What earlier psychoanalysts dismiss as narcissism becomes self-affirming because it is not an embrace of sameness and closure, which Irigaray identifies with maleness, but a lyric of multiplicity. Like Barnes's texts, Irigaray's undermines what she calls the "currency of alternatives and oppositions" (70). She writes in the shadow of Lacan and, without naming him, disputes his view of sexual difference that negates women.

The second essay, as its translator notes, echoes the first in its continuing meditation on woman-to-woman relationships, now shifted from lovers to mother and daughter. The daughter speaks to the mother from her undifferentiated state (in male psychoanalytic terms, the preoedipal): "I would like us to play together at being the same and different. You/I echoing endlessly and each staying herself" (61). Here as in the earlier essay, the question of sameness and difference has a set of parameters quite removed from standard models that pass over the preoedipal to concentrate on the role of the Father in the construction of sexual difference. It allows for difference in the context of resemblance, just as lesbian discourse does. Irigaray's essay fills a descriptive gap in male theory, then deliberates on the damage done when the woman is "trapped in a single function – mothering" (66). She both stresses the complexities and the sensuality of the mother-daughter connection and acknowledges the limiting dichotomy, mother-woman, in the referential world.

Chodorow also ruptures the Freudian/Lacanian insistence on the primacy of the father's role in structuring female sexuality. Unlike Irigaray, however, she is less interested in reformulating difference than in delineating differentiation. She connects difference with a model reducing the mother to the "not-me" thus obliterating her as a subject. She stresses instead the process of the daughter's struggle to differentiate herself from the mother, the fluidity rather than the fixity of gender difference, and the potential slippage in heterosexual orientation for women because of their bonds with the mother.

Beneath the surface of their conventional prose, the three "little girl" stories anticipate a number of these feminist currents. The stories are held together not only by their common narrator but by the common interrogation of gender and sexuality that shadows the text. In all three stories, a young woman tells a story to a lady. The narratives themselves are stories of one kind of seduction or another, seductions that have one younger and one older participant. The stories about seduction imprint on the narrative situation a forbidden atmosphere – the seduction of female by female, by older of younger, with the erotics of the mother-daughter trope shadowing the shadows. The narrator herself has the absolute autonomy usually reserved for men. She travels all over Europe, alone or with her sister; she decides how long she will stay, how she will live, when she wants to leave one place and move on to another. The narratee, the mysterious "Madame," we know less about. But the narrator wants her to listen. *"Nicht wahr,"* she says; *"n'est-ce pas,"* "is it not so?" – always seeking information, looking for assent. Even in the midst of the stories themselves, the narrator intrudes with direct address or little asides to her listener so that we never forget she is a "little girl" telling her stories to "a lady": "'Then this last autumn, before the last winter set in (you were not here then, Madame)'" or "'Sometimes it is beautiful in Berlin, Madame, *nicht wahr?*'" (15). Of course the narrator is not a little girl at all, but a precocious young woman who implicates herself and her sexuality even as she seems with innocent nonchalance to be recounting some other woman's story to the presumably attentive "Madame." Her three stories, increasingly overt in their sexual content, are themselves a fictional seduction of the older "madame" by the young narrator, Katya.

In "Cassation" a mysterious older woman tries to convince Katya to come and live with her and take care of her child.[16] Literally, that is, sexually, it is not a seduction story, yet there hangs over it a sexual atmosphere not unlike that of *Nightwood.* Originally "A Little Girl Tells a Story to a Lady" and first published in 1925, the story was revised and retitled "Cassation" for *Spillway.* The new title, come upon long after Barnes's Paris days and her denial of her own involvement with women, stresses what is now the standard reading of all the *Spillway* stories: the fascination with the void, with negativity, with the abyss at the heart of the world. Such a reading also connects "Cassation" to *Nightwood,* but it misses the radical nature of the text's questioning of conventional gender difference and sexuality. As usual in Barnes's fiction, plot is a minimal pretext. Katya several times sees a mysterious and dramatic woman in a cafe; one day they are drawn together and the woman invites the girl home. After they have lived together for a year, the woman, Gaya, asks Katya to stay forever to care for her mentally vacant child. Katya refuses, leaves, returns to say good-by and finds Gaya in bed with the child, both making the same wordless sound of vacancy.

The plot operates in a world of unconventionally marked gender and sexual likeness. The only man in the story is Gaya's husband, a sort of feminized ghost. He is little, dainty, dreamy, uncertain; he appears infrequently and does not participate in the action. Gaya does attribute to him what several generations later would be called "the power of the weak," the mark of woman. Conversely, the women, both Katya and Gaya, are independent and autonomous. In their year together they take walks, admire military cannons, and have intellectual conversations about philosophy and the state of civilization. During these brief scenes in the first half of the story, the women in their assertive autonomy generally occupy positions conventionally marked as masculine rather than as feminine. But within this reversed gender structure, there are still differences in power. The older woman has the active/male role, the younger, the passive/female role. Katya does what Gaya asks.

Halfway through the story, however, there is a shift in power. In the first half of the story, Gaya has been the stronger force, leading the girl home, ensconcing her in a bedroom for a year, treating her in part as a child, in part as an intellectual equal. When, in the story's second half, Gaya must finally become mother to her vacant child because of the child's growing need for care, the power shifts to the participant narrator. Katya exercises a masculine power of refusal in ignoring Gaya's pleas to stay, and Gaya, in turn, is reduced to childlike helplessness.

This then is the gendered structure of the story: the women marked by traditional masculine traits, the man by traditional feminine ones; the women present, the man absent. The reversal that drives the narrative comes when the older woman must assume the "trap" that Irigaray describes, the most institutionalized female role possible – the role of the mother. When she does so, the power dynamic shifts and with it the positions filled by the two women. The "little girl" now controls the action. The mother cannot prevent her going and collapses into vacancy. This gendered narrative is written in language charged with sexual meaning complementing/complicating the structure. Throughout the story the two women, though never lovers, act out child/mother relationships like those referenced in the passages of "Go Down Matthew." Reading particular scenes and particular turns of phrase in the light of that chapter illuminates the sexual subtext of the narrative.

Early in the story, the women go home together:

"Then one evening we came into the garden at the same moment. It was late and the fiddles were already playing. We sat together without speaking, just listening to the music, and admiring the playing of the only woman member of the orchestra. She was very intent on the movements of her fingers, and seemed to be leaning over her chin to watch. Then suddenly the lady got up, leaving a small rain of coin, and I followed her until we came to a big house and she let herself in with a key. She turned to the left and went into a dark room and switched on the lights and sat down and said: 'This is where we sleep; this is how it is.'" (14).

This scene resembles that of Robin and Nora's first meeting in *Nightwood*, when they are brought wordlessly together at a circus with a lioness bowing in recognition. In "Cassation" the women's first meeting begins with Katya walking elsewhere, looking at the statues of emperors (who look like widows, in keeping with the story's gender reversals), when she suddenly thinks of the cafe and the tall woman she has seen there. She returns; Gaya is there and speaks to her for the first time in a "'voice that touched the heart'" about her home with its Venetian paintings "'where young girls lie dreaming of the Virgin'" (13). The narrator sums up for Madame: "'I said I would meet her again some day in the garden, and we could go home together, and she seemed pleased, but did not show surprise'" (14). Then follows the passage quoted above. As in the *Nightwood* scene, the two women come together silently, one leaves suddenly, and the other follows. In between, they focus not on a lioness, but on the intensity of the only woman member of the orchestra. Here it is not the recognition of the animal appropriate to Robin's beast-self, but sexual difference, that only woman musician, that sends them home to the bedroom. Once there, the narrator takes time to describe the massive dimensions and great disorder of the room, but saves her most lavish description for a great war painting, which runs together "'in encounter'" with the bed. On it "'generals, with foreign helmets and dripping swords, raging through rolling smoke and the bleeding ranks of the dying, seemed to be charging the bed, so large, so rumpled, so devastated'" (14). So much for men in the bedroom.

In this narrative preparation, the two women have been drawn together by the repetitions of chance and the power of a woman's music; conventional expectations lead the reader to expect a sexual encounter. Here they are in front of the bed, the narrative action has been stopped to point to male violence, and then? In any popular lesbian pulp fiction, they might fall onto the bed, overwhelmed by Destiny or True Love. In "Cassation," they are prevented from so doing; a child lies in the center of the pillows, "'making a thin noise, like the buzzing of a fly'" (14). The charged atmosphere shifts from incipient sexuality to the needs of the child. But Gaya does nothing except drink a little wine; insist that Katya stay; throw herself on the bed, her hair spread around her; and fall asleep. Later that night she puts Katya to bed as she might a child, or a young lover, by loosening and braiding her hair. Katya stays a year.

After that year together, when the condition of Gaya's child worsens, Gaya, in the central monologue of the story, tries to convince Katya to stay and care for the child. She promises to be like her mother, her servant; she denies their previous intellectual sharing:

"'Now you will stay here safely, and you will see. You will like it, you will learn to like it the very best of all. I will bring you breakfast, and luncheon, and supper. I will bring it to you both, myself. I will hold you on my lap, I will feed you like the birds. I will rock you to sleep. You must not argue with me – above all we must not have arguments, no talk about man and his destiny.'" (18)

The sexual undercurrents of their coming together have earlier been bound up with Gaya's playing at the mother's role. Faced with actually mothering her own helpless child, the woman of power has become the suppliant who wishes to make her friend into her child's caretaker. As she continues her plea, she literally confuses her own child with Katya; friend and child become the same, as if Katya could fill in the vacancy of Gaya's daughter. Her actual daughter cannot provide the companionship that both Chodorow and Irigaray stress is basic to the mother-daughter relation; instead, the child's mental absence calls only for the mother's caretaking role. Not only is Gaya confronted with the institution of motherhood, but experientially she must mother a child who can never be her companion. To avoid such mothering, Gaya tries to convince Katya to become her child's caretaker; in her speech, she merges Katya as caretaker with Katya as daughter-substitute. Were she successful, she, like Nora in *Nightwood*, could have her intimate as her child and be both her companion and her caretaker. But Katya, her independence threatened by Gaya's attempts to make her a dependent "daughter," rather than a playful intimate, refuses. Her need for differentiation, as Chodorow might say, is as great as Gaya's confusion between her desire not to mother at all and her need for a daughter-companion. Their parting, like their meeting, is shadowed by longing:

"Then Madame, I got up. It was very cold in the room. I went to the window and pulled the curtains, it was a bright and starry night, and I stood leaning my head against the frame, saying nothing. When I turned around, she was regarding me, her hands held apart, and I knew that I had to go away and leave her. So I came up to her and said, 'Good-bye my Lady.' And I went and put on my street clothes, and when I came back she was leaning against the battle picture, her hands hanging. I said to her, without approaching her, 'Good-bye my love' and went away." (19)

Katya now has the power that initially was Gaya's. In the final scene, Gaya is no longer differentiated from her vacant daughter. She sits beside her child, imitating her mad sound, the seductive woman-turned-mother-turned-child fallen into the void.

Read in the context of "Go Down Matthew," this story confirms its configuration both of difference in likeness and mother-child dynamics between women intimates. Of course the story is "about" cassation, as Gaya's long monologue and the ending indicate. But it is also about a little girl telling a story to a lady, one woman speaking to another about attraction, the power of women, the devastation of motherhood, and the conflation of child and intimate. It assumes a female world, then gives up the shifts in power, conventionally marked masculine and feminine, as a comment on the consequences of the ultimate female role – mothering.[17]

The second story in the sequence, "The Grande Malade," continues the subtexts of gender and of sexuality/nurturance.[18] Its original title, "The

Little Girl Continues," connects it to "A Little Girl Tells a Story to a Lady," just as its revised *Spillway* title, "The Grande Malade," is linked to "Cassation" in its implication of annulment by disease. Unlike the earlier story, however, its unconventional structuring of gender implicates the male as well as the female characters. Again the story involves pairs of the same sex. Significantly, although the plot purports to be about a heterosexual couple, Moydia and Monsieur X, we never see them alone as a couple or hear anything of their relationship. Instead, the narrative construction subverts the ostensible focus of the plot by concentrating on the couples, Moydia and her sister, Katya, and Monsieur X and his patron, the Baron. Katya, here again active and autonomous, is both narrator and participant. The story is of a cap, a cape, and a pair of boots, all marking transgression of gender and blurring of lines of difference. Katya has given up flowered hats in favor of a cap. Only the women listen to her, whereas men adore her sister Moydia. Moydia is feminine difference in this pair marked by female likeness. If "Cassation" is shadowed by the sexuality of the mother-daughter trope, "The Grande Malade" suggests instead the problematic attraction of father-daughter couples. Moydia chooses as her lover Monsieur X, who himself is paired with the Baron, a man of "aged immaturity" who taps around after Moydia with his cane. With the Baron she is a gamine, teasing him in her childlikeness, sitting in his lap, playing either the "'kitten or the great lady as occasion demanded'" (24). He plays the passive but receptive older "father" to her spoiled child.

The story opens with Katya's description of Moydia's physical beauty. Its first half establishes them as a pair, always together, walking in the Tuileries, hanging lace curtains over their beds to smoke and talk of lovers. They differ in their appearance; Moydia is clearly feminine, while Katya has her trousers and her cap like her father's. The sisters are like, an inseparable "we," but different not only in their appearance, but in their relation to father figures. Katya wants to be her absent father; Moydia wants to take him as lover, substituting for him the available presence of the old Baron.

The males in the story, however, spend more time with each other than with the sisters. Monsieur X seems particularly unsuited as a lover for Moydia: "'He was the protege of a Baron. The Baron liked him very much and called him his *"Poupon prodigieux,"* and they played farces together for the amusement of the Fauberg. That was the way it was with Monsieur X, at least in his season when he was, shall we say, the belle-d'un-jour and was occupied in writing fables on mice and men, but he always ended the stories with paragraphs *très âcre* against women'" (24). Moydia leaves town to visit her actual father, the one who lives so strongly in the imagination of Katya. During her absence Monsieur X dies with the Baron at his side. The narrative's only repeated passage, its doubling appropriate in a story where likeness defeats conventions of sexual difference, re-counts Monsieur X's death and refers obliquely to the unconventional strains of the story. Katya tells Madame of Monsieur X's death: "'When the Baron saw that Monsieur X was truly going to die, he made him drink. They drank together all night and into the morning. The Baron wanted it that way. "For that," he said, "he might die as he was born, without know-ing"'" (27). A page later Katya repeats the scene and the quote for Moydia when she returns from her visit. What is it that Monsieur X doesn't know? Among other things, surely, that his ties to the Baron were greater than those to Moydia.

Katya asked the Baron for something of Monsieur X to give as a remem-brance to Moydia. He gives her Monsieur X's cape. Given the fame of Djuna Barnes's own cape, familiar to all who knew her in Paris at the time of the story's publication in *This Quarter* (1925), it is difficult not to see that story's cape as something of a private joke. But more than that, it marks a further transgression of gender identity, passing from a man of uncertain sexuality to a woman who, in wearing it always, as the story tells us, comes to resemble her dead lover. By wearing his cape, she becomes not only a masculinized woman who replaces the feminized man, but also the "protege" of the old Baron/father with whom she earlier has had such a sexually coy relationship. Meanwhile the boots that Monsieur X had ear-lier promised to Katya are quite forgotten. So while Moydia puts on a man's cape, Katya must forgo her man's boots; for both, clothes mark their move away from boundaries of gender identity toward an ambigu-ous center, "neither one and half the other" as Matthew O'Connor says in *Nightwood*. The matrix of gender and sexuality in "The Grande Malade" is not that of "Cassation," yet both stories are shadowed by outlawed trans-gression of difference boundaries. In their undercurrent of familial eroti-cism and their fascination with likeness and difference within that like-ness, they anticipate the overt emergence of these ideas in *Nightwood*.

"Dusie," like *Nightwood*, brings the undercurrents to the surface. Pub-lished in a collection called *American Esoterica* (1927) and not included in *Spillway*, perhaps because of its unambiguous lesbian subject matter, "Dusie" directly anticipates many of *Nightwood*'s preoccupations. Like other homosexual texts, the story's very existence challenges theories of sexual difference. Within its theoretical structure of sameness, difference appears at the textual level in the variety of women presented, but partic-ularly in the condemnation of one who commits an act of violence. Like *Nightwood*'s Jenny, Dusie disappears before the narrative closes. The women who remain, like Nora and Robin, participate in the familiar mother-daughter-lover configuration.

The story is set entirely in a world of likeness. In Madame K's lesbian salon there are no men, only women with different roles. Questions of conventional gender give way to an explicit focus on sexuality. Dusie is the prototype of *Nightwood*'s Robin. She dresses in trousers, plays with dolls and toy soldiers, has many women lovers who call her pet or beast "according to their feelings."[19] In a description that looks forward to Matthew's *Nightwood* speech on the third sex as "uninhabited angels," the narrator says, "You felt that you must talk to Dusie, tell her everything, because all her beauty was there, but uninhabited, like a church, *n'est-ce-pas*, Madame?" (78). Like Robin she has brief outbursts of temper coupled with an unheeding absence. She has a "strong bodily odor" not yet elaborated as the earth-flesh, fungi perfume of *Nightwood*. Her movements are "like vines over a ruin," just as Robin recalls the "way back" of prehistory (78). Others talk in front of her about her death. But she doesn't notice, and "that made it sorrowful and ridiculous, as if they were anticipating a doom that had fallen already a hundred years" (79). Other descriptions look forward just as directly both to the character and the language of *Nightwood*.

Clarissa anticipates Jenny just as Dusie does Robin. Both Clarissa and Jenny are thieves of others' lovers. Both mark difference in their female worlds; they counterpoint the other pairs of women lovers by their acts of violence and their narrative disappearances. Both are completely dependent on everyone they know. Jenny, the squatter, lives by appropriating others' words and loves. Clarissa seems "as if she lived only because so many people had seen and spoken to her and of her. If she had been forgotten for a month, entirely by everyone, I'm sure she would have died" (77). She knows how to teach evil, just as Jenny does; and the story's brief action, Clarissa's mutilation of Dusie's foot, shares the power of physical violence with *Nightwood*'s carriage scene in which Jenny attacks Robin, making bloody scratches on her face. In both scenes the violence has a sexual context: after the carriage ride, Robin goes with Jenny as lover to America. Clarissa says to Dusie, "You must think, too, about the most terrible virtue, which is to be undefiled because one has no way for it; there are women like that, grown women, there should be an end . . ." (81). These are the last words the "little girl" overhears before she falls asleep. When she awakes, Dusie is asking her to leave the bedroom. When she returns, Clarissa is gone and Dusie's foot is crushed. In this context, it is difficult not to hear the sexual implications of "defiled."

Set against this violence, the mother-daughter-lover dynamic in Dusie's relation with Madame X is warmer, but no less problematic. Though the story does not address the dynamic as directly as *Nightwood* does, it shares the novel's ambivalence about mothering one's lover. Dusie's dolls and tin soldiers, her vulnerability, and her self-absorbed absence signal her childlikeness. She clings to her lover, Madame K, as "The only reality." Madame K is mistress of the house, a large, very full blonde Frenchwoman who, the narrator reminds us, is childless. When she is with Dusie, she looks "like a precaution all at once" (77). The narrator says she does not fear for either of them because of the way they "were with each other always" (81). In the final moments of the story, when Madame K returns from a visit to her own mother[20] and finds Dusie with her foot crushed, she takes the foot in her lap and says to the narrator: "You see how it is, she can think no evil for others, she can only hurt herself. You must go away now" (82). Her maternal protectiveness, like Nora's of Robin, is unable to prevent Dusie's defilement. Despite this failure, the story, like "Cassation" before it and *Nightwood* after, makes clear how bound up with sexuality women's attempts to nurture are in Barnes's work.

"Go Down Matthew," with its discourse on the third sex as uninhabited angels, with Robin as Nora's "child" and lover, works out more elaborately what we see in Dusie as a character, just as *Nightwood* contains the story of Dusie, Clarissa, and Madame K writ large. What is missing in *Nightwood* is the "little girl" as narrator. Indeed the little girl's role in "Dusie" is considerably reduced from what it was in her first story, "Cassation," where she is half of the pair central to the story, and from "The Grande Malade," where she puts the story of Moydia in relief by her difference from her. In "Dusie" she is more strictly a narrator and less a participant, though she does consent to stay with Dusie when Madame K goes off and thus can report something of the goings on between Dusie and Clarissa. But clearly her role is fading. In "Dusie" she no longer has a name; in *Nightwood* she disappears altogether. The novel's narrative voice sounds like that of the unseen birds in Robin's hotel room – present but not assigned to a character.

"Dusie" has a related figure for its narrative and that of the other "little girl" stories. In Dusie's room are two canaries, "the one who sang and the one who listened" (76). As the "little girl," the one who is only a year younger than Dusie, sings her stories to "Madame," she becomes increasingly explicit in the sexual nature of her tales. We never learn how Madame responds, but we listen as Barnes works her way toward the exploration of gender and sexuality that is most fully presented in "Go Down Matthew." From "Cassation" with its shadow story about mothering, through "The Grande Malade" and its sexual uncertainty, to "Dusie" and *Nightwood* where lesbianism and meditation on inversion preoccupy the central characters, Barnes puzzles over likeness and difference, self and other, sexuality and gender. That these same puzzles are now crucial to feminist theory makes Barnes's place in a lesbian canon less important than her prescient raising of issues still hotly debated generations after she wrote her stories of seduction.

NOTES

1 Bertha Harris, "The More Profound Nationality of their Lesbianism: Lesbian Society in Paris in the 1920's" in *Amazon Expedition*, ed. Phyllis Birkby et al. (New York: Times Change Press, 1973), 77–88; Tee Corinne, in a slide show on lesbian images in art at a panel, "Old Dykes Tales: The Diversity of Feminist Experience," National Women Studies Association Conference, Douglass College, June 1984. Not all recent assessments by lesbians have been negative, however. See, for example, Monique Wittig, "The Point of View," *Feminist Issues* 3 (Fall 1983), 63–69.

2 Andrew Field, *Djuna: The Life and Times of Djuna Barnes* (New York: G. P. Putnam's, 1983), 37.

3 Field, 233. For example, Anaïs Nin wrote her admiringly about how Nin's own work had been influenced by *Nightwood*, but Barnes didn't answer her letter.

4 For a delineation of that literature in connection with Barnes's contemporary Radclyffe Hall, see Esther Newton, "The Mythic Mannish Lesbian: Radclyffe Hall and the New Woman," *Signs* 9 (Summer 1984), 557–75.

5 Catharine Stimpson, "Zero Degree Deviancy: The Lesbian Novel in English" in *Writing and Sexual Difference*, ed. Elizabeth Abel (Chicago: University of Chicago Press, 1982), 244.

6 For details of this history see Hester Eisenstein, "Introduction" to *The Future of Difference*, ed. Hester Eisenstein and Alice Jardine (Boston: G. K. Hall, 1980), xv–xxiv; Hester Eisenstein, *Contemporary Feminist Thought* (Boston: G. K. Hall, 1983), and Alison Jaggar, *Feminist Politics and Human Nature*, (Totowa, N.J.: Rowman and Allanheld, 1983).

7 This distinction between oppression and repression became shorthand for contrasts between American and French "feminisms" in the 1980s. See, for example, Alice Jardine, "Prelude: The Future of Difference" in *The Future of Difference*, xxv–xxvii, and Margaret Homans, "'Her Very Own Howl,'" *Signs* 9 (Winter 1983), 186–205.

8 For a discussion of Kristeva and Irigaray in the context of French "feminist" theory, see Josette Feral, "Antigone or the Irony of the Tribe," *Diacritics* (Fall 1978), 2–14.

9 Chodorow, "Gender, Relation, and Difference in Psychoanalytic Perspective" in *The Future of Difference*, 3–19. For a full discussion of her ideas, see *The Reproduction of Mothering* (Berkeley: University of California Press, 1978).

10 *Nightwood* [1936] (reprint edition New York: New Directions, 1961), 136; other citations are noted by page in the text.

11 Herbert Blau, "Disseminating Sodom," *Salmagundi* 58–59 (Fall 1982–Winter 1983), 237.

12 *Ladies Almanack, showing their Signs and their tides; their moons and their Changes; the Seasons as it is with them; their Eclipses and Equinoxes; as well as a full Record of diurnal and nocturnal Distempers:* Written and illustrated by a Lady of Fashion [1928] (reprint edition New York: Harper and Row, 1972), 24–26.

13 For a lesbian reading somewhat critical of Barnes's presentation of the Barney circle, see Karla Jay, "The Outsider among the Expatriates: Djuna Barnes' Satire

on the Ladies of the *Almanack*" in *Lesbian Texts and Contexts,* ed. Karla Jay and Joanne Glasgow (New York: New York University Press, 1990), 204–16.

14 For a discussion of boundary fluidity in lesbian relationships, see Beverly Burch, "Barriers to Intimacy: Conflicts over Power, Dependency, and Nurturing in Lesbian Relationships" in *Lesbian Psychologies: Explorations and Challenges,* ed. The Boston Lesbian Psychologies Collective (Urbana: University of Illinois Press, 1987), 126–41. For issues of incest in Barnes's life, see Mary Lynn Broe, "My Art Belongs to Daddy: Incest as Exile, The Textual Economics of Hayford Hall" in *Women's Writing in Exile,* ed. Mary Lynn Broe and Angela Ingram (Chapel Hill: University of North Carolina Press, 1989), 42–86.

15 Luce Irigaray, "When Our Lips Speak Together," translated and with an introduction by Carolyn Burke, *Signs* 6 (Autumn 1980), 66–79; "And One Doesn't Speak without the Other," translated and with an introduction by Hélène Vivienne Wenzel, *Signs* 7 (Autumn 1981), 56–67. Both these essays are very subtly wrought and deserve a full reading which space does not permit here. Irigaray's work also stresses woman and language and thus is a particularly promising intertext for Barnes.

16 "The Grande Malade" in *Selected Works of Djuna Barnes* (New York: Farrar, Straus and Cudahy, 1962), 19; first published as "The Little Girl Continues" in *This Quarter* 1 (1925), 195–200.

17 For a full delineation of the difference between mothering as "institution" and as "experience," see Adrienne Rich, *Of Woman Born* (New York: W. W. Norton, 1976).

18 "Cassation," *Selected Works,* 25; first published as "A Little Girl Tells a Story to a Lady," *Contact Collection of Contemporary Writers* (Paris: Three Mountains Press, 1925), 5–10.

19 "Dusie" in *American Esoterica* (New York: Macy-Masius, 1927), 78.

20 As in "The Grande Malade," actual parents are absent from the story proper. Barnes saved parental confrontation for *Ryder* and *The Antiphon.*

10

Marthe Rosenfeld

Modernity and Lesbian Identity in the Later Works of Nicole Brossard

Although there is no unique style that characterizes the work of all lesbian writers, it is not surprising that Nicole Brossard, the most famous lesbian poet of contemporary Quebec, should also be "resolutely modern" in her textual practice.[1] A writer who seeks to convey a way of life that runs counter to the norms and values of the dominant culture is likely also to challenge the institutions that perpetuate those norms: the literary canon and the language of tradition. In an informative book entitled *Les mots et les femmes* (1979), Marina Yaguello emphasizes the priority of the masculine over the feminine gender in French grammar; she demonstrates moreover how French words in the course of history have acquired meanings that convey negative images of women (115–47, 149–63). Brossard's early awareness that language, as a system of communication, transmits the cultural codes of a society accounts for her faith in the transformative power of experimental writing even in the early 1970s, when the liberation of Quebec still aroused her deepest feelings (1970:3–6). Not until the middle of that decade, when the author had chosen to identify as a feminist and as a lesbian, did she move beyond the theories of "new writing" to struggle with other women against the sexism and restrictiveness of the official language (Forsyth 1981:16–20). Indeed it is this quest for a medium of expression outside of the mainstream that elucidates the intersection between Brossard's lesbian-feminist identity and her postmodernism.

Because the meanings of words such as "modernism," "modernity" and "postmodernism" change according to the culture in which they are defined, a brief history of these movements from a francophone perspective might be in order here. Since *modernité* grew out of modernism, there is no visible demarcation line that separates these two periods from each other.[2]

In early twentieth-century France, a shift in attitude toward the arts began to manifest itself. Apollinaire, with his unusual poetry, epitomized this new spirit and its rejection of art's mimetic approach to nature. Similarly, by reducing all shapes to their geometric components, experimental painters such as Braque and Picasso transformed the concepts of space and of the human figure. Cubism with its multiplicity of perspectives also influenced the younger generation of poets to avoid ordinary descriptions. Instead of reproducing exterior reality, they juxtaposed images without regard to logic and thus communicated the rapidity of the modern age (Balakian 1959:50–69). In 1916 the Dadaists, expressing the utter confusion of a world at war, cast systematic doubt on everything except chance (Balakian 1947:127–41). A few years after the end of the hostilities, the surrealists, having overcome the initial nihilism of Dada, tried to revitalize the language, impoverished by the mediocre fiction of that period (1959:112–13). Attentive to their stream of thought, the surrealists would give free play to the association of words whose unusual combinations could explode in a brilliant image. With its free-flowing imagery and its minimum of preconceived ideas, surrealism increased the autonomy of the readers as interpreters of poetry (1959:114–15).

The novel, however, with a few exceptions, continued to stagnate. In 1932 Nathalie Sarraute began to jot down the minute inner movements, the impulses, the conflicting sentiments which bump against each other on the threshold of consciousness in *L'Ere du soupçon* (1956:ii–iv). By illuminating the profusion of sensations that often accompany, follow, or precede a dialogue, Sarraute invited her readers to experience for themselves the inner dramas of her anonymous people (72–74). But the preoccupation of the author of *Tropisms* (1939) with the subterranean movements that form an integral part of everyone's existence made it necessary for her to challenge the traditional novel with its individualized characters, its linear plots, its chronological time (1956:103–24). Thanks to her lonely experimentations, Sarraute became a pioneer of the *nouveau roman*.

In the novels of Robbe-Grillet, objects, passions and different versions of the same event are presented to the reader through the eyes of a narrator whose vision is both limited and fragmented. Unlike the surrealists, who sought to attain a higher form of reality by fusing the states of dream and of wakefulness, the new novelists, in true postmodern fashion, insisted on the purely fictional character of their work (Robbe-Grillet 1963:165–69). Similarly, in *Writing Degree Zero* (1953), Roland Barthes underscored the self-reflective nature of postmodern writing (44–52). In a world divided by factionalism, conflicts, and strife, "alienated writing" would seek its own self-transcendence, its own peculiarities, sounds, and functions, just as the *nouveau roman* had no other reality outside of its own narrative.[3]

It was in the 1960s that the ideas of postmodernism gained ground in Quebec, precisely at the time of its cultural revolution, a period often referred to as *La Révolution Tranquille* (Gould 1990:2–10). Given Brossard's early adherence to the principles of modernity, it is not surprising that *Un livre* (1970), her first novel, should read like an archetype of the *nouveau roman* in Quebec (1990:64). For, unlike many other Quebec novels of that period, which dealt with the land, the snow, the ever-increasing family, this book questioned the relationship between fiction and reality, between words and meanings, between the printed lines and the blank spaces. But the more the text turned inward, the more the female narrator vanished from the scene.

In this essay I plan to show the relation between Brossard's identity as a lesbian and her formalist approach to writing in two of her later works: in *Amantes* (1980b), translated as *Lovhers* (1986), and in *Picture theory* (1982). From that time onward Brossard was able to distill her experience as a lesbian in such a way that her words communicate not only her personal desire but the essence of sapphic love.

An avant-garde composition consisting of poems and prose passages, *Amantes* deals with the lovemaking of four lesbians who are staying at the Barbizon Hotel for women and who learn to articulate their feelings as well as their thoughts by associating with their own kind. To evoke the atmosphere of this female space, Brossard experiments with both form and typography. Divided into five parts by means of black and gray pages, illustrated with photographs of the New York skyline, and printed with a variety of types – capital letters, small letters, italics, blank spaces – this book immediately challenges our reading habits as well as the unidirectional character of patriarchal systems of thought. Similarly, the traditional concept of literature as a succession of masterpieces created in isolation by individual geniuses has given way to a more communal vision of literary creation (Forsyth 1981:10). That is why numerous quotations from other lesbian writers – Adrienne Rich, Monique Wittig, Louky Bersianik – embellish *Amantes*.

By showing how the subversive love between two women is related to their quest for a new language, Brossard also brings out the connection between lesbianism and postmodernism. Unlike traditional literature, whose texts refer for the most part to an objective reality, the words of *Amantes* create their own mental space. In fact what characterizes the writing of this book is the breaking up of the sentence with its subject, verb, predicate sequence into word-clusters, units that are no longer attached to one another by conjunctions, adverbs or punctuation:

concentrées dans l'île (4) amoureuses
picture theory / juillet la mer
dire l'intention des langues (28)

If the reader tries in vain to restore the grammatical order, it is because postmodern writing rejects the determinism that underlies the traditional narrative form. To express an open-ended reality, one that mirrors the dreams, hopes, and desires of women-loving women, the lesbian writer must also redefine all the words that have been contaminated by centuries of patriarchal ideology.

For example, the concept of memory, to which Brossard devotes a section entitled MA MEMOIRE D'(AMOUR), is a word that needed to be reexamined because the official memory, by ignoring or maligning women, has separated us from each other and from our past. Consequently Brossard links the nostalgic quest for our history to the physical love between women. Moreover, unlike the word that has been restricted in the dictionaries of the dominant culture to mean "remembrance of past events," memory in the work of Brossard also connotes the arrival of a bright future, a Utopian future which helps women to live in the present:

la nuit venue lorsque de mèche
nos fronts se souviennent des plus belles
délinquances, on bouge un peu la main
pour que s'ouvre sous nos yeux
la mémoire agile des filles de l'utopie
se déplaçant en italique
ou en une fresque vers toutes les issues
(70)

Likewise, in order to describe the pleasure of lesbianism without resorting to heterosexual language, Brossard found it necessary to alter the definition of the word *skin*. Unlike the dominant sexuality with its emphasis on penile penetration, lesbian loving has no single sensual center.[4] Disproving the image of superficiality that the mainstream culture has given to the expression "only skin deep," Brossard illustrates how "a woman's skin sliding on a woman's skin creates a slipperiness in the meaning of words and makes a new version of reality and fiction possible" (Wilson 1981:18). In *Amantes*, the knowledge derived from sensations of taste and touch enables the lesbian lovers to rediscover a multidimensional language.

If Brossard found it necessary as a lesbian writer to question grammatical structures and dictionaries, as a devotee of *modernité* she felt the need to reject traditional writing with its linear time and its binary system of opposition: man/woman, culture/nature, activity/passivity, intellect/feeling. It is precisely the author's rebellion against these manifestations of the "straight" mentality that accounts for the paramount importance of the spiral in her work from *L'Amèr* (1977) onward. This shape, which appears in everything from seashells to nebulas, from the flight of birds to the movement of planets and stars, enables the female writer to explore new analogies, new rhythms, a new way of relating with the world and of being. In postmodern texts by women each spiral repeats the same words but in so doing adds another element to the previous notation, thus advancing the turn of the coil every time (Wilson 1981:11). For example, the following spiral of *Amantes* brings out in a rhythmical flow of words the joy of yielding to temptation:

j'ai succombé à toutes les visions
séduite, surface, série et sérieuse

j'ai succombé à la vision claire
des végétations et des événements
matinales, . . .

j'ai succombé à l'écho, au retour,
à la répétition. *au commencement*
des vertèbres était la durée
une réplique essentielle à tout instant
dans la joie que j'ai de toi, . . .
(67, 69, 72)

Another spiral of that book makes the connection between the texture of the words and the taste of a kiss:

. . . et nous imaginons de nouvelles moeurs avec ces bouches mêmes qui savent tenir un discours, les nôtres au goût des mots au goût du baiser . . .

les faits sont tels que le projet du texte et le texte de projet s'accomplissent au goût des mots, au goût du baiser. je sais que tu m'es réelle / alors (13, 21)

A synthesis of all of Brossard's previous books, *Picture theory* (1982) resumes some of the major themes of *Amantes*, but it delves more deeply than the love poems into the issue of lesbianism and writing. One of the reasons why Brossard insists so vehemently on this question is her belief that women's literary expression is of paramount importance because it can change the world. However, in order to achieve this transformation, lesbians should be at the origin of the meaning they give to their lives (Cotnoir et al. 1982/1983:191). For the capacity to name and redefine the world depends largely on our place in the language. Since the French idiom, with its unequal gender structure, mirrors the heterosexist appropriation of the class of women by the class of men, Brossard chose lesbian-

ism not only because she passionately loves people of her own sex, but
because she seeks to alter the language.

Written from a lesbian-feminist perspective, *Picture theory* beckons the
reader to travel through five different areas of artistic creation, the five
chapters that constitute the book. "L'Ordinaire" introduces us to the characters of the novel as well as to its spiral composition. "La Perspective"
evokes the relationship between the female narrator and Claire Dérive,
her lover. The third chapter, entitled "L'Emotion," underscores the sense
of well-being that characterizes feminist utopias, especially when Amazons show solidarity with one another in pursuit of common goals. "La
Pensée," the most important chapter in the book, announces the arrival of
a sister poet, a contemporary Sappho whose genius will enable her to reshape the language. In the last chapter, this dreamlike image of the poet
comes into clear focus; she is emulated by other women, for she can interact with them by means of the hologram that helps to illuminate aspects
of the associative memory and of other thought processes.

In an interview with the lesbian-feminist journal *Vlasta* published five
years ago, Brossard emphasized the significance of expressing one's personal truth (Triton 1983:35–37). But the difficulty of articulating our intimate thoughts in patriarchal societies accounts for the importance the author attaches to the solidarity of women. It is not surprising therefore that
the female characters of *Picture theory* acquire their sense of self by living
together one summer in a communal setting. Breathing the sea air of a
holiday resort on the New England coast, they discuss their youth, the
stilted images of women in mainstream films, the danger of confusing
"father time" and the time of Amazon friendships. ". . . Nous sommes
cinq au lever du soleil à . . . voir éperdument la mer, prononçant d'une
manière atonale des phrases complètes et abstraites liant la vie et la parole
dans l'heure horizontale" (80). The frequent use of the feminine plural indicates not only that the women are pooling their energies but also that
they challenge one another to communicate their ideas, ideas which will
give them a new sense of being in the culture: "Je disais . . ." noted the
lesbian narrator ". . . qu'un témoignage utopique de notre part pouvait
stimuler en nous une qualité d'émotion propice à notre insertion dans
l'histoire" (85).

When preceded by the definite article, the word *histoire* often denotes
that branch of learning which relates and analyzes the "important events"
of the life of a people. However, since meanings, values, and notions of
reality have been shaped by centuries of patriarchal cultures, women as a
class have been excluded from this narrative. While certain francophone
feminists seek to inscribe a female presence into the language by using
such terms as *hystoire, écrivaine, auteure,* Brossard tends to redefine existing words and thus to produce a form of writing that breaks the continu-

ity of patriarchal culture.[5] As our experiences and perceptions have no credibility in that culture, the attempt to translate into words those "fictions" that are our realities becomes a utopian venture. In Brossard's *Picture theory*, the utopian quest arouses a quality of emotion conducive to women's insertion into history, that word having acquired the dual meaning of a female presence here and now as well as in the future.

But if women can become part of history by means of their communal efforts, it is lesbianism that enables them to express their own view of the world in new and modernistic terms. One of the ways in which the author links the themes of sapphic love and language is through the world of the senses. Surface/skin, in *Amantes*, constitutes an avenue of approach to sensuous and verbal knowledge. In *Picture theory*, however, the vast expanse of touching is explored to attain the body of the beloved as well as the art of writing: "sa main me touchait comme une raison / écrire allait devenir un souci permanent" (56). If Michèle Vallée, the narrator, and her lover, Claire Dérive, choose words for their sound and their evocative power rather than for their meaning, it is because they do not wish to see their poetry retrieved by existing cultural institutions:

je reprenais les sons
autour de sa bouche, les liaisons
presque sans accent la fièvre sonore
(64)

Although *Amantes* and *Picture theory* both link lesbian sexuality to language and to literature, it is the latter book that brings together lesbian poetry and postmodernism. In the arts this quest for new forms is related to the concept of abstraction. To accelerate her progress toward that goal, the narrator of *Picture theory* uses a vocabulary rich in the symbolist tradition: forest, water, sea, angel, helmet (Cotnoir et al. 1982:183). The following poem, for example, conjures up a scene of freshness that is at once lesbian and abstract:

Claire Dérive est entrée dans la forêt
et les songes emportée par la vision
du temps qui s'écoule entre ses lèvres
elle entend la pluie qui danse sur son casque
elle traverse la forêt ruisselante
et déterminée comme l'est sa bouche
Claire Dérive est dans la rosée
l'horizon, allongée entre mes cuisses
(71)

Exposed at the end of the second chapter to "l'abstraction vitale," the lesbian lovers have become symbolic characters, mythical figures who announce the coming of a poetess: "her through whom anything can happen" (Cotnoir et al. 1982/1983:129).

The arrival for the first time in history of a female subject in the language is evoked in different ways: plays on words, scene shifts without transition, travels back and forth between Paris, Montreal, and Curaçao. But more important than these signs of modernity in announcing the advent of the female poet who "makes contact" is the spiral, a form that Brossard relates to lesbian sensibility. In *Picture theory,* as in *Amantes,* phrases and analogous sentences build on each other to form an ever-widening curve, a spiral that challenges the linear structure of traditional fiction even as it favors the development of the texts' lesbian-feminist themes. "C'est elle," writes the narrator of *Picture theory* as she envisions the coming of the female author, "il faudrait la voir venir, virtuelle à l'infini," "je la vois venir," "je la vois venir les femmes synchrones au matin chaque fois plus nombreuse," "je la vois venir dans l'angle lorsque la phrase se divise en deux" (118, 165, 169, 189, 192). Similarly the repetition of the phrase "peau la langue monte au cerveau" takes on the quality of a chant, a recitative which also announces the arrival of her who generates meaning in words (194, 198–99, 201–2, 205). Indeed the issue of woman's position in the language looms so large that the spiral now moves in a centripetal manner toward that focal point (Danis 1987:39).

The utopian quest is a major theme linking *Picture theory* to *Amantes.* These two works point to a reimagined space where lesbians live in harmony with each other. Moreover, both novels illustrate the paramount importance of language as a means of expressing female-centered societies. In her transformation of Wittgenstein's picture theory, Brossard has shown how lesbianism challenges the limitations of a philosophy that views the concepts of language and of picture as synonymous terms. Instead of being captive in a two-dimensional model of reality, the lesbians in Brossard discover words while making love, and the radiance that emanates from this lovemaking, like a laser beam, alters the picture into a holographic three-dimensional image.[6]

In *Amantes* as well as in *Picture theory,* Brossard develops a polyvalence of meaning, a new form of writing that communicates the intensity of lesbian relationships as well as the momentous significance of female subjectivity in the language that has excluded women and lesbians as agents of thought and action. Rooted in the present and looking toward the future, Nicole Brossard's postmodernism is linked inextricably to her lesbian-feminist vision of the world.

NOTES

I am indebted to Janine Ricouart for her excellent bibliography in an unpublished paper entitled "Problématiques de l'homo-identité chez Marie-Claire Blais et Nicole Brossard," M/MLA Convention, St. Louis, Mo., 5 November 1988.

1 In an essay entitled "L'Epreuve de la modernité ou/et les preuves de modernité," Brossard explains the changes that have taken place since the end of the nineteenth century with regard to the issue of modernism. The words of the poet Rimbaud "Il faut être absolument moderne" have now become "résolument moderne." For an explanation of Brossard's attitude toward modernity, see her book *The Aerial Letter*, trans. Marlene Wildeman (Toronto: The Women's Press, 1988c), 68–76.

2 When francophones speak of *modernité*, anglophones use the expression "postmodernism." For contrasting points of view, see Caroline Bayard, "Postmodernisme et avant-garde au Canada, 1960–1984," *Voix et Images* 10.1 (1984), 39.

3 Roland Barthes uses the phrase "alienated writing" to express the uncomfortable position of the modern writer in a world without cohesion or unity. For useful insights, see *Writing Degree Zero*, pref. Susan Sontag, trans. Annette Lavers and Colin Smith (New York: Hill and Wang, 1977), xvii–xviii.

4 In her book *Pure Lust: Elemental Feminist Philosophy* (Boston: Beacon Press, 1984), 245, Mary Daly brings out the importance of surface knowledge and of touching, and she explains Brossard's contribution to this realm of knowledge.

5 Late-twentieth-century changes in the French lexicon often involve the feminization of words or the search for new etymologies. Linguistic innovations to facilitate the expression of lesbian or feminist realities have taken place in anglophone countries as well.

6 For a detailed explanation of the connection between the hologram and the idea of a lesbian utopia in Brossard's later work, see Lorraine Weir, "From picture to hologram: Nicole Brossard's grammar of utopia," *A Mazing Space: Writing Canadian Women Writing*, eds. Shirley Neuman and Smaro Kamboureli (Edmonton, Alberta: Longspoon/NeWest, 1986), 349–52.

11

Linnea A. Stenson

From Isolation to Diversity:
Self and Communities
in Twentieth-Century Lesbian Novels

We each have our reasons for wanting to know everything there is to know about women. She who has been mystery for centuries is coming out. We who have not made common cause since the fall of the great matriarchies, we are coming together (watch out).

Elana Nachman, *Riverfinger Women* (1974)

In the late nineteenth century, scientific literature appeared that debated whether homosexuality was a "vice indulged in by weak-willed, depraved individuals, an acquired form of insanity, or a congenital defect that indicated evolutionary degeneracy" (D'Emilio 1983:15). The disease model eventually won out, and the locus of homosexuality shifted from behaviors or acts engaged in by individuals, to the individuals themselves. Thus the homosexual, the "congenital invert," was born.

Among the works of the nineteenth-century sexologists, Havelock Ellis's *Studies in the Psychology of Sex: Sexual Inversion*, published in 1897, proved to be the most influential in its study of "female inversion." Lillian Faderman notes that for many nineteenth- and early twentieth-century women, a relationship between women that included genital sex was inconceivable (1981:251). However, there were doubtless thousands of women who did have sexual relationships with women, and who, because of the growing awareness of "female inversion," internalized the pathological view of their relationship put forth by Ellis.[1] In confirming the existence of the "third sex," Ellis "established the mystique of the 'true lesbian,' a mystique which was subsequently accepted by many lesbians themselves who then became transvestites and 'butches' because such behavior demonstrated *ipso facto* that they were the genuine article, that they must be taken seriously and not forced into heterosexual patterns" (Faderman, 245). Lesbian communities were formed, where a "self-conscious society of women who now identified themselves as 'inverts'" gathered in one another's company (Faderman, 250).

What visions does literature reflect written by and about those who became known as "inverts" or "lesbians" around the turn of the century? How were these female communities characterized? How have these visions changed over time? How are the lives of lesbians of color and working-class lesbians portrayed? Because the novel, at its roots, has been primarily a white, middle- and upper-class product, explicit treatment of lesbian themes in literature from working-class communities and communities of color is scarce, especially through the first half of this century. In thinking about fictions written in the twentieth century that deal with lesbian communities, I am particularly interested in the relationship between self-identity and its effect on community. If "identity" refers to the ideas and feelings an individual has about herself, what happens to lesbian communities when lesbians have, as part of their identity, a view that they are pathological? morbid? congenitally defective? The formation of identity-based communities, shaped by the shared or mutual experiences and identities of those who belong, can only reflect who the communities are made up of, and literature predominantly will reflect those who have had the leisure and resources to write. As lesbian identity has moved through changing social and cultural attitudes, fictional lesbian characters have moved from individual isolation to a greater sense of diversity within the many communities to which they belong.

Carroll Smith-Rosenberg writes in her pioneering article, "The Female World of Love and Ritual: Relations between Women in Nineteenth-Century America," (1975), that "nineteenth-century women routinely formed emotional ties with other women" and that these "deeply felt, same-sex friendships were casually accepted in American society" (1). These communities of women, or "romantic friendships," as Lillian Faderman calls them, were furthered toward the end of the nineteenth century as the early feminist movement began to open up education and career possibilities for women, who began to enjoy an independence they had not had previously (1981:178). However, this love between women began to be seen as threatening to the social order. Faderman writes that

the concern over the ramifications of women's increasing independence; the sexologists' theories which came along at a most convenient time to bolster arguments that a woman's desire for independence meant she was not really a woman;

and the poetry and fiction of the French aesthetes which provided anxiety-provok-
ing images of the sexual possibilities of love between women – guaranteed that
romantic friendship, which had been encouraged by society in the past, would
now be seen in a different, and most antisocial, light. (238)

The turn of the century found a new and hostile position formed about
female friendships and communities, where changing social and cultural
attitudes actively worked to discourage the behavior they had earlier
worked to foster.[2]

One obvious example of this change is particularly evident in a comparison of the works of Sarah Orne Jewett and Willa Cather. Many of
Jewett's women are involved in loving relationships with one another.
Cather, who grew as a writer in an entirely different social and cultural
environment than Jewett, leaves no mention of love between women in
her fiction. Despite Jewett's advice to the contrary, Cather patently refused to show that women had any love interest between them. In 1908,
Jewett wrote to Cather about Cather's story "On Gull's Road" that "'the
lover is well done as he could be when a woman writes in the man's character, – it must always, I believe, be something of a masquerade . . . and
you could almost have done it as yourself – a woman could love her in the
same protecting way – a woman could even care enough to wish to take
her away from such a life, by some means or other'" (quoted in Faderman
201–2). Doubtless, Cather had internalized the popular notions of the perverse nature of female friendships and chose to hide love between
women, despite her own long-term relationship with Edith Lewis.

As women's independence grew, so did antifeminism. In the early part
of this century, influenced by the hostile social climate, novels by white
middle- and upper-class lesbians overflowed with the pathological view
of their sociosexual communities. As well, after World War I, sexual strictures loosened and literature that dealt specifically with lesbianism became more popularly read (Foster [1956] 1975:240–41). Faderman notes
that "Earlier writing, if it treated lesbianism openly, focused on explaining
the 'problem' to heterosexuals, or it showed the lesbian characters trying
to adjust, with varying degrees of success, to the demands of the straight
world. Lesbianism was the major conflict of the story" (406). This early
treatment of "invert" literature reached its first peak in 1928, with the
publication of Radclyffe Hall's *The Well of Loneliness*.[3] Hall's influence and
the succeeding scandal that her novel created cannot be underestimated.
Hall's novel has become the one novel by which all other novels dealing
with lesbianism are measured.

In what I can see only as an ironic footnote, Havelock Ellis himself
wrote the introductory commentary for the novel, wherein he noted that
"the relation of certain people . . . to the often hostile society in which they

move, presents difficult and still unsolved problems" (Hall 1981:6). Indeed, Radclyffe Hall saw her "inversion" as a natural act of God, and challenged society's view of homosexuality as abhorrent practice. Stephen Gordon's character seems not only a blend of some sort of prebirth cause, hinted at in her parents' desire for a male child and Stephen's own masculine physical makeup, but in her father's indulgence of her masculine psychological characteristics as well. Stephen feels lonely and isolated, without an understanding community, her father her only friend. Stephen has yet to learn that the "loneliest place in this world is the no-man's land of sex" (79). Her isolation is furthered by her misadventure with Martin Hallum. Stephen finds Martin a true friend, and sees their friendship as one between two men. When Martin declares his love for her, she is struck with a "kind of dumb horror, staring at his eyes that were clouded by desire" (98). Through her rejection of Martin Hallum, Stephen begins to sense that there is something wrong with her; in this, she has accepted the expectations of her class and time and believed that any woman who desired male prerogatives must be congenitally abnormal.

Stephen decides to live in Paris, where she "'might make some sort of home, . . . work here – and then of course there are people . . .'" (248). Puddle, her tutor and friend, understands Stephen's loneliness, and thinks "'Like to like! Like to like! Like to like!'" (248). At the onset of World War I, Stephen finally finds her community in the women's ambulance corps:

Side by side with more fortunate women, worked Miss Smith who had been breeding dogs in the country; or Miss Oliphant who had been breeding nothing since birth but a litter of hefty complexes; or Miss Tring who had lived with a very dear friend in the humbler purlieus of Chelsea. . . . Their nerves were not at all weak, their pulses beat placidly through the worst air raids, for bombs do not trouble the nerves of the invert, but rather that terrible silent bombardment from the batteries of God's good people. (271)

With these women, "a battalion was formed . . . that would never again be completely disbanded . . . never again would such women submit to being driven back to their holes and corners. They had found themselves" (272). I think the women of this community bond through their shared guilt or shame at their abnormality, eager to show they have good hearts and minds despite their inversion. When word comes that the war is over, the women seem happy, but "funny, old, monosyllabic Blakeney with her curly white hair cropped as close as an Uhlan's – Blakeney who had long ago done with emotions – quite suddenly laid her arms on the table and her head on her arms, and she wept, and she wept" (295). The women have had their first taste of real community, despite the hardships of the war. "Not a woman of them all but felt vaguely regretful in spite of the infinite blessing of peace" (295). Stephen's first experience with a community to which she surely belongs is positive; she and the other women feel useful and proud of themselves and who they are. Later Stephen reflects on the women of her wartime community: "England had called them and they had come; for once, unabashed, they had faced the daylight. And now because they were not prepared to slink back and hide in their holes and corners, the very public whom they had served was the first to turn round and spit upon them; to cry: 'Away with this canker in our midst, this nest of unrighteousness and corruption!'" (405). Stephen believes that "Persecution was always a hideous thing, breeding hideous thoughts – and such thoughts were dangerous" (407), to the community from the outside as well as polluting the thoughts of those within.

Because of her wartime meeting with others of her kind, Stephen has her first real glimpse of the numbers of women like her. In postwar Paris, Stephen and her lover Mary Llewellyn finally venture into Valérie Seymour's salon world, where "men and women who must carry God's mark on their foreheads" meet (352). Stephen's turn to community is not for herself but for Mary's loneliness: ". . . to her own kind she turned and was made very welcome, for no bond is more binding than that of affliction" (356).

When Stephen and Mary experience the "tragic night life of Paris" (378), we get our first real glimpse of Hall's opinion of the community to which lesbians belong. It is not beautiful, nor a truly happy experience. Stephen arrives at

that meeting-place of the most miserable of all those who comprised the miserable army. The merciless, drug-dealing, death-dealing haunt to which flocked the battered remnants of men whom their fellow men had at last stamped under; who, despised of the world, must despise themselves beyond all hope, it seemed, of salvation. There they sat, closely herded together at the tables, creatures shabby yet tawdry, timid yet defiant – and their eyes, Stephen never forgot their eyes, those haunted, tormented eyes of the invert.

Of all ages, all degrees of despondency, all grades of mental and physical ill-being, they must . . . yet dance together . . . and that dance seemed the Dance of Death to Stephen.

Bereft of all social dignity, of all social charts contrived for man's guidance, of the fellowship that by right divine should belong to each breathing, living creature; abhorred, spat upon, from their earliest days the prey to a ceaseless persecution, they were now even lower than their enemies knew, and more hopeless than the veriest dregs of creation. (387–88)

Stephen finds the community awful, humiliating, and miserable, as do the readers. Certainly in this section, we read Hall's plea for understanding and an end to persecution, but the overall sense is that it will not come in Stephen's lifetime. We understand that this is the only community that can be expected for the invert until the day that justice and equality is done for those tortured souls marked by God.

As I think about this view of community, it is clear to me that it reflects the social and cultural expectations of the invert enforced by the dominant norms. Throughout the novel, Hall pleads for understanding of her self and community, but her pleas are colored by the pathological identity attributed to her characters, no matter how they attempt to live out their lives. I think that in a hostile world, where identity is formed with a strong sense of congenital deformity, combined with the view that one is morally depraved, the formation of an identity-based community can reflect only a negative view, since the individual identities and mutual experiences of being social pariahs can lead only to a lesbian community that sees itself as sexually and socially diseased. The text ends on a cry from Stephen's kind, the "one voice, one demand; her own voice into which those millions had entered. . . . 'God,' she gasped, 'we believe, we have told You we believe. . . . We have not denied You, then rise up and defend us. Acknowledge us, oh God, before the whole world. Give us also the right to our existence!'" (437). If nothing else, the reader might feel pity for the invert and her kind. After all, the invert can be kind and good and noble, as we see when Stephen gives Mary to Martin Hallum so that Mary, the "real" woman, may live the life she was meant to live. But it cannot be forgotten that Stephen and her kind view themselves as sexually and socially diseased.

It seems important to me to note here that Radclyffe Hall's vision of lesbian community was not the only one in existence at the time; indeed, the Parisian lesbian community of the 1920s to which Hall belonged was much less wrapped up in the self-loathing that permeates her novel. Certainly, Hall's identity was strongly influenced by the work of the sexologists; however, writers such as Renée Vivien and Natalie Barney took much of their identities from French literature of the nineteenth century, in which the lesbian character was a romantic figure. Through positive identities and a unique lesbian self-awareness, "Vivien and Barney were proud *of* homosexuality . . . [which they] considered a thrilling distinction" (Rubin 1976:x). As a work of propaganda, *The Well of Loneliness* perhaps achieved some level of the tolerance Hall hoped for, but it's evident to me that the tolerance never reached the level of a "thrilling distinction." Vivien and Barney were not interested in propaganda or tolerance for themselves so much as rooting out and fostering the growth of a positive identity and community for lesbians. Many of the lesbians of the Parisian community derided Hall's novel, and an American sociological study of lesbians in the 1920s and 1930s found that "'almost to a woman, they decried its publication,'" believing it did more harm than good for their community (Faderman, 322). However, its familiarity to the public at large and continued influence even today point to its importance, for better or worse.

After the publication scandal of *The Well of Loneliness*, "as is usual in cases of censorship the long range result was wide publicity . . . [and] the number of novels giving attention to variance swelled to a second peak in the middle Thirties" (Foster, 241). Outside of the Parisian community of lesbian writers, Gale Wilhelm introduced two novels with lesbian themes in the United States in the 1930s. The tone of Wilhelm's first novel, *We Too Are Drifting* (1935), differs from Hall's in that the lesbians are not quite so pathetic or abominable, although the novel does hold on to the sense that the lesbian is a martyr figure. The lesbian community present in *The Well of Loneliness* disappears. Instead, we find the protagonist, Jan Morale, the only "true" lesbian in the story, isolated from any larger community.

We Too Are Drifting revolves around Jan's attempt to disentangle herself from an ill-fated affair with a married woman, Madeline. Jan meets Victoria Connerly, a young woman with whom she falls deeply in love. The plot is complicated by Madeline's refusal to let Jan go and by Victoria's imminent engagement to "a nice young man." When a planned holiday between Jan and Victoria must be canceled because Victoria's family has planned a long vacation that includes the presence of the man her parents hope she will marry, all is over between Jan and Victoria. Jan tells Victoria, "There'll be things like this and you'll get used to them . . . I've got used to them. You see, my dear, you'll never be able to say to your family I'd rather go to the mountains with my friend than go to Chicago with you. . . . It's one of those things we can be sorry about but we can't grieve" (108–9). Like Stephen Gordon, Jay does right by the woman who does not truly belong to her kind. At the close of the novel, Jan watches the departure of Victoria, her family, and her fiancé. Jan stands separate and far off so Victoria cannot see her, and she watches as "the girls swarmed around Victoria and kissed her carefully because of their mouths and hers and said, Good-bye, good-bye, good-bye! and Victoria smiled at them and . . . stepped up and waved" (117). Jan does not belong to this world of smiling girls and fiancés; she is left alone at the close.

Another of Wilhelm's novels, *Torchlight to Valhalla* (1938), had a considerably happier ending. Once Morgen and Toni meet each other, they find that each is what the other has needed and wanted. The novel closes with the promise of a long, lasting relationship. It would also seem that Morgen and Toni live in a slightly more accepting world. In one passage, Morgen goes to see the family doctor about a problem that is never named. The doctor responds "I've finished with you professionally. I can't say to you this is wise or that is unwise. I can say find out the difference between the real and the false. You'll have to rely on your instinct and I know it's perfectly reliable because you're a sensible girl" (86). It would seem that much had changed in the ten years since Hall's novel had been published. Morgen finds acceptance, from her doctor and her family friend and neighbor, no matter what her decision.

In my reading of lesbian novels of this time period, I find an interesting shift. While the characters do not "thrill" to the distinction that marks them, neither do they dwell on it. Each novel hints at a possible cause for the sexual orientation of their main characters, but does not give much in the way of the lengthy explanation or self-examination that characterizes *The Well of Loneliness.* The lesbian characters are both extraordinary in some manner: Jan is a brilliant artist who makes woodcuts, Morgen is a writer who has her first novel accepted at age twenty-one. Both, by inheritances from their fathers, seem to have plenty of money to support themselves, so they can remain independent of any male figure, and therefore are not a part of the female community of married women or single women seeking husbands. As well, they are independent of any larger lesbian community that may exist. Because both novels are set in and around San Francisco in the 1930s, where there was "more open discussion of sexuality in sophisticated circles . . . [and] a small but stable group life was forming" (D'Emilio, 22) for middle- and upper-class white women, it is interesting to note that lesbian communities are entirely absent from each of the novels.

Lesbian fictional literature (especially of novel length) throughout the twentieth century reflects disproportionately the experience of white, middle- to upper-class, well-educated lesbians. Barbara Smith (1977) notes that

any discussion of Afro-American writers can rightfully begin with the fact that for most of the time we have been in this country we have been categorically denied not only literacy, but the most minimal possibility of a decent human life. . . . The political, economic, and social restrictions of slavery and racism have historically stunted the creative lives of Black women. (169)

As well, lesbian literature by white and middle- to upper-class lesbians reflects their own insularity by rarely including characters whose race and/or class is different from their own.[4] Hostile social attitudes made it nearly impossible for lesbians to move out of a small, safe group of acquaintances. Certainly this insularity points to the difficulty lesbians had in crossing race and class lines. Lesbians generally found one another where they socialized, worked, or went to school, which were (and often remain today) homogeneous settings in terms of race and class. As well,

financial independence from men was vital to the growth of an independent lesbian identity. Given the isolation of diverse groups of lesbians
from one another, it is not surprising that lesbian novels rarely depict their
characters crossing class and race lines.[5]

The New Negro Movement or Harlem Renaissance (approximately
1924–33) saw a flowering of middle-class African-American women writing. At the time, African-American writers were "certainly aware of the
images, primarily negative, of black people that predominated in the
minds of white Americans . . . [and these writers' works] were conditioned by the need to establish 'positive' images of black people; hence,
the exploration of self, in all its complexity, could hardly be attempted" (B.
Christian 1985:235). If women writers were concerned about the "exotic"
and "loose" images of African-American womanhood, the presentation of
lesbianism in their fiction could only complicate matters. Ann Allen
Shockley (1983) believes that "those Black female writers who could have
written well and perceptively enough to warrant publication chose instead to write about Black women from a heterosexual perspective. The
preference was motivated by the fear of being labeled a Lesbian, whether
they were or not" (84). Nonetheless, there was an active and open gay and
lesbian community in Harlem during the 1920s and 1930s. Oral inter-
views, flyers for dances, and blues songs all point to a "free-wheeling,
wide open tolerance" (Weiss and Schiller 1988:26) of difference, which included differences in sexual orientation. However, this tolerance did not
extend to the inclusion of explicit lesbian themes in literature.

Nella Larsen's *Passing* (1929) hints at lesbianism between her two female protagonists, Irene Redfield and Clare Kendry. Deborah E. McDowell, in her introduction to the novel, writes that while the story is "super-
ficially Irene's . . . account of Clare's passing for white and related issues
of racial identity and loyalty, underneath the safety of that surface is a
more dangerous story – though not named explicitly – of Irene's awakening sexual desire for Clare" (Larsen 1987:xxvi). Through the many sensual
descriptive narratives of the women and their meetings, the alert reader
can read the implicit desire of Irene for Clare. It is only through Clare's
death at the close of the novel that Irene's feelings for her are put to an end
as well. McDowell notes that "the idea of bringing a sexual attraction between two women to full narrative expression is . . . too dangerous a
move" and that Clare "becomes a kind of sacrificial lamb on the altar of
social and literary convention" (xxx).

Other African-American women wrote of their sexual attachments to
women. Angelina Weld Grimké (1880–1958) wrote poetry that suggests,
through its subtle coding, women-identified relationships. Alice Dunbar-
Nelson (1875–1935) chronicled her lesbian affairs in her diary, written
from 1921 to 1931.[6] However, African-American writers, as well as white

women writers, seemed unable to break the social strictures of the time to write explicitly and openly about lesbian self-identity, much less about the lesbian communities they surely inhabited.

Why else might lesbian communities disappear from the novels set in the 1930s? John D'Emilio writes that

On the one hand, cumulative historical processes – the spread of capitalistic economic relations, industrialism and the socialization of production, and urban growth – were shaping a social context in which homosexual desire might congeal into a personal identity. As men and women who were inclined toward their own sex took on a self-definition as homosexual or lesbian, they searched for others like themselves and gradually created a group life. On the other hand, a pervasive hostility, expressed through religion, law, and science, kept homosexuality submerged and constrained gay people from openly acknowledging their presence in society. . . . For men and women who surmounted these hurdles and managed to stumble upon collective manifestations of gay life, the prevailing ideology imposed a burden of self-hate and encouraged them to interpret their sexuality in individualistic terms as an aberration, a flaw, or a personal failing. (22)

I believe that the complexity of factors during the time contributed to this "invisibility" of lesbian communities in literature. Tolerance or acceptance of one lesbian might be greater than tolerance or acceptance of whole communities of lesbians. Wilhelm herself was a fairly widely read and well-reviewed writer, receiving high praise for her work from a number of major publications including *The Nation* and the *Saturday Review of Literature*. Given the political climate in the 1930s, it is a wonder that she was published at all.[7] I wonder if it wasn't calculated on Wilhelm's part (much as Hall's work was calculated) to present to her readers a vision of lesbians that was not so frightening – if there is only one or two of "them," there's nothing for the heterosexual majority to worry about. As well, the characters are artists, and the public perhaps was more forgiving of artistic peculiarities. Given the publicity that Hall's work aroused, and the extremely degraded condition of Hall's fictional community, perhaps later novels wanted to shy away from the kind of negative image that could be invoked at the presentation of lesbian communities in all their intricacies. As well, perhaps an open acknowledgment of the fledgling lesbian community could only mean discovery and danger for those who belonged to it. Whatever the reasons, this absence of community is notable throughout fictional works into the 1950s.

The 1940s and early 1950s brought considerable changes to lesbian communities. World War II brought an influx of single women into major metropolitan areas. Their newfound independence and economic strength gave them freedoms they had not had since World War I. As well, they tended to live in highly sex-segregated communities, which allowed lesbians to find one another in a way that had been nearly impossible before. The growth of the number of bars that catered exclusively to homosexuals began to foster a group identity. The publication of the Kinsey reports startled the American consciousness with scientific evidence that the frequency of homosexual activity, for both women and men, was significantly higher than previously thought. Finally, the publication of Donald Webster Cory's *The Homosexual in America* in 1951 presented a new view of the homosexual: that of a persecuted minority. I think all of these factors played into the "bloom" of lesbian literature that occurred during the 1950s, which included (along with the "pulp" novels) works of such note as Claire Morgan's *The Price of Salt* (1952).

John D'Emilio writes that "among lesbians, a primary relationship with a lover, a circle of friends, or social activities in the home may have offered emotional sustenance, but they also structured a view of one's sexuality as an exclusively private matter" (1983:32–33). In novels the community tends to be the two women, still isolated from others, who manage to remain together at the close. Invariably, it is at some high price – children are lost, money is lost, families disown and disinherit their daughters, one of the characters is killed or kills herself. The conflict of the novel shifts from being that of lesbianism to being that of prejudices the world holds against lesbians, which bring the bad fortune to them, not the other way around.

This view, of one's sexuality being a private matter and community being small in number, is supported in Morgan's novel. The love between Carol, a woman in the middle of a nasty divorce and child custody suit, and Therese, a younger woman who breaks off her engagement to a male art student, defies the view that lesbians are immature or pathological. Instead, we have some understanding that society's attitude is the problem, not the love between two women. Carol tells Therese that "'in the eyes of the world it's an abomination,'" but Therese replies, "'You don't believe that'" (189). The complications of lesbianism are seen in terms of the difficulty in living in a world where same-sex love is viewed as horrible, not in the love itself. In a letter later in the novel, Carol writes to Therese that

between the pleasure of a kiss and of what a man and woman do in bed seems to me only a gradation. . . . I wonder do these men grade their pleasure in terms of whether their actions produce a child or not. . . . It is a question of pleasure after all, and what's the use of debating the pleasure of an ice cream cone versus a football game. . . . But their [the custody lawyer's and the court's] attitude was that I must be somehow demented or blind (plus a kind of regret, I thought, at the fact a fairly attractive woman is presumably unavailable to men). Someone brought "aesthetics" into the argument, I mean against me of course. I said did they really want to debate that – it brought the only laugh in the whole show. (246)

This points to a much more sophisticated understanding of self-identity, and one that is explicitly defiant in the face of social norms. In this novel, a distinction is drawn between internal and external definitions of self and self-worth. This marks a dramatic shift in the consciousness of lesbian characters that will influence the self-identity of protagonists in subsequent lesbian novels.

The circle that comprises the lesbian community in *The Price of Salt* is that of Carol, Therese, and Abbie, a long-time friend of Carol's. Abbie has been in a relationship with Carol in the past, and Therese and Abbie have a "tacit rivalry" (108) for Carol's affections. Carol's husband found out about the relationship between Abbie and Carol, and when Therese and Carol go on a cross-country trip, he sends a detective to follow them and get damning evidence to use against Carol in the custody suit. In the end, Therese and Carol manage to stay together, and Carol even suggests that they live together. However, the price that is paid for their happiness is that Carol completely loses any right to see her daughter.

The lesbian "pulp" novels during the 1950s and the early 1960s have a slightly different version of community. Isolation gives way to wider communities: those of the bars. Certainly, bars provided a social center and a haven of sorts for lesbians, and a growing sense of community identity for them. In an interview, Audre Lorde and Maua Adele Ajanaku note they went to the bars to meet other lesbians, and met racism as well (Weiss and Schiller, 54). In these novels the characters drink excessively; their lifestyles seem self-destructive. Certainly, the social condemnation they lived with contributed to the self-destruction and alcoholism. Ann Bannon's "Beebo Brinker" series is the most widely known among these novels, but there are a number of others.[8] Nonetheless, these novels point to the growth of diverse group identities.

It is salient to note the general political climate for the homosexual of the 1950s. The McCarthy era ushered in the "homosexual menace," and no one in America was safe from "perverts" who were unstable, undesirable, and morally bereft. Local police departments took their cue from the federal government and began an intense campaign of harassment that would last past the Stonewall riots. Joan Nestle (1987) writes of the time that

we had the images of smashed faces clear in our memories: our lovers, our friends who had not moved quickly enough . . . [but] the ones that reached into our minds, that most threatened our breathing . . . the words *hate yourself because you are a freak, hate yourself because you use your tongue, hate yourself because you look butch and femme, hate yourself because you are sexual.* (38)

The 1950s also was a time when lesbians gained a more public courage: in 1955 Del Martin and Phyllis Lyon founded the Daughters of Bilitis (DOB), whose goal was to "educate lesbians and the general public about lesbianism, and to provide a social gathering place outside of the bars" (Weiss and Schiller, 49). The DOB published *The Ladder,* which was filled with political news, fiction, and poetry.

The roots of activism grew in the 1960s. The feminist movement heightened women's sense of inequality in the public and private spheres and raised women's political awareness. With the advent of the civil rights movement, many lesbians and gays openly began to picket for civil rights for homosexuals. Unlike the student, antiwar, and black power movements, early lesbians and gays sought acceptance into American society, rather than resisting it. This growing political movement exploded in New York on the night of June 27, 1969, with what the New York Mattachine Society called in its newsletter "The Hairpin Drop Heard Round the World" (D'Emilio, 232). At the Stonewall Inn, a bar that catered to a clientele made up largely of young people of color and drag queens, police officers conducted what they thought would be a routine raid. As a lesbian was being led to the patrol car, she put up a struggle. Suddenly the crowd began to throw whatever it could get hold of, and the bar was torched. The rioting lasted a few nights, and before the end of July, lesbians and gay men formed the Gay Liberation Front. The entire experience radicalized lesbians and gay men, who openly became active in a number of other protests, rallies, and meetings across the United States.

Lesbian literature of the 1970s reflects this great change in the lives of lesbians. The political upheaval of the 1960s, culminating in the Stonewall riots, gave lesbian literature a decidedly political flavor. The few lesbians who appear in novels of the 1930s through the 1950s grew in number to a "lesbian nation" – a vision of community that extends well beyond the privatized perspective of earlier years.

Elana Nachman's *Riverfinger Women,* published in 1974, presents such a political vision of community.[9] The community in which the Riverfinger Women live is not without its precedents. Inez knows where she has come from:

The bartenders are incredibly masculine and wear their hair in those slickbacked ducktail haircuts that people wore in the fifties. They wear work overalls or jeans, and stick their hands in their pockets when they aren't busy, smoking Camels without ever taking them from their mouths unless someone orders a drink. . . .

They seem like icebergs, like caricatures and yet, at closing, their women or their friends come and talk to them and they are suddenly as sympathetic and kind, mopping up the bar, with no more money to haul in for the mafia, as the most gentle social worker in San Francisco. These women, I think, are my true fore-mothers. They became strong and independent in isolation. They may seem to me all caught up in roles, they may never agree with me about what's important, what a political act it is within the state to be a lesbian, an act of defiance – never-theless, they committed that act and gave me the courage to commit mine. I love them. (173–74)

That the novel is clearly about a lesbian community is present from the very beginning, as Inez Riverfingers sits down to write out the stories, saying "these are our lives, these are our lives, these are our lives" (7). The stories of these women "touch each other and make the start of a common life, the beginning idea about community. There are all the places where the story falls apart and something else shows through – an isolation, a terror, a hunger to shape that isolation and terror into some kind of love for ourselves" (14), and they shape themselves into "tough, strong, proud: free women" (16). The novel lyrically moves forward and backward in time to trace Inez Riverfingers's "dream of my women, the world where all women are strong and beautiful, even me" (59–60).

The power of the novel rests in Inez Riverfingers's voice, which is not only her voice but the voice of her community as well. The vision and voice of this community is radically different from *The Well of Loneliness*. Inez knows that in writing these stories, the "pornographic novel of my life" (3), she is shaping both her own identity and the identity of her com-munity. It is outsiders, the men, who will see the stories as "porno-graphic" because the stories are about lesbians. Inez writes because she must tell about the "first powerfulness in knowing what our hungers are, that they may not be taken from us and be sold by Tampax or Pepsi-Cola" (15). It is the "vision of who we are and who we can be, a race of intact human beings unafraid to give to each other, one to one, in specific ways, and more than one to one, in groups, in the new ways we are learning. To give, each time, the vision of each woman" and "this woman is of course myself" (60). Nachman's novel ends with Inez thinking of the "'happy ending to the pornographic novel of our lives'" (183). The voice of Nachman's community has moved from pain and despair to a voice that celebrates women together.

The combination of the homophile movement and the black civil rights movement blossomed into a large number of short stories, letters, poems, and essays about the experience of lesbians of color. It is not until 1974, with the publication of Ann Allen Shockley's *Loving Her*, that we have the first open and explicit lesbian novel by an African-American woman. Shockley's novel revolves around Renay, an African-American woman pianist forced by pregnancy into a marriage with an abusive man, and Terry, a rich white woman writer. Renay manages to win custody of her child, who had been staying with her grandmother. Renay's husband, in a drunken fit, takes the child for a ride in his car, and she is killed in the ensuing accident. Renay leaves Terry for a short time, but returns to her in the end, with the promise of a long-lasting relationship.

The novel deals directly with homophobia in African-American communities. Renay decides it would be for the best not to tell her best friend about her relationship with Terry, reflecting:

Black women were the most vehement about women loving each other. This kind of love was worse to them than the acts of adultery or incest, for it was homophile. It was worse than being inflicted with an incurable disease. Black women could be sympathetic about illegitimacy, raising the children of others, having affairs with married men – but not toward Lesbianism, which many blamed on white women. (31)

The novel also confronts racism directly. When Renay is in Terry's apartment, the white cleaning woman shows up and assumes Renay has taken her job. In addition, Terry has forgotten to leave an envelope of money for the woman, and she accuses Renay of taking it. Terry later says that that is "'positively ridiculous,'" but Renay responds "'Uh-huh. Maybe to *you*.' Sometimes Terry could be so damn naive. But Terry had never lived in a black world" (53). Terry herself is confronted by the racism of the apartment owners, who ask her and Renay to move out, because "when Negroes move in, there follows a rash of them" (60). Terry and Renay manage to pull through, because, as Renay says, "'it's nice to know in all the world's confused state, we can think like this about one another. If we can, then there must be others like us who can feel and love and live together despite everything else, and even in this smallness, make the world a better place'" (64). Shockley's community of women survives, although at great cost. The novel gives us a vision of a lesbian community that can overcome racism and classism (although it helps that Terry is independently wealthy), where women of color and white women can learn to survive and abide with one another.

Shockley's novel was met with acclaim as well as harsh criticism (Roberts 1981:35, entry 181). My sense is that much of the harsh criticism came from African-American male reviewers (with whom Shockley has never been on very friendly terms), who, rather than focusing on the literary problems with the novel, instead vented their sexist and homophobic rage.[10] Whatever the criticism, *Loving Her* was a landmark novel for its treatment of the life of an African-American lesbian, as well as for its beginning look at race and class issues within the lesbian community.

Other novels of the 1970s also speak of the diversity of lesbian communities. June Arnold's *Sister Gin*, published in 1975, deals with a fifty-year-old closeted woman who turns into an angry and "out" political activist. When Su, the main character, finally integrates her "proper" self with the angry madwoman/alter ego Sister Gin (who early in the novel appears only when Su is drunk), she comes into her own power. When Su joins a "bridge club," organized by a seventy-seven-year-old woman, a front for a vigilante group that punishes the local rapists, she dreams of "all women . . . in a field of brilliant green, buoyed up by unbelievable green – gathered in a giant sweep all yellow and blue and scooped it into one untouchable safe sea of women" (92). This community of older lesbians believes in, and acts for, righting the wrongs of women's oppression. As well, the characters in the novel are a refreshing change from the youthful lesbians found in most other novels. Su's turn to a positive identity for herself leads her into a constructive community life.

Jane Rule produced a number of works in the 1970s. Rule's lesbian communities tend to be more integrated with the life of the characters' family of origin, most notably *The Young in One Another's Arms* (1977) and her later work, *Memory Board* (1987). Certainly, her classic *Desert of the Heart* (1964) will always be a favorite, and has been reintroduced to a new generation of readers through the (not always faithful to the novel) film. The 1980s have witnessed a vast number of lesbian novels published, ranging from serious subjects to pure "bodice-ripping" romances, from utopian literature and science fiction to lesbian detective fiction. What is most common in these novels is that, for the main character, community is more diverse and means more than one other woman with whom the main character will spend her life. Lesbianism is presented in a positive light, as an "expression of sisterhood and health . . . a cause for celebration" (Faderman, 406). Characters are fully realized and integrated in their lesbian identities, and their communities provide helpful, supportive space for their collective struggle against the homophobic world. This is not to say that lesbian communities are monolithic in nature. Nor is this to say that lesbian communities in literature have dealt with the racism and classism reflected in earlier novels. Instead, as more and more books by lesbians about their communities are published, I hope that issues of race and class are explored more fully.

Lesbian fiction has developed through this century in a way that parallels the development of lesbian self-identity. When the disease model of homsexuality gave way to more current theories of sexuality, so did fiction by lesbians. Growing political awareness, fostered by the homophile, feminist, and civil rights movements, contributed much in the way of nurturing a lesbian self-identity that rejected traditional norms for women and heterosexual marriage patterns as a standard for self-worth. As authors' self-identity has strengthened and become more positive, so too has fictional self-identity. Lesbian authors and characters have moved from an isolated existence to one that celebrates the plurality of their identities and their intersections with many diverse communities.

NOTES

1 One of the more interesting places to find evidence of sexual relations between women is in the accounts of "passing" women. These cases also provide some of the rare glimpses into the lives of working-class lesbians and lesbians of color. "Passing" provided protection for lesbian relationships, and, as important, offered substantial improvement in economic status for women who then could work for "male" wages. See "Passing Women" in Jonathan Katz's *Gay American History* (1976), 209–79.

2 Before the work of the sexologists became part of public discussion and women's relationships and communities came under social, medical, and psychological scrutiny, nineteenth-century women's fiction is full of stories and novels about these romantic relationships. Works such as Louisa May Alcott's *Work: A Story of Experience* (1873), Sarah Orne Jewett's *Deephaven* (1877), and Florence Converse's *Diana Victrix* (1897) all revolve around blissful and romantic relationships between two women. As the pathological model of lesbianism seeped into the social consciousness, women's literature changed.

3 Other notable publications by women in 1928 that dealt with lesbianism, either implicitly or explicitly, included Virginia Woolf's *Orlando* and Elizabeth Bowen's *The Hotel*.

4 One instance where an African-American lesbian appears in a white lesbian's work is in Ann Bannon's *Women in the Shadows*, published in 1959. Tris, a minor character in the narrative, ends up negating both her black identity and her lesbian identity (Roberts, 30, entry 155). Paula Christian's *Edge of Twilight* (1959) and *This Side of Love* (1963) have a continuing character, Toni Molina, a Hispanic woman. She turns out to be emotionally unstable and a thoroughly unlikable woman. Even as minor characters, lesbians of color generally don't fare well in fiction by white women.

5 My thanks to Susan Wolfe and Julia Penelope for helping me to clarify this notion of lesbian isolation in literature.

6 Gloria T. Hull discovered Alice Dunbar-Nelson's discussion of her woman-identified relationships in her diaries; Hull also uncovered a letter and love poems written by Angelina Weld Grimké to other women during her research with Grimké's papers at Howard University. See Hull, "Researching Alice Dunbar-Nelson: A Personal and Literary Perspective" in *But Some of Us Are Brave*, and "'Under the Days': The Buried Life and Poetry of Angelina Weld Grimké" in *Conditions* 5 (1979), 17–25.

7 John D'Emilio notes that in the 1920s plays dealing with lesbianism were driven from the New York stage, that booksellers were targeted for reprisals for selling such material, and that in 1934 the motion picture industry banned any portrayal of homosexuality on film (131–32).

8 Many of these "series" are out of print. Naiad has recently reissued *Chris* by Randy Salem, which is one of a number of works by this author. Paula Christian's series of novels, beginning with *Edge of Twilight*, was reissued by Timely Books in 1978.

9 Elana Nachman now publishes under the name Elana Dykewomon.

10 A male reviewer in the September 1975 edition of *Black World* wrote of Shockley's novel: "This bullshit should not be tolerated" (Shockley 1983:92–93). This response seems not unlike the ones that greeted Alice Walker's *The Color Purple*.

12

Erin G. Carlston

Zami and the Politics of Plural Identity

Identity politics. The politics of location. Coalition politics. Under different names and in various manifestations, the idea of a politics produced by multiple experiences of subjectivity and addressing the needs, problems, and desires springing up at their intersections, has taken root in feminist theory and praxis in this decade. Offering as it does the possibility of a collective political agency that yet does not suppress difference, the "politics of location" seems capable of avoiding many of the pitfalls of both radical and deconstructive feminisms, and even of providing a model of pluralistic politics to other progressive movements.

Audre Lorde's *Zami: A New Spelling of My Name* (1984c) is an early, important attempt to articulate a politics of location in a work of fiction. Though similar in many of its premises to Bernice Johnson Reagon's groundbreaking "Coalition Politics: Turning the Century," *Zami* seems rather more complicated and subtle than Reagon's piece, particularly in its treatment of "identity." To the idea of coalition between individuals Lorde adds the concept of "positionality," or individual identity as an unstable construct, constantly (re)produced both by and within the social matrix, and by the subject's conscious creation of her self. In this regard Lorde prefigures more recent theoretical work by writers like Chandra Mohanty, Gayatri Spivak, and Trinh Minh-ha, while presenting a unique vision of the construction and uses of subjectivity.

Lorde describes identity in *Zami* in several different ways, although all the categories she defines are involved with and depend on each other. Identities can be given, that is, constructed by forces outside the subject, and made accessible to or imposed on her by their prominence as socially recognized and articulated categories. Race is this sort of identity; in the context of the novel, race would seem to be "innate" or "natural" rather than constructed, and there is no doubt that Lorde emphasizes blackness as the first, both chronologically and in significance, of Audre's identities. It is also, however, the first to become *linguistically* available to her, always already embedded in the social context of language. And as I will try to show, she describes her relation to her racial identity in such a way as to problematize blackness as a wholly natural or self-evident category.

Identities can also be constructed and chosen by the subject, either positively – as when Audre names herself a poet – or reactively, in contrast to another category of identity, as when Audre and her crowd of gay-girls define themselves in opposition to the butch-femme bar scene in Greenwich Village. Finally, an identity can be both chosen and essential, or at least essentialized in Lorde's mythology. Lorde mythologizes her sexual identity in this way, deliberately ahistoricizing lesbianism to link it with her maternal/ethnic heritage at the same time that she describes its numerous and changing configurations in her own and others' lives.

Audre's first identity, then, is as a black West Indian. Race is foregrounded immediately in the novel when Lorde begins her first chapter describing the racism Audre's immigrant parents encounter in America. Audre's experiences of race are narrativized differently from her other experiences of identity; the narrator intervenes frequently to interpret events in the light of her mature consciousness of racism. When she recounts the story of the Fairies and the Brownies, for example, she notes, "In this day of heightened sensitivity to racism and color usage, I don't have to tell you which were the good students and which were the baddies" (*Zami*, 27–28). These interventions often take the form of prefaces to chapters or italicized passages. This constant, self-conscious analysis of racism accompanying the chronological narrative has the effect of lending young Audre a perceptiveness about race that the narrator claims she did not in fact have at the time. In chapter 10 she describes her parents' silence about racism, their unwillingness to explain why they can't eat in the dining car or to answer her questions when they are refused service in a soda fountain. Yet she understands enough to be outraged by the waitress's behavior and to write a letter to the president about it; to the reader, who has already read the narrator's comments on racism in the middle of the chapter, it seems that Audre grasps the meaning of racial injustice almost instinctively.

Young Audre's intuitions about race make it appear as a given, a determining factor in her life from the moment of her birth. But the narrator's commentary reminds us that it is her culture's obsessive and constantly articulated awareness of race that allows her to be so aware herself. Skin color may be given, but race is constructed, both by a racist society and by the individual reacting to that society. If Audre's racial identity seems self-evident, for example, her light-skinned mother's is not; Linda's boss thinks she is Latina until he sees her darker-skinned husband – and promptly fires her. Linda's racial identity, and its material consequences, emerge from quite a complicated set of socially mediated assumptions and judgments. And, if Audre is born West Indian, she also writes, "I *grew* Black as my need for life. . . ." (58; my emphasis). Being black is both something she *is* and is aware of from the beginning of her story, and something she *becomes* as her experiences of race and racism produce the significance of that identity.

Being a poet, in contrast, is clearly an identity Audre chooses, even though when Lorde describes her genesis as a poet she locates it at a very early age and links it to more fundamental or essential identities. The section headed, in boldface, "How I Became a Poet" both highlights the conscious, chosen moment of becoming, and rewrites it as an element of her story indissociable from her relation to her mother/her mother's language. This section is not, apparently, about being a poet at all; it is, first, about her mother's West Indian English and then about Audre's erotic awareness, as a child, of her mother's body. The passage could, in fact, equally well be titled "How I Became a Lesbian," and the implication, though subtle and uncommented, is clearly that the identities – West Indian, her mother's daughter, lesbian, and poet – are inextricably entwined.

There are other sources of Audre's poetry, however, more specific to her individual experiences and choices; for example, her peculiar perception of the visual world, due to her early nearsightedness, also seems intrinsic to her evolution as a poet. Seeing clearly and learning to read, write, and speak nearly simultaneously, she begins to define herself as a poet at the time, more precisely identifiable than for those who gain these skills one by one, when she first acquires control of her visual/linguistic world.[1] The first thing she learns to write is her own name, which she rewrites, in defiance of her mother, because the word "Audre" without a "y" is aesthetically pleasing to her; in an artistic (re)vision of her identity, she names herself. The importance of the written word in creating identity is reiterated elsewhere in the novel. In the title, for example: "*Zami*" is "[a] Carriacou name for women who work together as friends and lovers," a new spelling of Lorde's name that once more links her ethnic and sexual identities and writing. Or again, when Audre resolves at the age of five to "make up a story of my own"; or finds, years later, that the lesbian pulp novels don't discuss love triangles like the one she is involved in and knows that "that meant we had to write it ourselves . . ." (48, 213). These words are, of course, embedded in the text that they prophesy, a novel that writes (about) identity.

The way Lorde tropes writing in *Zami*, her self-referential language, underlines her sense of identity as a product of the dialectic between social inter-(re)action and self-(re)creation. Biddy Martin and Chandra Mohanty have claimed that Minnie Bruce Pratt's use of "conventionally realist and autobiographical narrative" in *Yours in Struggle* is essential to any treatment of identity politics (1986:94). While acknowledging the value of Pratt's work, I must take exception to the assertion that conventional narrative strategies – realism, shoring up the author/narrator as unified subject, and so on – are the only adequate way to address this issue. By maintaining a tension between the roles of the author, the narrator, and the protagonist of *Zami*, intercalating a variety of stylistic devices into the text, and pointedly calling the work a bio*myth*ography, Lorde emphasizes that a life is a *story*, produced as dialogue between a subject and society, and, most importantly, open to rewriting. This is certainly not the only valid approach to issues of identity either, but I would argue that it is highly effective in *Zami*. It is crucial to our understanding of Lorde's concept of subjectivity to realize that Audre's identity as a poet, while rooted in her given identities, as West Indian and child of her mother, and closely tied to her lesbianism, is, finally, chosen, an act of control and (self) creation.

If, in *Zami*, being black is the self-conscious experience of a given ethnic heritage, and being a poet is the self-conscious rewriting of given experience, being a lesbian seems neither one nor the other. The narrator gives us clues, hints, partial definitions, suggestions of influences on Audre's sexual orientation from the beginning of her narrative. But in marked contrast to the analysis of race and racism, there is no accompanying commentary on the significance of lesbianism until late in the novel, when Audre is already firmly established in the Village gay-girl scene. And in contrast to her early declaration of poetic identity, there is not, in fact, a section titled "How I Became a Lesbian." Lesbianism is made to seem self-evident by being associated with the deepest roots of Audre's ethnic identity, and manifested in some of her earliest childhood experiences. That this is an artifice, however, part of Lorde's mythologizing of her own life, is suggested by the fact that there is neither an awareness on young Audre's part of the significance of those experiences, nor a narrator's intervention to explain it to us. Lorde inserts certain remarks and episodes into the text and lets us deduce, from their (juxta)position and in the light of her later development, a meaning that they did not (seem to) have at the time.

In her first chapter, Lorde writes about Grenadian women and *zami*, the tradition of woman loving that Audre, by implication, inherits through her mother. She places her mother on the lesbian continuum, offering her first definition of dykes as "powerful and women-oriented women" (*Zami*, 15). Later, Audre will amplify that definition, describing the women she is attracted to as "either gay, or so strongly women-oriented that being gay became only a question of time or opportunity." Being gay, then, is a function of personal/sociohistorical circumstances; being women-oriented is a given, like being a woman. She emphasizes this point in the heavily sexualized descriptions of her childhood encounter with Toni, and of her mother's spice mortar and her own menarche. This latter chapter marks the moment when Audre, the novel's protagonist, begins to converge with Audre the narrator and comes into possession of the knowledge that the narrator has had all along. It recounts her discovery of the relation between West Indian culture (symbolized by the spice mortar), her own female sexuality and sexual power, and her relationship with her mother, now overtly eroticized in the sexual fantasy she associates with the day of her first menstruation. From this point in the novel on Audre is an adult, her mother's equal – she realizes at the end of the chapter that they are the same height – and the conscious teller of her own story.

It may seem somewhat odd, then, that Audre's description of her adolescent sexual development remains unanalyzed, unannotated, as it were. She mentions stages in her investigation of her sexuality without explaining or even hinting at how she arrived at them, as if a whole process of reflection and change were taking place "off camera," or never took place at all. We are told that other people assume that she's gay – first Ann, then Ginger – but not why they might have thought that. Later, when she begins to describe the lesbian community in the Village, she talks about the bars, the Daughters of Bilitis, *The Ladder;* but how she found them, who led her to them, what she thought of them at first, remain mysterious. It is not that she recounts a sexual coming-of-age that is entirely free of anxiety or conflict; she says that she was uncertain about having an affair with a woman, that she was nervous before making love to Ginger. What she doesn't tell us is how or why she began to consider sexual relationships with women in the first place. Here, where we might expect Audre the protagonist to share in the narrator's insight, the narrator instead mimics Audre's aphonia, refusing to name in retrospect what was perhaps unnameable at the time, to use a vocabulary of explanation acquired later to reinterpret that for which at first she had no words. The effect of this (feigned?) muteness is to romanticize and essentialize her sexuality, as if it had since childhood been too obvious, too fundamental to remark. Yet at the same time, because in her childhood neither she nor others had words for it, it was not determining in the way that race was, nor consciously perceived and available for analysis in the same way.

When Audre does begin to analyze her sexuality, there is a point where she converges with the narrator again, elaborating on her earlier definition of women-orientation. When Audre leaves Eudora, she arrives at the awareness that informed the narrator's earlier characterization of her mother as a dyke and her invocation of her Grenadian heritage as the source of her sexual identity. At this point in her story, she realizes for the first time that her lesbianism extends beyond the fact of being involved in a sexual relationship with another woman.

[I felt] a new determination to finish something I had begun, to stick with – what? A commitment my body had made? or with the tenderness which flooded through me at the curve of her head over the back of the chair? . . . I felt myself pass beyond childhood, a woman connecting with other women in an intricate, complex, and ever-widening network of exchanging strengths. (175)

Claiming her participation in a network of women-oriented women as the basis of her sexual orientation, Audre goes on to describe the mutations of her *gayness*, the ways she chooses to shape her fundamental, "given" sexual nature.

Audre's sexuality sometimes takes forms that are defined by their difference from other configurations of sexual identity. She and her friends identify themselves as a group in opposition to butch-femme lesbians: "Being gay-girls without set roles was the one difference we allowed ourselves to see and to bind us to each other" (205). This notion of "antagonistic" identities, which are constructed as what is opposed to or outside of another identity, is a crucial part of Lorde's concept of identity. Audre's first chosen identity *group* (as opposed to identity) is the Branded, her circle of high school friends who, like the gay-girls, "never talked about those differences that separated us, only the ones that united us against the *others*" (81). At the same time she identifies with the Branded, she finds that she is not accepted by other poets in her high school because she is black.[2]

The experience of being marginalized within every group with which she identifies becomes a constant in Audre's story, until she finally claims and transforms that experience as the basis of her politics of location. As early as high school she becomes involved in leftist politics and begins to perceive herself as a revolutionary; when the cold war sets in she finds herself grieving for the Rosenbergs while trying to hide her homosexuality from her leftist friends. As a lesbian she is suspected by the left, other black women, straight society; as a black woman she is discriminated against by whites, both straight and gay; as a black woman who is neither butch nor femme, she has no place in gay bars. In addition, during the period when she lives in the Village, Audre hides the fact that she is a poet and, especially, that she is a *student*, from the bohemian circles in which she moves.

The addition of these last categories of identity perfectly illustrates the concept of "positionality" or "a politics of location." Being a student is clearly neither an essential identity nor even a static, if constructed, one. Within a specific sociohistorical context, however, it can be as determining in an individual's experience as a more apparently fundamental identity. In Audre's case, being a student is, at a particular period of her life, tied up with her class, race, and sexuality, and relevant to her sense of subjectivity in the same way. What is common to all these experiences of identity is the impossibility, for Audre, of wholehearted allegiance to any one. Not entirely conforming within any community or identity group, she threatens and is threatened by all of them (224). And so her constant, uncomfortable awareness of her ineradicable difference within any given situation or group becomes, eventually, a consciously articulated loyalty to difference itself.

Being women together was not enough. We were different. Being gay-girls together was not enough. We were different. Being Black together was not enough. We were different. Being Black women together was not enough. We were different. Being Black dykes together was not enough. We were different . . . we could not afford to settle for one easy definition, one narrow individuation of self. (226)

It is important to note that, for Lorde, working out these differential relations is never a purely reactive project, or one that depends on a dualistic vision. Each of her "antagonistic identities," while it may be produced in opposition to one other identity, is an element in a network of multiple identities, some oppositional, some contingent, and some largely unrelated. Because the subject, Audre, *moves* within this network, her relation to any particular identity or identity group is never wholly and permanently that of the Other, nor of the Othering. Philosopher Linda Alcoff comments on this phenomenon as it applies to gender in the work of Lorde and other women of color: "I have simply not found writings by feminists who are oppressed also by race and/or class that place or position maleness wholly as Other" (1988:412).

The result of this strategy is that no identity can ever be perceived as entirely centered, "pure," or hermetic. Lorde makes this clear early in the novel; remember young Audre's confusion about her light-skinned mother's racial identity. The same principle may be at work, more subtly and humorously, in the account of Audre's first writing assignment for elementary school, when the pupils are supposed to construct sentences from words clipped out of newspapers. While the other students compose neutral declarative sentences, young Audre clips out an ad and writes "I like White Rose Salada Tea," decorating the sentence with a picture. Her strong sense of subjectivity, her verbal creativity, and her aesthetic sensitivity are thus filtered through the medium of white consumerist culture. Lorde's point would seem to be that even her identity as a (black socialist feminist) poet is not separable from the language and society in which she produces her poetry.

Lorde's emphasis on distinct identities that are, nonetheless, "impure" and nonstatic allows for the possibility of "identification" (in the sense of empathy) and coalition, without neutralizing difference. (This may help account, incidentally, for the reaction of many of *Zami*'s readers who feel that they can "identify" with Audre despite having had vastly different life experiences.) Furthermore, by relativizing her identities – Audre *feels* more or less black, more or less lesbian, according to circumstances – Lorde avoids essentialism without denying the effective reality of her position at any given moment. The fluidity of her categories of identity both hierarchizes them within a specific sociohistorical context, and allows for the possibility of a rearrangement of their configuration at any time.

Lorde's recognition of difference as an incessant displacement of *interior* as well as exterior boundaries is perhaps her most radical, insightful contribution to the whole notion of identity politics. She acknowledges the need for occasional retreat into one, stable position, but insists that this can be only a temporary construction. This provisional positionality is perhaps equivalent to what Bernice Reagon calls "home"; and, like Reagon, Lorde understands it as "a place to refuel and check your flaps" (225) before returning to the space of coalition building and political action. As Reagon writes, "In a coalition you have to give, and it is different from your home. You can't stay there all the time. You go to the coalition for a few hours and then you go back and take your bottle wherever it is, and then you go back and coalesce some more" (1983:359).

While Reagon speaks in terms of coalitions between individuals with self-evident and static identities, however, Lorde is describing an internal coalition; her temporary treaties, alliances and compromises are with her selves, her multiple and overlapping sexual and racial identities. Martin and Mohanty write of Minnie Bruce Pratt's work, published in the same year as *Zami*, that

> it unsettles not only any notion of feminism as an all-encompassing home but also the assumption that there are discrete, coherent, and absolutely separate identities – homes within feminism, so to speak – based on absolute divisions between various sexual, racial, or ethnic identities. . . . The "unity" of the individual subject, as well as the unity of feminism, is situated and specified as the product of the interpretation of personal histories. . . . (1986:192)

It is striking how similar their description is to the tendencies I have been attempting to identify in Lorde's work, even as they advocate a very different narrative technique. Like Pratt's work, *Zami* is "a complicated working out of the relationship between home, identity, and community that calls into question the notion of a coherent, historically continuous, stable identity . . ." (1986:195). As I have said, the fact that Lorde's novel also calls into question the possibility of a coherent and historically continuous autobiographical *text* only strengthens her work.

It could be argued that Lorde is less persuasive when she is most essentialist, namely, in her treatment of female sexuality, which she describes, as Alcoff would say, as a "place where meaning can be discovered,"[3] and in her romanticization of Audre's lesbianism. Interestingly, Martin and Mohanty describe the same phenomenon in Pratt's work. "Only one aspect of experience is given a unifying and originating function in the text: that is, her lesbianism and love for other women, which has motivated and continues to motivate her efforts to reconceptualize and recreate both her self and home" (202). It is difficult to know how to interpret this, unless it is, in both texts, a defense of the "naturalness" of homosexuality against a dominant ideology that insists that it is "unnatural" and "acquired" and that therefore homosexuals can "change." But perhaps it is more useful to read Lorde's novel, at any rate, as an attempt simply to problematize all prevailing definitions of essential and nonessential traits, and to defend lesbianism against the charges sometimes leveled that it is a white, Western, bourgeois practice, by tying sexuality indissociably to her own ethnicity and culture: to her mystical, mythologized West Indian heritage.

Carriacou, in the West Indies, is the place where Audre and the novel have their genesis and to which they return in her last paragraphs. "Home," for Audre, is a mythical place she has never seen, that does not exist on any map of the world she knows. It is, clearly, different from what Reagon calls "home," which Martin and Mohanty ultimately define as "an illusion of coherence and safety based on the exclusion of specific histories of oppression and resistance, the repression of differences even within oneself" (196). Reagon's "home," as I noted earlier, seems closer to that space represented in *Zami* by Harlem: "[t]his now, here, was a space, some temporary abode, never to be considered forever nor totally binding nor defining . . ." (*Zami*, 13). Audre's relation to Harlem, the "place of [her] mother's exile," becomes the paradigm for all her fluid constructions of identity (104). This "place to refuel" is not fictional in the sense that Carriacou is a fiction, but, rather, to be taken as real only as long as it has to serve as what Alcoff calls "the point of departure." In other words, any identity, as a temporary construct, must serve the real political/emotional needs of the moment rather than the other way around.

You had to have a place. Whether or not it did justice to whatever you felt you were about, there had to be some place to refuel and check your flaps. In times of need and great instability, the place sometimes became more a definition than the substance of why you needed it to begin with. Sometimes the retreat became the reality. . . . For some of us there was no one particular place, and we grabbed whatever we could from wherever we found space. . . . (225–26)

The difference between these temporary and essentially "unreal" retreats and the mythological Carriacou marks a point where Lorde departs from and elaborates on ideas of "home" and "location" in the other works I have discussed. What Lorde recognizes, I think, is that actually living a politics of location can be exhausting; what she deals with, that the other writers do not, is, simply, the danger of emotional burnout and the imperative necessity of a source of revitalization. The decision to freeze a particular configuration of her multiple identities, briefly to choose one place as center, gives her only a momentary breathing space. But Carriacou, as an internal and fictionalized concept of centeredness, is a more permanent source of power. It is, of course, "an illusion of coherence and safety," but an illusion recognized and utilized as such: as myth. Like all Edenic myths, the stories Audre tells herself and us about Carriacou and *zami*, about her erotic relationship to her mother and her connection through her own body to primal sources of wisdom, function as heuristic devices, bringing order and meaning to the concatenation of circumstances that shape her material existence. Her "real," biographical relationships – to her ethnic heritage, her mother, other women, her body – are charged with conflict, pain, the necessity of constructing a politics flexible enough to be responsible to all her voices and strong enough to let her survive her multiple oppressions. It is Audre's evocation of mythological Carriacou – a fiction that is potent precisely because it is fiction and so uncompromised by materiality – that lends her politics that strength. What Lorde seems to be suggesting is that her identity politics needs to draw on a mystical, spiritual vision, a "truly private Paradise" (14) to which she can at least imagine return, and where she can find the power to rewrite her life/story.

NOTES

1 It would be interesting to consider the implications a simultaneous acquisition of spoken and written language might have for the development of a poetic style heavily dependent on aural patterns, as Lorde's is.

2 In the interview with Adrienne Rich reprinted in *Sister Outsider* (1984a), Lorde adds that in the group where she found support during this period and later for both her poetry and her blackness, the Harlem Writers' Guild, she was "never really accepted" because of her homosexuality (91). It is not, of course, possible simply to add this piece of information to the mythologized version of the story; it is perhaps more useful to ask why she chose to leave it out when writing her novel. The answer may be simply that she already had enough

documentation of her multiple marginalities, though there are certainly other possibilities.

3 Alcoff, 434. This article is worth quoting at length for the cogent analysis it gives of the kind of strategies Lorde deploys in *Zami*. Alcoff's theory merges "identity politics" with a conception of subjectivity that draws on poststructuralist critiques of the subject without reverting to nominalism. (I should note that, while Alcoff is working with the concept of gender, her analysis is applicable to any category of identity; for the word "gender" in this passage we can, I believe, substitute "race" or "sexual identity.") Alcoff writes, "it seems both possible and desirable to construe a gendered subjectivity in relation to concrete habits, practices, and discourses while at the same time recognizing the fluidity of these. . . . We must continually emphasize within any account of subjectivity the historical dimension. This will waylay the tendency to produce general, universal, or essential accounts by making all our conclusions contingent and revisable. . . . I assert that the very subjectivity (or subjective experience of being a woman) and the very identity of women is constituted by women's position. However, this view should not imply that the concept of 'woman' is determined solely by external elements and that the woman herself is merely a passive recipient of an identity created by these forces. Rather, she herself is part of the historicized, fluid movement, and she therefore actively contributes to the context within which her position can be delineated. . . . Therefore, the concept of positionality includes two points: first, as already stated, that the concept of woman is a relational term identifiable only within a (constantly moving) context; but, second, that the position that women find themselves in can be actively utilized (rather than transcended) as a location for the construction of meaning, a place from where meaning is constructed, rather than simply the place where meaning can be *discovered* (the meaning of femaleness)" (431, 434).

Compare this formulation to Lorde's description of her first menstruation, and a similar line from another of her works. In *Zami* she writes that "within [my uterus] was a tiding ocean of blood beginning to be made real and available to me for strength and information" (78). And in the interview cited in the preceding footnote she says, "What understanding begins to do is to make knowledge available for use" (1984a:109). The juxtaposition of these quotes suggests that, with menarche, Audre reaches a conscious understanding of a sort of primitive, unconscious knowledge contained within every female body by virtue of its sex.

13

Diane Griffin Crowder

Separatism and Feminist Utopian Fiction

The period 1968 to 1985 saw one of the greatest concentrations of feminist utopian fiction in U.S. history, with a new work appearing on average once every ten months. In the five-year span 1975–79, twenty-four utopias by women were published in the United States alone.[1] This explosion of works went against a trend. Whereas the second half of the nineteenth century produced a plethora of utopian stories (including many feminist works), the twentieth century was the era of dystopian fiction depicting the horrors of the future à la *1984* (Bartkowski 1989:7). Utopias are the literature of hope, and the liberation movements of the late 1960s renewed the possibility of a better world. It is noteworthy that this utopian upsurge was almost entirely limited to works inspired by the feminist movement – there is no significant body of utopian literature by men in this period.[2]

Yet these novels are not merely a throwback to the first wave of feminism. These neofeminist utopias differ in two crucial respects from their predecessors of the nineteenth and early twentieth centuries. First, with rare exceptions, utopian writers of the 1970s and 1980s doubt that education, technology, and normal political processes can bring about the desired changes. Second, the feminist and gay/lesbian liberation movements of the 1960s and 1970s freed writers to examine problems of sexuality and to posit lesbianism as an alternative in a way not possible before. As a result, a majority of newer feminist utopian fictions portray all-female utopias that exist either in worlds without men, or at least in clearly separate spaces. In this study I look at the reasons for such a separatist vision and trace its evolution through three stages.

Clearly it was the revival of feminism that stimulated an outpouring of feminist utopian literature. Beginning in France with Wittig's *Les Guérillères*, written in the heady days following the student revolution of

1968 that spawned the neofeminist movement there, utopian ideas were necessary to the new movement. Like any revolutionary ideology, feminism requires both an analysis of the evils of this world and a vision of the better world towards which we struggle. In the 1970s, the commercial success of feminist utopian fiction and the reprinting of earlier lost works like *Herland* or *Mizorah* indicated a hungry readership for these novels.

But the issue of why women wrote and eagerly read these works is more complex than simply an expression of the renewed rise of feminism. Modern feminist utopias in general, while certainly arising out of a desire to imagine a more perfect world, seem to respond even more to other needs. Perhaps foremost is the need to explore fully the oppression of women and to express the deep-seated rage such oppression causes. I think my own reaction is typical. I bought and read all the utopian works I could get my hands on, and felt a powerful emotional response to most of them. These novels gave me a fictional representation of the unexpressed anger I felt at abuses I saw daily but felt powerless to stop. They also gave me models of female characters who were not helpless, who did in fact stop the abuses one way or another, and who often along the way created worlds of real beauty. I could for a few hours imagine myself in these utopian worlds and come away with a modicum of hope that, despite the depressing evidence of my daily newspaper, we could in fact make a better world. But my visceral response was clearly marked by two stages: the release of anger preceded, and was often more powerful than, the yearning to live in the utopian world.

If "a lesbian is the rage of all women condensed to the point of explosion,"[3] then it is not unreasonable to conclude that the rage of all women, when condensed to the point of explosion, will produce lesbian texts. The two earliest modern utopian texts (and the novels that had the greatest influence on the development of the genre) both recognize the importance of expressing this repressed anger. And it is noteworthy that these works, Wittig's *Les Guérillères* and Russ's *The Female Man*,[4] are both overtly lesbian. (A list of all literary works cited in this essay is at the end of the essay.) The utopian vision occupies only a portion of the novels. Much of the narrative space explores in detail how men as a group have benefited from the oppression of women, and the resultant physical and psychological damage to women. Wittig and Russ both use satire, irony, humor, and violence to force the reader to confront her oppression in our world and to provoke her outrage.

Interestingly, both novelists also choose to split the female hero into multiple characters, bringing to bear different viewpoints on male oppression. If, as some critics maintain, a crucial aspect of most modern feminist utopias is the movement from isolation to community among women,[5] that community is embedded in the very narrative structure of *Les*

Guérillères and *The Female Man*. In the former, there are no individual characters at all. The feminine plural pronoun *elles* in the body of the fiction parallels the lists of female names that punctuate the text.[6] The "guérillères" make war, make love, work, sing, and play as a group. In true epic style, Wittig tells us the story of an entire people creating a new world, whose history she and Sande Zeig later write in *Lesbian Peoples*.[7] The lists of names evoke women's stories from all cultures, now to be reinterpreted in the context of a postpatriarchal world.

Joanna Russ splits her narrative "I" into the four "Js": Jeannine, Joanna, Janet, and Jael. Each is an aspect of the writer's and reader's possible stances toward the evils of our world and the possibilities for a utopian future. In a ploy that becomes common to later novels, Russ presents not only a utopian future but a possible dystopian future as well. Janet comes from Whileaway, the utopia where men disappeared centuries ago as a result of a "plague." Only late in the novel do we encounter Jael, who lives in a dystopian world where the "war of the sexes" is literal and still going on. Jael is pure rage, enacting the retribution that Whileawayans have erased from their history and that Jeannine cannot even imagine. Jeannine, who valiantly tries to fulfill our culture's image of femininity, "enjoys being a girl," to the evident disgust of Joanna. The latter, a savvy, angry, and aware feminist of our present, gradually evolves away from her focus on men to become a lesbian.[8] This splitting tactic allows Russ to explore the tensions between rage and despair, passivity and aggression, fear and hope, that underlie feminist utopianism.

The use of satire and irony, as well as the emphasis on criticizing our world and expressing anger, mark these early lesbian utopias. They are an explosion of female awareness and outrage that has no parallel in earlier utopian fiction. But they also respond to a second need – a desire for a concrete plan of action. How can we get from our present dismal situation, so thoroughly depicted in the dystopian sections of these novels, to the utopian world? For Russ and Wittig, there is clearly an enemy, and it is not impersonal social structures, but the power men, as individuals and as a group, wield over women. In both of these works, and in d'Eaubonne's *Les bergères de l'apocalypse*, the utopian society is all-female and has been earned only through armed revolt – an ultimate war of the sexes in which men who will not see reason are eliminated. Wittig includes detailed plans for organizing and carrying out the revolt, turning sexism itself against men. Only those men who "having understood our language / and not having found it excessive / have joined with us to transform the world" (128) and survive "the longest most murderous war . . . ever known, the last possible war in history" (127–28).[9] Russ only gradually reveals that the "plague" that eliminated the men on Whileaway was in fact a war like that Jael is fighting against Manland.

Jael says, ". . . the Whileawayan flowers nourish themselves on the bones of the men we have slain" (211).

Does this mean that lesbian utopian fiction is "man-hating"? Certainly many male critics reacted to these novels as if they gloried in violence. Yet Wittig and Russ both take care to document the necessity for war by showing how women have tried without success all less drastic means of gaining freedom. Some of the funniest passages in *The Female Man* show Joanna and the other characters trying to escape the Catch-22 position of women in our culture. Further, violence by Russ's women is almost always a defensive response to attacks by men. Russ has noted, however, that male critics and readers react with distress at the perceived violence of women against men (1981). She anticipates this reaction in the novel itself, quoting male attacks on feminist works: "Shrill . . . vituperative . . . no concern for the future of society . . . selfish femlib . . . needs a good lay . . ." (140). Wittig also quotes male thinkers such as Freud and Lévi-Strauss, but in a context where the violence caused by their ideas becomes the evident justification of the women's revolt. The "guérillères" laugh and bare their teeth.

Wittig and Russ clearly do not expect male supremacy to wither away without a fight. But their goal is not a female supremacist future where men are enslaved.[10] As Russ herself says, "The feminist utopias, to the degree that they are concerned with 'the battle of the sexes' (and most are) see it as a long, one-sided massacre whose cause . . . is male supremacy" (1980:248). This is the real enemy. As Lefanu notes (concerning Russ), ". . . an attempt to deconstruct notions of masculine and feminine is more of a transgression against the male law than is a radical separatism" (1988:176). Wittig goes even farther perhaps than Russ, making the cultural construction of gender itself the focus of battle. The "war" is therefore one of language and meaning, which must become a literal war only because men will not give up the division of humanity that forces female humans to become "female men."

Les Guérillères and *The Female Man* are innovative, in both form and theme, complex works that stand alone within the genre. Both are lesbian utopias that nonetheless reject the siren song of innate female superiority in favor of clear-eyed analysis of the cultural basis of male supremacy. They incarnate the radical political analyses of the first period of the neofeminist movement. Their separatist utopias envision a world where gender does not exist. The inhabitants of these utopias are unique in the literature, incarnating the entire range of human possibilities.

The second phase, running roughly from 1975 to the mid-1980s, is the period of greatest activity in feminist utopian fiction, both lesbian and heterosexual. (The latter are, however, in a distinct minority.) While the influence of Russ and, to a lesser extent, Wittig, is ubiquitous, important differences reflect the evolution of American (and, in a different way, French) feminism. These differences concern the relation to our present, the nature of the utopian worlds and the theory of feminism underlying them, and the ways to create utopia from our present situation.

In Russ and Wittig, our present is also the present of at least some characters. Joanna and Jeannine come from patriarchal cultures very similar to our own, and the analysis of our culture is central to the novel. In *Les Guérillères*, "elles" are in the process of evolving away from our culture, and the narrative makes frequent reference to it in the present tense that dominates the novel. Our world *is* the dystopia, except for Jael's world in *The Female Man*.

In the novels of the second phase, our present is usually long past. The characters confront male supremacy either as history (the remembering rooms of *The Wanderground*, for instance) or as futuristic dystopias that occupy parallel spaces with the utopia. In *Walk to the End of the World*, for instance, Charnas creates a patriarchal nightmare world where women are literally slaves. The heroine, Alldera, escapes at the end to find the female utopia depicted in the second novel, *Motherlines*. Our present is in the distant historical moment preceding a catastrophe that has led to creation of these worlds. While the dystopia is based upon exaggerating tendencies in our society, it is recognizably a different world.

In the two novels that do incorporate our present, the heroine from our time is seen as mad. Connie, in Piercy's *Woman on the Edge of Time*, may be hallucinating the utopian (and dystopian) future as she is confined to a mental asylum, while the courier in Sheldon's "Your Faces, O My Sisters" inhabits a mental utopia revealed to be a figment of her imagination when she is raped and murdered in our real present.[11]

This tendency to place our present in the past and to contrast utopia with a future dystopia has the (unintended?) effect of displacing criticism from our world to a fictional one. Whereas present reality was dystopian enough for Russ and Wittig, by the late seventies, writers seemed to feel they must create grotesque parodies of patriarchy as foils for their ideal worlds. Perhaps the superficial progress towards feminist goals in our real culture made writers think our world would not seem bad enough. Readers would need to have the hidden excesses of·male supremacy exposed through the device of a fictional dystopia in which the veneer of egalitarianism was stripped completely away.[12] While the reader recognizes that the horrors of these dystopias are clearly rooted in our society, in fact these nightmare worlds are not our own.

As numerous critics have pointed out, there is surprising agreement on what the utopian world will look like.[13] Anarchic, communal, close to nature, egalitarian, centered on people rather than on things, most of these worlds fit what Williams terms the "Arcadian" model.[14] With very few exceptions, these utopias are all-female and lesbian. It is clear that most writers, as Williams notes, "seem unable to imagine a world free from male oppression unless they eliminate men entirely" (1985:232). It is no accident that this period of the late 1970s and early 1980s witnessed the development of this theme. At this time, many lesbian feminists abandoned the social constructionist theories that undergird the radicalism of a Wittig in favor of essentialist theories of gender.[15]

Simply put, men are *by nature* incapable of inhabiting utopia. Lesbian separatists differ widely on the question of whether men are inherently oppressive or whether it is patriarchal culture that must be eliminated, as the diverse articles in the Hoagland and Penelope anthology (1988) reveal. Yet all the lesbian separatist utopias I have found in this second phase depict men as inherently violent, hierarchal, incapable of humane, or even human, relationships with women, children, the earth, or other men. As Keinhorst says of these writers, "Faced with the task of portraying men as non-oppressive and as whole human beings, their imagination fails" (1987:97).

When male characters do encounter a lesbian utopian culture, their first impulse is to rape, or to take over. In the witty and profound short story, "Houston, Houston, Do You Read?," three astronauts from our time are transported to the all-female future. Under the influence of a kind of truth serum, one tries to rape, another believes himself God's messenger to take over these "lost daughters," and the third insists on men's vital role in human society. One of the women responds:

Of course we enjoy your inventions and we do appreciate your evolutionary role. But you must see there's a problem. As I understand it, what you protected people from was largely other males, wasn't it? . . . But the fighting is long over. It ended when you did, I believe. We can hardly turn you loose on Earth, and we simply have no facilities for people with your emotional problems. (93)

The men are humanely destroyed.

Even the one lesbian novel that does portray profeminist men denies them the possibility of entering the female utopian society. Gearhart's *The Wanderground* includes a group of men, the "Gentles," who have rejected the masculinist cities and formed their own group to overcome male values. They develop their own telepathic powers to parallel those of the women, but Gearhart makes it clear that it is of a totally different nature. Men and women are almost different species.

These separatist utopias provide a fictional space for imagining what a world based upon female values might look like, just as women-only spaces in the real world give us freedom to explore what we might become without the pressures of male hegemony and violence. The relief from that pressure can be euphoric, and reading these novels provides a needed escape from the evils of everyday life in modern society. It is understandable that lesbian writers and readers found real joy in these fictions.

But this privileging of "nature" contains within it the seeds of its own destruction. First, by positing a fixed, biologically determined female nature, these novels leave little hope that we in the real world can achieve the kind of society shown. For, if men are irretrievably tainted and cannot change, then we can only win if we kill them all off. But one of the primary traits essentialist feminists attribute to women is nonviolence! Unlike Wittig's warriors and the inhabitants of Whileaway, the women in most of these novels abhor killing.

Second, the theory of a feminine "essence" leads inexorably to the tyranny of "political correctness" that dominated many lesbian communities of this period. Rejecting the idea that gender itself is artificially imposed to maintain male power, essentialist theories view certain traits as "female" and "male." A good lesbian is supposed to eliminate all "male" traits and develop only "female" qualities. While the lesbian list differs from what our culture defines as "feminine," it is no less arbitrary and no less confining. This essentialism makes some of the lesser novels of this period static and bland.

Given a belief in innate traits, creating utopia from dystopia is problematic. The lesbian novels I have read generally don't show positive change coming about through political and social revolution. Only a very few heterosexual works, including Piercy's *Woman on the Edge of Time* and LeGuin's *Always Coming Home*, show men voluntarily working with women to eliminate male dominance. In all other cases, men become increasingly violent as women press for more freedom.

Unlike our nineteenth-century predecessors, these novelists do not believe that education will work. Reasoning with men, showing the injustices of sexism and the benefits of equality for all, fails. Confronted with the facts about rape and abuse of women and children, imprisonment of women within their homes, genital mutilation, economic enslavement, the feminization of poverty, the failure of even moderate reforms like the ERA, and the other horrors of current life for women, our writers conclude that men will not give up their power without a fight. But, unlike Wittig and Russ, the majority of these authors reject the option of fighting back. Instead, in example after example, the women flee to safer ground and establish their own societies, carefully protected from intrusion by men. Whether these lesbian spaces are on a segregated Earth (*The Wanderground, Motherlines*) or on other planets colonized by women (*Daughters of a Coral Dawn*), women opt for separate, if not equal.

Like Gilman and Lane before them,[16] other authors choose to eliminate men in fantastic ways that do not satisfy our need for a concrete blueprint for action. Although these writers are enraged by the violence done to women in our culture, they are often curiously reluctant to portray violence against men. Instead we find earthquakes (*Herland*), plagues ("Houston, Houston"), or the revolt of the earth itself (*The Wanderground*).

Thus, in this second period we find a proliferation of lesbian and feminist utopias depicting attractive worlds, but which often are based upon a philosophy – essentialism – that deprives readers of any realistic means of attaining the better world. These utopias are truly "nowhere." There is a kind of pessimism under the rosy surface of these fictions.[17]

As the 1980s wore on, feminist utopian fiction reflected a growing feeling of hopelessness. The gains feminists had made in the 1970s came under attack in Reagan's 1980s. Women's presses and bookstores that had mushroomed in the 1970s began to close. Homophobia turned to violence against lesbians as well as gay men. Sturgis (1989) summarizes the trend thus:

In the 1980s, mainstream media discovered "postfeminism." Separatism was not popular in feminist or even lesbian-feminist circles, and most women-only spaces happened by accident. In women's fantasy and science fiction, the woman hero took center stage, solitary, unsupported by female friends, lovers, kinfolk, mentors, protegées, or peers. In fantasy, Jungian-style dichotomies prevailed – good/evil; dark/light; male/female – with similar result: women were paired with men but strangers, if not rivals, to each other.[18]

Sturgis also notes the prevalence of horror and dystopia in fiction of the 1980s.

Indeed, in this third phase, the sheer quantity of utopian fictions slowed to a trickle, and most of those published after 1984 (a prophetic date!) either are dystopias like Wittig's *Across the Acheron* and Atwood's *The Handmaid's Tale* or are ambivalent toward (if not critical of) separatist all-female utopias. In such different novels as *The Shore of Women* (1986) and *The Gate to Women's Country* (1988) we again find a violent male world confronting a peaceful mostly female world. But, unlike novels of the 1970s showing separatist environments, the central question is not how to maintain the separation but whether, how, and when, to integrate the male and female worlds. As Sturgis notes, the "worlds of women only . . . seemed to have vanished," and these new works "took the absence of men as tragic deficiency rather than great opportunity" (1989:2). Even though they share certain structural similarities with earlier utopias, these two works are hardly utopian in outlook.

In other cases, such as *A Door into Ocean* (1986) and *Native Tongue* (1984), female characters struggle to maintain or establish separatist utopias against overwhelming odds, but the novels stress their difficulties, rather than reveling in the new worlds.[19]

It is obvious that the real world has overwhelmed the lesbian and feminist utopian impulse. As Bartkowski says in reference to *The Handmaid's Tale*: ". . . by the time Atwood sets out to tell her tale, the world is already changed so that a promissory rhetoric of hope is rendered naive. . . . The 'what if' has shifted from a terrain bright with daydreams to a mute field of nightmarish whispers" (1989:133).

The dystopian visions of Atwood's *The Handmaid's Tale* and, in a much more allegorical vein, Wittig's *Across the Acheron* locate the nightmare in our own time and place. Gilead, Atwood's theocracy, is set in the 1990s and incarnates the agenda of the New Right. Her hero, Offred, can remember her feminist mother participating in the movement of the 1970s, and Atwood is careful to supply a realistic account of how the New Right took over in the United States. Wittig takes Dante as her model and shows contemporary culture as a series of circles of hell in which the "damned souls" are female.[20] Lesbians inhabit the limbo of a lesbian bar, refugees from the horrors of heterosexuality. Only those lucky and persistent enough to "find the words" to describe paradise can, like the hero Wittig, join the angels in their potluck supper on the hills above San Francisco. Neither writer needs to invent a futuristic dystopia. The here and now is bad enough.

Interestingly, neither Atwood nor Wittig uses biological determinism to explain the extreme male dominance and violence they depict so graphically. Atwood's men are corrupted by power, and her dystopia is clearly political and religious in motivation. Wittig's novel explores the psychology of oppression and why some of the damned souls refuse to leave Hell. In several episodes, the damned souls fear the monsters – lesbians – which they have been told devour those who escape. In others, the damned souls prefer the hell they know, and in which they have carved a niche for themselves, to the unknown paradise they can barely imagine. Wittig also reveals the economic and political barriers confronting women, but insists that escape is possible if we avoid the twin traps of despair and collusion.

Separatism in lesbian and feminist utopian fiction thus reflects the evolution of lesbian experience, from the explosion of anger and hope in the early 1970s to the dreams of lesbian community of the late 1970s and early 1980s, and finally, by the mid-1980s, to frustration and pessimism engendered by the conservative atmosphere. But I see a positive side to this movement. Like the early utopias of *Les Guérillères* and *The Female Man*, the dystopian fictions of Atwood and Wittig reject the profound pessimism of essentialist thinking that denies any real possibility of change. If the problem lies not in our natures but in our political and social structures, then we can heed the warnings and find realistic solutions. Lesbian separatism thus becomes a viable strategy for building our strengths, while we work to eliminate the very concepts of gender and oppression.

Literary works cited; in chronological order of original publication:

1880 Lane, Mary E. Bradley. *Mizorah: A Prophecy*. Reprint. Boston: Gregg Press, 1975.

1915 Gilman, Charlotte Perkins. *Herland*. New York: Pantheon Books, 1979.

1969 Wittig, Monique. *Les Guérillères*. Paris: Minuit. English translation: Avon, 1973.

1974 Charnas, Suzy McKee. *Walk to the End of the World*. New York: Berkeley Books.

1975 Russ, Joanna. *The Female Man*. New York: Bantam.

1976 Piercy, Marge. *Woman on the Edge of Time*. New York: Fawcett Crest.

1976 Sheldon, Alice (James Tiptree, Jr., and Raccoona Sheldon). "Houston, Houston, Do You Read?" (pages 36–98); "Your Faces, O My Sisters! Your Faces Filled of Light!" (pages 16–35). In *Aurora: Beyond Equality*. Vonda N. McIntyre and Susan Anderson, eds. New York: Fawcett.

1976 Wittig, Monique, and Sande Zeig. *Brouillon pour un dictionnaire des amantes*. Paris: Grasset. English translation: *Lesbian Peoples: Material for a Dictionary*. New York: Avon, 1979.

1977 d'Eaubonne, Françoise. *Les Bergères de l'Apocalypse*. Paris: Jean-Claude Simoën.

1978 Charnas, Suzy McKee. *Motherlines*. New York: Berkeley.

1978 Gearhart, Sally Miller. *The Wanderground: Stories of the Hill Women*. Watertown, Mass.: Persephone Press.

1984 Elgin, Suzette Haden. *Native Tongue*. New York: Daw.

1984 Forrest, Katherine V. *Daughters of a Coral Dawn*. Tallahassee: Naiad Press.

1985 LeGuin, Ursula K. *Always Coming Home*. New York: Harper and Row. Bantam, 1987.

1985 Wittig, Monique. *Virgile, Non*. Paris: Minuit. English translation: *Across the Acheron*. London: Peter Owen, 1987.

1986 Atwood, Margaret. *The Handmaid's Tale*. Boston: Houghton Mifflin.

1986 Sargent, Pamela. *The Shore of Women*. New York: Crown.

1986 Slonczewski, Joan. *A Door into Ocean*. New York: Arbor House. Avon, 1987.

1988 Tepper, Sheri S. *The Gate to Women's Country*. New York: Doubleday. Bantam, 1989.

NOTES

1 Carol Farley Kessler, ed., *Daring to Dream: Utopian Stories by United States Women, 1836–1919* (Boston: Pandora Press, 1984), 9. For general introductions to feminist utopian fiction, see: Marleen Barr, ed., *Future Females: A Critical Anthology* (Bowling Green, Ohio: Bowling Green State University Popular Press, 1981); Marleen Barr and Nicholas Smith, eds., *Women and Utopia* (Lanham, Md.: University Presses of America, 1983); Elaine Hoffman Baruch and Ruby Rohrlich, eds., *Women in Search of Utopia: Mavericks and Mythmakers* (New York: Schocken Books, 1984); Frances Bartkowski, *Feminist Utopias* (Lincoln: University of Nebraska Press, 1989); Diane G. Crowder, "Amazones de . . . demain?:

La fiction utopique féministe et lesbienne," *Amazones d'Hier, Lesbiennes d'Aujourd'hui* 2, 4 (1984), 19–27; Pamela Tucker Farley, "That Wrench of the Mind," *Hysteria* 2, 1 (1983), 25–30; Peter Fitting, "'So We All Become Mothers': New Roles for Men in Recent Utopian Fiction," *Science-Fiction Studies* 12, 2 (36) (1985), 156–183; Annette Keinhorst, "Emancipatory projection: an introduction to women's critical utopias," *Women's Studies International Forum* 14 (1987), 91–99; Sarah Lefanu, *In the Chinks of the World Machine* (London: The Women's Press, 1988); Carol Pearson, "Women's Fantasies and Feminist Utopias," *Frontiers* 2, 3 (1977), 50–61; Natalie M. Rosinsky, *Feminist Futures: Contemporary Women's Speculative Fiction* (Ann Arbor: U. of Michigan Research Press, 1984); Joanna Russ, "Recent Feminist Utopias" in *Future Females*, Marleen Barr, ed. (Bowling Green, Ohio: Bowling Green University Popular Press, 1981), 71–87; and Jane B. Weedman, ed., *Women Worldwalkers: New Dimensions of Science Fiction and Fantasy* (Lubbock, Tex.: Texas Tech Press, 1985).

2 Peter Fitting, "For men only: a guide to reading single-sex worlds," *Women's Studies International Forum* 14 (1987), 101–17, explores in detail why female separatist utopias are the only possible ones. In his important bibliography of gay and lesbian science fiction, Eric Garber lists some gay male utopias, but I have been unable to find them and cannot comment on their content. See Garber, *Uranian Worlds: A Reader's Guide to Alternative Sexuality in Science Fiction and Fantasy* (Boston: G. K. Hall, 1983). It would be interesting to explore why the gay/lesbian liberation movement inspired so little utopian fiction by gay men positing an all-male world.

3 Radicalesbians, "The Woman-Identified Woman," leaflet reprinted in *The Ladder* 11–12 (1970) and in *For Lesbians Only: A Separatist Anthology*, Sarah Lucia Hoagland and Julia Penelope, eds. (London: Onlywomen Press, 1988), 17.

4 Russ's novel appeared in 1975, two years after the translation of *Les Guérillères*, but an early version of the utopian portion was written as a short story, "When It Changed," in 1970 and published in 1972 in Harlan Ellison's collection *Again, Dangerous Visions* (New York: Doubleday). Thus, it is fair to say the ideas behind Russ's novel were at least germinating within a couple of years of the publication of Wittig's novel in French, and before the English translation appeared. Publishing history of "When it Changed" is from the introduction to the story in *Kindred Spirits: An Anthology of Gay and Lesbian Science Fiction Stories*, Jeffrey M. Elliot, ed. (Boston: Alyson Publications, 1984), 43–44.

5 Thelma J. Shinn, "Worlds of Words and Swords: Suzette Haden Elgin and Joanna Russ at Work" in *Women Worldwalkers*, Jane Weedman, ed. (Lubbock, Tex.: Texas Tech Press, 1985), 207–22, notes that Russ has moved from celebrating the solitary female hero to exploring community and sisterhood. Keinhorst, Bartkowski, and other critics have also remarked on the development of community in utopian fiction by women.

6 Unfortunately the English translation of *Les Guérillères* uses "the women" to translate "elles." This badly deforms what Wittig was doing in the novel. She explicitly avoids the use of "femmes" (women) in this and later works. In "The Mark of Gender," *Feminist Issues* 5, 2 (1985a) Wittig explains her theory of language and gender. She says: "In *Les Guérillères*, I try to universalize the point of view of the *elles*. The goal of this approach is not to feminize the world but to

make the categories of sex obsolete in language. . . . By turning my *elles* into *the women* [the translator] destroyed the process of universalization. All of a sudden, *elles (the women)* stopped being *mankind*. . . . [woman] is one of those gender-marked words . . . which I never use in French. For me it is the equivalent of slave . . ." (9–10). For Wittig, the lesbian writer must suppress gender altogether. See also her articles "The Point of View: Universal or Particular?" *Feminist Issues* 3, 2 (1983), 63–70, and "The Trojan Horse," *Feminist Issues* 4, 2 (1984b), 45–50.

7 For a treatment of the epic mode in *Les Guérillères*, see Hélène Wenzel, "The Text as Body/Politics: An Appreciation of Monique Wittig's Writings in Context," *Feminist Studies* 7, 2 (1981), 264–87.

8 See Farley, op. cit., and Bartkowski, ch. 2 for further discussion of these characters.

9 The presence of the young men at the end of the novel is problematic. Since the "elles" of the novel is a universalizing shift in the language, and since Wittig is perhaps the most radically antiessentialist writer I know, these young men must be considered as members of the "guérillères" – socially constructed as members of the all-female utopia of the "elles" – precisely because they have negated their own male privilege by joining with the "guérillères." Wittig has repeatedly reiterated her materialist and social constructionist stance. See her "One Is Not Born a Woman," *Feminist Issues* 1, 2 (1981), 47–54, and "The Straight Mind," *Feminist Issues* 1, 1 (1980), 103–11. Both articles have been reprinted in Hoagland and Penelope, op. cit.

10 Critics too numerous to list have noted that women writers don't imagine utopias where our current sexist situation is reversed. Mixed matriarchies in which women hold power over men are a staple of antifeminist writing by both men and women, as Russ explores in "*Amor Vincit Foeminam:* The Battle of the Sexes in Science Fiction," *Science Fiction Studies* 7 (1980), reprinted in *Gender Studies,* Judith Spector, ed. (Bowling Green, Ohio: Bowling Green University Popular Press, 1986), 234–49. Role-reversal novels by women either are clearly intended as satire, or are dystopian. Gert Brantenberg's *Egalia's Daughters: A Satire of the Sexes* (originally published in Norwegian as *Egalias døtre* in 1977) (Seattle: The Seal Press, 1985) exemplifies the former, while Marion Zimmer Bradley's *The Ruins of Isis* (Norfolk, Va.: Donning, 1978) is typical of the latter.

11 Carolyn Rhodes, "Method in her Madness: Feminism in the Crazy Utopian Vision of Tiptree's Courier" in *Women and Utopia,* Marleen Barr and Nicholas Smith, eds. (Lanham, Md.: University Presses of America, 1983), 34–42, discusses how this madness works as a feminist device in Tiptree's story.

12 An interesting aspect of this is the use of Arab and Muslim models for the future dystopia. The "bad world" removed from the present-day United States not only in time but in culture as well. Russ's *The Two of Them* (New York: Berkley, 1978), Ursula K. LeGuin's *Always Coming Home* (New York: Harper and Row, 1985), and Marion Zimmer Bradley's *The Shattered Chain* (New York: Daw, 1976) all incorporate dystopias featuring veiling, purdah, and other devices that evoke Islamic cultures. Given the dates, one could speculate that heightened awareness of Islamic culture caused by the OPEC oil crisis and the Iranian revolution of the mid- to late 1970s influenced this development.

13 See previously noted work by Pearson, Lefanu, Keinhorst, Russ, Barr, Crowder, and Fitting for overviews of social organization in these utopias.

14 Lynn F. Williams, "'Great Country for Men and Dogs, but Tough on Women and Mules': Sex and Status in Recent Science Fiction Utopias" in *Women Worldwalkers*, Jane Weedman, ed. (Lubbock, Tex.: Texas Tech Press, 1985), 223–35.

15 Alice Echols, *Daring to Be Bad: Radical Feminism in America 1967–1975* (Minneapolis: University of Minnesota Press, 1989) gives a very clear history of the rise of "cultural feminism" or essentialism in the American feminist movement. Echols maintains that by 1975 this tendency was the dominant philosophy. This same trend developed in France with the hegemony of the group "Psychanalyse et politique," and the theories of Luce Irigary, Hélène Cixous, and Julia Kristeva. All three of these writers maintain that, because of the potential for motherhood, women have certain essential characteristics such as nurturance and nonviolence. These theories underlie the development of the notion of "écriture féminine" as set forth in Cixous's "The Laugh of Medusa" ("Le Rire de la Méduse," *L'Arc* 61 [1975], 39–54; English translation *Signs* 1, 4 [1976]: 875–93). Wittig went into voluntary exile in the United States at about the time these essentialist theories achieved dominance over the French feminist movement. The very important manifesto by the publishing collective of *Questions féministes*, "Variations on Common Themes," is one of the most lucid analyses of the different trends in feminism, and especially of the dangers of what they call "féminitude," that one can find. Originally published in *Questions féministes* 1 (Nov. 1977), it is reprinted in English in *New French Feminisms*, Elaine Marks and Isabelle de Courtivron, eds. (New York: Schocken, 1981), 212–30. The introductions to this invaluable book by Marks and de Courtivron are excellent histories of the French movement. For a more recent survey, see Claire Duchen, *Feminism in France* (London: Routledge & Kegan Paul, 1986). See Annie de Pisan and Anne Tristan, *Histoires du M.L.F.* (Paris: Calmann-Levy, 1977) and the anonymously edited *Chronique d'une imposture: Du mouvement de libération des femmes à une marque commerciale* (Paris: Association Mouvement pour les Luttes Féministes, 1981) for the influence of "Psychanalyse et Politique" and eyewitness histories of the French movement.

16 I include Charlotte Perkins Gilman's *Herland* (1915) and Mary E. Bradley Lane's *Mizorah* (1880) here because both novels were rediscovered and reprinted in the late 1970s (1979 and 1975, respectively) and had an influence on writers of this period. *Herland* has become part of the feminist canon. *Mizorah* is less well known, but quite interesting. The "catastrophe" that eliminated men in *Mizorah* is my personal favorite. Legislation has deprived men of the vote for one hundred years in order to allow women to clean up the corruption that followed the Civil War. The women discover parthenogenesis the minute they have access to science labs. Stripped of political power and biological usefulness, the men simply wither away.

17 Of course, male readers recognize this immediately, and react with predictable discomfort. One of the few male critics to take this body of work seriously is Peter Fitting, in "For men only: a guide to reading single-sex worlds," *Women's Studies International Forum* 14 (1987), 101–17. He argues that works like

Motherlines, The Female Man, and "Houston, Houston" call not for a world without men but for a world without male values. Further, he believes the device of the all-female utopia forces the male reader to recognize his position of power in our society, and to acknowledge that he must change radically if men are to enter utopias. He criticizes the most successful mixed utopia, *Woman on the Edge of Time,* for allowing men to see the needed changes as external, not requiring men *as men* to change. While I think Fitting makes many valid points about how the male reader can approach these utopias, I do not believe writers like Gearhart and Charnas want only to eliminate male values. As Fitting himself says of these novels, ". . . it was easier to imagine an end to the sex/gender system by eliminating men than to try and 'rewrite' them" (108). In Gearhart's case, even men who reject male power are suspect.

18 Susanna J. Sturgis, "Editorial Memories & Visions, or Why Does a Bright Feminist Like You Read That Stuff Anyway?" Introduction to *Memories and Visions: Women's Fantasy and Science Fiction,* Susanna J. Sturgis, ed. (Freedom, Calif.: The Crossing Press, 1989), 3.

19 Merril Mushroom's *Daughters of Khaton* (Denver: Lace Publications, 1987) is a true separatist utopia. According to Julia Penelope (personal communication), the novel was written in the late 1970s, although not published until 1987. It therefore properly belongs in the period of works like *The Wanderground,* rather than to the late 1980s under discussion, and does not negate my argument.

20 Since Wittig eschews the words *women* and *men,* only the gender of the nouns in French indicates the gender of the "damned souls" ("âmes damnées") and of their torturers ("ils"). It is their social position, revealed by the linguistic sign, that is in question and not some essential "feminine" or "masculine" nature. If only lesbians inhabit paradise, it is because only lesbians have moved out of the dichotomy defining "women" and "men." See "One Is Not Born a Woman" and "The Straight Mind" for Wittig's explanations of why lesbians are not "women."

14

Louise Kawada

Liberating Laughter:
Comedic Form in Some Lesbian Novels

So all the history, all the stories would be there to retell differently, the future would be incalculable; the historic forces would and will change hands and change body – another thought which is yet unthinkable – will transform the functioning of all society.

Hélène Cixous, "Sorties" in The Newly Born Woman (1986)

Where's the energetic wit, the looney outlook, the frivolity, the lightness of comforting laughter? It has become fashionable to know and unfashionable to feel, and you can't really laugh if you can't feel.

Rita Mae Brown, In Her Day (1988)

Two contemporary Lesbian novelists, Rita Mae Brown and Lisa Alther, in *Rubyfruit Jungle* and *Other Women,* have done much to engender laughter and feeling. In both novels, old myths about limitation are replaced by new myths of potential and vision for the future. Brown and Alther celebrate women's sexuality, something that seems in both writers to be a starting point for self-awareness and healing creative energy. Their fiction, moreover, is open-ended, suggesting process and renewal, and not closed with the summary approval of behavior corrected. The conclusions of their novels do not rise perhaps to the visionary level that Cixous suggests; in many ways the idea of comedy as a compelling vision rather than a moral taskmaster is still so new that these novelists can only suggest the genesis of that idea. Nonetheless, the fiction here is exemplary of a new comic mode, for it exhibits the power of a laughter that is universal, along with the affirmation of connections made and love shared.

A mode too often deployed to castigate rather than to celebrate, comedy has for a long time now seemed in need of some restoration work done on its soul. Women writers, and in particular, Lesbian writers, already marginalized and in possession of different truths, have begun to reshape the template of comedic form. In the recent past, the prototypical comic plot scored its conventional success by reintegrating the misfit or the regenerate back into the communal fold. Harmony was restored, and the "happy ending" was symbolically rendered with a marriage that affirmed both the status quo and the status of the patriarchy. Not much to laugh at here for any woman.

Gradually, though, through what Hélène Cixous and Catherine Clément call the "cracks in the overall system,"[1] women have learned to speak out, open up new perspectives, and challenge the sanity of conventional wisdom. Often the vehicle for this exploration has been a revised expression of comedic form that has privileged the spontaneous and zany, the marginalized and the disempowered.

Independent of and yet simultaneous with the marked increase in women's comedic expression is a body of theoretical writing that articulates newfound potential for both women and comedy. The critical writers that I shall consider here briefly as a prologue to a discussion of Brown's and Alther's novels are the Russian critic Mikhail Bakhtin and the French feminist writers Hélène Cixous and Catherine Clément. Though the subjects of their discourse (Bakhtin on Rabelais and the festive folk humor of the Middle Ages and Cixous and Clément on the need to locate and affirm the tremendous powers within women's psyche) have ostensibly little to do with each other; nonetheless, their theories often anticipate and support each other with uncanny prescience.

Bakhtin, in *Rabelais and His World,* describes the characteristics of carnival or festive folk humor used by Rabelais and at the same time expresses a nostalgia for the rich, earthy, sometimes ribald, and always deeply celebratory life that Rabelais and the spirit of his times displayed. Carnival laughter, as Bakhtin indicates, was a broad laughter, not only in its expression of bawdiness but also in the universality of its scope and participants. Everyone took part in the carnival or unofficial feast, the people's respite from the somberness of the church or feudal law. The festive laughter that resulted was a release and a form of bonding. The carnival, moreover, was an open-ended form that instilled within its participants the imagery and feeling for growth, change, and renewal. Hierarchies of class were dropped for the day. Most importantly, carnival was a permissible "crack in the system," a time when the world could be seen and experienced in a different light. Bakhtin gives special emphasis to this point:

As opposed to the official feast, one might say that carnival celebrated temporary liberation from the prevailing truth and from the established order; it marked the suspension of all hierarchical rank, privileges, norms, and prohibitions. Carnival was the true feast of becoming, change, and renewal. It was hostile to all that was immortalized and completed.[2]

The speech of carnival was more direct, frank, and even vulgar; and the essence of carnival was figured in what Bakhtin names as "the grotesque body." The grotesque body exhibited convexities and protuberances, excesses and secretions, "a brimming-over of abundance" that implied sexuality and fertility.[3] This description, with its emphasis on bodily functions, growth, and contiguity of that body with the rest of the world, was hardly the description of the classic body: static, with ideal proportions, the perpetual object of the arresting gaze.

Cixous and Clément reiterate many of Bakhtin's comments, although in more radical, women-centered and visionary ways.[4] Their prose, particularly that of Cixous, speaks with a lyric intensity, thus lending a measure of apocalyptic permanency to Bakhtin's intimations of utopian promise within carnival's liminal moments of release.

Cixous describes the feminine body in terms that are similar to Bakhtin's valuation of the grotesque body, citing qualities that had previously been inadmissible, shameful, even dangerous. The woman for Cixous is one who has never

held still; explosion, diffusion, effervescence, abundance, she takes pleasure in being boundless, outside self, outside same, far from a "center," from any capital of her "dark continent," very far from the "hearth" to which man brings her so that she will tend his fire, which always threatens to go out.[5]

Moreover, this body exceeds and abolishes boundaries between itself and the entire world. Like Bakhtin who insisted on the grotesque body as one "blended with animals, with objects,"[6] Clément also perceives this fabulous contextuality of body and world as well as its profound implications for the release of pleasure and reordering of perceptions. In a description of Hieronymus Bosch's *The Paradises,* Clément observes:

Nature and Culture abolished, all bodies mingled: animals, fruits, and humans in the same intertwining. Flowers penetrate, fruits caress, animals open, humans are like instruments of this universal *jouissance.*[7]

The apocalyptic promise uttered here (i.e., the division between nature and culture to be abolished) is picked up in a later essay in *The Newly Born Woman* by Cixous. Here she sees civilization's tendency to dichotomize, to order thought by pairings (day/night; man/woman; culture/nature) as a way of maintaining hierarchical and phallocentric modes of thought. After naming the pairings, Cixous reflects:

And all these pairs of oppositions are *couples*. Does that mean something? Is the fact that Logocentrism subjects thought – all concepts, codes and values – to a binary system, related to "the" couple, man/woman?[8]

In his analysis of carnival, Bakhtin envisioned a classless society with hierarchies removed at a political level. Here, however, Cixous would break down even those deeply ingrained patterns of thought, far more subtle and elusive than any political codification. In calling for this fusion of divisions, moreover, Cixous and Clément are privileging a Lesbian perspective that (re)fuses ideas of otherness and superiority in a relationship. To enter into that perspective where binary divisions, hierarchies no longer have meaning is to renew oneself, become whole, and experience a sense of joy and renewal long after the carnival is over. The promise of such a vision begins to enact itself in the earliest comedic Lesbian novel, Rita Mae Brown's *Rubyfruit Jungle.*

Rubyfruit Jungle opens with a large ironic joke upon itself. Carrie, the stepmother of Molly Bolt, accuses Molly (all of age seven) of having sexual relations with the boy next door. Never again – woefully for Carrie – will she have occasion to make such charges. Meanwhile, Molly learns she is "Ruby Drollinger's bastard"[9] and that Ruby, in Carrie's eyes, was not a paragon of moral excellence. Molly runs away that night only to find no one has stayed up waiting for her. In one stroke she has learned of her origins and attained impeccable certification as an outsider.

Molly, in short, is an ideal comic heroine in what Bonnie Zimmerman calls "the Lesbian novel of development."[10] According to Zimmerman the Lesbian heroine is closer to the male actor in a bildungsroman, for she, unlike her female counterpart in a novel of awakening, is more likely to experience freedom, rather than defeat or resignation. Moreover, the bildungsroman spirals upward toward a conclusion that is marked by affirmation and a stronger sense of self-identity.

Molly functions in the novel as a picaresque heroine, a role that by the fundamental likability of the energy it expresses automatically garners some reader support. In her journey from her childhood and adolescence in the South to her film degree earned at NYU, she undergoes several experiences that confer upon her not only likability but strength, courage, and feisty savvy. One of her first rites of passage occurs when Carl, her stepfather, acknowledges she is more intelligent than his own children; shortly after, he dies. A second "turning point" takes place at the Univer-

sity of Florida, where Molly falls in love with her roommate and is expelled by a dean who is herself probably gay. The incident is important on
two counts: First, Molly, unlike earlier Lesbian heroines, has dared to
knock on the closet door of institutional respectability. Second, the incident arouses a sense of betrayal and hypocrisy that almost overwhelms
Molly and puts an end to her innocence. Again, Molly's experiences follow the paradigm, for, as Zimmerman points out, a necessary passage in
the Lesbian novel of development is a passage between innocence and
experience and a recognition, thereby, of the full consequences of Lesbian
love.[11]

After this incident, Molly hitchhikes to New York City and finds an unlikely mentor in Chris, who is homeless, black, and gay. Chris enables her
to survive, but more strategically he sets up an occasion for Molly to see
herself as a heroine. She considers his offer to travel to the West Coast but
holds off, saying:

Something tells me I have to stay in this ugly city for awhile. . . . It's like I'll make
my fortune here or something. Remember those old children's stories where the
young son goes out on the road for adventure and to make his fortune after he's
been cheated out of his inheritance by his evil brother? (151)

This is the fairy tale of the dispossessed, an appropriate one for Molly;
and fairy tales by nature are comedic, for their form relies upon the up-
turn of good fortune to bring the tale to a satisfactory resolution. Molly
does "make her fortune" through the use of her wits and her emotional
resilience, as well as her uncompromising sense of self. No hero ever pursued the golden fleece with more single-minded intensity than that which
Molly directs toward a working out of what is right for her.

As with any self-respecting hero or heroine, tests come along to
challenge Molly's integrity. An aging, wealthy woman, for example, offers
to provide Molly's keep and tuition in exchange for her sexual attentions.
Molly opts for the difficult route of self-sufficiency, but is not beyond
some unscheduled "borrowing" of film equipment when it comes time to
finish her senior project. With Ulysses-like energy and a sense of practical
shrewdness, Molly makes circumstances favor her, without engaging in
any act that would diminish her sense of self.

If Molly merely paid private allegiance to her identity, she would be a
rare enough commodity in today's society, but hardly heroic; nor would
Rubyfruit Jungle, despite its bawdiness, leveling wit, and outrageous diffusion of energy be comedic in the fullest sense. Molly has received validation from her stepfather, Carl, but her real parentage has remained
shrouded in mystery and derogation, and her relations with Carrie have
been, at best, strained. A sense of remembering the past and healing the

gaps in understanding begins in a lovemaking session with an older woman, when Molly is asked to name her private fantasy. In her response, Molly, indirectly at least, affirms her union with her mother, as well as the shared richness of female sexuality, as she reveals, "When I make love to women, I think of their genitals as a, as a ruby fruit jungle" (203). Ruby, of course, is her mother's name.

Molly's strongest and most valorizing moment of selfhood comes, though, when she returns home to film Carrie for her senior project. A life unfolds before her eyes, as Carrie, old, alone, physically worn down with age and cancer, tells Molly of her frustrations and jealousies, her desires and her pleasures. A recognition takes place between the women of their mutually strong-willed natures, which sometimes kept them apart. Their meeting ends with an admission of love, and Molly returns to New York to show the film and be graduated with the highest honors. The novel suggests a happy ending and closes on a note of reconciliation and love but does not token a stasis or an advocacy of old norms. Exactly because Molly is excluded from society and cannot get tracked in a job path that would assure her success, her dialogue with society is ongoing, and the novel cannot adopt the closure of traditional comedic form. "One way or another I'll make those movies" (246) is the concluding promise of the book, and one that carries the action and engagement of the heroine beyond the limits of the novel's ending.

Rubyfruit Jungle is an important pioneer text in women's comedy because it begins to break down so many of the old myths and stereotypes. Most obviously, the novel does away with the myth of the maladjusted homosexual. Molly is attractive, athletic, popular – and, with some help from the high school principal and the dean of women whom she discovers having an extramarital affair, she is also class president. Hardly a scenario from *The Well of Loneliness*.

Amid all the pranks, the sometimes bawdy humor, and the ribald language, *Rubyfruit Jungle* offers some strong commentary on the arbitrary definition of normalcy and its ways of subverting and twisting those who do not meet the definition. Throughout the novel, Brown shows us figures such as Leroy, Molly's early childhood friend, and Carolyn, a high-school companion, who resist and suppress their own homosexual leanings because of social pressure. In this novel, too, the myth of first-night heterosexual ecstasy suffers, as does that of marital bliss. Molly sees her old friend and onetime lover Leota Phantom (née Bisland) now married with two children: "Same cat eyes, same languid body, but oh god, she looked forty-five years old and she had two brats hanging on her like possums" (216).

The world in *Rubyfruit Jungle* is in upside-down carnivalesque upheaval. The down and outs, like Chris, who befriended Molly, receive high scores for their humaneness; while those who are accepted as authority figures (the dean of women, probably herself gay, who dismissed Molly from college on the basis of homosexuality) often fail. Bakhtin praised madness as a way of seeing the possible and new in a tired system. At one point in *Rubyfruit Jungle,* a character calls Molly "lunatic" (301) when Molly suggests that love between women is beautiful. Just before, Molly had described to this woman how advertising and its hawking of the "good life" ultimately exploit women and condone violence. Molly adds:

"You don't see ads of women kissing to get you to buy Salem cigarettes, do you?" She laughed. "That's funny, that's truly funny. Why the entire world must look different to you." (199)

Indeed it does, and the Lesbian writer seizes upon this anomalous perspective, this crack in the system, to try to change the system. The radical quality of the image presented here – two women kissing in a Salem ad – is so preposterous, so askew from Madison Avenue cool, that it amuses and prompts reflection. What are the constructs in our society that order and hierarchize sexual relations, that also sell violence and domination? And why is one image labeled as acceptable and the other as morally wrong?

Rubyfruit Jungle consistently seems to ask questions that too often go unframed and to voice (at least implicitly) answers to those questions. Making sense of the world (even if one has to turn it upside down), finding and affirming meaning, are important aspects of the novel's program. But to what extent is this epistemological quest a gender-related issue; does meaning matter more to women than it does to men?

Brown seems to structure the novel to point up differences in male and female sensibilities. At important moments, Molly is connected with the image of a raft and the implied notion of Huck Finn. Even Molly's Aunt Florence sounds like a recreation of the Widow Douglas and her "siviliz-ing" ways. Molly bemoans her situation:

She ran on and she got me for this offense and that offense as well as one hundred trespasses. She's gonna make a lady out of me that summer, a crash program. She was going to keep me in the house to teach me to act right, cook, clean, and sew and that scared me. (33)

On the one hand, the Huck comparison reflects Molly's role as *picaro,* but it also forces a subtle measuring of the two protagonists. Although Molly's future is uncertain at the close of the novel, her direction and accomplishments are clear. Huck, on the other hand, seems committed more to action than direction, and his tale finds closure in the maelstrom of pranks and Missouri voodoo played on hapless Jim. Brown offers a more explicit reading of male/female perception in her comparison between Molly's retrospective of Carrie's life and the films made by the other (male) students, who focused their artistic energies on gang rapes, Martian attacks, and nuclear destruction in a hail of tinfoil balls. The rhetorical point of Molly's film is the discovery of meaning, while the message of the others' "works" is to insist on the absence of meaning, the violent and violated strata of contemporary existence.

Rubyfruit Jungle, as I have indicated, performed an enormous amount of groundbreaking work in transforming the Lesbian novel from a *vie privée* text of exclusion to a work that could recover and extend the idea of comedy. Lisa Alther's *Other Women,* published more than a decade after Brown's book, stands in affirmation of the changes set in motion. Both books enjoyed an immediate success, some indication, perhaps, that the general readership was responsive to reading about Lesbian issues in fiction. *Other Women* is a less polemical, more imagistic book than *Rubyfruit Jungle* and works at a quieter archetypal level to show the deep inner resources of strength women possess.

The book opens with Hannah surmising Caroline's Lesbian leanings, even before a therapy session begins:

The woman was standing with her hands on her hips, her weight on one leg. An athlete. Probably a lesbian. I wonder how long it will take her to tell me. I wonder if she knows.[12]

Caroline knows, of course, and tells Hannah immediately:

"I'm a lesbian," Caroline announced. . . . Hannah shrugged. O yes, she thought, and what did you have for breakfast? (23)

The dialogue between the Lesbian and the straight world is established immediately; moreover, in an advance beyond the single controlling perspective of Molly, the reader of *Other Women* hears both the spoken and the inner conversation of the main characters and is privy to special information about their lives. For example, Hannah seems to Caroline to be "fresh from the contract bridge-playing circuit," (23), but the narrator has already informed the reader of other details in Hannah's life:

But she'd been taken by surprise too often. Four years old and your mother dies of typhoid. Abandoned by your father at five. Nineteen, and your husband is killed in battle. Two children dead in bed from carbon monoxide. (19)

Along the lines of less catastrophic data, the reader also knows that Hannah has tried several times to quit smoking; that she is addicted to reading romances; that once in introducing her second husband she forgot his name; and that while training in psychotherapy, she had formed a very deep relationship with Maggie, her instructor and mentor. Caroline comes eventually to learn all this, and the knowledge, which both levels and enriches Hannah's image, enables a more even-handed dialogue between the two women. Just as importantly, the reader, who almost always has a clearer view of both characters, enters into the substance of the dialogue as a mediator, or third-party therapist, to some extent. The demand of this novel, after all, is not approbation – Lesbianism as an accepted lifestyle is a given here – but rather a beneficent sense of making peace with ourselves and with each other and of sharing in the awareness of life as carnival.

Caroline is a test case for whether or not someone can learn to adopt this celebratory perspective. She is, as the reader soon learns, the offspring of diehard do-good parents who practice charity with more virulence than vision. No domestic demand (such as Caroline's needs as a child) could ever be any match for pain abstractly categorized as the Homeless, the Poor, the Dispossessed. Naturally enough, Caroline uses their perspective to organize and color her own mental landscape, and a sunset over Lake Glass reminds her of how her brain felt at the moment: "raw beef pounded flat by a cubing hammer" (27).

Gradually, with Hannah's help, Caroline begins to see different exterior and interior landscapes. Toward the end of her therapy, Caroline, a weaver by avocation, presents Hannah with a shawl she has woven of a sunset over Lake Glass. Caroline's dreams change from terror-filled ones to dreams of "dark, healing stillness" (370). A line from Hannah keeps echoing at fortunate moments – "The miracle is all around you" (329). Even Caroline's cat, Amelia, for a split second, provides Caroline with the occasion to participate in the miraculous:

Amelia turned her head, met Caroline's gaze, and slowly blinked her yellow-green eyes. Her mouth looked as though it were smiling. Caroline was struck by her gratuitous beauty. Why did such a silly, friendly, aloof, graceful creature exist at all, with her totally unnecessary patches of tan, black, and white? *Open your eyes and see what you see when you're not set to see the horror.* Amelia was a miracle. (30)

At this time, too, Caroline begins to open outward to other people. She makes a foray into the straight world, attending a party with Brian, a hospital physician. The party, hosted by a silicone-endowed suburbanite, is virtually a parodic rendering of festival, with its stylized glitter, tony hors d'oeuvres, and self-conscious banter. Caroline, feeling inept and out of synch, ends up taking refuge in a closet (of all places) and calling her friends. Shortly after that particular evening, perhaps to right the scales of justice and pleasure, Caroline goes home with a woman she has met in a sauna. The meeting is one of pure satisfaction and desire unencumbered by any obligations or needs. The encounter brings to mind Cixous's reflections on Lesbian love: "Elsewhere she gives. She doesn't measure what she is giving, but she gives neither false leads nor what she does not have."[13]

Finally, having centered and secured her sense of identity, Caroline again returns to her former lover, Diana. The relationship ultimately will not work out, but Caroline has reached a point where she can assume the risk-taking and the leave-taking on her own.

Diana, a loom, a cat – these are images that stand like signposts along Caroline's journey to health; but they also signal the potentially numinous, the realm of the feminine archetypal. On many levels, *Other Women* presents images that foreshadow and virtually enable Caroline's growth and healing. While sitting in Hannah's office each week, Caroline glances at certain objects that, on a suggestive level, help instruct her. On the wall behind Hannah is a tapestry of two women in Eden, smiling and eating apples. Resting on the windowsill is a gray stone Venus, with protruding belly and breasts. In the corner is a bark painting of a "bizarre leaping creature called a mimi spirit" (49), given by an Australian aboriginal to Hannah's mother before he died of typhoid fever. And on the other side of the office is a photograph of a snowy field, at first glance the Virgin Mary if vision were skewed another way. Together these images endorse and suggest guilt-free pleasure, the carnivalesque life-generating female body, the wildness and spontaneity that exceeds civilization's repressive codes, and the control and choice in framing the images of perception. Much of Caroline's progress in therapy is documented by her ability to read the iconography and internalize the power of these images.

As with *Rubyfruit Jungle*, *Other Women* ends with a sense of new life and new possibilities, rather than with a sense of defined order and a restoration of social norms. Hannah and Caroline walk toward the lake, its ice already having melted in the warm spring sun. The narrator observes:

The lake spread out below them, a soft pewter color under the overcast sky. All the ice had melted. Summer was coming. They heard a clamor in the trees bordering the yard. Looking up, they saw that the branches, swollen with new buds, were filled with chattering yellow evening grosbeaks, fresh from more balmy lands, sporting their jaunty masks like revelers returning from a Caribbean carnival. (380)

The scene is, of course, in the sense Bakhtin intended the term, a veritable carnival, with its released sense of joy and reason to celebrate. Nor does the reader have any reason to suspect that this carnival will be only a liminal moment of celebration; for a very deep and lasting bond seems now to exist between Hannah and Caroline, and many old misconceptions and self-destructive myths have been put aside.

In retrospect, perhaps the strongest, most potent forces these novels exhibit is the power of the erotic, or, as Audre Lorde puts it, "a resource within each of us that lies in a deeply female and spiritual plane, firmly rooted in the power of our unexpressed or unrecognized feeling."[14] At the close of *Rubyfruit Jungle*, Molly comes back to Carrie, the "mother" who nurtured her, and we hear in the filming sessions Carrie's own acknowledgments of her desires, her failing and fading physical body and its sexuality, and her connectedness with Molly. Likewise, in Caroline's sessions with Hannah, we come to learn of both women's sense of eros and their affective desires and needs. It seems that for self-identity as well as for the act of writing and the possibility of comedy this sense of eros is absolutely necessary, for it empowers, brings joy, enables feeling. As Audre Lorde further explains:

The very word *erotic* comes from the Greek word *eros*, the personification of love in all its aspects – born of Chaos, and personifying power and harmony. When I speak of the erotic, then, I speak of it as an assertion of the lifeforce of women, of that creative energy empowered, the knowledge and use of which we are now reclaiming in our language, our history, our dancing, our loving, our work, our lives.[15]

The "erotic," as Lorde defines the term, shares much with other ideas and terms that have special importance to women and comedy. First of all, "erotic" is akin to the French feminist term *jouissance*, a play-filled ebullient sense of sexuality that can also be a pun on *j'ouïs sens* – I hear meaning.[16] It also suggests Henri Bergson's *élan vital* or "life force," used to define mind as something always in the process of creating. Bergson, in his *Laughter* (1911:8–22) cited the mechanistic and the absent-minded as fundamental sources of laughter and as something quite other than this vitalistic principle that affirmed the true comedic spirit. Finally, the "erotic" also aligns itself with Bakhtin's sense of utopian promise within comedy, for Lorde's definition of the "erotic" suggests living each moment at its fullest, most uncompromising level. To do so would be to abrupt meaninglessness and to absolve the false dichotomies between mind and body, Logos and feeling. To live in the spirit of the erotic would also enable all of us to see the world anew and to adopt with Rita Mae Brown the Cartesian formula, "*Rideo, ergo sum* – I laugh, therefore I am."[17]

NOTES

1 Hélène Cixous and Catherine Clément, *The Newly Born Woman*, translated by Betsy Wing (Minneapolis: University of Minnesota Press, 1986), 7.

2 Mikhail Bakhtin, *Rabelais and His World*, translated by Helen Iswolsky (Bloomington: Indiana University Press, 1984), 10.

3 *Rabelais*, 64.

4 A parallel between Cixous and Clément and the relation of their work to Bakhtin's writings on Rabelais has been observed by Mary Russo in her article "Female Grotesques," which appears in *Feminist Studies/Critical Studies*, edited by Teresa de Lauretis (Bloomington: Indiana University Press, 1986); see especially pp. 211 – 23. Russo concludes, as I do, that "Carnival and carnival laughter remain on the horizon of a new social subjectivity" (226). She also, however, takes Bakhtin to task for failing to "incorporate the social relations of gender in his semiotic model of the body politic . . ." (219). Given the fact that Bakhtin's intent was to write a study of Rabelais, I have no argument with his methodology and only gratitude for the flexibility and applicability of his scholarship.

5 *The Newly Born Woman*, 91.

6 Ibid., 27.

7 Ibid., 23.

8 Ibid., 64.

9 *Rubyfruit Jungle* (New York: Bantam Books, 1977), 8. Subsequent page references will appear in the text of the article.

10 "Exiting from the Patriarchy: The Lesbian Novel of Development," from *The Voyage In: Fictions of Female Development*, edited by Elizabeth Abel, Marianne Hirsch, and Elizabeth Langland (Hanover and London: University Press of New England, 1983), 246.

11 "Exiting," 247.

12 *Other Women* (New York: New American Library, 1984), 19. Subsequent page references will appear in the text of the article.

13 *The Newly Born Woman*, 100.

14 *Sister Outsider* (Trumansburg, N.Y.: The Crossing Press, 1984), 53.

15 Ibid., 55.

16 I am indebted to Betsy Wing, who provides a most useful, often essential, gloss to her fine translation of *The Newly Born Woman*.

17 *In Her Day* (New York: Bantam, 1988), xii.

PART IV

(Op)positional Aesthetics: Creating Lesbian Culture(s)

Introduction

Lesbian identity is, as we stated earlier in this book, grounded in Lesbian sexuality, women's love for other women. It is true that patriarchal societies have discouraged the expression of Lesbian sexuality, suppressing both Lesbian sexual acts and openly Lesbian texts. Even in the latter half of this century, mainstream ideology continues to marginalize Lesbians, who reject institutionalized heterosexuality and hence threaten gender roles central to male oppression of women.

Existing tenuously in the margins of patriarchal culture, Lesbians create alternatives to it, using the Lesbian body as a metaphor, metamorphosing both world and self. Since we are, as Marilyn Frye (1980:97) has said, "something which there is no such thing as," we create ourselves out of ourselves. As in Lesbian sexuality, so in Lesbian culture the Lesbian is both subject and object, self and other. Hence, the Lesbian writer "writes" the Lesbian body, and the Lesbian reader finds herself in the mirror of the text, both attempting to inscribe identity and Lesbian culture.

We (Julia and Susan) take the position that Lesbian sexuality is the basis of Lesbian identity, and a positive sense of Lesbian identity the basis of Lesbian cultures. Others contend, however, that it is difficult to identify Lesbian culture(s), because definitions of "culture" are problematic. Ann Ferguson, for example, in her essay "Is There a Lesbian Culture?" (1990), took exception to "objectivist" approaches to culture, arguing that the mere possession of a number of common social attributes was inadequate: any set of shared attributes might be identified in a group of individuals, who might or might not recognize themselves as a culture. Finding the "identity" sense of culture problematic because women who declined to identify as Lesbians (regardless of their sexual and affectional relationships with other women) would be excluded from membership in Lesbian culture(s), Ferguson opted instead for what she termed a "dialectical approach," one which saw "lesbian cultures as potential cultures of resistance within historically specific patriarchal cultures" (84).

Interestingly, such a definition precludes Lesbian cultures except under patriarchy, suggesting that a Lesbian culture that successfully resisted patriarchy, perhaps to the point of replacing it, would evaporate, leaving . . . what? A loose gathering of cheerful, communal bisexuals, one might presume. Lesbian identity, for Ferguson as for us, inheres in women-only sexual relationships. However, as we pointed out earlier in this book, the term *identity* has several definitions, each making specific use of a notion of "sameness." Women who are sexually involved with other women, but who fail to identify as Lesbians – that is, who deny their sexuality and/or consequently refuse to recognize that others share it – will neither participate in the creation of Lesbian culture nor contribute to a Lesbian movement. They will perceive and describe their Lesbianism as a personal, bedroom issue, a stance that fosters isolation rather than sisterhood, and which creates subcultures rather than cultures. In contrast, we view a fully *realized* Lesbian identity as the product of a shared sexuality and self-acknowledgment as well as of identification with other Lesbians, and believe that our definition situates Lesbian identity historically *while* maintaining some (sexual) continuity across periods and groups. Unlike Ferguson, we regard Lesbian identity and Lesbian community as interdependent, and see both as critically important in creating and transmitting Lesbian culture.

Our (Julia's and Susan's) personal experiences in coming out at different periods in U.S. history (and therefore in very different contexts) indicate that Lesbians have begun to create our own cultures, cultures that in turn contribute toward a shared culture. When Julia came out in the 1950s, she emerged into a gay subculture, a world of gay males, bars, and role-playing. There she discovered others like her, made new friends, developed a social life, and experienced a sense of liberation and play. The gay male world, however, played into and off of gender stereotypes, alternating between emulating and camping them. Few Lesbian bars existed, and some gay male bars discouraged Lesbian patrons by mandating that they wear skirts (thereby effectively excluding all but the most "feminine" Lesbians).

In contrast, when Susan came out in the 1970s, it was into a Lesbian culture. Olivia Records had released record albums by Lesbian performers and with Lesbian lyrics. *Sinister Wisdom* and *Conditions* began publication; Lesbian presses (Out and Out Books, the Naiad Press, Daughters, and Diana Press) had a number of Lesbian titles in print. There were Lesbian potlucks, concerts, and dances; softball teams, organizations, and hotlines. Lesbian gatherings and Lesbian artifacts gave Susan a sense of empowerment as a Lesbian.

Julia has said in "The Lesbian Perspective" (1990:102) that as Lesbians we occupy a dual position, "simultaneously oppressed by a society in which we are unwanted and marginal and envisioning for ourselves a culture defined by our values, with Lesbian identity at its core." The essays in this part of *Sexual Practice / Textual Theory* suggest ways in which Lesbian writers and readers envision and move toward Lesbian culture, disrupting patriarchal (con)texts and creating Lesbian positions in/from which to speak. Lesbian aesthetics not only emerges from but serves to create Lesbian space.

Marks's "Lesbian Intertextuality" (published in *Homosexualities and French Literature: Cultural Contexts/Critical Texts* in 1979 and reprinted here) implicitly adopts an ambiguous, multilayered definition of "Lesbian," at least for Lesbian characters. Tracing historically the literary images of Lesbians available to Lesbian readers, Marks notes that "Women have always loved women" (this volume, p. 271) and that Lesbian characters have been drawn from "life" as well as "born in the words of the text" (p. 271). Historical figures who become fictional characters (re)create Lesbian history, providing us with a sense of a continuous past: "they play an important role in the reader's imagination" (p. 271). The use of real names validates Lesbian existence.

Marks analyzes alterations in "the Sappho model," contrasting images of Lesbians in literature by male French writers with those provided by women writers. In male prose, the Lesbian has been made to seem either incomprehensibly feminine or (as a tribade) imitative of men, a woman who "has value as a sexual being only in so far as she participates in the worship of the phallus" (p. 276) (since, in the male literary stereotype, the tribade's clitoris, like her sexual appetite, was depicted as unusually large, she at once copies grotesquely and validates heterosexuality). As a consequence, when French women writers produced texts in which "The experience of loving a woman . . . [was] *the* experience of awakening" (p. 277), critics misread them, judging them according to the patriarchal views of women (and therefore of Lesbians) prevalent during the period.

Feminist writers, however, have created Lesbian characters in order to "imagine a world before the domestication of woman, before the deliberate taming of her sexuality and her language. In such a world the woman who loves women and writes is the central figure in a new mythology" (pp. 277–78). What has happened in the development of Lesbian literature from Colette and Leduc is, according to Marks, nothing less than "a sexual and textual revolution" (p. 284). While each writer is connected in important ways to the social and literary contexts in which she writes/wrote, it is nonetheless true that the apocalyptic future Wittig envisions, unlike the "realistic" fictions crafted by Colette, has transformative power. Marks quotes a portion of Wittig's introduction to *Le corps lesbien* on the exclusion of men from Lesbian literature, the elimination of the male gaze in which the Lesbian is held as Object: "'Only the women's movement has proved capable of producing lesbian texts in a context of total rupture with masculine culture, texts written by women exclusively for women, careless of male approval'" (p. 286).

In *Le corps lesbien*, according to Marks, Wittig uses Lesbianism as a means of destroying male discourse and male stereotypes of women's bodies, preparing the way for the revolution that will undomesticate women. Wittig's I/you opposition is now entirely female, and patriarchal categories disappear, suggesting new possibilities for women in reading and in life.

For Marks, the Lesbian corpus draws upon the Lesbian body, transcending the stereotypes available in male texts, shattering patriarchal categories, transforming textual practices, and bringing about a sexual revolution. McNaron, too, ascribes transformative power to Lesbian sexuality. Because Lesbian sexuality is sexuality based on likeness, the Lesbian seeks images of sexual likeness in literature; finding them, she finds her sense of self affirmed by the texts she reads.

McNaron's essay is a personal history of her journey away from the heterosexual mirroring prescribed for women in patriarchal culture. Finding no self-affirming portrayals of Lesbians available, she began to read perversely, looking for evidence of likeness in characters and language not (consciously) formulated as Lesbian. Like Woolf in *A Room of One's Own*, McNaron suggests "a radical shift from gender opposition to gender likeness as a governing narrative and aesthetic principle" (this volume, p. 293). Her readings of (non-Lesbian) texts from Shakespeare and Milton to the television series *Cagney and Lacey* as well as those of coded Lesbian texts (by Dickinson and H.D.) demonstrate how each may be made to yield portrayals of the importance of same-sex bonding and celebratory images of Lesbian sexuality.

Seeking likeness is essential to the Lesbian reader response, then, because "images of sexual likeness . . . affirm our very existence" (p. 304) and provide an aesthetic that displaces heterosexuality as *the* formula for sexual passion. This new aesthetic may have personal and cultural consequences: it could "be of use not only to future lesbian artists but to any women wishing to affirm the power of their own sexuality or of their myriad connections with other women" (p. 305). Finally, looking into the mirror, Lesbians find self-definition, as La Belle (1988, quoted in McNaron 292) has suggested: "'The image in the glass is a "life companion," at once an otherness she can study and an intrinsic part of the ego as it comes into being. [The] wise woman . . . can use the alterity of the mirror image as a constituent of identity.'"

In contrast to McNaron, who describes Lesbian reading through the gentle visual metaphor of finding sameness in a mirror, Jeffner Allen uses physical violence as a metaphor for Lesbian poetics, in order to reflect its revolutionary potential. Lesbian writing is a war machine, according to Allen, capable of destroying patriarchal discourse and freeing women.

Allen's "Poetic Politics: How the Amazons Took the Acropolis" (reprinted from a 1988 issue of *Hypatia*) contends that, when Lesbian and feminist texts enter into discourse with each other, they "reconfigure fiction and reality," creating an "amazon intertextuality": ". . . by placing more and more female-defined signs in relation to each other, [they make] vanish patriarchal signifiers and signification," a field for creating "female freedom" (this volume, p. 318).

Juxtaposing the writing of Cixous and Wittig, Allen identifies the textual violence in both, violence that serves to eliminate the wedge between the poetic and the political. Although Cixous uses "a writing said to be feminine" and Wittig one that strikes at the dichotomies within sex and gender categories, the interactions between the two destroy language proper (patriarchal language) through the creation of female languages that "destabilize laws of gender-marked syntax and semantics" (p. 314).

The political power of an amazon poetics serves as a war machine, taking the Acropolis, blocking the "Athenian" wedge between poetics and politics, and turning "poetry's fictions into reality" (p. 310). Assimilationist readings of Lesbian and feminist writings, including the new French feminisms, says Allen, attempt to obscure the violence by which such writings provide "rigorous critique[s]" of male tradition or "turn it inside out until it is beyond recognition" (p. 311). The textual violence of the new French feminisms "emerges in spaces where patriarchal structures are absent–spaces which would expand and which are already female languages, cultures, histories" (p. 311).

For Parker, too, writing is a strategy, a strategy to establish Lesbian subjectivity. Because Lesbian identity structures Lesbian writing, Lesbian writing defies patriarchal ideologies of sex and gender, choosing the self as both subject and object. Lesbian writing occurs within a forbidden zone, one in which the "unspeakable" is spoken, creating Lesbian identity even as it "inscribes" it.

In "Under the Covers: A Synesthesia of Desire (Lesbian Translations)," Parker sees herself as engaged in double translation because, as a Lesbian, she must "translate the materiality of [her] daily experiences into an alien code." The male gaze is privileged in patriarchal code, but when she "speak[s]/write[s] as a lesbian the (gendered) center no longer holds." Creating a place for herself, "literally inventing new signs" (this volume, p. 322), Parker disrupts the patriarchal discourse that would relegate her to the margins. In so doing, she connects the intimate details of her personal life to a Lesbian aesthetic and to Lesbian identity – "how we know who we are" (p. 323).

Parker sees herself as passing, always, from fiction to fiction, from heterosexual to Lesbian, as "Jewish, North American, francophone, a student of signification" (p. 336), juggling signs and constituting her self as at once subject and object of desire, removing her self from the ideology of sex and gender. Careful to observe the differences among Lesbians, the identities that have constructed her, and which she constructs, Parker has learned "to play with the place of subjectivity that [she] covet[s]" (p. 324). Having chosen to speak as a Lesbian, having chosen "an identity that is unspeakable" (in the university where she works) (p. 323), she finds the plural subject even in herself, so as not to lose the richness of her identities or to obscure the identities of others.

In the course of her text, Parker explores the limitations imposed on her early life by sexism and heterosexualism, and the pain she has experienced since she chose "to be a lesbian" (p. 326) "in order to direct [her] political and sexual desire in a positive channel . . ." (p. 326). Citing Brossard, she notes that a Lesbian must constantly reinvent the world or risk erasure, and so sees herself constantly negotiating, passing back and forth across texts, daily using an equation to "plot a trajectory of lesbian desire" (p. 324).

To write as a Lesbian is to write from no space, from forbidden territory, in defiance of silence. The Lesbian identity is a structure, the Lesbian subject a strategy:

Resonating with (forbidden) joy and fear, LESBIAN draws power. . . . [As a primary identity it] is a structure or field that compels disruptive patterns of thinking and imagining. . . . To write (as a) lesbian is not to use language as a wo/man, but to inscribe a subject of desire that has rarely been spoken. . . . The lesbian subject has, of course, no dimensional existence as a physical fact, but is rather an intellectual/psychic strategy. Which is not to deny my body or the material circumstances of lesbian lives. (p. 328)

As Lesbian writing produces relationships between the body, the spirit, and the world, Parker writes and is written by Lesbian texts, in both English and French. Her present fiction is that her writing invents "those who are waiting to be born" (p. 330), placing her choice (of writing as Lesbian) within Brossard's "spiral of luminous energy, which encodes lesbian memory and connects us with our (radical) root, transmutes into a resonating crucible, a field and song of vision" (p. 331).

This part of the book concludes with an annotated partial bibliography of Lesbian literary criticism published in English from 1976 to 1989. In providing a summary and commentary on criticism readily available through major libraries, Garber herself contributes toward the emerging fields she documents – those of Lesbian writing, criticism, and publishing in Lesbian contexts.

15

Elaine Marks

Lesbian Intertextuality

So the first problem of mythic thought is that women must be domesticated.

Claude Lévi-Strauss

Every text is absorption and transformation of a multiplicity of other texts.

Julia Kristeva

Women have always loved women. The investigation and quarrels about causes do not interest me here, although in other contexts they may illuminate and incite. My corpus, composed of written texts, fiction and nonfiction, many fragments, by women and men, mostly French, from Sappho through Baudelaire to Wittig (the Lesbos-Paris axis), proposes other enigmas. Through a network of anecdotes – formalized gossip that gives pleasure – and proper names – those of the protagonists who transmit and receive messages – I shall attempt to elucidate models and impose prophetic fictions.[1]

WHO'S WHO

Fictional characters are of two kinds. There are those who are born in the words of the text and those whose existence in a text is due to a prior existence in what it is difficult not to call "life." Most women writers and many famous and infamous women in history have become fictional characters of the second kind. Because of their double heritage they play an important role in the reader's imagination. It would be insufficient to talk about lesbianism and literature in France and mention only the better-known characters.[2] Space must also be allotted for rumor about Louise Labé and Clémence de Bourges, the Duchesse de Berry and Mlle de Mouchy, Marie Antoinette and Mme de Lamballe, George Sand and Marie Dorval, Germaine de Staël and Juliette Récamier, as well as for facts about Adrienne Mounier and Sylvia Beach, Marie Laurencin and Suzanne Morand, Colette and the Marquise de Belbeuf, Lucie Delarue-Mardrus and Germaine de Castro, Natalie Clifford-Barney and a host of women including Renée Vivien, Liane de Pougy, Romaine Brooks, the Duchesse de Clermont-Tonnerre, Dolly Wilde.

Name-dropping in this instance is an essential preliminary activity, for if Gomorrah, as Colette observed in a criticism of Proust, is not nearly as vast or as well organized as Sodom, it is nonetheless a small, cohesive world in which connections between bed and text are numerous. This is particularly true during the *belle époque,* when, in the wake of an emerging feminist movement, women writers, many of whom were lesbian, appeared on the French literary scene. They came from America and England, from the demimonde, from the bourgeoisie. A central figure in this constellation of "Sapho 1900, Sapho cent pour cent"[3] is Natalie Clifford-Barney, an American living in Paris who had great wealth, many paramours, and a prestigious salon. She was a crossroads of lesbian associations and appeared, barely fictionalized, in the texts of many of the writers of the period: as Moonbeam and Miss Flossie in Liane de Pougy's *Idylle saphique* (1901), as Miss Flossie in Colette's *Claudine s'en va* (1903), as Lorély in Renée Vivien's *Une femme m'apparut* (1904), as Geraldine O'Brookomore in Ronald Firbank's *Inclinations* (1916), as the Amazon in Rémy de Gourmont's *Lettres intimes à l'amazone* (1927), as Evangeline Musset in Djuna Barnes's *Ladies Almanack* (1928), as Valérie Seymour in Radclyffe Hall's *The Well of Loneliness* (1928), as Laurette in Lucie Delarue-Mardrus's *L'ange et le pervers* (1934). Only George Sand has been the imputed model for as many literary heroines.

The Natalie Clifford-Barney connection takes us farther afield to Marie Souvestre, whose fashionable boarding schools for girls – Les Ruches at Fontainebleau and Allenswood near Wimbledon Common – have been used as referents in texts as diverse as Eleanor Roosevelt's *This is My Story* (1939), Dorothy Strachey Bussy's *Olivia* (1941), and Michael Holroyd's biography of Lytton Strachey (1968). Natalie Clifford-Barney attended Les Ruches after Marie Souvestre had left France for England, but she was already involved in the kind of *amitié passionnée* that precipitated Marie Souvestre's departure. Through an early American lover, Eva Palmer, mentioned by Renée Vivien in *Une femme m'apparut* and by Colette in *Mes apprentissages* (1936), Natalie Clifford-Barney was invited to visit Bryn Mawr College. Gertrude Stein, whom she knew, but not intimately, in Paris, used the lesbian relationship between M. Carey Thomas, president of Bryn Mawr, and Mary Gwinn in one of her first novels, *Fernhurst* (1904–1905, published in 1971). Bertrand Russell also refers to the intense Bryn

Mawr scene in the first volume of his autobiography (1967). In the convergence of anecdotes and proper names a paradigm emerges. From Natalie Clifford-Barney to Marie Souvestre and M. Carey Thomas, from Parisian alcoves to a woman's school or college, we are obliged to acknowledge the inevitable presence of the Sappho model.

THE SAPPHO MODEL

Sapho, Sappho, Psappha, Psappho, the lesbian from Lesbos. A confusion of facts, a profusion of semantic and phonemic connotations emanate from and surround the name. The small, ugly, lewd nymphomaniac and the beautiful poetess and muse coexist in the mind of the contemporary reader. They are part of a fragmented tradition through which we can formulate the outlines of a myth intended, like so many others, to domesticate woman's sexuality as well as, in this particular case, her relation to language.

Sappho and her island Lesbos are omnipresent in literature about women loving women, whatever the gender or sexual preference of the writer and whether or not Sappho and her island are explicitly named. Through her own poetic fragments she is the unwitting initiator of three apparently distinct models, which have, in fact, a common origin: the older woman who seduces beautiful young girls, usually in a school or by extension in a convent or bordello; the older woman who commits suicide because her love for a younger man is unrequited; the woman poet as disembodied muse. The first model has its origin in those poems in which Sappho, the persona, speaks about the young women – Atthis, Anactoria, Gongyla – whom she desires. In the Greek and Latin literature that came after Sappho and in many later European texts this model, with its disguised references to the mother-daughter incest taboo, was discarded, except for its pornographic, comic value, in favor of the two others more palatable to the transmitters of a patriarchal code. It was Plato who, in referring to her as the tenth muse, (in an epigram that may be apocryphal) removed Sappho from the sexual arena, thereby allowing for the greatness of her poetry. Ovid, in the fifteenth and last letter of his *Heroides*, "Sappho and Phaon," codified into one legend the double model of Sappho the poet and Sappho the woman burning with corporeal lust who, because of her desperate love for Phaon, leapt from the Leucadian cliffs into the sea. The suicide model includes such prominent progeny as Phaedra and Dido and should not be forgotten in the larger corpus of lesbian intertextuality.

Although there is no evidence in Sappho's poems to corroborate the notion that she did indeed have a school, religious or secular, for young women, the gynaeceum, ruled by the seductive or seducing teacher has become, since the eighteenth century, the preferred locus for most fictions about women loving women. The conventions of this topos are simple and limited, signifying in their constraints the marginal status of lesbians and lesbianism. In general men play secondary roles as fathers, spiritual advisers, or intrusive suitors. The younger woman, whose point of view usually dominates, is always passionate and innocent. If, as is usually the case when the author of the text is a woman, it is the younger woman who falls in love, the narrative is structured so as to insist on this love as an awakening. The older woman as object of the younger woman's desire is restrained and admirable, beautiful and cultivated. If the older woman plays the role of seducer-corrupter, as she does in texts written by men, she is intense and often overtly hysterical (although this does not prevent her from being admirable in her intensity). Whoever plays the aggressive role, the exchanges between the older and the younger woman are reminiscent of a mother-daughter relationship. The mother of the younger woman is either dead or in some explicit way inadequate. Her absence is implied in the young woman's insistent need for a good-night kiss. The gynaeceum, particularly when it is represented by a school, also controls time. Time limits are set by the school calendar whose inexorable end announces the fatal separation, which may involve a death. Temporal structures reiterate the almost universally accepted notion that a schoolgirl crush is but a phase in the emotional development of the young woman, something that will pass. The denouement in these lesbian fairy tales is often brought about by a public event during which private passions explode.

The lesbian fairy tale based on the Sappho model is written by men of letters in the eighteenth and nineteenth centuries and by women and men of letters in the twentieth. I have chosen the term fairy tale in order to accentuate the distance from an apparent, transparent "real" and to insist on structural similarities between diverse fictions: the stock characters and stock situations; the rude or blissful awakening of sleeping beauty; the lesbian as good or bad fairy who is fate. The system of relationships in lesbian fairy tales, the reiterated network of obsessions reinforce an ideological system of stereotypes based on a synthesis of religious and psychological dogma.

Some of the texts that must be included within the Sappho model, whether they are written by women or by men, whether or not the gynaeceum is the locus, present, in strikingly similar terms, an explicit apology for lesbianism: the "Apologie de la secte anandryne" in *L'espion anglais,* "Delphine et Hippolyte," *L'idylle saphique, Claudine en ménage,* passages in *Le pur et l'impur* and the *Stances à Sophie.* This apology, made by a female character, is not to be understood as authorial endorsement of women loving women; on the contrary, the intention may be ironic. But it does point to a specific mode of discourse that is a significant feature of lesbian intertextuality.

The "Apologie de la secte anandryne" contains the first and most complete formulation of this discourse. The text is composed of a speech purportedly delivered on 28 March 1778 by Mlle de Raucourt, who was in fact a celebrated actress, lesbian, and active member of the flourishing *secte des anandrynes*. Mlle de Raucourt is a narrator thrice removed in the chain of reporting, since it is Mlle Sapho who is telling her story to a male narrator who is writing it to a friend and to the reader. This combination of remote narrative distance with the use of characters for whom there are referents beyond the text is frequent in writing about lesbians. Brantôme employs similar devices in his *Vie des dames galantes* and Colette in *Le pur et l'impur*. Lesbianism often appears in literature as something about which one has heard and perhaps, because lesbianism is considered unusual, it requires the kind of validation that only real names can confer.

The speech forms part of the initiation rite during which Mlle Sapho, a novice, is presented to the other members of the sect by her mother-teacher Mme de Furiel. (The mother-daughter, teacher-pupil categories are referred to constantly, as is the notion of model. The mother-teacher incubus is a model for the daughter-pupil succubus, who will in turn become a model.) The terms of the argument are quite simple: men, although they are initially exciting, provide inadequate physical and moral satisfaction; men are responsible for woman's physical suffering both in lovemaking and in the pains of childbirth: "Kisses will discolor your face, caresses will wither your breasts, your belly will lose its elasticity through pregnancies, your secret charms will be ruined by childbirth."[4] Men cause women mental suffering as well because they tire quickly of their wives. Heterosexuality is presented by means of such words as "pain," "blood," "slaughter," "care," "anxiety," "torment"; man is "perfidious," "fickle," "a cheat." The most important point in the argument is not, however, the perfidy of men but the glorification of the pleasures "true, pure, long-lasting and without remorse" ("Apologie," 170) that exist between women: "In the intimacy between women there are no frightening and painful preliminaries; everything is pleasure (*jouissance*); each day, each hour, each minute this attachment is easily renewed; it is like waves of love which follow each other unceasingly as do those of the sea" (271). This complete harmony, this constant pleasure, does not exist, according to the apology, between women and men. Delphine delivers the same message to Hippolyte, Miss Flossie to Annhine, Claudine and Rézi to each other. Colette suggests it, tentatively, in *Le pur et l'impur* and then retracts it. The possibility of this paradise of oceanic bliss can only occur in a woman's world, between *sisters* (265).

The "Apologie de la secte anandryne" is the one text in the corpus I have consulted that supplements this defense of lesbianism with an idyllic image of the continuity of the cult, the vision of a utopia in which "maternal tenderness" replaces the "unrestrained passion of men" (276), in which wealth is shared, in which elegance of dress and abundance of jewels are requisites of beauty and useful in proselytizing. The evangelical spirit is strong in the "Apologie de la secte anandryne." The goal of the sect is the conversion of all women, particularly aristocratic women, to lesbianism because lesbianism is the most natural, the most virtuous, and the most pleasurable way of life. This is a unique apology, an extreme and rare formulation of the Sappho model in which lesbianism has an equally glorious past, present, and future. I cannot help but wonder about the identity of the unknown author.

FROM LASCIVIOUS TRIBADE TO REVOLUTIONARY SIGNIFIER

Images of the lesbian are related in any given time and place to prevalent images of women. They are influenced by the same fear, loathing, or ignorance of female sexuality apparently subsumed by male (and in their wake female) psyches under the broader category, mysteries of life and death, or universal misogyny and gynophobia. From Martial to Brantôme the lesbian character is, within the context of the male anecdote, grotesque, an exaggeratedly comic version of the Sappho model reduced to her sexual preference. She is generally referred to as a tribade, from the Greek verb *tribadein,* meaning to rub. The tribade lies on top of her partner, whom she rubs with her unusually large clitoris. The tribade is lascivious because she enjoys what she does and grotesque because she imitates a man. The tribade is a social menace because, so the rumor runs within the text, she often succeeds. The burning question thus arises: does one woman lying on top of another and rubbing constitute adultery? By means of this male obsession the tribade is assimilated into accepted patterns of heterosexuality and enters into fiction. In the texts of Martial, Lucian, and Brantôme, who incorporates and recapitulates his predecessors, the tribade is always seen at a distance; she is talked about, reported on, spied on. This distance reinforces her status as a weird, comic object. But were it not for the hyperbolic and hypothetical size of her clitoris she would be completely incomprehensible. The tribade has value as a sexual being only insofar as she participates in the worship of the phallus. The phallus is always present as prime mover in the lesbian discourse of male scriptors.

The lesbian who appears in prose texts by male writers of the eighteenth, nineteenth, and twentieth centuries may be a possessed hysteric, a charismatic evangelist, or a lascivious glutton guilty of profaning either the law of God or the natural law or both. She tries to seduce a younger woman and sometimes succeeds. She is often responsible for the death of a male figure. She is always an outlaw, a powerful challenge to one of society's most cherished principles, sexual order. The world of the text in which she appears is immediately thrown into confusion. The confusion ends with her death or disappearance, or that of her victim, or of her male antagonist. From Martial's Bassa and Lucian's Megilla, model tribades of antiquity, to the lesbians of Diderot, Balzac, Proust, and Sartre, the female homosexual incarnating the Sappho model has moved from a small corner of the canvas to a central position. The comic, lascivious tribade lives on in the demonic corrupter, but in general the imitation of the male is less pronounced than the affirmation of incomprehensible femininity.

The lesbian in lyric poetry written by men, from Pontus de Tyard's "Elégie pour une dame énamourée d'une autre dame" to Pierre Louÿs's *Chansons de Bilitis,* bears little resemblance to her prose sister. The discourse on lesbians in prose narrative tends to reproduce some culturally accepted derogatory point of view on women loving women, whereas the lyric poem tends to represent the lesbian as synonymous with a mysterious world of feminine pleasure. The prose narrative usually uses the lesbian for social or psychological censorious reporting on aberrant female behavior; the lyric poem projects through the lesbian an unattainable dream of erotic love in the absence of the censor.

A major thematic transformation takes place when women begin to write about women loving women. The experience of loving a woman is, for the narrative voice, *the* experience of awakening, the revelation of an unknown, unsuspected world which, once glimpsed, can never be ignored. It is a momentous discovery whose importance within the text and beyond was until recently obscured by the weighty screen of psychological misreadings. Women's narratives were examined for signs of deviant behavior that would reveal simplified, vulgarized Freudian categories. The lesbian had to be a pre-Oedipal polymorphous perverse child, full of rage because of an early, deprived relationship with the mother, obsessed with death, voraciously hungry for love, exorbitantly demanding and dependent. Critics reveled in images of alimentary deprivation that would prove the prevalence of the oral element in the affective life of the lesbian character. Indeed, whatever happened to the lesbian within the text, she was submerged from without by the ruling orthodoxy.

Recent feminist critics have reversed these judgments, turning condemnation of regressive behavior into exploration of uncharted modes of affectivity. Hysteria and oceanic feeling are exalted. The Minoan-Mycenean civilization that preceded the Oedipal institution of patriarchal law is glorified. What began a long time ago as the domestication of Sappho has become a concerted effort to imagine a world before the domestication of women, before the deliberate taming of her sexuality and her language. In such a world the woman who loves women and writes is the central figure in a new mythology.

COLETTE, THE FOREMOTHER

Colette, the foremother, left God out and was accused by the morally serious and believing of frivolity. Critics, female and male, took their revenge. Silence or banter surrounded her six-year liaison with the Marquise de Belbeuf. The text which she considered to be her most important, *Le pur et l'impur,* was either ignored or treated as a bizarre excrescence. The preponderant role played by women, alone and together, in her writings, as mothers and daughters, as sisters, as friends, as lovers, received less recognition than the more obvious but fundamentally less important relationships between women and men. Colette occupies a privileged place and therefore takes up most space in a study of lesbian intertextuality. Her texts, like Brantôme's *Vie des dames galantes,* recapitulate an earlier tradition, but they also announce new departures. In 1900, for the first time since Sappho, the narrator Claudine in *Claudine à l'école* looks at another woman as an object of pleasure and without any excuses describes her pleasure. A great revolution had begun:

She is like a cat caressing, delicate and sensitive, incredibly winning. I like to look at her pink little blond's face, her golden eyes with their curly lashes. Beautiful eyes that are always ready to smile! They oblige the young men to turn around when she goes out. Often, while we are chatting at the door of her excited little class, Mlle Sergent walks past us to go to her room, without a word, staring at us with a jealous, searching gaze. Her silence tells my new friend and me that she is furious at seeing us get on so well together.[5]

Everyone is looking at Aimée Lanthenay: Claudine, the young boys, Mlle Sergent. Voyeurism, in contrast to what transpires in male novels, is neither secret nor cerebral. It is a public activity. The originality of Claudine's voyeurism is that it is directly related to her appetites. What is less original are Claudine's insolence and impertinence, the marks of the titillated and titillating schoolgirl whose desire for Aimée and later for Rézi recalls the presence of the lesbian in many turn-of-the-century texts, a male creation, the summum of naughtiness.

From Colette's Claudine to Violette Leduc's Je and Thérèse, to Monique Wittig's J/e, female voyeurism gains in intensity as it focuses on the relation between the self and the other. At the same time the stereotypical posturing of the curious adolescent characteristic of Claudine progressively diminishes, finally disappears. The movement from Claudine to J/e is a movement from self-consciousness in culture to self-consciousness in writing, from an attempt at portraying new attitudes in an old language to an attempt at creating a language capable of speaking the unspoken in Western literature – female sexuality with woman as namer.

"Lesbian" is a word the narrator "Colette" never uses, and "homosexual" is reserved for men. Her female characters who are attracted to women have no labels. They do, however, fall into two major, quite traditional groups: the impudent, perverse younger woman like Claudine and perhaps Renée Vivien; the mannish woman like the Baronne de la Berche in *La fin de Chéri* (1926) or la Chevalière in *Le pur et l'impur*. The narrator's attitude toward them oscillates between a maternalistic protection – protection from the uncomprehending male, protection from the "ordinary reader" who may be smirking – and a series of mild attacks in which these women are variously seen as "childish," "infantile," "adolescent," "crude," "promiscuous," or "deluded." Within this spectrum female homosexuality is sanctified by comparisons to the mother-daughter relationship. This occurs initially and most powerfully in "Nuit blanche," a prose poem in *Les vrilles de la vigne* (1908):

Because I know that then you will tighten your embrace and that if the rocking of your arms does not calm me, your kisses will become more tenacious, your hands more loving, and that you will give me pleasure as an aid, as a supreme exorcism which will drive out the demons of fever, of anger, of unrest . . . You will give me pleasure, leaning over me, your eyes full of maternal solicitude, you who are seeking in your passionate friend, for the child you never had.[6]

All of "Colette's" empathic attitudes toward women loving women are contained within this image and will be repeated in nonlesbian situations: in the relationships between "Colette" and "Sido," between Chéri and Léa, between all those who love passionately and exclusively. What is involved is someone younger needing protection, someone older offering a refuge and caring. The younger person receives pleasure, but the older person who gives pleasure is searching. The quest is not for the mother, the mother is always there, but for the child. The female figure who dominates in Colette's female hierarchy is the mother figure, Sido crying, "Where are the children?" It is also the role of the mother who loves to preside over the sexual ritual, which without her presence is incomplete.

Le pur et l'impur restates all the forms of lesbianism and all the narrative commentary on women loving women that appear in Colette's texts from 1900 to 1932. Colette is writing with and against Marcel Proust. It is obvious that the publication of *A la recherche du temps perdu* encouraged her both to deal directly with homosexuality, female and male, and to present images of female homosexuality different from Proust's febrile Gomorrah. Within the French literary tradition *Le pur et l'impur* takes its place in the exclusive company of André Gide's *Corydon* (1924) and the overture of Proust's *Sodome et Gomorrhe* (1922) as a rare example of explicit narrative commentary on homosexuality. "Renée Vivien," one of the texts included in *Le pur et l'impur*, was published in a limited edition in 1928. The mid- and late 1920s, particularly in England, were *anni mirabili* for novels by women that depict important lesbian characters or references to women loving women. It is unlikely that Colette was familiar with Virginia Woolf's *Mrs. Dalloway* (1925) or her *Orlando* (1928), or with Rosamund Lehmann's *Dusty Answer* (1927), but she did know of Radclyffe Hall's *The Well of Loneliness* (1928), and she obviously knew the screen version of Christa Winsloë's *Mädchen in Uniforme* (1931), for which she wrote the French subtitles.

Le pur et l'impur is a restless text. The narrator "Colette" struggles to maintain a deliberate and decent distance through time, texts, and translations from the variety of pseudonymous women loving women, the exotic, extinct species on which she reports: la Chevalière, Renée Vivien, Amalia X———, Lucienne de ———, and the Ladies of Llangollen. "Colette" intrudes on and retreats from the text, which is an organized mélange of reporting (anecdotes, portraits) and commentary (maxims and generalizations). The women who love women occupy the central parts of *Le pur et l'impur*. They are preceded by Charlotte, the woman who feigns pleasure to please her young male lover, and Don Juan, who gives, according to his accounting, more than he receives, and followed by male homosexuals whose "theatrical cynicism" and "childishness" are redeemed by their capacity, which the narrator insists lesbians lack, to forget the other sex completely. The only couple in *Le pur et l'impur* to receive the narrator's benediction and admiration is the couple formed by two men. "I find it in me to see in pederasty a kind of legitimacy and to acknowledge its eternal character."[7] In the volume, which "will treat sadly of pleasure" (31), this is the unique relationship that is not depicted by the narrator as an unequal exchange: one partner giving, the other receiving, in an ultimately self-destructive pattern.

Whether it be in the occasional discordance between narrative commentary and reporting, or in the shifts of tone from lyrical to ironic to lyrical, or in the sudden eruptions of moral and psychological rhetoric, the text, like the androgyne and like Renée Vivien, "wanders." The exclusive text abounds in contradictions and paradoxes that reflect the narrator's variable points of view about women loving women, about what constitutes feminine/masculine behavior. Ambiguity is sustained on all levels of the text. From the mixture of real and pseudonymous anthroponyms – "Colette," Marguerite Moreno, la Chevalière – emanates a genre ambiguity (is it autobiography? is it fiction?) that mirrors the sexual ambiguity (is it female? is it male?). There is an implied equivalence between textual and sexual androgyny and travesty. The pages on la Chevalière and her group constitute an indeterminate text in which older, aristocratic women in tuxedos, wearing monocles, instruct their lower-class protégées in the ways of the respectable world. The narrator employs "these women" to insist on the sadness (her point of view), not the ridicule (but she has an eye for that too), of their impossible masculine masquerade and to reveal their ineradicable appurtenance to a woman's world. They gather together "uneasy," "haunted," in a cellar restaurant in Montmartre, seeking "a refuge, warmth and darkness" (169). There, safe temporarily from male intrusion, they indulge in an activity more subversive than love-making: they communicate with each other in woman's language. "I reveled in the admirable quickness of their half-spoken language, the exchange of threats, of promises, as if, once the slow-thinking male had been banished, every message from woman to woman became clear and overwhelming, restricted to a small but infallible number of signs" (69). "Slow-thinking" but dangerous, the image of the heterosexual male emerges in the guise of a retarded brute whose shadow is always present in the narrator's commentary as a reminder to her and to the reader of the certain danger that lurks outside and within "these women." The narrator's pleasure in the spectacle of women signaling together partially corrects the constant menace and the pervasive sadness that permeate the text. It is as if, near the end of the tour, the guide discovered a fragment of what it was she had been looking for initially and had been unable to locate because the site was so cluttered. When the male is removed, when the subterranean space is occupied uniquely by la Chevalière and her group (which includes the narrator-guide), the masks fall, the women temporarily, hesitantly, come out.

The transition in the text from la Chevalière to Renée Vivien is from a nonliterary to a literary milieu of the *belle époque* and from a shy discreet butch to a vulgar *femme de lettres*. The narrator quite clearly prefers, in its purity, the unwritten, "half-spoken" woman's language of la Chevalière and her group to the "cynical opinions" and the sentimental imitative poetry of Renée Vivien. The third category of women who love women is represented by Amalia X——— and Lucienne de ———, the fourth by the Ladies of Llangollen. It is as if the narrator were testing herself against the portraits of these women in order to determine whether or not she was a lesbian, in order to determine the limits of her understanding and her compassion. "Colette's" central obsession is with the women who imitate men (la Chevalière, Lucienne de ———, Lady Eleanor Butler) and thereby violate what would seem to be the narrator's fantasm of an exclusively woman's world. "You see, when a woman remains a woman, she is a complete human being. She lacks nothing, even insofar as her *amie* is concerned. But if she ever gets it into her head to try to be a man, then she's grotesque. What is more ridiculous, what is sadder, than a woman pretending to be a man?" (86). This judgment, pronounced by the wise Amalia X———, an aging Tunisian Jewess who functions here as a second narrator, represents, I think, the simplest but most profound of "Colette's" conclusions. The woman who imitates a man, either in love or in literature, is not an acceptable model for a woman who loves women.

Because the narrator saves them for the end, the reader assumes that the Ladies of Llangollen will be the uniquely successful couple. But the Ladies of Llangollen are set up to fall from the narrator's grace in the course of her writing about them. The pastoral tone of the introductory hymn to the Ladies' mutual love – "I want to speak with dignity, that is, with warmth, of what I call the noble season of feminine passion" (91) – is not sustained. The idyllic aura that surrounds the multiple images of togetherness, "the magic of this radiant friendship," is dissipated slowly by a change in point of view. Light mockery transforms the perfect couple into a pathetic, fragile couple. The final step is the destruction by implication and direct castigation of the original ideal image. "As usual with perfectly happy people, the younger woman neglected all means of expression and, mute, became a sweet shadow. She was no longer Sarah Ponsonby, but a part of that double person called 'we.' She even lost her name, which Lady Eleanor almost never mentioned in the diary. From then on she was called 'Beloved' and 'Better Half' and 'Delight of my heart'" (97). "Colette" interpellates Lady Eleanor Butler and accuses her of three crimes: eliminating Sarah Ponsonby's identity, behaving like a man, and creating, through her diary, a fabulous fiction. The narrator challenges "stouthearted Eleanor's" version of the Ladies of Llangollen by imagining Sarah Ponsonby's subversive diary. The text ends with a curious reversal: a short letter written by Sarah Ponsonby after the death of Lady Eleanor Butler in which she speaks neither of her sorrow nor of her lost friend but, like Colette's mother "Sido" in *La naissance du jour* (1928), of flowers that may bloom. Although "Colette" is obliged to accept the report of the Ladies of Llangollen's fifty-year idyll, her comments betray her suspicion that it was a romantic delusion systematically sustained by Lady Eleanor Butler through her diary. But if the couple composed of women together is doomed a priori, the woman alone who loves women is privileged. She has for "Colette" a *magie suggestive* that belongs to the mother-teacher-seducer exemplified by "Sido" and "Colette" herself, the signifiers of the Sappho model.

The narrator's moral and psychological conclusions, which the reader distills from the totality of the text, imply that "Colette" is not nearly as interested in lesbians as she is in women and the possibilities of their survival. She attempts to locate, through an exploration of female sexual behavior and frequent modulations in point of view, what apparently works, what really goes on and at what price. Unlike her successors in the examination of the "dark continent" of female sexuality, Violette Leduc or Monique Wittig, Colette does not focus on lovemaking or the celebration of the female body. Rather she insists throughout *Le pur et l'impur* that "In no way is it passion that fosters the devotion of two women, but rather a feeling of kinship" (92), by which she means "similarities." Women who love women come together in Colette's world because they are fleeing from a painful experience with a man and are looking for a *retraite sentimentale*, "Sido's" warmth with its attendant garden and animals. Lesbianism is a *pis aller*. It is a copy of either mother-daughter or male-female love or both.

If homosexual and heterosexual coupling are unsatisfactory, if promiscuity is undesirable, then what remains is the single woman writing alone about woman's sexuality. The narrator "Colette" is almost never implicated in sexual activity, but is always, like her male predecessors, reporting on the activities of other women. When she removes the Sappho model from the schoolroom, she keeps it for herself. In Colette's ultimate expression of the Sappho model, Sappho fills her erotic needs through her creations and her readers.

THE DEATH OF GOD/THE BIRTH OF THE LESBIAN-FEMINIST

There is no one person in or out of fiction who represents a stronger challenge to the Judeo-Christian tradition, to patriarchy and phallocentrism, than the lesbian-feminist. After the end-of-the-century wailings over the death of the ideal God, after the aesthetic retreats and constructions of the dandies in life and art, after the liberation of the male imagination through surrealist techniques, after the existentialist images of male fraternity – the band of courageous brothers facing nothingness together, or battle, and creating heroic portraits of man's dignity, man's fate, man's hope – the women began, ever so slowly, to see connections between production and reproduction, to masturbate consciously, to explore the "dark continent," and to write. The most subversive voices of the century are, and will be, in their texts. Because they are trying to displace the phallus, they propose a new pleasure and a new imagery. They propose new relationships to gender and pronouns, to the jejune past, the hysterical present, and the luminous future. They do not intend to save the world because salvation died with God, but to create hyperbolic, sensuous fictions that illuminate possibilities for the woman as narrator and the woman as reader.

What breaks down in this new prophetic universe is the God-ruled phallologocentric system and the imaginative sensibility it exploited. As outsiders to traditional gender semiotics, innovative lesbian-feminist writers invent new forms. The established relations between the traditional female/male love story and the mythology used to transmit the story are no longer operative. The veneration of male figures and the need for their approbation disappear and with them the old categories of patriarchal solid space and past time. The elimination of the female/male opposition within the text does not, of course, eliminate feminine/masculine as biological entities or cultural signs, but the absence of the masculine figure from the text makes it possible to diminish a primary source of conflict and to reinterpret such historically male-created negative images of femininity as the Medusa, the witch, or the hysteric. The I/you opposition remains, but the other is now also familiar, familial – a sister, a friend.

The differences that we find in the textual representation of female homosexuality in Colette, in Violette Leduc, and in Monique Wittig are related significantly to the literary and social codes of the periods in which these writers began to write. There would seem to be homology between Colette and the *belle époque*, between Leduc and the flowering of French existentialism, between Wittig and the formalist-feminist movements of the late sixties and early seventies. Colette's mother figures, Leduc's young schoolgirls, and Wittig's Amazon women recall and reproduce the *monstres sacrés* of the theater world, the precocious, anguished young women who haunted the existentialist cafés, the romantic feminists and revolutionary feminists of the French women's liberation movement. The temporal distance between the narrative "I" and the other or others is also revealing: "Colette" is always looking back nostalgically to an exotic past in which women dominated the stage; Leduc as "I" struggles and desires in a present perfect; Wittig's *guérillères* and slashed "I" are installed in an eternal repetitive present that is already from the reader's point of view an apocalyptic future. Colette tells a fairly traditional story, remaining within the narrative norms established by nineteenth-century "realistic" fiction. Leduc also remains within this tradition, although she disrupts it thematically by insisting explicitly on the narrator's subjectivity, on her deepest feelings of shame and desire. Wittig, on the contrary, is working within another tradition in which the narrative conventions of plot and character have been, like the first person J/e, dismembered.

From Colette through Leduc to Wittig a sexual and textual revolution has taken place. The lesbian in literature has undergone a radical transformation from impertinent young woman, fragile couple, solitary writer, ecstatic schoolgirl, to aggressive lover and namer. The images recurrent in Colette's texts of two women seeking refuge or lying voluptuously in each other's arms and the lyrical descriptions of passionate adolescent lovemaking in Leduc's novels bear little resemblance to the gluttonous cannibalism of Wittig's truncated, anonymous J/e. Only the presence of the Sappho model remains constant, although the manner in which it informs the text is very different in *Le pur et l'impur* from what it is in *La bâtarde* and *Thérèse et Isabelle* or *Le corps lesbien*. In *Le pur et l'impur,* Sappho is mentioned only once in the derogatory phrase "the Sapphos met by chance" (93). In *La bâtarde* and *Thérèse et Isabelle*, Sappho is never mentioned, and in *Le corps lesbien*, Sappho, the ruling muse, is invoked twenty-two times. The frequency of the name is almost as great as in the poems of Renée Vivien. But if Sappho's name is absent from *La bâtarde* and *Thérèse et Isabelle*, Sappho is inevitably present in the gynaeceum in which the protagonists spend their time seeking each other and making love. Sappho is also present in the narrator's passion for her mother, a passion which, in *La bâtarde*, has as its obsessive maternal object the grandmother and, in the later volumes of Leduc's autobiography, is focused on Simone de Beauvoir. But more importantly Sappho dominates intertextually as she does in *Le corps lesbien*, through the insistence on the physical symptoms of desire, the visceral awareness of the female body, and the endless repetitions. In Sappho's own fragments the symptomatology of love, expressed by such rhetorical devices of repetition as anaphora and anadiplosis, focuses on the exchange between psyche and soma.

Repetition underlines the obsessive nature of Sappho's, Leduc's, and Wittig's texts and reveals the writers' fantasms. But these texts go beyond idiosyncratic sexual preferences toward the creation of a new mythology in which the female body is undomesticated: "If I meet you suddenly, I can't speak – my tongue is broken; a thin flame runs under my skin; seeing nothing, hearing only my own ears drumming, I drip with sweat; trembling shakes my body and I turn paler than dry grass. At such times death isn't far from me."[8]

To undomesticate women would mean to change the relationship between nature and culture and seriously to alter the configuration of culture as we knew it. This can only be realized through the creation of images powerful enough to impress themselves on the reader's mind and to resist the pressures of misinterpretation. Sappho's texts provided the elements for a new perception of female reality, but representatives of the dominant culture fashioned from these elements the myth of romantic love, using the millennial equivalence between woman and death. Sappho is much more concrete in her poetry. She is suggesting equivalences between the physical symptoms of desire and the physical symptoms of death, not between Eros and Thanatos. The female body's initial undomestication takes place in Sappho's texts. The body and its reactions are given poetic importance. The female body and the female persona's attitudes might have become a legitimate topos for lyric poetry. But the domestication process set in almost immediately, and Sappho's texts by both conscious and unconscious misinterpretations were incorporated into a tradition in which the independence of the female body was taboo.

There were, between Sappho and Violette Leduc, women writers who attempted to liberate women from the most obvious legal and social injustices. And although some of these writers – Christine de Pisan, Germaine de Staël, George Sand, Colette – did attack a fundamental source of woman's plight, sexual oppression, they never presented sufficiently challenging counterimages. It may well be that only a committed lesbian-feminist writer can, within our culture, succeed in transmitting cogent images of undomesticated women. In her preface to the English edition of *Le corps lesbien*, Monique Wittig situates her text among others that have lesbianism as their theme:

a theme which cannot even be described as taboo, for it has no real existence in the history of literature. Male homosexual literature has a past, it has a present. The lesbians, for their part, are silent – just as all women are as women at all levels. When one has read the poems of Sappho, Radclyffe Hall's *Well of Loneliness*, the poems of Sylvia Plath and Anaïs Nin, *La bâtarde* by Violette Leduc, one has read everything. Only the women's movement has proved capable of producing lesbian texts in a context of total rupture with masculine culture, texts written by women exclusively for women, careless of male approval. *Le corps lesbien* falls into this category.[9]

Violette Leduc is the only French writer Monique Wittig acknowledges as a predecessor. It is obvious that the scenes in *La bâtarde* and in *Thérèse et Isabelle* in which the young girls make love are acceptable to Wittig not merely because females are making love but because the narrator as lesbian is describing her own experience. The lesbian is no longer the object of literary discourse seen from an outside point of view. She is her own heroine:

The hand was wandering through whispering snow-capped bushes, over the last frosts on the meadows, over the first buds as they swelled to fullness. The springtime that had been crying its impatience with the voice of tiny birds under my skin was now curving and swelling into flower. Isabelle, stretched out upon the darkness, was fastening my feet with ribbons, unwinding the swaddling bands of my alarm. With hands laid flat upon the mattress, I was immersed in the selfsame magic task as she. She was kissing what she had caressed and then, light as a feather duster, the hand began to flick, to brush the wrong way all that it had smoothed before. The sea monster in my entrails quivered. Isabelle was drinking at my breast, the right, the left, and I drank with her, sucking the milk of darkness when her lips had gone. The fingers were returning now, encircling and testing the warm weight of my breast. The fingers were pretending to be waifs in a storm; they were taking shelter inside me. A host of slaves, all with the face of Isabelle,

fanned my brow, my hands.
She knelt up in the bed.
"Do you love me?"
I led her hand up to the precious tears of joy.[10]

The text concentrates obsessively on the actions being performed. Love-making occupies a central place in the text, although not all of the text, as in *Le corps lesbien*. But it is in large part what the text and the narrator's adventure through life are all about. These are the privileged moments, this is the paradise and the epiphany. Violette Leduc has deliberately chosen a lyrical style through which to produce the effect of joy and ecstasy. The syntax changes to accommodate longer sentences that attempt to recreate the rhythms of expectation, tension, and diffusion and to recount the gestures of both partners. Through a traditional nature code, springtime, with its flowers and its storms, invades the text associating with the pleasures of lovemaking the pleasures of an awakening and a renewal. It is, of course, a verbal pleasure, the moment in the writing of the narrator's greatest command over her language. The power of the word and the pleasures of the female body are intimately related. Lovemaking is the primary source of inspiration. It opens and defines a world whose existence had been suspected but never so explicitly stated. Within the context of lesbian intertextuality Violette Leduc is indeed the first French writer to take us beyond the Sappho model to Sappho's own texts – the lesbian writer writing as lesbian. But the power of this image of female lovemaking is weakened in *La bâtarde* by the autobiographical nature of Leduc's enterprise. As soon as the narrator and the text move out of the gynaeceum into a male-dominated world, the female body can no longer occupy the center of the stage. Because the gynaeceum and schoolgirl love are so invested with intertextual connotations and because Violette Leduc uses traditional nature codes for metaphoric support, *Thérèse et Isabelle* is not nearly as original or as disturbing a text as *Le corps lesbien:*

In this dark adored adorned gehenna say your farewells m/y very beautiful one m/y very strong one m/y very indomitable one m/y very learned one m/y very ferocious one m/y very gentle one m/y best beloved to what they, the women, call affection tenderness or gracious abandon. There is not one who is unaware of what takes place here, which has no name as yet. . . . Not one will be able to bear seeing you with eyes turned up lids cut off your yellow smoking intestines spread in the hollow of your hands your tongue spat from your mouth long green strings of bile flowing over your breast, not one will be able to bear your low frenetic insistent laughter. The gleam of your teeth your joy your sorrow the hidden life of your organs your nerves their rupture their spurting forth death slow decomposition stench being devoured by worms your open skull, all will be equally unbearable to her. . . .

At this point I invoke your help m/y incomparable Sappho, give m/e by thousands the fingers that allay the wounds, give m/e the lips the tongue the saliva which draw one into the slow sweet poisoned country from which one cannot return. . . .

I discover that your skin can be lifted layer by layer, I pull, it lifts off, it coils above your knees, I pull starting at the labia. . . .[11]

In *Le corps lesbien* Monique Wittig has created, through the incessant use of hyperbole and a refusal to employ traditional body codes, images sufficiently blatant to withstand reabsorption into male literary culture. Wittig has taken Sappho out of the gynaeceum in which she had been confined for so long. She has brought her back to Lesbos and placed her among the Amazons. A recognizable social context, itself a purveyor of labels, has been replaced in *Le corps lesbien* by a stylized decor composed of conglomerate elements of the Sappho and Amazon legends: islands, a beach, the sea, the color violet, strong female bodies, uniquely female names. This hymn to the lesbian body is also a hymn to the body from Lesbos who is not only lover, writer, muse, but potent goddess, the central figure of a new mythology. There would seem to be little doubt that for Monique Wittig, who has the passion of the true believer, lesbianism is a cause, the only conceivable rallying point for the elaboration of a woman's culture. As an ideology on which to impose a fiction, the possibilities as well as the risks of lesbianism are enormous. Monique Wittig has chosen, in this text, to use lesbianism as a means of destroying the accepted male love discourse as well as the accepted male literary stereotypes about the female body. The destruction begins with the "farewells" of the first sentence and continues through reiterated parodies of sacred literary texts to the torturing, beating, flaying, peeling, devouring, vomiting, and caressing of female flesh. The physical exchange between J/e and Tu is reminiscent at times of a *pas de deux*, at times of a boxing match, at times of a surgical operation. But destruction of one order of language and sensibility implies creation of a new order. The J/e of *Le corps lesbien* is the most powerful lesbian in literature because as a lesbian-feminist she reexamines and redesigns the universe. Starting with the female body she recreates through anecdote and proper names a new aqueous female space and a new female time in which the past is abolished. She is, in fact, the only true anti-Christ, the willful assassin of Christian love.

Provocation exists at every level of the text: in the monotony of the lists, in the female endings attached to masculine proper nouns, in the typography, and in the verbal violence. J/e names the hitherto unnamed. The desperate desire for impossible union is described through the trajectories traced by fingers, hands, tongue outside and inside the body. The female body, whose every part is enumerated, destroyed, and reassembled is the alpha and omega of Wittig's fiction. In the beginning is the body and at the end; an indestructible body, singular in the text, but signifying the potentiality of all female bodies.

No one since Sappho herself has made a greater contribution to lesbian intertextuality than Monique Wittig. Not only has she restructured elements of the Sappho model, eliminating the enclosed spaces of school or convent, cellar restaurant or alcove, but she has transformed the image of Sappho by associating Sappho's verbal power with the physical power of the Amazons. Wittig has abandoned any attempt to insert Sappho into male culture. *Le corps lesbien* is a textual and cultural gamble. It is a courageous aspiration toward the creation of a linguistic behavior that would, by its very existence, prepare the way for the undomestication of women. Whatever the ultimate fate of the book and the revolution it solicits, it does herald the second coming of Sappho.

Because the corpus of texts that contain the Sappho model is small, any major alteration in the angle of vision transforms the entire body, illuminating forgotten fragments, suggesting new correspondences. The poems and stories of Renée Vivien, for example, begin to emerge from almost complete oblivion under the new lighting. Instead of dismissing them as poor imitations of the Baudelairean lyric or as examples of the inferior "feminine" writing of the *belle époque,* we can now see them as interesting attempts by a lesbian to write as a lesbian about lesbianism. As our awareness of the Sappho model grows, a writer such as Renée Vivien takes her place within a canon that has been until this century an exclusively male creation. Perhaps the most tenacious and pernicious element in this creation, reiterated by almost every writer, female and male, with the exception of Monique Wittig, is that lesbianism implies a nostalgic regression to the mother-daughter couple and is therefore not viable. A text such as *Le corps lesbien* is not concerned with psychological causality. Lesbian intertextuality will never be the same.

NOTES

1 This paper was nourished by four texts: Mary Daly, *Beyond God the Father* (Boston: Beacon, 1973); Jeannette Foster, *Sex Variant Women in Literature* (Baltimore: Diana Press, 1975), originally published in 1956; Jules Michelet, *La sorcière* (Paris: Garnier-Flammarion, 1966), originally published in 1862; Edith Mora, *Sappho* (Paris: Flammarion, 1966). I discovered, after my article was completed, Bertha Harris's delightful essay "The More Profound Nationality of Their Lesbianism: Lesbian Society in Paris in the 1920's," in *Amazon Expedition: A Lesbian-Feminist Anthology,* ed. Phyllis Birkby, Bertha Harris, Jill Johnston, Esther Newton, Jane O'Wyatt (Washington, N.J.: Times Change Press, 1973), 77–88.

2 Martial's Bassa, Lucian's courtesans. Sapho in Brantôme's *Vie des dames galantes* (1665); Mlle Hobart in Hamilton's *Mémoires de la vie du Comte de Gramont* (1713); Mlle d'Eon, Mlle de Raucourt, Mme de Furiel, Mlle Sapho in "Apologie de la secte anandryne" (1784); the Mother Superior in Diderot's *La religieuse* (1796); Camille in Latouche's *Fragoletta* (1829); Mlle de Maupin in Gautier's *Mlle de Maupin* (1835); Margarita-Euphémia Porrabéril, Marquise de San Réal and Paquita Valdès in Balzac's *La fille aux yeux d'or* (1835); Sapho, Delphine, and Hippolyte in Baudelaire's *Les fleurs du mal* (1857); Sappho and the friends in Verlaine's *Parallèlement* (1867); the black woman in Mallarmé's "La négresse" (1866), and the two nymphs in his "L'après-midi d'un faune" (1875); Suzanne Haffner and the Marquise d'Espanet in Zola's *La curée* (1871), and Nana and Satin in his *Nana* (1879); Madeleine, Pauline in Maupassant's *La femme de Paul* (1881); Sapho in Daudet's *Sapho* (1884); Bilitis, Sappho, Mnasidika in Pierre Louÿs's *Chansons de Bilitis* (1894); Claudine, Aimée and Luce Lanthenay, Mlle Sergent, Rézi, Miss Flossie in Colette's Claudine novels (1900–1904); Mlle Vinteuil and "son amie," Albertine, Léa, Andrée, Odette, Gilberte, Mme Verdurin, Oriane de Guermantes, Rachel in Proust's *A la recherche du temps perdu* (1913–1927); Marie Bonifas in Jacques de Lacretelle's *La Bonifas* (1925); la Chevalière, Renée Vivien, Amalia X———, Lucienne de ———, the Ladies of Llangollen in Colette's *Le pur et l'impur* (1932); Inès Serrano in Sartre's *Huis clos* (1944); Céline in Christiane Rochefort's *Stances à Sophie* (1963); Je, Isabelle, Hermine in Violette Leduc's *La bâtarde* (1964) and Thérèse, Isabelle in her *Thérèse et Isabelle* (1966); the *guérillères* in Monique Wittig's *Les guérillères* (1969), and J/e in her *Le corps lesbien* (1973).

3 Phrase used by André Billy in his *L'époque 1900* (Paris: Editions Jules Tallandier, 1951), 227.

4 "Apologie de la secte anandryne," in *L'espion anglais ou correspondance secrète entre Milord All'Eye et Milord All'Ear* (London: John Adamson, 1784), vol. 10, 274. The first four volumes of *L'espion anglais* were written by Mathieu François Pidanzat de Mairobert. The authorship of the last six volumes is unknown.

5 Colette, *Claudine à l'école. Oeuvres complètes* (Paris: Flammarion, 1948), vol. 1, 21.

6 Colette, "Nuit blanche" in *Les vrilles de la vigne. Oeuvres complètes* (Paris: Flammarion, 1949), vol. 3, 219–20.

7 Colette, *The Pure and the Impure,* trans. Herma Briffault, Introduction by Janet Flanner (Harmondsworth: Penguin, 1971), 118.

8 Sappho, "He is more than a hero" in *Sappho,* trans. Mary Barnard (Berkeley and Los Angeles: University of California Press, 1958), no. 39.

9 Monique Wittig, *The Lesbian Body,* trans. David LeVay (New York: William Morrow, 1975), 9.

10 Violette Leduc, *La bâtarde,* trans. Derek Coltman, with a foreword by Simone de Beauvoir (New York: Farrar, Straus, and Giroux, 1965), 84.

11 Wittig, 15, 16, 17.

16

Toni A. H. McNaron

Mirrors and Likeness:
A Lesbian Aesthetic in the Making

As an avid reader from childhood, I looked in vain for images of the girl and woman I was and was becoming. I did not find her. Girls functioned in essentially passive roles, supporting boys in one way or another. As my reading went from Dick-and-Jane to Shakespeare and Dickens, women characters typically concentrated on their "knight" or some more modern equivalent. Once having found him, they settled into marriage, hoping to live as happily ever after as they had in earlier fairy tales. If there were women without men they were depicted as pinched, depressed, predatory. They were either desexed or sexually avaricious.

Once a feminist, I began to analyze this pitiful situation; once a lesbian-feminist, I found my analysis becoming ever clearer. Sexuality for women was presented in only one dress – heterosexuality. I simply did not find high or low art in which the lives of lesbian women or women together was represented as possible or desirable. From my yearning for what was absent, I began to look for any signs of gender likeness;[1] from this position of deprivation I began formulating the theory behind this essay. I asked myself an obvious question: what would happen if readers looked for evidence of likeness in characters and language? The results have been far more impressive and extensive than I had foreseen; the terrain significantly broader than I could have imagined.

In 1929, Virginia Woolf argued that the historical function of women was to serve as mirrors in which men will find themselves reflected back at twice their real size. As someone who minored in mathematics and adored fractions, I understand only two paths to this fantasy reflection: either the woman must make herself half her real size so that the illusion of greatness will pertain to the viewer without his having to do anything at all, or the woman must inflate her responses to whatever her needy looker does so that normal or usual acts will seem grand. In both instances, the work is done by the image-making woman, and in either case she involves herself in a lie so close to the bone as to run the risk of destroying whatever separate self she might have.

In 1988, Jenijoy La Belle published her study of fictive and real women in relation to mirrors.[2] From the sheer force of her cumulative examples, it would appear that our heterosexist culture keeps indoctrinating women to perform Woolf's frightening role. Though much of her book sets out the negative, even fatal, aspects of a woman's looking for her identity in a mirror, La Belle concludes with work on mostly recent scenes written by women determined to expropriate one of patriarchy's oldest symbols of our superficiality and turn it into a tool through which women may come to know ourselves better, more particularly, more deeply. Speaking of this more affirming process, La Belle says, "This is a constant affirmation of personal presence through the division of self into both subject and object. . . . This act of objective self-recognition institutes a bifurcation, but at the same time can be used by women to break down the conceptual barriers between mind and body. . . . The image in the glass is a 'life companion,' at once an otherness she can study and an intrinsic part of the ego as it comes into being. [The] wise woman . . . can use the alterity of the mirror image as a constituent of identity" (1988:185). I find it worth noting that two of the three examples La Belle uses to illustrate her more positive assertion come from books by lesbians or about lesbian relationships (Alice Walker's *The Color Purple* and May Sarton's *Mrs. Stevens Hears the Mermaids Singing*).

In her outline for the possible course of British fiction in the future, Virginia Woolf made the comment that such novels might attempt to depict a situation in which "Chloe liked Olivia." In this now-famous passage from *A Room of One's Own*, Woolf describes a hypothetical scene in which two women work together in a laboratory. They watch and watch over one another and, in that seemingly simple action, reverse hundreds of years of women's gaze. All women are conditioned to regard those who are our gender opposites as the most interesting and worthy objects of our attention. On the simplest social level, such osmotic instruction yields a ready group of young girls waiting to embrace compulsory heterosexuality even if that means turning away from their particular Chloe and Olivia. Stories of such redirection of attention are all too plentiful: who among us has not been called by a high-school girl friend canceling plans for doing something in order to go on a "real" date with some boy who bothered to ask at the last moment? And how many women tacitly give up contact with devoted women friends at the time of their marriage, thereby short-circuiting a relationship sometimes of many years' standing, often never making our way back to that deep connection with one of our own kind?

What Woolf proposed in *A Room of One's Own* is a radical shift from gender opposition to gender likeness as a governing narrative and aesthetic principle. We can tell from her excitement at the prospect of resulting scenes that she feels the charge of that mirroring at least as powerfully as she does the more socially accepted opposition. However, such representations within literary genres are still viewed by women and men alike as somehow not quite as stimulating or vivid, not as susceptible to "erotic" action as scenes in which a man figures.

Not only did Woolf theorize a radical departure from heterosexual dominance in fiction, but she demonstrated what it might feel like in novel after novel (e.g., *Mrs. Dalloway* [1925], *To the Lighthouse* [1927], *The Years* [1939]). Here I will use material from her early work, *Night and Day* (1919) as typical of Woolf's representations of an aesthetic freed from heterosexual hegemony.

Throughout *Night and Day*, the relationship between Mary Datchett and Katherine Hilbery draws me to it more strongly than do any of the more conventional heterosexual alliances. Shirley Garner has argued this point quite persuasively in her essay, "'Women Together' in Virginia Woolf's *Night and Day*":[3] "When they are together, the manner and intensity of their responses to each other suggest that they feel the affection and attraction of lovers, not merely of friends. . . . Their love for each other is most often inferred rather than known, understood rather than stated, shown indirectly rather than directly" (Garner, 325). The authorial language is generally less certain, the conversations between them have a directness absent from all other converse except for a few exchanges between Katherine and her mother, and the aura surrounding them virtually every time they are together possesses a sexual tinge that is unmistakable to anyone interested in theories of likeness. Though her unwillingness to risk her relatively privileged social and economic position prevented Woolf from developing anything like a lesbian relationship in this novel, she nonetheless represented much the same thing in the intimate scenes between these two extraordinary women.

One example will have to suffice for this argument. Both women are at one time or another in love with the same man – an archetypal setup in fiction and life for opposition to assert its hegemonic cultural position. What Woolf does in this 1919 novel reminds us of contemporary feminist instances of women's resistance to seeing each other as enemies fighting for the same prize. Sensing Ralph's love for Katherine, Mary decides to put aside her own personal hurt at being rejected in order to tell Katherine. Her reasons are worth listening to:

I've told you . . . because I want you to help me. I don't want to be jealous of you. And I am – I'm fearfully jealous. The only way, I thought, was to tell you. . . . [Mary] seemed to have lost her isolation; she was . . . happier than she had ever been; she was bereft; she was rejected; she was immensely loved. Attempt to express these sensations was vain and moreover, she could not help believing that, without any words on her side, they were shared. Thus for some time longer they sat silent, side by side, while Mary fingered the fur of the skirt of [Katherine's] old dress. (276–78)

Surely this scene illustrates the essential charge behind allowing Chloe to like rather than compete with Olivia. To make the claim "I like you" suggests some degree of personal pleasure in the presence of another and so may already carry a sexual potential. Why else has it been so fraught for heterosexuals to try and have friends of the opposite sex? When liking is based on likeness, with all the trust that familiarity and commonality implies, the connection often becomes electric, and Woolf knew it.[4] Her comment that Mary sensed *without any words on [Katherine's] side* that her feelings were returned in kind – were "like" in the sense I am using the term – is a theme Woolf would reiterate in her fiction, criticism, and personal writing. In a journal entry, she described a tea with Katherine Mansfield and her husband, John Middleton Murry, a leading establishment critic. While Woolf reported finding Murry's comments pointed and a mark of his erudition, she gave herself away by saying that once he had left the room for some reason, she and Mansfield had been able to cover much more ground much more rapidly. She posits a shorthand based on a principle of sexual likeness to which she would give flesh in her novels.

Turning to a consideration of what lesbian-feminist consciousness might contribute to literary study, I want to trace a path through some literature that clarifies this relatively unknown subject. It might seem to go without saying that lesbians are drawn to likeness rather than to opposition, at least in terms of sexual passion. Yet, because all children are conditioned to heterosexuality, and because heterosexuality does contain the power and excitement that does inhere within systems of opposition, history and practice have given us many lesbians who have acted out masculine/feminine dynamics, sometimes in dress itself but more often in role behaviors within relationships – the classic butch/femme syndrome.[5] As Judith Roof has shown in her article, "The Match in the Crocus: Representations of Lesbian Sexuality,"[6] most male depictions of lesbian relationships have substituted a phallic situation or rhetoric for the absent penis, leaving the reader/viewer undisturbed in his or her comfortable habit of seeing all human relationships through such a limited filter. It has been within the systematic growth of lesbian-feminist analysis of culture and psychology that real-life lesbians have come to understand these adopted modes of personal representation. Only within such a context have we been able to choose to alter them in favor of something more nearly approximating a valuing of self and other as expressing sexual likeness.

In such representations, sexuality will not be located as it has tended to be in male-identified stories. Precisely what is seen by conservative Freudians as a "lack" will provide a much-widened canvas on which to sketch lesbian sexuality. As Roof remarks, "We can't see (lesbian) sexuality because it is no single point but is everywhere at once" (Roof, 110). This simple fact, based on anatomy, has allowed many a closeted lesbian writer or painter to present her truest sexual messages through the use of images in Nature, which embraces a diffuse system of signs and meaning analogous to certain aspects of human exchange. This fact is what is now empowering many lesbian-feminist readers to break such codes in writers like Willa Cather, Edna St. Vincent Millay, H.D., Dickinson, and Elizabeth Bishop.

Of course feminists of all sorts are implicated in the business of asserting the power of connections between women – gender likeness. Twentieth-century feminism began under a banner that proclaimed sisterhood to be powerful rather than catty or boring. Later critiques of this declaration, made by women of color, working-class women, and lesbians, have been well founded and have led to more rigorous and self-reflective work and action. In writing about the power of likeness, I in no way mean to revert to those earlier stances, which essentially silenced diversity among women.

Attractions possible within situations or images involving sexual likeness, however, lie at the heart of much of men's fear and anger about the women's movement: men sense, at times without knowing how to articulate their fear or discomfort, that if women look across lunch tables or day care center meetings at other women, they may move an inch or two away from their historical place as reflecting men. What many men fear losing in this tiny but paradigmatic shift is what Woolf understood when she spoke of women as mirrors ready to reflect men at twice their size.

If our modern sense of irreparable fragmentation causes us to seek integration, then there are satisfactions to be gained from various image echoes at the base of all social relationships. Beginning with a look into our bathroom mirrors, I would posit that the most satisfying "return" comes from seeing there a face that more or less coincides with our inner sense of self. If that mirror casts back an image too dissonant with our own self-concept, we wind up split at some root and crazed. Each of our relations casts back an image that can be located on this continuum from such nightmare reflections to a sense of total identification between outside and inside. If I look across social or intimate space at another woman, there is less dissonance than if I gaze at a man. On this obvious fact is based the entire edifice of heterosexual attraction: that system is constructed on the militant belief that dissonance is the stuff of sexual excitement. We are all encouraged to think, then, that less is happening or at stake when Chloe watches Olivia instead of Oliver.

Lesbians often question this dominant construct, since at our best we subvert the cultural formulae for sexual passion. Our artistic representations, then, will also tend to reflect something quite different from the body of such work. Tension may indeed be replaced by something more nearly resembling what Milton had Eve describe as "that smooth watery image." But an absence of tension based on gender opposition does not equate with an absence of excitement, as many feminists know who have experienced just how energizing it can be to work or play with other women.[7] Woman-to-woman exchanges often include a sense of satisfaction often lacking from comparable events involving a man or men. In fact, in phrasing this last sentence, I kept wanting to use "parries" as the cognate term for "exchanges," and therein lies meaning far beyond diction.

By looking to self rather than other for one's images, be they personal or artistic, we can gain a double vision with the attendant potential critical advantage. Lesbian-feminist scholars are in a unique position to resist dichotomous thinking if we can stand the rigor of the alternative ambiguities. We have been told that in sexual matters, opposition is all, but many of us have rejected that message in favor of likeness. If one thing that is supposed to be is not, then why not question all Platonic splits – good/evil, white/black, male/female, right/wrong, order/chaos, mind/body, spirit/matter, light/dark, even hard/soft feminist scholarship. Lesbians, by a simple but profound shift in our gaze of attraction, are positioned as thinkers and theorists poised to lead the way within the larger spheres of feminist thought toward a rejection of the very notions of either/or-ness. Furthermore, we may be able to dramatize both in our lives and our research the ability to hold seeming oppositions in ideological solution without having to come down on one side or the other.

Having set out the possibilities, let me pose a few operative questions: What would happen to generic considerations and even to language use, especially metaphors, if likeness were to become a governing principle behind aesthetics? Won't lesbians have something unique to contribute to such questions and to the building of such an aesthetic? What happens when we read literature with an eye to language that affirms likeness of various sorts? What really happens to our western aesthetic if we find it exciting and powerful that Chloe liked Olivia? And what will we read if we look with eyes drawn to likeness rather than to opposition?

The last question is easiest to answer. When I read *La Morte d'Arthur,* I cannot avoid the fact that the king refuses to recognize his wife's amorous goings on for as long as absolutely possible in order to keep his bond intact with his knight, Lancelot. Similarly, Camelot is lost forever not because of Guinevere's infidelity, since virtually everyone playing the courtly love game was unfaithful to someone, but because another noble man broke fealty with his lord. Reading Shakespeare, my eye finds a feast of dramatic presentations illustrating the Bard's fierce pull toward sexual likeness accompanied by often violent punishments for admitting or expressing that inclination.[8] In *Romeo and Juliet,* Mercutio is sorely vexed by Romeo's falling in love rather than continuing to play the field at no cost to their bond of likeness. Similarly, Romeo breaks his vow of pacificism and runs furiously off to murder Tybalt not when Juliet's hot-headed cousin mocks Romeo himself but only when he harms Mercutio, Romeo's "consort." In *The Merchant of Venice,* a more somber Antonio is full of dark melancholy which he never can or will explain, caused as far as I can see by Bassanio's having broken their tight bond by seeking Portia's hand and fortune. In the insidious world of *Coriolanus,* the title character is far more intimately involved with Aufidius, his archenemy, than he is with Virgilia, his silenced wife. For Aufidius's part, he expresses his welcome to the man who has bested him on no less than twelve occasions with these strangely homoerotic words:

but that I see thee here,
Thou noble thing! more dances my rapt heart
Than when I first my wedded mistress saw
Bestride my threshold. . . . I have nightly since
Dreamt of encounters 'twixt thyself and me;
We have been down together in my sleep,
Unbuckling helms, fisted each other's throat,
And waked half dead with nothing.
(4.5.121–32)

In his late work, *The Winter's Tale,* Shakespeare has Polixenes explicitly blame Hermione for coming between him and his idyllic relationship with Leontes, now her husband. Their heterosexual romance not only mirrored and confirmed the theological fall, but (more importantly for Polixenes) caused a rift between the two young men who thought of themselves as "twin lambs."

Shakespeare also treats what happens to women who affirm likeness in such plays as *A Midsummer Night's Dream, As You Like It,* and *The Winter's Tale.* By the end of *A Midsummer Night's Dream,* all three instances of female friendship and community have been sacrificed in order to achieve the conventional happy ending: Hippolyta has been abducted by Theseus, who himself boasts of having wooed her with his sword; Titania has been forced to give the changeling boy to her husband, the tyrannical Oberon, thereby reneging on her promise to his mother to raise him as she herself would; Helena and Hermia have broken their childhood bonds because Hermia believes Helena has joined with the two men, deserting not only her but their sex, to make fun of her. Once their friendship is shattered in favor of compulsory heterosexuality, they literally lose their voices: the two young women remain entirely silent throughout the final act.[9] In *As You Like It,* as Rosalind continues to ask Celia for sustenance, only to carry her renewed strength to her heterosexual lover, Orlando, Celia is understandably driven to excoriate Rosalind for trying to have it all. Only in *The Winter's Tale* can Shakespeare allow intimacy between two women, Hermione and her faithful court lady, Paulina, to endure. That becomes possible, however, only through the extreme measure of making it seem that one of the women is dead for sixteen years. Obviously, sexual likeness both drew and terrified the playwright, as it would many after him.

Milton makes a centrally important statement on this matter in *Paradise Lost* (1962). Amidst various lapses into blatant misogyny, he sets the scene in Book 4 where Eve awakes to life for the first time. She tells Adam about hearing

a murmuring sound
Of waters issu'd from a Cave and spread
Into a liquid Plain, then stood unmov'd
Pure as th' expanse of Heav'n; I thither went
With unexperienc't thought, and laid me down
On the green bank, to look into the clear
Smooth Lake, that to me seem'd another sky.
As I bent down to look, just opposite,
A Shape within the water's gleam appear'd
Bending to look on me, I started back,
It started back, but pleas'd I soon return'd,
Pleas'd it return'd as soon with answering looks
Of sympathy and love; there I had fixt
Mine eyes till now, and pin'd with vain desire,
Had not a voice thus warn'd me, What thou seest,
What there thou seest fair Creature is thyself,
With thee it came and goes.
(11.453–68)

This is a quintessential example of mirroring as a powerful modality for representing likeness. What she sees appeals to her tremendously, and

this arresting image holds her with great force. Only after direct intervention by a heavenly voice, and then reluctantly, does she move away from
her self in the lake, following the invisible voice until it leads her to Adam,
asleep under a plantain tree. Though she admits he is "fair indeed and
tall," she goes on to tell him, "yet methought less fair, / Less winning soft,
less amiably mild, / Than that smooth wate'ry image: back I turn'd /
Thou following cri'd'st aloud, Return fair Eve, / Whom Fli'st thou?
Whom thou fie'st, of him thou art, / His flesh, his bone" (11.478–83).

At the end of this story of birth and self-awareness, Eve says that she
"yielded,"[10] and from that moment saw "How beauty is excell'd by manly
grace / And wisdom, which alone is truly fair." The passage is followed
by a sexual scene of Adam and Eve in their Bower of Bliss watched over
by a leering Satan. Interestingly enough, he expresses what he sees as
"bliss on bliss," a perfect example of the kind of mirror metaphor I believe
so often reflects the power of likeness. To Satan, who sees himself as thrust
into hell, Adam and Eve do represent a kind of hateful sameness simply
because they dwell together in a region of sublime love. But to Eve, who
has just recounted her initial meeting with herself, Adam seems quite different, even if acknowledged as superior according to some artificial criteria.

I see this scene as an archetypal instance of what I am arguing. Eve is
"taught" by prescript that she needs opposition but she intuits from her
own senses a primal attraction to those images which give us back ourselves though in totally separate forms. Again, I in no way mean to essentialize "lesbians." Rather, I am asserting that no matter how a given
woman may practice her lesbianism, at the root of her attraction lies a
fundamental, even if subconscious, recognition of the power of sexual
likeness as the basis upon which to build relationships.

From the examples above, I would argue that affirming the attraction to
sexual likeness in various artistic media will at the very least change our
perspective on certain figures within white male European literature. An
even more salient application involves reading so-called coded women
writers from earlier eras to see how many of them are writing subtexts
which celebrate all sorts of Chloes liking all sorts of Olivias. Two of the
best loci for such study occur in the poetry of Hilda Doolittle, or H.D. as
she called herself to mask gender, and of Emily Dickinson, America's lady
genius whom we all admire but about whom many of us have very little
to say in the way of intelligent interpretation.

Emily Dickinson sought in many of her poems to establish a "home" for
herself, since she felt distinctly and painfully out of place in the social
world of mid-nineteenth-century Amherst. Writing deeply coded poems
about her homoerotic feelings, she leaves a rich depository from which to

draw as I think about the power of sexual likeness.[11] I want to speak briefly about only two of these gems, but there are literally hundreds of such poems waiting for a lesbian-feminist interpretation to give them sense. First is #533:

Two Butterflies went out at Noon –
And waltzed upon a Farm –
Then stepped straight through the Firmament
And rested, on a Beam –

And then – together bore away
Upon a shining Sea –
Though never yet, in any Port –
Their coming, mentioned – be –

If spoken by the distant Bird –
If met in Ether Sea
By Frigate, or by Merchantman –
No notice – was – to me – .
(1960:260)

How do I know that the two butterflies are female? Partly because I have read thousands of poems by heterosexual white men for whom celebrating equality is not a major theme; mostly because of the coded context surrounding these particular lepidoptera. Stepping through the Firmament suggests escaping patriarchal constraints; the observers who might have seen them in heaven are masculinized and then oblivious (what do two women "do" remains the query to this day). Americans in the nineteenth century were certainly not used to mentioning the coming of same-sex lovers. This sexual fantasy asserts two like creatures doing something risqué and dangerous but also something exciting and "shining."

In #288, known by many as one of her childhood ditties, Dickinson openly asserts the importance of likeness. "I'm Nobody! Who are you? / Are you – Nobody – Too? / Then there's a pair of us! / Don't tell! they'd advertise – you know! / How dreary – to be – Somebody! / How public – like a Frog – / To tell one's name – the livelong June – / To an admiring Bog!" (1960:133). Admittedly wry, this poem nonetheless becomes distinctly more serious if looked at through a lesbian-feminist lens. Not only is the poet ecstatic over the mere possibility of finding someone like herself, but she understands that if they really are alike, they must keep it secret or the larger world will make a spectacle of them – like monkeys in a zoo. The second stanza becomes a politically radical statement about preferring nobody if it can be shared to somebodyhood if one has to look across at a divergent image – that "admiring Bog" that echoes Eve's words to Adam in *Paradise Lost,* a work Dickinson knew thoroughly. Lest anyone think this reading too far-fetched, let me quote in its entirety one of Dickinson's clearest poetic declarations of woman love: "To own a Susan of my own / Is of itself a bliss / Whatever realms I forfeit, Lord, / Continue me in this" (#1401, 1960:600). Not to understand this as a sexual preference for likeness is simply to refuse the poem's terms.

Turning to H.D., we come to a complicated woman who not only survived analysis with Freud but profited from it, someone who seized upon the Helen of Troy myth as a perfect opportunity not only to give America one of its only epic poems, but more importantly to explore ancient terrain seen from a woman's eye, an eye that welcomes goddesses rather than being fixated only on gods. Because of the length and density of this work, I feel it wiser to focus on one of her shorter, so-called imagist poems, since it will illustrate the kind of coded likeness I am exploring. In "The Helmsman" (1957:7–8), H.D. takes an unspecified "we" through an elaborate landscape as they flee inland from a "you" who has always wanted them. In the first twenty-four lines, "we" occurs sixteen times, establishing an equality between these obvious lovers stepping "past wood-flowers," "wood-grass," breaking "hyssop and bramble," feeling "the clefts in the bark." At one point, images of repeated pairings become so forceful that it would take sheer determination to falsify this into a heterosexual love poem. The lovers "parted green from green," felt "the slope between tree and tree – / a slender path strung field to field, / and wood to wood / and hill to hill / and the forest after it." Not only is this a coded love scene but the actors are individuals of the same sex, two women to be exact. I assume the sex is the same because of the exact repetition of the images used; I assume they are women by the language suggesting female sexuality within that mirrored imagery in which H.D. expresses their journey to sexual climax. When I read poems like this, I do not find them less exciting than John Donne's or Anne Sexton's. Quite the contrary: I find them totally engaging precisely because they affirm an electric charge present in my own life. The aesthetic representation corresponds with my experience at least in part because it takes its origin in Hilda Doolittle's.

I want now to focus on one contemporary novel and several films and television programs in which a distinct lesbian aura or subtext exists for the reader or viewer seeking instances where likeness has power and excitement. In Toni Morrison's well-known early work, *Sula* (1975), Barbara Smith finds ample evidence for a lesbian subtext. In her germinal article, "Toward a Black Feminist Literary Criticism,"[12] Smith asserts that no lesbian can fail to respond to the charged scenes between Sula and Nel as girls or to the ending of the novel as representations of lesbian attraction. The fact that the narrator tells us they dreamed each other before they actually met sets the stage for a kind of Eve-like, Edenic awakening. Morrison gives it to us in the scene in which the two girls, on the verge of womanhood, lie in the summer grass and dig holes in the dirt. Their paradisal moment is very short-lived, because Nel, the consistent initiator in this scene, modulates from play into some kind of angry restlessness when her stick breaks. From that moment on, the scene shows the girls filling the single hole made from the merger of their individual ones with increasingly ugly objects, fouling the very sexual playfulness in which they have so recently luxuriated.

Part of the difficulty in resolving this scene stems from the author's not being able to envision any other than a phallic representation of sexuality. Of course Nel's twig breaks – it is not her best tool – and her resulting frustration, anger and rejection of the possibilities of that moment come from her sudden feeling of inadequacy. Sula does not share this feeling and so begins to pull away from their bonded place. From this scene onward, she and Nel gradually cease to value the likeness that once empowered them until their ties are broken entirely when Nel marries and when Sula makes love with Nel's husband. Significantly, from the point of view of my thesis, what we are asked to watch at the end of the wedding ceremony is not two old friends smiling into one another's eyes, but Sula's back as she walks resolutely down the sidewalk of Nel's house, away from her self and away from her attachment to Nel, away from Medallion itself. Equally significant is the fact that Morrison makes it unmistakably clear that Nel does everything imaginable to avoid looking squarely at the gray ball that begins to float just to the side of her field of direct vision. If she had been able to turn and face it, she might have understood much sooner, perhaps even in time, that her sense of lack did not come from Jude's absence at all but from Sula's. The depth of her final grief wail is a powerful measure of the consequences of refusing the draw toward likeness in an effort to conform to culture's scripted preference for opposition.

If we consider briefly more popular forms of representation, some fascinating conclusions present themselves. For several years, one of the most popular prime-time commercial television programs in America was the police drama, "Cagney and Lacey." The program did everything it knew to enforce compulsory heterosexuality – Mary Beth's happy marriage to her particularly lovable Harvey; Chris's series of affairs brought on by her blatant "sex appeal," which lurked just under her canny sense of detective work and her quick wit; a change of actors in response to public objection to the original woman who played Chris because she seemed too "masculine" or dykey. Yet week after week, in places like the ladies' locker room at the police station, their enclosed car, or tense interior spaces in which one or both were at risk, thousands of Americans watched close-up exchanges (verbal and physical) between these "partners."

Two such scenes left permanent images in my memory. The first is of Chris's having been held hostage in a shed by a psychopathic killer until Mary Beth and her backup forces capture him. While the male officers are trying to determine just what has happened, Mary Beth rushes into the shed to cradle her partner, who, now that the ordeal is over, has collapsed in terror. The camera rolled for significant seconds on a silent scene, a special feminist pietà if you will, and I felt mirrored in ways seldom experienced.

The other memorable scene comes late in the series' history, after Chris's father has died his alcohol-related death and before she has admitted her own drinking problem. Both Mary Beth and Chris's current boyfriend know she needs help, but he is too codependent to do more than try to contain her drinking by watching over or cajoling her – futile tactics in the face of Chris's massive denial, anger, and hurt. Only Mary Beth loves her sharply and unselfishly enough to confront her, and in a remarkably dramatic incident (which won an Emmy), Mary Beth does precisely that. At one point, Chris physically fights her and Mary Beth just holds on to her until she can surrender to the harsh truth coming from her friend. Again, I was riveted to the screen, feeling a woman-centered power based in the likeness of the two actors, a power much more convincing and exciting than the frantic or mushy efforts of Chris's boyfriend, even though the script would have us believe he is the focus of her attention.

Any consideration of popular cultural images of lesbian likeness must include commentary on films that have seemed to be about us. If I think of *Personal Best* and *Lianna* as illustrative of this trend, I must say that neither affirms my thesis about the power of likeness, because both maintain a heterosexual point of view. Furthermore, the characters portraying so-called lesbian life seem more nearly to be tropes for something else the writer/director wishes to convey to his/her audience. "Lesbians" seem in movies of this sort to be particularly cruel stand-ins for a male fantasy about women's sexuality left unchecked by social conventions.

Technically and in terms of content, in *Personal Best* the audience's gaze is no different than it is in films where women are being looked at by actual men. Furthermore, by the last frame, the "lesbian" character has been saved from her dangerous tendencies. In the love scene, viewers watch two adolescent "male" bodies, further coded into classic cultural definitions of butch/femme or classic literary stereotypes of evil/good. The sexual initiator is dark-haired while her companion (and the movie's real "heroine") is blond.

Lianna, while focusing on two adults and being more sympathetic towards women's relationships with one another, nonetheless perpetuates

in a seemingly unself-conscious way the old and essentially abusive heterosexual myth of the teacher/student "romance" with all the dynamics
of imbalance present in any such inappropriately structured, power-
based liaison.

In order to find commercial films that participate in the kind of argument I am offering, I must turn to stories whose manifest plot has little to
do with what an audience would term "lesbian." As with "Cagney and
Lacey," it would seem that in a culture as militantly heterosexist as ours,
directors feel at liberty to show the possibilities for same-sex mirroring in
a positive light only when they are telling such a (safe) story.

Movies that stand out in my experience as being as moving in their
scenes of women or men seeing genuine likeness when they look at one
another are *Julia*, the story loosely based on Lillian Hellman's life, and
Women in Love, the film made from D. H. Lawrence's novel supposedly
about relations between the sexes. In each case, the actual emotional center of a production advertising itself as being very much about heterosexuality lies in scenes between persons of the same sex. In *Women in Love*, it
is the charged wrestling scene between Birkin and Gerald. Coming as the
climax to one of their numerous and intense conversations, the energy
that flares out in these few silent moments overtakes all other sexual or
romantic images in a predictable film about the emptiness at the heart of
modern life. The camera seems to be reveling in this scene, casting it in a
distinctly sfumatoed light, playing off the men's bodies so lovingly when
compared with the brittle glare under which so many of the scenes of sexual opposition are played out. As in the case of Woolf's *Night and Day*,
when I recall this film years after seeing it, scenes between two of a kind,
scenes constructed around the principle of the pull of likeness, appear in
sharp detail while much of the rest has faded.

In *Julia*, once again the camera makes a great deal of mirroring between
Julia and her girlhood/lifelong woman friend. Literal mirrors are often
used as the angle of vision – in restaurants as well as houses, suggesting
the importance of this same-sex bond in public as well as private space.
More subtle devices for mirror imaging include reflections in store glass
windows and on the surface of a lake in one of the most powerful and
moving scenes between the two women. All such visual effects heighten
the subtext of this film, that is, Lillian's ancient tie to her friend, in whose
face she finds a slant on her self and for whose life she is finally willing to
risk her own. Scenes between her and the men in her life, including
Dashiell Hammett, have a cinematic flatness in comparison.

For those readers and viewers who, like me, hunger for work that portrays the power and attraction within images of sexual likeness because
they affirm our very existence, accumulating actual instances is an essential act of reader response. To begin then to theorize about what our data

might signify, not only for us but for critics of these modes, becomes an act of immense potential.

Let me conclude by saying that analyzing images of sexual likeness or mirroring systematically and across several centuries and genres could begin to give the feminist literary community an alternative aesthetic to the thrust and parry, sticks and bowls school with which we are all too familiar. This alternative aesthetic could then be of use not only to future lesbian artists but to any women wishing to affirm the power of their own sexuality or of their myriad connections with other women.

When I look into a mirror, I am likely to see a reflection like me. Living within patriarchal culture as women is often like looking into mirrors with no silvering – we look and find either nothing at all or a face of the other against whom we must attempt the always-arduous task of self-definition. In psychological terms this means that our ideas of "woman" remain perforce deeply masculinized – we know as yet very little about all that being a woman might entail.

Lesbian writers and critics may be leaders in the fascinating enterprise of determining for ourselves what our selves might be. However, lesbians still battle the traditional and paradoxical view of us that we want to be men, and some of us have lived inside that paradox historically and often – bravely. But some of us insist on retaining the vision Eve had before she was forcibly led away to embrace compulsory heterosexuality, a vision full of powerful attraction, playfulness, and ease.

NOTES

1 Through this essay, my use of "sexual likeness" refers to something quite literal: one woman (or man) seeing another woman (man) rather than a representational opposite (woman seeing man or man seeing woman). On another level, I intend the term to signify literary representations of likeness through using various mirroring devices such as exact repetition of words or phrases or reliance on actual self-images found in looking glasses, watery surfaces, or other reflectors.

2 Jenijoy La Belle, *Herself Beheld: The Literature of the Looking Glass* (Ithaca: Cornell University Press, 1988).

3 In *The (M)other Tongue* (Ithaca: Cornell University Press, 1985), 318–33.

4 For this particular understanding of same-sex liking, I thank my colleague, Jacquelyn Zita, professor of women's studies and philosophy.

5 Contemporary research on the resurgence of butch/femme practices within lesbian cultures, particularly on the West Coast, is revealing a much more complex matrix within which some lesbians are "playing" with roles in an often self-conscious effort to fragment rigidly constructed gender presentations. For an engaging study from a cultural anthropological perspective, see the work of

Kath Weston, especially a forthcoming essay, "Do Clothes Make the Woman? Gender Theory and Lesbian Eroticism." I find such arguments enticing and provocative, but remain clear that even in such resurgence, at the heart of both the power and the playfulness is the clear knowledge that under the costumes there exist two creatures who are alike in some crucial ways.

6 In *Seduction and Theory,* ed. Dianne Hunter (Urbana, Ill.: University of Illinois Press, 1989).

7 Even as I assert the power of women-centered activities experienced by many heterosexual women, I realize that others do not like or enjoy spending time with only women for a number of reasons, both personal and culturally determined.

8 Like many others, I am indebted to Eve Sedgwick for her work on Shakespeare's images of male bonding of a homoerotic nature.

9 For a fuller discussion of how this comedy enforces heterosexuality at the expense of women's bonds with one another, see Shirley Nelson Garner, "*A Midsummer Night's Dream:* 'Jack shall have Jill; / Nought shall go ill,'" *Women's Studies* 9 (1981), 47–63.

10 I am again indebted to Jacquelyn Zita, who, in reading of a draft of this essay, pointed out that it may be women's "yielding" that creates the whole arena of the sexuality of difference. This suggestion is quite provocative and deserves more development than I have space for here.

11 For the clearest work to date on Dickinson's woman-centered and lesbian-bodied imagery, see Paula Bennett's chapter on Dickinson in *My Life a Loaded Gun: Dickinson, Plath, Rich, and Female Creativity* (Boston: Beacon Press, 1986), or her full-length treatment of the poet in *Emily Dickinson: Woman Poet* (New York: Harvest Wheatsheaf, 1990).

12 "Toward a Black Feminist Criticism" in *But Some of Us Are Brave,* ed. Gloria T. Hull, Patricia Bell Scott, and Barbara Smith (Old Westbury, N.Y.: The Feminist Press, 1982), 257–75.

17

Jeffner Allen

Poetic Politics:
How the Amazons Took the Acropolis

Lesbian and feminist writing makes actual – logically and materially – worlds in which females choose freely the course of our lives. The startling repercussions of these textual worlds take by surprise, and devastate, patriarchal institutions that would control the distribution of meaning, value, and physical goods against the self-defined interests of each woman.

By lesbian and feminist writing I include, as a partial list: the use of words, dialects, and manners of speaking that strike a liberating resonance among groups of women; diaries; deliberate mistakes in the addition of a bill, when women do not have enough money to purchase basic necessities; the exchange of notes to make known the depths of friendship and passion; lesbian and feminist philosophy. The random appearance of this list belies rigid separation of texts into "practical" and "theoretical" categories. Common to each instance of lesbian and feminist writing cited is a commitment to a textual action I will call: poetic politics.

I. FOUR THESES ON POETIC POLITICS

Poetic politics is defined uniquely by each instance of lesbian and feminist writing, and by their shifting interconnections. Some instances of lesbian and feminist writing may be so bold that they transform entirely the field of textual action, at least for some readers. We can articulate major claims of poetic politics, nevertheless, while keeping in mind the inevitably perspectival character of any such description.

Thesis 1

Poetic politics speaks the fortunes of a people in such a way that that fortune might be real.

Thesis 2

Poetic politics sets forth, by retrieval and by invention, elements vital to the production of meaning: language, culture, and corporeal self. A poetic politics posits connections between women's control of the production of meaning and women's shaping of our sexualities and our bodily powers.

Thesis 3, the entanglement of freedom

In poetic politics there speaks not one for all, but each for herself. How I speak myself as lesbian or feminist, or as both, is specific to how I experience my selves, is multiple in meaning, resists normative classification. To the extent that how I speak myself is alive, a quality more readily felt than thought, it interacts with the creation of meaning by each woman, with the fortunes of all women.

Thesis 4

The aesthetics, ethics, and ideologies at work in poetic politics give rise to textual worlds which differ, and which may conflict.

This study of poetic politics will focus on the distinctive configuration of these theses in the works of Hélène Cixous and Monique Wittig, writers situated frequently in the heterogeneous movement called the new French feminisms. To be sure, Cixous and Wittig are vigorous in their pronouncements of nonrelatedness to one another, and with good reason. There is an insurmountable opposition between the "feminine textual breakthrough" proposed by Cixous, which utilizes "a writing said to be feminine" and seeks the recovery of a feminine symbolics, and the "political semiology" developed by Wittig, which aims at ending the categories of sex and gender by study of language and ideology (Cixous and Conley 1984:51, 60; Wittig 1980:103).

My choice of Cixous and Wittig as major points of reference in poetic politics is based primarily on their perspicuous understandings of the textual production of meaning and its effects and, not incidentally, on a readerly delight in some of their texts. An uncompromising affirmation of female control of the creation of meaning is fundamental to the writings of both Cixous and Wittig, as is the affirmation of female language, embodiment, and experience as sites where meaning is created. Both writers offer the additional advantage of a steady production of book-length publications through which issues in poetic politics can be traced, Wittig beginning with *The Opoponax* in 1964, and Cixous with *Dedans*, 1969.[1]

These two accomplices in poetic politics will be found, however, in the company of a third. My own approach to their texts is neither literary criticism, which has been done excellently by others, nor a history of recent conflicts in the French lesbian/feminist movements.[2] *I propose, instead, a philosophical reflection on poetic politics and the process of meaning constitution.* Such a proposal may seem to run against the grain of claims by both Cixous and Wittig that philosophy is antithetical to empowering female thought. Cixous, in one of her many critical remarks on the solidarity of philosophical inquiry with logocentrism and phallocentrism, writes, "The philosophical constructs itself starting with the abasement of women." Wittig contends that the categories of sex, which enforce the social dominance of women by men, are "those two great axes of categorization for philosophy" (Cixous 1980b:92; Wittig 1978). Although in agreement with what I take to be the spirit of these statements, I claim that lesbian and feminist writing can rewrite any field of inquiry, and that it already has accomplished such a rewriting of philosophy.[3]

Like much of the new French feminisms, my philosophical approach will shape itself not by writing about texts, but by engagement in textual invention. Reference to texts by Cixous and Wittig will be grounded in what I take to be some of the strongest, boldest elements of their respective poetic politics, a selection that shifts the contours of the new French feminisms by situating them in a context that is more American than European, and more feminist than postmodern. In the case of Cixous, many writings prior to her statement, "the enigma of heterosexuality . . . it is behind me" (Cixous and Conley 1984:66), will be abandoned.[4] If such choices appear arbitrary to some, they also give opportunity to find how one poetic politics constitutes itself.

II. TEXTUAL VIOLENCE

The textual action of lesbian and feminist writing takes the right to determine what a poetry and a politics might be. It nullifies mandatory separation between that which has been designated the "poetic" and the "political." No longer can a text be classified the product of either a statesman or a poet, a philosopher or a feminist, a writer or a political activist. The wedge that has constructed the "poetic" and the "political" as discrete categories and dictated the laws that govern their combination is removed by the textual violence of this writing. The practice of a textual violence at once poetic and political is affirmed decisively by Cixous:

Poetry is/and (the) Political
Sorties: Out and Out

Attacks/Ways Out/Forays
(Cixous and Clément 1986:63)

The political power of a literary work with a new form is, Wittig argues,
like a Trojan Horse. It

> operates as a war machine, because its design and its goal is to pulverize the old
> forms and formal conventions. . . . Eventually it is adopted, and even if slowly, it
> will work like a mine. (Wittig 1984:49)

The wedge

The Athenian illusion that poetry and politics ought to be separate has
masked for too long, in Western cultures, the subtext from which that illusion arose: the claim of a single poetic politics to make real the fortunes of
all. The Acropolis, Athens' "higher city," has protected this subtext, legis-
lating that those who are not at its origin may be poets or statesmen, but
not both. Or that one might be both if in possession of a poetic politic that
is mimetic and dulcet – imitative, soothing, agreeable – a servile imitation
of its own. In contest for admission to the city, many a poet has exhausted
herself and never been said to win.

The Athenian laws of textual production justify their rule of poetry and
politics by claiming a privileged epistemic access to knowledge of the
truth. The Athenian Citizen in Plato's *Laws* declares, "Our whole polity
has been constructed as a dramatization of a noble and perfect life . . . one
which indeed can be produced only by a code of true law." Socrates offers
in support of his expulsion of poetry from the *Republic*, "It would be imp-
ious to betray what we believe to be the truth" (Plato 1961: VII 817b, IV
719c). This tenuous justification takes on verisimilitude when Socrates
fabricates the history of a long-standing quarrel between poetry and philosophy, a tradition that would perpetuate the banishment of poetry and
prevent the exercise of poetry and politics by hands other than his own.

The textual violence of lesbian and feminist writing blocks the wedge
by affirming that which Socratic tradition would disinherit: poetry, her
bold and unsettling character. Against Socrates, whose views of poetry
and "her spell" in a "well-governed city" lead him to testify, "we really
had good grounds then for dismissing her from our city since such was
her character" (Plato 1968: X 607b) – poetry is freed to become a furious
complex of characters that turn the Athenian city into an illusion and
poetry's fictions into reality.

Today a new form of the wedge, assimilationist claims and expectations, would conceal the textual violence of lesbian and feminist writing.
This wedge would separate lesbian and feminist writing, including the
new French feminisms, from their history as a distinctive textual move-

ment. By obfuscation of their historic exercise of violence, it would reinstate the Same: the Athenian laws of textual production. In the wake of assimilation, women are written about without any reference to actual texts by female authors, as is the case with continental philosophers such as Derrida and Foucault. Or the new French feminisms are mentioned, but only by coupling female writers with male counterparts. Much as Simone de Beauvoir has been read against a background of Sartrean philosophical presupposition, missing the import of her concerns, new French feminist writers are read as accessories whose task is to respond to, correct, deviate from, and enhance, male-defined theoretical projects.[5]

Assimilationist claims argue in support that writings by Cixous and Wittig reflect a traditional academic training: Cixous references Freud and Lacanian psychoanalysis, Genet, Heidegger, and Derrida, and Wittig cites influence by Barthes, Brecht, Proust, and Russian formalism. Both Cixous and Wittig cite the importance of works by Marx.[6] Assimilationist readings of the new French feminisms fail to note that texts such as those by Cixous and Wittig mention the classic male tradition in order to dismiss it by rigorous critique, or to turn it inside out until it is beyond recognition.

The lacunae

Suppression of the textual violence of the new French feminisms fails, for the lacunary origins of these and other lesbian and feminist writings resist all attempts to institute the Athenian laws of textual production. Both Cixous and Wittig claim a strong rapport with female authors: Cixous writes of her bonds with Clarice Lispector and Marguerite Duras, and Wittig indicates her connections with Sappho, Djuna Barnes, Natalie Sarraute, and members of the group *questions féministes*. Yet the question of textual situation is more than a matter of influence, for the violence of the new French feminisms emerges in spaces where patriarchal structures are absent – spaces which would expand and which are already female languages, cultures, histories. Cixous tells of those "spaces containing a certain amount of useful and necessary knowledge in order to carry out another type of work which would be on the side of femininity" (Cixous and Conley 1984:63). Wittig writes of the "intervals that your masters have not been able to fill with their words of proprietors and possessors . . . the gaps, . . . all that is not a continuation of their discourse" (Wittig 1973:113, 114). *Les Guérillères*, Wittig's book of female writer-warriors, concludes,

TO WRITE VIOLENCE
OUTSIDE THE TEXT
IN ANOTHER WRITING
THREATENING MENACING
MARGINS SPACES INTERVALS

WITHOUT PAUSE
ACTION OVERTHROW
(Wittig 1973:143)

The power of the lacunae derives not from an essentialist separation of female and male traditions, but from the historic fact of the linguistic and other activities that take place in such sites. For Cixous, the institutions of phallocentric language are firmly displaced by a lacunary feminine language:

For as soon as we exist, we are born into language and language speaks (to) us, dictates its law, a law of death: it lays down its familiar model, lays down its conjugal model. . . . (Cixous 1981:45)

A metaphoric language opens up a life space for Cixous, "Up high, I lived in writing. I read in order to live . . . there was little place for metaphor in my existence, a very restricted space, which I often annulled" (Cixous 1977:29). For Wittig, it is because the female warriors of *Les Guérillères* create shared linguistic spaces that they can name, and in so doing end, phallic control of language –

They [*Elles*] say, the language you speak poisons your glottis tongue palate lips. They say, the language you speak is made up of words that are killing you. They say, the language you speak is made up of signs that rightly speaking designate what men have appropriated. (Wittig 1973b:114)

They say, I refuse henceforward to speak this language, I refuse to mumble after them the words lack of penis lack of money lack of insignia lack of name. (Wittig: 1973b:107)

Recognition of male appropriation of language is accompanied by the decision of each female to determine the language, or languages, she will speak, a choice that is made, for both Cixous and Wittig, in a specifically female context. For Cixous, the context is that of a feminine writing that disperses the space of death:

It was mortally cold, the truth had set, I took the last book before death, and behold, it was Clarice, the writing. . . . The writing came up to me, she addressed me, in seven languages, one after the other, she read herself to me, through my absence up to my presence. (Cixous 1979:48)

For Wittig, the context is a lesbian writing whose power imbues a subjectivity, *j/e*, the lesbian "I." *J/e* is not one, nor is *j/e* split. As Wittig indicates in *The Lesbian Body, j/e,* with the power of /, the bar, overturns all expectations of heterosexual discourse:

Your whole body is in fragments here. . . . I [*j/e*] speak to you, I yearn for you with such marvelous strength that all of a sudden the pieces fall together. (Wittig 1976:112)

In the space of a female bestowed life, Cixous affirms poetry: its phonic and oral dimensions, its bodily materialization of language, and its source in female desire. Such a poetizing grants an open space that brings each woman to writing: "Woman must put herself into the text – as into the world and into history – by her own movement" (Cixous and Conley 1984:63). Wittig claims poetry as a catalyst for transformation in women's lives. In *Crossing the Acheron,* Wittig shows that Virgil failed to attain paradise not because he was pagan but because, without desire or hope, he lost passion for an actual paradise here and now and wanted to destroy his works. Wittig, a poet of desire and hope, reworks female syntax and semantics to write that which has been without words: the space of freedom threatened with extinction, "the music of the spheres and the voice of the angels" (Benegas 1985:97; Wittig 1985d:110).

Just as language is not a static framework to which new contexts are attached as clothes are hung on a line, the female languages determined by Cixous and Wittig are not ethnographic details added on to language, but a shift in what is language. *It would be a misunderstanding to conceive the textual violence of Cixous and Wittig's writing as an external tool that manipulates language, rather than as a creation of meaning that makes real the claim that language, or more accurately, languages, are informed by ethnographic limits.* To be forbidden language, to be poisoned by a language not one's own, are not psychological, or individual dilemmas. Experience that the language, or languages, one exercises are distinct from that language which would impose itself is not "merely" an autobiographical confession, but a dispersal of philosophical, literary, and political discourses about "language itself." As Jewish, Algerian, lower middle-class when young, and a woman, Cixous states she had to deal with the fact that language, the material from which writing is drawn, was lacking for her. "'You can read, adore, be assailed,'" she was told, "'But writing is not granted to you.' . . . Writing was reserved for the elect" (Cixous 1977:20). A battle for a language of one's own begins early, also, for the young female students of Wittig's *Opoponax*. Françoise Pommier, already alienated from the vitality of language, "makes round, fine letters with her pen that stay right between the two lines without sticking out" (Wittig 1966:31). Catherine Legrand, heroine of the *Opoponax*, resists the rule of the dominant language and refuses to hold a pen correctly during writing class (Wittig 1966:32).

A pulverization of "language proper" is effected by the interaction and singularity of female languages that destabilize laws of gender-marked syntax and semantics. The impact of Cixous's observation that there is not one feminine discourse, but thousands of different kinds of feminine words, and of Wittig and Zeig's *Lesbian Peoples: Material for a Dictionary* (1979), is to demonstrate that *the plurality of female languages is textual violence* (Cixous and Clément 1986:137). The violence of these languages is not the centralized and seemingly monolithic force of the wedge, but a starting on all sides at once, the character, Cixous maintains, that makes a feminine writing, or a fracturing and extension into space that is like Pascal's circle, whose center is everywhere and whose circumference is nowhere, a character, Wittig states, of lesbian writing (Cixous 1981:53; Wittig 1979:65). These feminine languages announce themselves in Cixous's texts: "a language that resonates in each national language"; "the language of my mother"; "the language that speaks/is spoken by women when no one is listening to them to correct them"; the language of Promethea, she who speaks burningly, she who has not cut the cord that connects speech to her body and who does not know how to speak otherwise (Cixous 1977:28; 1983:184). Each of these languages is, Cixous insists, a political act of resistance:

For a long time it has been in body that women have responded to persecution, to the familial-conjugal enterprise of domestication, to the repeated attempts at castrating them. Those who have turned their tongues 10,000 times seven times before not speaking are either dead from it or more familiar with their tongues and their mouths than anyone else. (Cixous 1976:886, 887)

The lesbian languages in Wittig's texts are animated by "the original language of 'letters and numbers,'" which the ancient Amazons did not relinquish . . . a language which, according to the legend, "was capable of creating life or of 'striking' death" (Wittig and Zeig 1979:94). "OLULU, OLULU," modulated according to different rhythms, speeds, volumes, the famous cry of triumph of the Tritonians, conqueresses and amazons from Libya, disempowers languages whose rigid, rigorous, repressive construction would effect a permanent representation of female oppression (Wittig and Zeig 1979:119).

The longer one moves in the lacunae, the more readily the textual violence of lesbian and feminist writing defines itself as the creation of meaning that is exercised by each female language. Female control of the production of meaning constructs a pandemic poetic politics that makes real not one history, but many. It aims not to establish a correct line of female inheritance, but to make a claim of noninheritance, based on the female experience that knowledge cannot be possessed. The languages that are created and freed in the works of Cixous and Wittig pass on textual worlds without dictating a right over them, a freedom without legislation, in rivalry to excel in the rejection of servile ideology and in invention. As the sites of a poetic politics in which female fortunes are remembered and invented by each in the company of those whom she chooses, the lacunae effect cataclysmic upheavals in textual history and produce their own textual worlds.

III. THERE IS NO "POLITICS OF DIFFERENCE"

Lesbian and feminist poetic politics challenge the current designation of women's writing, and in particular, of the new French feminisms, as "the politics of difference." "The politics of difference," a term that has achieved prominence among contemporary continental and feminist theorists, is a misnomer.

"A writing said to be feminine," the political strategy of Cixous, claims to draw upon the lacunae of female writing, each with its languages and politics, and thereby to affirm a politics of differences. Feminine writing dissolves the logic of difference organized according to a hierarchy of opposition and, Cixous declares, makes of difference "a bunch of new differences." For Cixous, the affirmation of differences, one of which is "woman," forms a politics of female survival that dislodges the rule of the Same. A claiming of differences stops racism and misogyny, "two ways of not letting the other exist, of cancelling, of excluding, or of occulting the other," and brings to an end that history in which differences are at no moment tolerated or possible (Cixous and Clément 1986:67, 70, 71, 83; Cixous 1980a).

The "political semiology" of Wittig, in contrast, claims the lacunae in their individuality by abolishing "differences" and "difference." Any difference that constitutes concepts of opposition between categories of individuals is, Wittig maintains, the product of an oppressive ideology. This includes the difference identified as "woman," for as Wittig argues with admirable consistency:

What makes a woman is a specific social relation to a man, . . . a relation which implies personal and physical obligation as well as economic obligation. (Wittig 1981:53; 1982:64; 1979:115)

Apart from the rule of identity, both "differences" and "difference" are empty concepts. One is not born a woman or a man, and just as there are no slaves without masters, there are no women without men.

There can be, moreover, no "politics" of difference. When posited as "difference," the "margin," the "other," the new French feminisms are represented as a reactive movement, mesmerized by the mechanisms of power that enforce the Same. Female control of the creation of meaning is depicted as a single voice which, for unexplained reasons of birth, destiny, or mere happenstance, is stationed permanently on the outskirts of the Acropolis and barred from entrance. Without the dignity of their self-chosen names – "a writing said to be feminine," "political semiology," etc. – the plurality that constitutes the political power of the new French feminisms is not addressed.

The new French feminisms constitute themselves by refusing "the politics of difference," by rejecting that ideology whose fixity and universality of claim would erase the indigenous aspects and the particularity of female languages and experience. This refusal is textual violence, an act in which being spoken for is displaced by a fluid speaking of self with selves. As a valuation of self, it is a deliberate offense which is one, although not the only, historical condition for the possibility of female survival.

The rejection of "the politics of difference" opens a space, moreover, for the formulation of issues still to be resolved. Cixous affirms a politics of differences, but in such a way that her writing tends toward an ideology of difference. Wittig rejects all ideologies of difference, but underestimates the relevance of some differences that are historically constituted.

That difference which is feminine, Cixous argues, exceeds the rule of signification and is, therefore, beyond ideology. "Feminine" and "masculine," "man" and "woman," designate that which cannot be classified inside a signifier except by force. The feminine, and more precisely, the feminine libidinal economy which Cixous characterizes as "neither identifiable by a man nor referable to the masculine economy," is abundant, endless. The feminine escapes the signifier as a living structure: a biological difference based on drives which are radically different for women than for men, and a product of history and culture (Cixous and Conley 1984: 51, 56, 57; Cixous 1976:28; Cixous and Clément 1986:81–83).

Cixous's affirmation of femininity as "the precursory movement of a transformation of social and cultural structures," makes femininity, written outside anticipation, into a messianic text of the future. "Women-poems," the "poems like open palms," are to organize and care for the regeneration and vitalization of other (Cixous 1981:50, 53; 1976:879; 1980a). Messianism and maternity intertwine in Cixous's texts, which resist the patriarchal disparagement of the pleasures of pregnancy, but at the risk of making motherhood prescriptive for females. Messianism, maternity, and heterosexuality are mandated:

I do not believe in that [artificial insemination] at all. . . . I do not sing the praise of the union of women, because it is wrong . . . but as one knows, a child is made together. It takes two, a man and a woman. Besides this child precisely needs two. (Cixous and Conley 1984:66)

As Wittig succinctly remarks, this is "An anti-homosexual racism, whose function is to poeticize the obligatory character of the 'you-will-be-straight-or-you-will-not-be'" (Wittig 1980:107). Even in *Le Livre de Promethea*, in which Cixous explicitly rejects bisexuality and writes the love of women with women, H. describes herself, "I am born mother, like all the girls," and Promethea is named, "a woman, a child, a mother" (Cixous 1983:150; 1976:890, 891).

The ideology of difference is more successfully brought to an end by Wittig, whose texts make real her maxim, "Neither gods nor goddesses, neither masters nor mistresses" (Wittig 1985c:35). Her theory of writing tends, however, to a formalism that does not take into account the relevance of diverse female languages and experience. Wittig's claim that ideology is displaced when a literary text reduces language to be "as meaningless as possible" and turns language into a "raw," "neutral," material to be worked (Wittig 1984b:47–49), does not admit those nonformal elements that might account, in part, for how language is worked in some ways rather than others, for instance, as lesbian writing rather than as heterosexual discourse. This omission is unexpected, for the formalism that pervades Wittig's theory of writing is not predominant in that writing itself. The material base that informs her theory of writing breaks through formalism and enables theoretical articulation of women's concrete situations. Wittig's *Paris-La-Politique* calls in that city, a city in name only, where

one is like the wolves that howl from freedom and famine, their flanks exposed to the wind while the others with the mark of the collar have a full stomach and a shining fur (Wittig 1985c:41).

for food, drink, and shelter, the first necessities for a space in which one can breathe more freely.

Amidst the conflicts in Cixous and Wittig's assessments of the relation of ideology to female languages and experience, "the politics of difference" is dismantled from all sides at once. At their best, the texts of Cixous and Wittig displace the ideology of difference by the practice of new forms of textual violence: the uprooting of their own narratives, especially insofar as they preserve the imprint of ideology; the creation of meaning that is unrecoverable by ideology, and which is, therefore, dangerous to the rule of the Same. While the practice of textual violence is dangerous to itself, danger is an element in which lesbian and feminist writing thrives.

IV. AN AMAZON INTERTEXTUALITY

Poetic politics transforms textual reality not by a single strategy, but by a combination of strategic shifts. A turnabout of realities occurs when lesbian and feminist writing, by placing more and more female-defined signs in relation to each other, makes vanish patriarchal signifiers and signification. Piece by piece, syntactic and semantic innovations pile up and, by the power of their presence, reconfigure fiction and reality. Luci Maure, of Wittig's *Les Guérillères*, gives one instance of how multiple methods of meaning constitution magnify their effects when she cries,

> . . . to the double echo the phrase of Phenarete, I say that that which is is, I say that that which is not also is. When she repeats the phrase several times the double, then triple, voice endlessly superimposes that which is and that which is not. (Wittig 1973b:14)

An initial judgment that the effects of Luci Maure's cry are more imagined than "real," may be followed by an awareness of their surprising reality. Objections that the new French feminisms do not engage a narrative style that portrays "reality" according to a representational concept of truth and do not offer step-by-step proposals for action miss the possibility that there may be numerous politically efficacious styles of lesbian and feminist writing. A related charge of elitism has tended to accept the biases of literature of engagement, for which language is but a tool for liberation. The frequent assumption of this criticism, that there is a single, linear language common to women, ignores the plurality of female languages and the strength of their nonconformity.[7] Indeed, as females experiment ourselves in words on paper, our texts become an outpost of lesbian and feminist cultures.

Common to the strategies of lesbian and feminist writing, and defined uniquely by each, is a field of textual action that might aptly be termed: amazon. If an amazon text is a text of female freedom, then the texts of lesbian and feminist writing constitute an amazon intertextuality. Such texts may be considered by and about amazons, whether Cixous's *Le Livre de Promethea*, in which "H." calls Promethea, bearer of female languages and life, "my amazon," or Wittig and Zeig's *Lesbian Peoples*, in which "all the companion lovers called themselves amazons. Living together, loving, celebrating one another" (Cixous 1983:89; Wittig and Zeig 1979:5).

Feminine writing, Cixous claims, is an action of strategic value, for it expresses what has been silenced. The poetic is political in the most efficient and ensnaring sense because it takes place in language (Cixous and Conley 1984:65; Cixous 1981:53; 1976:879; 1980a). Wittig affirms that writing and action are inseparable,

I am a woman who writes of women and for the liberation of women. It is the same act: I cannot dissociate the two terms. It engages my body, my desire, my dreams, and my hope. (Wittig 1974:12)[8]

She shows, in *Crossing the Acheron*, that the text is an excellent site for a female offense, so often is the enemy an ideology that induces servitude without exercising a direct, physical presence (Wittig 1985d:81). While admitting that some militant actions advance women's liberation more immediately than does feminine writing, Cixous insists,

And to live, I need to do what I am doing. So, do I have the right to do it? . . . I justify myself . . . I believe it is useful, and I think that it can be useful only on condition that there be a women's movement. (Cixous and Conley 1984:59, 60)

So primary is the women's movement to the production of texts in rupture with masculine culture that, Wittig states, "if the women's movement dies, I die. My person would lose all reality, all sense" (Wittig 1974:12; 1976:ix).[9]

Once banished by patriarchy, the ensemble of amazon texts articulates its histories, from the warriors of Dahomey, Patagonia, the Caucasus, to Sakundeva, rebel queen in Cixous's *The School at Madhubai*, and Panza and Quixote, heroines of Wittig's *The Longest Journey* (Wittig 1985b; Cixous 1986). The record of Aeschylus in the *Eumenides*, and of those who have held the power to write and to preserve that record, has perpetuated the history of amazon defeat and Athenian victory at the Acropolis. Yet the record of a loss so overwhelming as to constitute the end of amazon endeavor is far from universal. An amazon intertext has been suppressed, not for lack of records by which it might speak its fortunes, but because how the amazons took the Acropolis might displace male, Western, philosophical culture.

In the records of this writer, the Acropolis has been taken not just once, but over and over again. The amazons have gone to Athens to avenge the wrongs done an amazon queen, to recapture a hill still marked by traces of an ancient amazon city, to engage in a textual production of meaning that befits these and related events.

On the Acropolis, that symbolic site from which male-defined institutions have attempted to rule, the amazons pitched their camp after they mastered the surrounding country and approached the city with impunity (Plutarch 1914:XXXVI.4–XXVII.2; Aeschylus 1959: lines 684–90; Cleidemus 1973:103–4). On Ares' Hill they set up their camp and fortified that place with walls and towers as a new fortress-town. The Athenians were routed and driven back by the women as far as the shrine of the Eumenides. The fact that the Amazons encamped almost in the heart of the city is attested both by the names of the localities there and by the graves of those who fell in battle.

The Acropolis has been taken, as well, by an Athena whose verdict before the Athenian judges was not that recorded by Aeschylus. Athena's supposed defense of the laws of Apollo, "my task is to render the last verdict / And I cast this stone for Orestes" (Aeschylus 1959: lines 662–720), is thereby recast.[10] Instead of the illusory Athena, "motherless daughter of Zeus' head," there speaks an Athena, ancient Libyan amazon, founder of that city which was given her name and from which she, like poetry, was expelled. In the contest of languages and life, Athena, amazon, dismissed by tragedian and philosopher for reasons of character, history, and her friends, casts a final verdict – for freedom made by each woman's words and hands.

NOTES

1 As a chronological point of reference, Wittig's *Opoponax* (1964) is the earliest of the new French feminist texts. Cixous's *Le Prénom de Dieu* (1967) and *L'Exile de James Joyce* (1968) do not take up gender issues, which she first considers in *Dedans* (1969). The first major book by Luce Irigaray that is gender related, *Speculum de l'autre femme*, was published in 1973. The widely held belief that Julia Kristeva "is also, among the major theoreticians writing in France, the only woman – and that makes her contribution even the more noteworthy as she challenges a long Western tradition of male-dominated thought," is given voice in Leon S. Roudiez's "Introduction" to his translation of *Revolution in Poetic Language* and is a serious misrepresentation. Kristeva's *Recherches pour une semanalyse*, which does not deal directly with gender issues, appeared in 1969, and her *La Révolution du langage poétique*, in 1974.

2 Texts of particular usefulness either for study of literary criticism of Cixous and Wittig's writing, or for historical analysis of recent events in the French lesbian/feminist movements include: Verena Andermatt (1979); Noni Benegas (1986); Diane Griffin Crowder (1983) and (1985); Christiane Makward (1978); Michele Richman (1980); Marthe Rosenfeld (1988) and (1984); Namascar Shaktini (1982); Hélène Vivienne Wenzel (1981).

3 In addition to the numerous and diverse instances of lesbian and feminist writing to be found in books, anthologies, and journals such as *Hypatia: A Journal of*

Feminist Philosophy, see also *The History of Women Philosophers,* ed. Mary Ellen Waithe, a four-volume series forthcoming with Martinus Nijhoff.

4 While Cixous never relinquishes entirely the ideology that motherhood is a necessary element of any symbolics, her texts, such as *Le Livre de Promethea* and *La Bataille de Arcachon,* reject bisexuality and heterosexuality as normative and establish other directions of inquiry.

5 Simons (1986) develops a reading of Beauvoir that is independent of Sartrean presuppositions.

6 A direct criticism of French, male, poststructuralist thought is developed by Wittig (1980), "The Straight Mind."

7 Feminist theorists in the United States have expressed reservations at attempts to import French feminisms into lesbian and feminist writing in the United States. A charge of "exoticism" has developed which, for this writer, is well addressed to the publishing industry and the academic institutions that have supported the works of French female writers to a far greater extent than similarly experimental, theoretical work by American authors. Nevertheless, the new French feminisms' concern with language is not exclusively academic. Outside the United States, groups of women who live apart from academia, for instance, the French Canadian *Visibilité Lesbienne,* conduct experiments in female syntax and semantics which, in addition to their own concerns, share much in common with the new French feminisms.

8 See also Rosenfeld (1984:241).

9 See also Makward (1976:13). Cixous and Wittig recognize the need for a plurality of political actions, including those outside the texts of writing. The written text is limited, Cixous claims, because a part of the world cannot write and because truly unlivable events do not have a writing. For Wittig, the exercise of a new language requires a parallel action in social history, or, as she demonstrates in *Les Guérillères,* that females seize all weapons.

10 Athena, according to Aeschylus, votes for Orestes, who has killed his mother, Clytemnestra, to avenge the death of his father, Agamemnon. Athena votes against Clytemnestra, who has killed Agamemnon to avenge his murder of her daughter, Iphegenia. (See Aeschylus [1959: lines 662–720]). For reference to Athena the amazon, and the history of Athens as an amazon city, see W. K. C. Gutherie (1955:107); Wittig and Zeig (1979:11, 12); Herodotus (1973:103, 104).

18

Alice Parker

Under the Covers:
A Synesthesia of Desire (Lesbian Translations)

Using the related concepts of *translation* and *passing*, I want to de-sign a space of lesbian subjectivity. As translation moves from one semantic system to another, passing is an exchange of codes that permits movement between cultural locations, prototypically passing from one race to another. As we will see, these movements call into question and destabilize the codes involved. As a woman, a feminist, a lesbian, I translate the materiality of my daily experiences into an alien code, a code that is always already phallic and patriarchal, and which e(xc)ludes me. The only way I can speak/write is by passing as an-other. The subject position, the "I" I try to occupy is (presumed to be) male and heterosexual. Further, Woman, the sign of my given gender, is a place of representation for me in a sociotext that makes self-knowledge difficult by privileging the male gaze. I watch my self being seen. The stories that I will recount about my "life" are all fictions, mediated by my assigned place in a Jewish family with bourgeois pre-tensions, by my geocultural and professional locations.

But when I speak/write as a lesbian the (gendered) center no longer holds. The fact that I speak in the place of the Other problematizes the authorizing discourses that would like to keep me at the margins, or, indeed, invisible. In assigning myself a place, literally inventing new signs, I create breaches in what Michèle Causse calls the "androlect" that at once writes me and reduces me to insignificance (1988:1). The first order of business is to evacuate the place of Woman, an object of phallic/male desire, which, as Nicole Brossard notes, "hangs over our heads like a threat of extinction" (1988b:134).

But this is a tricky operation, because, as Monique Wittig observed, the category of sex "sticks" to a woman (1982:68); the moment I open my mouth "you," my interlocutor, put me in my "proper" place, the place of Woman, my place of assignation in the sex/gender system. Further, following Luce Irigaray we know that the sex/gender system is monosocial and monosexual (men addressing men), as Teresa de Lauretis reemphasizes in a recent article, based on a phallic model (the "Oedipal contract"), and an economy of the same (Irigaray 1984:132–33; de Lauretis 1990:132 et passim). "Resistant" readers recognize personal pronouns, in particular the subject of discourse, by not-too-subtle markers as white, bourgeois, male, and so on, while the syntax of traditional grammar positions woman as object (as in the social sciences she is not the agent but is rather acted upon).

The work on pronouns in lesbian-feminist texts, the violent rending of the subject (*j/e*) in Monique Wittig's *Le corps lesbien* (1973a), is an effort to foreground concealed ideology in supposedly neutral grammar, and to "lesbianize" both the subject and the object of discourse (Wittig 1985a:11). I too am learning radical strategies to disrupt linguistic functions, I am learning to focus on gender/power arrangements in order to tease out patriarchal privilege as it inheres in heterosexualism (Sarah Hoagland's term in *Lesbian Ethics* [1988]), family arrangements, and the exchange of women and children, all of which legitimize abuse and neglect. How, I ask myself, do I avoid phallic patterns, the tyrannical "I" and the hegemonic "we"; how do I write so that I neither occupy your space nor put you in your place, so that I speak only for myself while encouraging you to articulate your desire? How do I use the plural subject or indeed the word *lesbian* without losing the rich variety of our skin tones, of our national and class differences, of the textures of our hair?

I see translation and passing as back-and-forth movements between androlect and gynolect, between female and lesbian; they disrupt phallo(go)centric structures that reinforce the law of the father(s) and reduce me to bio-graphesis, and to a false "origin" in the (m)other. "The personal is political," we learned in the seventies, and vice-versa – I was amazed recently to hear a friend declare that she thought this formula was a huge net intended to trap the politically incorrect; I was reminded how incomplete is my understanding, especially of the oppressions of class, and that we can never be vigilant enough. Lesbians writing are busy charting new paths between the individual and the ontological in order to reopen the question of epistemology, how we know who we are. What does it mean to choose an identity that is unspeakable, that I cannot name, for example, at the university where I work? Absence is a place of knowing in this text – I am allowed to *be* a lesbian, my ontological location is secure, as long as I do not use the word. It appears that this absence is a protective silence; paradoxically, I and my hypothetical university interlocutor know that the word *lesbian* has such power that it must remain veiled. Thus Alice Parker the lesbian is at once absent and present, "split at the root" (Rich 1986a:100–123), forced to speak with forked tongue, double-speak. Now we know from psychoanalytic theory that the subject is necessarily divided, absent and present, but the complex doubling of lesbian subjectivity is a heavy house to carry on my back as well as a protective cover.

"A lesbian who does not reinvent the world is a lesbian in the process of disappearing" (Brossard 1988b:127). Every day I engage in the work of double translation, in which there is no original and no target language. Psychic experience is pushed to the limit, following the structure of the per/verse. I trespass in an alien territory where my lesbianism knows uncertain limits. In the borderlands my only camouflage is my skin. Moving in the neural conduits of the brain I try out new commands, primal messages, rewriting the programs. "Perturbation, my sister, the hundred-headed woman" (Ernst 1968): I chose to be a teacher so that I could remain a student, learning, reading, writing, moving in the para-doxical. Translation for me is having several languages, as passing is not so much a question of covers as codes to play with, the polysemic potential of words on the tongue, tongues on the words. There are questions of ad-dress, who wears whose clothes; one thinks of a carnival or a masquerade. Criss-crossing: "tacking," I learned as a Mariner Scout, was a "zigzag" path you used in difficult seas or wind conditions, and to return your sailboat to its mooring when you could not sail straight in. Every day I shift my sails to catch the wind as I set my devious course.

I study dislocations: letters, words fly off in all directions, relieved of gravity, sentences turn in/side out, are upended like the "wrecked" planes in surrealist paintings. I am sentenced to begin again, unwrite, rewrite. Under the covers are certain *sig*nals: an in/tensity of the eyes, configurations of the hands. The lesbian body is the woman of the woman as we would say the other of the other. Passing changes its suffix to become pas/sage, a process that leads us undercover, under the covers, where we do not find anything we did not already know, as between the covers the story is at once written and read. The process is creative or it is deadly: if we do not invest in the pleasure of our bodies, the ecstasy of our spirits, we will become zombies in the service of the destroyers.

Re-citing the texts that inspire me, I have learned from the practice of recent writers to play with the place of subjectivity that I covet, to engage in a loving process with all of the surfaces of my language. I am nourished by many lifetimes, although the waters I navigate are not always clear. Negotiations (re-claimed from the crass world of commerce): from one language to another(s) and back, trans-actions, texts juxta-posed, sometimes just brushing against each other, a slight pressure of the fingers. How do you line up tongues? How do I hear what you are saying? In the end I may be able to abandon my masquerade, to pass as my "self," to translate my desire into words that do not sound foreign. Each day I invent a space in which to breathe, to write. Each day I remind myself that I am not free while my sisters are tortured, in Chile, in Soweto, in Bangladesh, in Beirut, on the streets of the United States of North American cities. Each day I use a "differential equation" (Brossard [1977] 1988a:45) to plot a trajectory of lesbian desire. Each day I try to decipher the voices of lesbians I see. Each day I reassure my lover(s); each day I need more space. Each day I write my name.

Every time I read I want to change my mind. A traffic in minds? "An image," says Djuna Barnes, "is a stop the mind makes between uncertainties" (1961:111). The mirror in which two are seen as one, reduced by half, reflects a picture on the wall behind my head (a Venus figure), the planes dissolve. The logic of the sentence predicates its own truth. Never, is my rule, give a straight answer. Stay in the space between the signifier and the signified, refusing signification. Neither facts nor autobiography (Cixous 1983:27) exist: I have a passion for living (on) the margins (of assigned subject positions), thus for slippage where "I" am difficult to apprehend; "I" pass as a configuration of the "real," the quotidian; I move in a world that I name with parentheses or quotation marks, like the title of Michèle Causse's latest fiction, a wordless diacritical/grammatical sign, "( )." I trans/late my self from one code to another. If I chose to "start" somewhere, it would be with a body on the waning side of middle age, a life which is phasing out like the crescent moon. Of course, there are no real or unmediated "facts." So why my body? Is it less reducible or mediated than the rest (Jewish, North American, the other categories of bio-graphesis that write me)? If subjectivity is produced by "interlocking systems of . . . social stratification" (de Lauretis, 1988:164), surely there are figures that enable us to understand the process – for example I feel that chance molecules of identity may bond, in my case the signs Jewish and lesbian, to produce a combination that displaces whiteness and middle-class, North American identity – mine are the refugees, the immigrants, suspended between cultures, whose domestic languages differ from the official tongue.

Then there is the question of address: "who produces cultural representations and for whom"? (de Lauretis 1988:168). How is *dress* hidden in *address* and *redress*? Michelle Cliff writes of the negotiations involved in "claiming an identity they taught [her] to despise," after she had spent many years learning to "pass" as white – passing from silence/speechlessness to speech, but of an/other (1980:6–7; 43–51).[1] This is a double travesty, trying to master the passages, the codes. When you claim a new identity you do not give up the others, nor is it a simple process of addition – there may be a shift of consciousness with attendant "ripple" effects on an entire milieu.

Nicole Brossard wonders what sort of relationship she would have to her body/gender in, say, Italian, or if the word *kimono* were in her daily vocabulary (1984:23). It is worth our while to ponder the kind of relationship black and Chicana, Native American and Asian-American lesbians have to their bodies. What would lesbian representation become under these circumstances? For me lesbian subjectivity consists of a continuous, active listening and interpretation, of a deconstruction of images of women that structure our seeing and of a visual grammar – the male gaze – that inhibits our perception. It is not just who is she, but who am I when I hear her voice, read her words.

Feminist consciousness is a fiction I invent (which is not to say that feminism does not exist as a political force) in order to survive in a patriarchal world in which the destroyers prosper – using, according to Carl Sagan's analysis, the most primitive, reptilian portions of their brains (1978:54–56; 62–64). It covers the entire surface of my skin in a rather uncomfortable way like goosebumps or hives. Late capitalism, communism, the fathers rule, and neither my skin nor my fictions protect me. Women, children, older people, the rain forests of the Amazon, the ozone layer, all unprotected species perish atrociously, in Palestine, Northern Ireland, Peru; whales and dolphins, my sisters off the coast of Japan, in "homelands" and on reservations, in El Salvador, Tanzania and many more strange-sounding places to my unpracticed ear.

I choose to be a lesbian in order to direct my political and sexual desire in a positive channel, as a medium channels spirits. Ethical short circuits engendered by heterosexualism, family ideology, and other abuses of power permit me only a ambivalent relationship with male colleagues and with the men in my own family. Women who are captives of this system, wonderfully mocked by Monique Wittig in her fiction *Virgile, non* (*Across the Acheron*) (1985d), inscribe disturbing deformities as well, unless alternate codes preserve them from idiocy. As my mental categories shift, I see my body not as female (a suspect term, like *feminine*), but as lesbian. If I redesign the world from the vantage point of lesbian desire, new images and patterns of perceiving emerge. The intertextual referents in this process move from Sappho, the Amazons, Egyptian and Ethiopian women, and the queens of Africa and ancient Europe to Renée Vivien, leaving space for the other lesbians occulted by his-story, the Natalie Clifford Barney and Gertrude Stein groups, Djuna Barnes and Colette, up to the radical feminists of the 1970s and 1980s. Although I pass as female and professional (genderless) in the everyday world in which I work, an underground lesbian culture, "an/other mother tongue" (Grahn 1984) nourishes my imagination like an artesian well.

Having arrived at it rather late in life, after a long marriage and two children, the choice to become a lesbian was not only "free" but a gift of the early seventies. Many women will never have this freedom or the space to experience such a decision. In looking back over my early life, and in refashioning an-other version of it in the light of permissions I now accord myself, I realize the extent to which misogyny and homophobia limited not only my choices but a recognition of the love (even passion) I felt for women. I remember my mother's reaction when I dared to associate the word *lesbian* with the director of our local Girl Scout council, and the scandal, from which I distanced myself with dis-taste, in my undergraduate dorm in the late fifties when two women were discovered together in a loving posture. A close friend who grew up in rural Alabama told me her dismay when she found herself attracted to a woman, an impulse for which she had no word except "crazy." I find that for women in the South, especially those from fundamentalist backgrounds, the word *gay* is decidedly sex-specific, relating only to men, and does not give use access to the word *lesbian* or to our varied sexuality. Just this week I donated many bags of unsold items from a community garage sale to a local relief agency staffed by older volunteers from various churches, who truly did not know who or what we were when I signed my name on behalf of the Tuscaloosa Lesbian Coalition. Obviously, if I do not continue to use the word I risk not only disempowering myself, but perhaps the sanity of a sister who has no language for her desire.

I certainly do not believe that lesbians will save the world or even ourselves from destruction. True, the category LESBIAN unsettles binary gender arrangements, as women loving women undermines patriarchal ideologies that control production and reproduction, that regulate the exchange, sexuality, and labor power of women, children, minorities. While participating in the "political process" (in the old way), and trying to create a cultural revolution, my strategy is to deny that the fathers retain all the power, the discourses, the war machines. Beginning with my own father, angry, tyrannical, abusive, alcoholic, and loving, supportive of an unwomanly education and career. I cannot pretend that I do not have two parents, or that in grieving a difficult childhood I can even stop there: I try to comprehend how what Alice Miller calls "poisonous pedagogy" and family pathology reach back through the generations.[2]

It must matter that mine is the first generation born into the "middle" class, still marginal, immigrant Jews possessed by self-loathing and a desire to pursue the American-Protestant dream, my anti-Semitic parents, card-carrying atheists, rejecting their roots. My mother, her anger surfacing in unpredictable ways (as did mine later with my own children), undermining a basic warmth and generosity, succeeded in loving only her youngest daughter; the sharp edge of her voice still can work its way up my spine. I hear it again when she talks to my daughter, her only granddaughter; girls, three of us and no sons – my father thought we were all "stupid." The bright side was a socialist heritage, a belief in the working class, and a faith in culture and intelligence. The paradox is that "class" is merely a pre-text in our country, obscured by a capitalist ideology of upward mobility, surplus value, overconsumption of goods, services, and resources. So many contra-dictions: I must have been encouraged to lie before conscious memory; duplicity is such a comfortable way of mind.

Resonating with (forbidden) joy and fear, LESBIAN draws power, although historically suppressed and silenced, from the displacements it enacts in the symbolic system. Think of the oxymoron, the *lesbian mother*, which unsettles not only patriarchal expectations for the reproduction of social institutions but the psychoanalytic formulation of subjectivity – and we should not underestimate the prescriptive psycho-sexual force of the Oedipal scenario. Similarly, the single (especially older) lesbian is a pariah who figures the stubborn refusal of and isolation from the comfort of pseudo-family (couple) arrangements. The level of discomfort that results from such illegitimate choices and exclusions may be excruciating. In small towns across North America gay men still use the cover of marriage. What protection do we as lesbians have from public censure? How do we keep from losing our children, our self-respect, our minds? Unwilling to give up my lover, my children, or the radical alternatives to nor/male social patterns, for years I juggled personae as if I had multiple personalities. More recently I have been learning to live with my ex-centricity, unraveling decades of socializing messages, stubbornly refusing to compromise my freedom, autonomy, or voice for the security of the couple. This has been the hardest road of all.

Lesbian identity is a structure or a field that compels disruptive patterns of thinking and imagining, "cerebral spinning" (Daly 1978:320; 1987:96). To write (as a) lesbian is not to use language as a wo/man, but to inscribe a subject of desire that has rarely been spoken. I have no choice but to blur "subject" and "confessional" positions, and to take responsibility, be responsive to the post-colonial United States of North American space into which "I" am inserted, as Adrienne Rich describes the process in "Notes Toward a Politics of Location" (1986a:210–31). The lesbian subject has, of course, no dimensional existence as a physical fact, but is rather an intellectual/psychic strategy. Which is not to deny my body or the material circumstances of lesbian lives. As soon as I speak my name as "I," an interlocutor (re)constructs the subject pronoun in whatever nominative gender s/he desires, appropriating, quite possibly, my syntactical location, the self I have tried to construct, reducing me to an "abject" position. The only desire structured into the symbolic system we call language is a phallic will to power that bars me as a woman, and how much more indignantly as a lesbian from speaking in my own voice. So I have to borrow other tongues, dress in drag as a fe-male, in order to be heard.

Now my habit of duplicity, of passing, stands me in good "stead" in this game; when I speak *I* do not mean what I say.

Writing a body that is marked with varied deformities and scars, a subject and object of lesbian desire, I am subject to the hesitations of "coming to terms." A woman in her fifties looks into the mirror, through the mirror, and sees some-one-else. I train myself to see the wrinkles, to observe my abdomen with its un-sight-ly bulges in profile. This is a chastening exercise, often repeated, to displace the smile and intensity (tension) of the eyes that try to trick me from the silvered surface – into believing I am younger, more attractive, more fe-male. Suddenly the process shatters into fragments, always lacking the courage of my convictions, born a rebel of rebels, my parents' best legacy. Looking at events, statements, pro-positions through a devious lens.

Nicole Brossard teaches us the many prisms of language, desire, the lesbian body, her spiral and hologram inscribing a utopic space for the imagination. I do not have to write sentences any longer – to sentence myself or any other lesbian. My syntax will be-come radical, come from deeply intuitive roots. I will come to know my own mind, the mind of the universe. Alice (*au pays des merveilles*) I was named by my older sister, a stroke of luck that keeps me negotiating on the far side of the mirror. This was not her only gift; there is a space of the soul I am just beginning to assess now that she has completed a final transition. She chose a difficult life. Karen, the channeler, told me that I would learn many more languages, and that I would teach those who are mute. That is, as they say, a tall order. What in fact could a lesbian practice of writing produce other than relationships between the body, the spirit and the word? The tongue, undertongue-tone-tow, the tide licking at the edge of the word as "we" know it.

In the mean-time, I study and write, rewrite, am written by lesbian texts, and by those who ponder the mysteries and hysteries of the universe, the infinitely great and infinitely small. I figure their figures. Playing in the spaces between stories, the lesbian story is neither more real nor more true, claims that no longer make much "sense," just more comfortable, more pleasurable. Is it possible to write a story that would save us from destruction? A story of skin brushing against skin, of the smell of women's bodies, of the silky feel of cheeks and lips, of hands reaching for each other, of voices linked in song, of your arms encircling my body in a gesture of reassurance, of fingers threading through all kinds of hair? You and I are not the same, so I have to learn your language, how you greet your mother, your daughter, the color of your/her eyes, how you twist your hair, the rituals you use to call your spirits, the names of your guides, your friends, how you light your fire, how you say your name, and mine. In passing I have been content to shuttle back and forth, to take few risks;

if I continue to seduce the fathers the last laugh will be on me. Passing from straight/norm-al to lesbian every living, working day. But my sisters are not all lesbians.

In an earlier version of this text I wrote "Only eros can materialize abstraction." Now the limitations of the term *eros* (like *agape* for that matter) disturb me. What I am seeking is a universal energy that can help heal the wounds: there are women I love in Mozambique, in India, in the United States, and they are mutilated. The women in Buchenwald, in Guatemala spoke to me before they were tortured and killed in Bolivia, in Liberia. So I must always know whose story I am telling, whose tongue I am speaking. What principle(s) can help us pass from class to class, from culture to culture, assess alien codes designed by male voices to protect their property, to isolate their wives, daughters, sisters, to keep the universal/univocal for themselves? My fiction at the moment is that when I write (as) a lesbian, I invent those who are waiting to be born. In a 1987 novel, the exiled Chilean writer Ariel Dorfman stages a revolt of the unborn, who simply refuse to emerge into a world of social horrors and political terror. An intriguing notion, this nostalgia for a new beginning is, of course, cultural suicide. But I make it a rule never to evaluate/para-phrase someone else's tragedy. The pain and complexities of exile are compounded when factors of gender and sexuality are introduced, creating a situation of continuous "othering" – call it translation and passing – for a Chilean poet who calls herself (regarding her first book) a "gagged muse," and even now "an echo torn out of another echo" (Diaz-Diocaretz, 1992:175). She asks: "Changing from language to language, do I actually travel or am I always in the same space but remain having the illusion that I have moved elsewhere?" (175). This is about perceptions and choices, about strategies for subjectivity, writing, survival.

We all speak many languages, and we also participate in culturally imposed or elective mutism. Sometimes when we are more eloquent we cannot hear a sound we are making. Survival depends on a nonreductive appreciation of diversity and complexity that cluster around two poles: responsibility (the ability to respond), and desirability (the ability to desire). How many of us have "shut down' with regard to one or the other? Life, in the student slang of the eighties, is "awesome." Enunciative strategies may become rituals of initiation. In my case, passing from a stable relationship into the unknown, learning to honor a choice that made me gasp for breath, has forced me to locate a new time/space from which to speak. In some way I needed my partner/lover to *be* a lesbian, for ontological support.

To choose lesbian identity is to eschew comfort, the security of fixed boundaries, the convenience of a recognizable category of nomination. Lesbian subjectivity is anomalous – which does not mean that we can dispossess ourselves of it by refusing the term *lesbian;* we can choose to think (of) it as mired in quicksand and dangerous, or, as Brossard has it, to regard the lesbian as writing on the side of pleasure (*jouissance*) and desire, as necessarily creative. Brossard's spiral of luminous energy, which encodes lesbian memory and connects us with our (radical) roots, transmutes into a resonating crucible, a field and song of vision (*champs/chant de vision*) (1988d:46). Who can work without desire, the energy that emanates from the cells and relates us to all other life? I pass from one zone to another, under(writing) the covers; I cannot write without feminist consciousness, without a global view. The multiple terrains opening on to lesbian subjectivity through codes of ex/change produce what I call a *synesthesia of lesbian desire*. I see the many prisms of lesbian desire as a kaleidoscope of astonishing colors and de-signs in many dimensions. According, recording, this desire is continuously displaced, without (an) object, never satisfied, continuously reborn – with all the jubilance of Michèle Causse's *Lesbiana* (1980) and its prototype, *The Ladies' Almanack* (Barnes 1972), and the erotic energy of Brossard's *Sous la langue/Under tongue* (1987b). Translation, passing: a round-trip ticket; mirror, mirage (*Le désert mauve*, Brossard 1987a:61); whom to let in, what to keep out; an original, a derivation. The substance of words, a controlled substance. Encoding lesbian desire we create our site/city, our country, a place to play ourselves.

Judy Grahn wonders if like Native peoples the lesbian "nation" (Johnston 1973) is spirit-related rather than family/blood related (1984:57). She sees our culture as "intersectional" (281), "diachromatic" (Lee Francis's term, quoted by Grahn, 278); passing gives us a perception of what she calls the "other side," engaging us in a process of crossing (273): "crossover journeys between genders, worlds" (260). We know the power of crossroads over which Hecate presides (273); we learn signs for transculture, the force of the rainbow (270). Translation leads to transformation; as double persons, through doubling "we can see into more than one world at once" (72). I personally have been undergoing a most amazing passage, from love and security through grief and sorrow to strength and enlightenment.

Three years ago I went through a life-rending breakup of a fourteen-year relationship. Besides our academic and community work, we were lovers, friends, family, collaborators. Ironically, I, who pride myself on trying everything at least once, was totally bereft of resources to deal with this new experience. How do you reorient a life, turn your heart around, face forward rather than backward? I am leaving intact my first effort to deal with the separation in writing, other than letters that I wrote compulsively, which are another kind of record that some day may be published. I chose to write in French not only because of the distance it afforded on the dynamics of the struggle to survive, but also because my favorite lesbian writers are francophone. Further, I was able to share this somewhat monstrous (malformed) document with some of the writers and benefit from their comments at an international seminar on lesbian theory hosted in Florence, Italy, by Liana Borghi in the summer of 1989. As for indiscretion, I make no excuses – the events of my own "life" have never seemed too sacred to share; further, transgression in this realm may help to demystify, to shatter the prison and silence (secret) in which lesbian lives have been immured. I do apologize to those of you who do not read French.

Depuis quatre mois je suis aux prises avec l'interlocution. Pendant quatorze ans le "je" dont je me servais com-prenait toujours un "tu," le moi appelait tout de suite un toi. Tu es redevenue pour moi une femme ordinaire, in-différente, une troisième personne. Etre lesbienne sans partenaire, en-visager les autres femmes comme objets de spéculation est un état d'esprit inédit. Etre lesbienne sans le toucher, sans les lèvres, sans les contours d'un corps à ma mesure me laisse non seulement un grand fonds de tristesse mais sans dé/finition. Je dérive dans un flot de mots qui a perdu sa structure, sa grammaire, son orientation. Où jeter l'ancre? Dans quelle terre informe poser des racines? Que mettre, comme le demande Michèle Causse, entre les parenthèses?

La dis-location est d'autant plus grave qu'idéaliste, j'ai vécu dans les nuages, j'étais absolument démunie. Ayant subie pas mal de déceptions dans une vie qui comprend maintenant plus de cinq décennies, je savais me protéger contre les hommes, le patriarcat, même le nom/non du père en pratiquant un langage de subversion, menteuse à l'occasion. Que devient pour moi par exemple l'éthique lesbienne sur laquelle je fondais une pensée, une alimentation intellectuelle? Là où il y avait une charge positive qui nourrissait mon espoir et une vision de l'avenir, une attirence qui dessinait une subjectivité lesbienne en expansion permanente, se trouve maintenant un abîme, un gouffre, un trou noir (noms marqués par le genre mâle), la terreur donc qui me répulse vers les marges de la création, qui me rend mon mutisme.

On me dit qu'il est trop tôt pour théoriser une rupture qui a failli me coûter la santé. Etrangère, oiseau de passage en migration permanente, je refaçonne l'imaginaire et une langue qui me permettra de nouvelles formes d'adresse. Qu'est-ce qui arrive si, ayant survécu le couple, ayant dépassé la troisième personne(s), je parle à la quatrième personne par exemple? A quoi cela ressemblerait-il? Y aurait-il moyen d'éviter non seulement la dépendance mais même la complémentarité?

En essayant de récupérer une voix (lesbienne) je me rappelle que *lesbienne* c'est aller toujours plus loin, s'en aller au bord, à la limite: n'est-ce pas cela que nous enseigne la physique théorique actuelle? Le chaos avec ses lois subtiles, la balance, qui me fait penser à cette déesse de la justice chez les Grec(que)s, qui l'ont sans doute héritée d'une époque plus loin, et qui s'appelait Dike, mot qui signifie "le chemin," "la voie" . . . "le passage" . . . "l'é-change" . . . "la réciprocité."

Là où était le silence sera une nouvelle aventure. Si la traduction c'est passer d'une langue dans une autre, quel avantage nous accorderaient plusieurs langues pour raconter notre histoire, pour façonner une écriture lesbienne? Entre le "je" neutre de l'interlocution, d'avant la sexuation, à puissance illimitée, tel que nous le décrit Monique Wittig dans une communication sur Natalie Sarraute, le je-femme et le je-lesbien il se produit tous les jeux possible ("Le lieu de l'action," 74). Ce sont des per-formances qui mettent en jeu les brèches, les failles de la langue pour dire les jouissances du corps et de la sensibilité lesbiens. Faillir serait renaître, une sub-version. Ne faire donc confiance ni à la langue maternelle ni à la langue paternelle, ni au sémiotique ni au symbolique. Quelle serait la langue qui ne nous dévalorise ni ne nous opprime? Quelle syntaxe nous permettrait d'inscrire nos désirs? Quelle lexique serait assez riche pour écrire le corps lesbien? Pour survivre il faut inventer tout cela, comme les esquimaux avec leur cent mots pour la neige.

S'il n'existe vraiment pas de frontières, comme nous le propose la nouvelle physique, si les courbes s'allongent devant nous dès que nous nous approchons des "limites" de l'univers, ne serait-ce de même pour la conscience humaine? Nous nous servons de si peu de notre cerveau. Les langues humaines elles aussi ont des morphologies arbitraires, effets de distinctions culturelles traditionelles aussi bien que de sociolectes locaux. Comment la lesbienne pourrait-elle éviter de voir plus loin, de se faire polylingue? Judy Grahn médite une langue secrète dont nous garderions la mémoire et que nous seules saurions réactiver (1984:19). La lesbienne se dédouble, lit les signes et les figures que ne sauraient interpréter les non-initiés. Le secret, ce qui ne se dit pas, des langues particulières, pleines de locutions à double valeur, c'est là où se reconnaissent les lesbiennes, dans l'île ou sur le continent (Brossard). Le danger c'est que je/nous risquons à tout moment de tout perdre si la liberté de le dire nous est refusé ou si nous nous interdisons cette liberté.

Autrefois, en fait jusqu'au vingtième siècle, la lesbienne qui "passait" acceptait de devenir un "homme" pour épouser celle qu'elle avait choisie comme partenaire. Les jeux "butch-femme" et érotiques nous font voir la diversité des statégies qu'ont adoptées les lesbiennes pour survivre avec nos désirs et nos différences. En relisant Joan Nestle (1987) et en discutant avec une jeune amie ses sentiments vis-à-vis certaines pratiques et fantaisies érotiques j'ai dû me rendre compte du rôle de la police intérieure qui nous dicte certains comportements et nous en prescrit d'autres. Voilà pourquoi je préfère négotier les limites, et cela de façon continue – nous ne savons pas encore ce que pourrait être une subjectivité et à plus forte raison une sexualité lesbienne. Entre deux langues, entre deux ou plusieurs lesbiennes, le monde est à recréer. Et la lesbienne solitaire, célibataire, c'est à elle seule de lire et de façonner son existence. Jusqui'ici pas de mot pour cela, la *différance,* mot utile qui met en cause notre liberté corporelle et temporelle.

Le lesbianisme, est-ce une pratique (sexuelle ou autre), ou un rapport inouï à l'autre (aux autres) lesbienne(s) – j'allais écrire *femme* ce qui me renverrait au système hétérosexuel dont je voudrais m'échapper – un rapport inédit à la langue, qui s'entendrait en "d'autres termes"? Les lesbiennes entre elles font glisser le sens; le genre devient un passage continu, une figure qui regarde autre-ment, qui s'harmonise avec elle-même, produit plusieurs voix, multiplie les résonances. Parce qu'il y a un excédant, un sur-plus. Le mot lesbien dérange les catégories, scandalise, met en mouvement toutes les particules, les ondes de mon être, m'excite, nouvelle attraction, gravité neuve. Le phénomène de passer, de découvrir un passage, comme toute traduction où il faut trouver le geste, le mot juste, demande une grande acuité mentale. Or je suis convaincue que la lesbienne est toujours aux écoutes, à la recherche de signaux, d'une langue à elle, une version originelle qui se fait reconnaître entre nous. Cela dépasse les codes conventionnels. Traduction simultanée, la subjectivité lesbienne serait une prise de position épistémologique/ontologique. Il s'agit de "traduire inénnarable" (Brossard 1986:25). La lesbienne serait l'intuition d'une espace libre de toute contrainte phallique, marquée de nos seuls désirs, une intuition nourrie, comme l'écrit encore N. Brossard, de toutes celles qui ont signé, qui ont laissé une signe (Brossard 1980b:108).

Synesthésie du désir lesbien, voilà ce que j'appele "l'entrelangue." Ce sont à la fois les espaces secrètes dans la langue, et les circuits qui relient les langues entre elles. Nous en apprenons les modalités chez les philosophes, les savantes chercheuses et les écrivaines lesbiennes; elles comprennent la révalorisation des termes fondamentaux de la philosophie et l'enrichissement de la lexique (Mary Daly, Monique Wittig et Sande Zeig, Jeffner Allen, Judy Grahn, Sarah Hoagland parmi d'autres); une nouvelle textualité – grammaire hardie, inconnue; pratiques syntaxiques, graphiques, poétiques (figurales); une in-tensité inédit; tonalité et modulation d'un érotisme savamment construit qui fait appel à toutes nos sur-faces. Comme lesbienne j'ai l'impression d'être un point d'origyne, un point zéro, un "centre blanc" (Brossard), d'où émane une énergie spéciale, une géométrie complexe, sans bords (fractals?) que moi seule saura traduire et que seules les autres lesbiennes sauraont lire.

A une année de distance de ce texte, porte parole d'une "vie" (laquelle?), d'un procès (dans les deux sense), je me rends compte d'une espace de perte, de collègues chéris, d'une soeur. Pas moyen de me tirer d'affaire, de conclure, de terminer cet écrit par une formule provocatrice. Sans doute ai-je travaillé dur pour récupérer un sens. Sans doute ai-je gagné une meilleure com-préhension des rapports entre le vécu et sa traduction. Ayant choisi de vivre entre deux femmes, de partager ma view et mes espoirs avec d'autres, la rupture ne me semble pas plus insensé qu'une relation devenue fiction par la distance psychologique et temporelle. La voix s'altère avec les circonstances. La mienne s'accorde à de nouveaux choix, à de nouvelles situations. Si j'ai perdu un partenaire j'ai retrouvé l'enfant abandonée et maltraitée (que j'étais) il y a si longtemps, et je me suis mise à l'aimer. J'apprends à me passer de la glace où j'ai cherché mon image pendant mon premier et seul amour lesbien, de jouir de la lumière que me renvoient les figures les plus diverses, y compris la mienne.

As the years accumulate, where am I? Amidst raw notes and ragged edges, have I learned to speak my name? I am seeing that there is life beyond stoicism and repression, after decades of "toughing it out." There is no healing without the expression of grief for the damage that has been done to us as women and lesbians, of which Minnie Bruce Pratt writes so eloquently in her prizewinning volume of poems, *Crimes Against Nature* (1990). I have given my self the gift of time, charting survival by the months now rather than the hours, writing journal entries, poetry, letters to friends near and far whom I had neglected or barely known. I traveled, made new friends, worked on classism, learned to cry. I exercised and re-oriented my diet. Trying to cope with insomnia and fits of depression, I wanted to run away, kill myself, escape my ex-lover and her new friend and the "community" that bore witness to my weakness and dismay. I had to give myself new permissions: therapy, like tears, had been forbidden. The knots inside are coming undone; I have learned patience, and how to recuperate the fragile self from the detritus of recent events. Central has been a spiritual journey, that has included a transcendental energy science, a medium, a psychic, astrology, quantum mechanics and the neurophysiology of the brain, the old and the new. We survive and we endure, and if we are forced to we even grow in the process. I have leased life anew, loving and living.

I am no longer certain how to distinguish desire from codependency/addiction.[3] Passing seems more and more like rereading, reinterpreting the codes, reworking the masks, the dis-guises. It is a radical refusal of a fixed place. A synesthesia of desire implies keeping all the channels open, discovering channels within channels, not a maze in which to conceal oneself, but alternative spaces to relate to one another. Beyond dependency on any person or ideology, what would it feel like to be properly attuned, to love oneself, to love all of the children regardless of race or class, to accept all of the variations on the theme of human sexuality? Suspended between my fifth and sixth decade, a lifetime is not long enough to learn all of the tongues with their endless accents. On the one hand my continuous rebellion as a lesbian, and on the other my recognition of our astonishing diversity prompts me to try terms like *polysexual*, and *multigendered*, keeping all of my options open, juggling the signs . . . the willful act of constituting my-self as a subject/object of desire re-moves me from the technology/ideology of the sex/gender system (de Lauretis 1990:passim). The more I pass the shiftier I become, like my children who never played with a toy the way the manufacturers had intended, or played a game according to the "rules." Passing is never unidirectional; it is always a travesty: some days I pass as "straight," others as a lesbian, andro/gynous, Jewish, North American, francophone, a student of signification, of mug shots.

There is no way to exit gracefully from such a text. I am learning that these things happen, even to lesbians, that even lesbians produce these kinds of scenarios. I am learning to use "even" with "lesbians." My partner reads a love letter, elaborately theoretical and embarrassingly sexual – in public – to a woman she only later acknowledges as her new lover; after a year her words still take my breath away. I who have had so much difficult finding a voice discover that my thoughts and writing terrify the woman I love, who wonders how she will ever tell her own story with such a lover as me. True, we cannot dismantle the master's house with the master's tools (Audre Lorde, 1984a:110–13), but how do we keep from turning them upon ourselves? How do we empower ourselves in language without (ab)using power? How do we speak and write without wounding each other by the sheer energy of our words? Paying back the language (and its authoritative practitioners) for the damage wrought, writing me as I am, refusing to say what I mean, mean what I say.

A women's studies student who spent the semester mired in the dilemma posed by the conflicts among her feminism, her family and upbringing, and her profession as a journalist breaks out of the "prison house of language" when she is able to say: "I have to get the *fuck* out of here," absorbing the shock of the term. How many years I spent thrashing about in "four-letter" words, jarring with my "mild" manners and "pleasant" smile, unable to access my anger! Many self-help books later I realize that I survived my radical choices (socialist, feminist, lesbian) with my addictions firmly in place.

Why doesn't the "eccentric subject position" (de Lauretis) I have chosen protect me from dependency and reactivity? When the channels are closed we cannot "come" alive, experience our desire. There is some comfort in anomaly, in resistance to what Trinh T. Minh-ha calls "incorporation" (1989:54). "To be lost, to encounter impasse, to fall, and to desire both fall and impasse – isn't this what happens to the body in theory?" (42). *That* body is of course only a dummy, a *woman's* body, colonized, not my body at all. How do we account for the collusion of women – even lesbians – in their oppression? Is Suzanne Pharr correct in her assessment of homophobia, that it all comes down to heterosexualism (1988)? However effective as political rhetoric, isn't this too reductive? To invent a life is a daily affair, the translation is never done.

My naiveté with regard to lesbian culture/ethics was based on a categorical error. What has been suppressed for this story to be told? Where are the obscure spots in the theory? Hadn't I forgotten the indeterminacy of signs and signifiers, the flexibility of any grammar? Had my utopian vision not repressed centuries of homophobia and misogyny, which was now returning with a vengeance? Isn't passing a failure of nerve, even nerve damage?

Into what master narrative were we inserted, not only before conscious memory but generations ago, that left us with so little courage in our own defense? Postcolonial analysis, for example, Trinh T. Minh-ha's work on the discourse of anthropologists that colonizes ("tames") but cannot capture the rich spirit life of the "natives" they study, affords some insights (1989). Paradoxically we lesbians are great risk-takers, choosing lives of constant challenge and danger. Many lesbians refuse to be domesticated, to play their part in the Oedipal drama. At what cost?

the woman who brings down the tower, stones tumbled
like skulls. What skill can keep us unstruck?
Me, or the child who has choked under stones,
who has seen me walk among them, split and broken.
(Minnie Bruce Pratt, 106)

I am at once the woman tearing down the tower and the child destroyed by it. I am the mother and the daughter, the outlander who pitches her tent at the edge of the reservation, prisoner and free, subject to the masterplot and alone with my desire. This has been a season of grief, of learning how to care for the self I was ready to cast away in favor of an other, a fragment here, a fragment there. Bless it and release it, they said, when I needed to spin and spin in my tears, until the core of pain could be revealed. I write these lines with my blood, the menstrual blood that no longer marks any seasons, the afterbirth I lost with my innocence in toxic spasms with my first child, aphasia, losing the connection between thinking and the word to speak it, the e-motion lacking all purpose. I have lost my blood sister, and another, who tried to take her place, temporarily staunching the flow of pain. I am beginning again, having buried the placenta. Perhaps this time I will not need my lover and she can be my friend.

Whatever illusions we may have of "passing" in the ordinary sense there are no hiding places either in practice or in theory. Women who are lucky enough to have homes are still indentured servants, when they are not hostages to the American Dream or some other princess scenario. An ex-steelworker friend with five children, whose estranged husband came back to share his suicide with the family one Christmas, said the dream began to crumble when she was about to be laid off, terrified to go to work for fear of injury, the final choice for the truly desperate, a last-ditch choice when the money ran out. My state (Alabama) prides itself on having ratified by the largest majority of any state yet an amendment to make English the official language of the state. This is an admirable move, given how little practice (much less expertise) the people and officials of our corner of Dixie have in the use of our native tongue, a tribute to our educational system and Reaganomics. The intention, however, was not to increase literacy but to reinforce the myth of homogeneity that keeps us in bondage, unable to hear/read each other's dialects and accents. The goal is to melt us all down like Southern vegetables that cook half a day, culinary delights of dubious nutritional value. The meltdown of revolutionary values and "individual rights" in the cauldron of late capitalism is proceeding on schedule, and few seem to perceive the danger. How do we lose our innocence without our hope, wonders Amy Tan; how do we keep laughing? (1989:239). You have to hold on to the pain, she suggests, while you peel back the skin, scars, flesh from mother to mother through the generations. For me, as a lesbian reader, this arresting figure leaves the morphology (the bones of heterosexualism) intact. More translation.

People starve in my state; infant mortality rivals that of "developing" countries; the shelters are full of battered and unwanted children, while the prolife movement is as strong as anywhere in the land. Not to mention our "national scandal," the homeless. There is food for despair and for laughter as we round the bend into the next century, as I curve into the homestretch of my life. I ponder the significance of three relationships in various stages of concluding, wondering how it will feel to be "just friends." How do we learn to appreciate differences, to risk new patterns, concepts, spaces? Misogyny and lesbophobia come from the same sources as anti-intellectualism, intolerance for theory ("foreign" ideas) in the lesbian community. How do we escape oppressive categories while we search for a name?

What formulas do we use to calculate the probabilities? How do we register the intricacies of lesbian desire, how do we create a space in the imaginary for it to speak? How do we attune our vocal chords to harmonize with themselves, teach them a new kind of music? My principal figure, synesthesia, is drawn from Baudelaire's "Correspondances" (1932). Our sensual and perceptual capabilities, he believed, co-respond, transmute, participate in a larger, ineffable whole he could only intuit. I intend synesthesia, as our first modern lesbian poet, Renée Vivien, tried to use a Baudelairian aesthetics at the turn of the century, to collect the polymorphous lesbian body, its deepest impulses, the spirit of women loving women in a process metaphor that is indeterminate and precise – the expanding ripples of many drops striking a watery surface, the intermingled waves of our many senses including those that yet have no name.

NOTES

1 Michelle Cliff explains the tyranny of racial/cultural passing as a one-way street where there is no looking back and there is a complete suppression of differences. It is precisely this sort of ideological trap (1980:6) that I am trying to deconstruct by reclaiming the term *passing* and opening it up. See especially the essay "Passing," but in the context of the others collected in Cliff's *Claiming an Identity They Taught Me to Despise*.

2 Alice Miller is a psychoanalyst who broke with the Freudian establishment over the issues of "drive theory" and the sexual abuse of children, the incest stories Freud rejected in favor of "hysteria." She turns the analysis of the Oedipal drama around to impugn the parents rather than the children. Although she is not a feminist, and has little critique of the institution of motherhood or the role of phallocentrism (patriarchal prerogatives) in the cycle of incest and abuse of women and children, she is useful as a child advocate, and for her analysis of abusive pedagogy. As a theoretician she is unique in her willingness to extend the insights of psychoanalysis beyond the individual and the family to the larger culture, to locate the pathology in history. See especially *Thou Shalt Not Be Aware: Society's Betrayal of the Child* (1986) or her earlier *The Drama of the Gifted Child* (1981).

3 In spite of the professional view of "self-help" books as popular or even vulgarized psychology – ironically the market demonstrates that we have become addicted to them as well as to our addictive behaviors – I have used works on dependency, shame, and recovery directed to various audiences, including Elly Bulkin's beautiful and brave *Enter Password* (1990) to gain insight into the spaces where love, desire and pleasure spill over into addiction. Thus I believe that the codependency/addiction literature may help feminist/lesbian theory with an overdue critique of the mystique of romantic love, of eroticism, and of course of family pathology. This literature has likewise had for me a liberating effect with regard to a personal spiritual journey.

19

Linda Garber, with Vilashini Cooppan

An Annotated Bibliography of Lesbian Literary Critical Theory, 1970–1989

Lesbian literary criticism has come of age, arriving in a varied proliferation of theoretical explanations and observations. In 1981, Bonnie Zimmerman's crucial essay, "What Has Never Been: An Overview of Lesbian Feminist Criticism,"[1] cited twenty-seven published and fourteen unpublished essays, including works of critical theory as well as essays in poetics and investigations of specific lesbian authors and/or works. In 1990, we found forty-one essays published from 1970 to 1989 on literary theory alone; a list of essays on specific lesbian authors and poets (or their works), theater and film criticism, linguistics, poetics, and published would include nearly five hundred journal articles published between 1970 and 1989 – without including book reviews.[2]

Sexual Practice / Textual Theory is one of a spate of books in lesbian literary criticism published or in progress since 1989. Academic presses have begun to solicit lesbian manuscripts, often for lesbian and gay studies series. In 1989, Amherst College advertised the first opening for a tenure-track appointment in English and women's studies specifically looking for a specialist in lesbian and gay studies. The *Gay* Nineties? Perhaps. But honey, the lesbians have arrived.

Significantly, we are here and represented more diversely than ever before. While academia and the traditionally pristine tower of its high theory remain dominated mostly by white scholars commenting on each other's ideas, the presence of women of color is felt in the best of contemporary lesbian theory. Barbara Smith's "Toward a Black Feminist Criticism" exploded on the scene in 1977 – the same year that Audre Lorde called on critics at the Modern Language Association to speak about *all* our differences (Lorde 1978) – and the shock waves have been reverberating through lesbian studies ever since. The most direct responses to Smith's call to theorize both sexual and racial politics in literature come from Elly Bulkin (1980c, 1982), Jewelle Gomez (1988), and Gloria Anzaldúa (1989), whose essays present an ongoing challenge to expand definitions of "lesbian" criticism.[3]

Defining "lesbian writing" has remained a central task of lesbian critical theory, but the terms in which critics address the question have shifted with the constantly changing concerns of both lesbian-feminist politics and academic feminist criticism. Preoccupation with who is or isn't, was or wasn't a lesbian is still with us. What was once called "lesbian sensibility" and presumed to include a multifaceted but recognizable set of linguistic, political, and emotional concerns (Arnold 1975; Arnold and Harris 1976; Harris 1977 and 1979; Desmoines 1979; Klepfisz 1979) is now being theorized more abstractly by some critics in terms of a poststructuralist lesbian "subject position" (Wittig 1983; Allen 1988; Case 1988–89). The explicit call to "name" ourselves and our heritage (Griffin 1975; Rich 1977 and 1978; McDaniel 1978; Stanley 1978; Zimmerman 1983) has taken back seat to an implicit assumption that our literature and theory are of central importance. Along with this shift goes the move from an exposition of negative depictions of lesbians (Griffin 1976; Harris 1977) to an interpolation of lesbian metaphors into the larger field of feminist criticism (Farwell 1988 [after Rich 1977]; Case 1988–89).

As lesbian literary criticism becomes more acceptable – in fact, downright fashionable – in literature and women's studies departments in the 1990s, it seems likely that our critical theory will continue to engage with and be influenced by academic theoretical trends in general. At the same time, however, our academic interests remain rooted in our various community and political priorities. It is not surprising, in this light, that some theorists since the late 1980s have addressed lesbian issues as *gay* issues, not primarily or only as women's issues (Dollimore 1986; Case 1988–89).

For some critics, the lesbian/gay/bisexual coalition politics of the AIDS era have engendered a move away from the woman-identified concerns of lesbian-feminist theory, which has its roots in the women's liberation movement of the 1970s. Or, as a prominent East Coast lesbian author recently remarked, "No one calls herself a 'lesbian *feminist*' any more!"[4] – implying a different sense of political community, albeit one that retains basically feminist principles. Theorists of this stripe might find the emerging lesbian, bisexual, and gay studies movement a more congenial milieu than the traditional lesbian venue of women's studies programs or English departments. The fate of the feminist and otherwise politically radical edge of the new lesbian and gay studies programs and centers at San Francisco City College, Yale University, and elsewhere remains to be seen, as does the outcome of UC Berkeley's reported commitment to a multi-cultural bisexual-lesbian-gay studies program.[5]

What this all means for the future is, of course, a matter of speculation. Historically, we have seen too many reactionary backlashes against women and homosexuals to believe carelessly in progress. But for now, we unquestionably are witnessing a dramatic increase in academic lesbian visibility and in the number of locations from which to practice lesbian literary criticism. From twenty-seven published articles in 1981, to nearly five hundred in 1989, to – who knows? – our own departments?, a striking and lasting influence on mainstream literary studies? "What had never been" has become a force to contend with.

NOTES

1 Zimmerman (1981). See annotated bibliography that follows for complete references to articles cited in this introductory essay.
2 Figures derived from *Lesbian Sources: A Bibliography of Periodical Articles, 1970– 1990,* by Linda Garber (Garland Press, Gay and Lesbian Monograph Series, 1993). This bibliography includes only those articles that were printed in nationally or internationally distributed periodicals.
3 I count an additional forty essays published between 1970 and 1989 that focus on specific black lesbian authors, poets, and/or their works, and thirteen that focus on Latina, Pacific-Asian, or Native-American lesbians (not including book reviews). Many other essays, especially in the late 1980s, consider works by lesbians of color and white lesbians together. – L. G.
4 Private conversation. – L. G.
5 As reported in the *San Francisco Sentinel,* May 31, 1990, page 1.

AN ANNOTATED BIBLIOGRAPHY OF LESBIAN LITERARY CRITICAL
THEORY, 1970–1989

"What Is the Function of Criticism in the Movement?" *Sinister Wisdom,* "Lesbian Writing and Publishing" 1, no. 2 (Fall 1976): 64–5.

Brief comments by Joan Larkin, Jan Clausen, Susan Sherman, Pamella Farley, Lyndall Cowan, Barbara Grier, Rita Mae Brown, and Rhea Jacobs on the role of criticism, its methods, the need for critics to criticize one another, and critics' obligation to demonstrate political commitment. Also discussed are the relations among critic, writer, and reader, and the implication of criticism for lesbian history.

Arnold, June, Sandy Boucher, Susan Griffin, Melanie Kaye (/Kantrowitz), and Judith McDaniel. "Lesbians and Literature" (Modern Language Association (MLA) panel, San Francisco, December 1975). *Sinister Wisdom*, "Lesbian Writing and Publishing" 1, no. 2 (Fall 1976): 20–33.

Arnold defines the lesbian-feminist novel as the voicing of every lesbian-feminist's unconscious struggle "to phrase what has never been," i.e., a lesbian history. She discusses the lesbian-feminist novel as a new way of writing: reinventing language, playing with form, rethinking humor. Marginal point of view is crucial; Arnold offers a formulation similar to the "standpoint epistemology" of Marxist scholarship of the time. Arnold insists upon the lesbian-feminist writer's responsibility to community life, terming the lesbian-feminist novel a revolutionary political action: "The dyke author is committed only to the truth, having no stake in placating the culture – no life to lose either."

Boucher, Sandy, et al. "Lesbians and Literature" (MLA panel, San Francisco, December 1975). *Sinister Wisdom*, "Lesbian Writing and Publishing" 1, no. 2 (Fall 1976): 20–33.

This reflection on three stories about lesbians written by Boucher locates each story in Boucher's life history and in the evolution of her ideas about lesbianism. Boucher's account of her coming out and coming to lesbian identity mirrors her account of the growth of lesbian literature over the past two decades.

Griffin, Susan, et al. "Lesbians and Literature" (MLA panel, San Francisco, December 1975). *Sinister Wisdom*, "Lesbian Writing and Publishing" 1, no. 2 (Fall 1976): 20–33.

Griffin discusses the silencing and self-censorship that haunted her writing as she worked toward the declaration of lesbian identity in her poetry and public life. She discusses the primacy of the mother/daughter relationship as a model of self-love and other-love, and comments on the distortion of that relationship in popular culture. Griffin concludes by noting the power of words: "I believe that it is extremely important to use that word, to be able to say: I am a lesbian."

Kaye(/Kantrowitz), Melanie, et al. "Lesbians and Literature" (MLA panel, San Francisco, December 1975). *Sinister Wisdom*, "Lesbian Writing and Publishing" 1, no. 2 (Fall 1976): 20–33.

Unlike the other speakers on this panel, Kaye talks about *reading* as a lesbian. She fuses brief critiques – of Kate Millet's *Flying*, Marge Piercy's *Small Changes*, Sandy Boucher's *Assaults and Rituals*, June Arnold's *The Cook and the Carpenter*, Joanna Russ's *The Female Man*, and Monique

Wittig's *Les Guérillères* – with a call for lesbian writers to continue to give their readers the "weapons" with which to perceive and fight their socialization and the "vision" of a newly imagined future. In focusing on lesbian readers, Kaye formulates some essentials of reader-response theory.

McDaniel, Judith, et al. "Lesbians and Literature" (MLA panel, San Francisco, December 1975; McDaniel discusses *Mrs. Dalloway* by Virginia Woolf). *Sinister Wisdom*, "Lesbian Writing and Publishing" 1, no. 2 (Fall 1976): 20–33.

McDaniel presents a reading of Clarissa in Virginia Woolf's *Mrs. Dalloway*. Focusing her reading on the question "Why not Sally?" (as Clarissa's lover), McDaniel posits that the task of lesbian literary criticism is synonymous with its method: the voicing of questions unasked by conventional criticism.

Arnold, June, and Bertha Harris. "Lesbian Fiction: a Dialogue." *Sinister Wisdom*, "Lesbian Writing and Publishing" 1, no. 2 (Fall 1976): 42–51.

Two lesbian-feminist novelists and critics discuss their own writing, the need to overcome one's desire for mainstream critical approval, pressure from the lesbian community to create only "politically correct" characters, and the importance of writing "the truth" despite what readers and critics want or expect. Arnold and Harris criticize lesbians who stay in the closet or present "acceptable," partial truths about women's and lesbians' lives. They posit a "lesbian sensibility," i.e., a "heightened awareness" of reality that is true to lesbian experience and which is challenged from all sides throughout a lesbian's life. They assert that lesbian writers are "inventing the world" through plot and language informed by "lesbian sensibility."

Rich, Adrienne. "It Is the Lesbian In Us . . ." *Sinister Wisdom* 3 (Spring 1977): 6–9.

Remarks read at a 1976 MLA panel on racism and homophobia in the teaching of literature. Rich asserts that it is "the lesbian in us who is creative, for the dutiful daughter of the fathers in us is only a hack." She discusses the rendering of lesbian experience "unspeakable," and comments briefly on the unspeakability of love between daughters and their mother figures, referring to the black woman and white woman who raised her. She concludes by calling on women's studies and black studies to account for lesbian existence, but does not explicitly call for multiracial lesbian studies.

Harris, Bertha. "What We Mean to Say: Notes Toward Defining the Nature of Lesbian Literature." *Heresies #3* 1, no. 3 (September 1977): 5–8.

In this dense, provocative piece, Harris defines lesbian literature (as it exists under patriarchy) as a literature of monsters, then examines the historical meaning of monsters and the monstrous. Harris calls for a rejection of lesbian literature modeled on heterosexual dynamics and discusses why lesbian literature is more than just a matter of "a woman plus a woman in bed." She notes the function of literary figures as lesbian role models: "Lesbians, historically bereft of cultural, political and moral context, have especially relied on imaginative literature to dream themselves into situations of cultural, political and moral power." She discusses popular novels as "monster stories" about lesbians and points the way to a transformation of the monster in contemporary "correct" lesbian fiction.

Smith, Barbara. "Toward a Black Feminist Criticism." *Conditions: two* 1, no. 2 (October 1977): 25–44; also *Women's Studies International Quarterly* 2, no. 2 (1979): 183–94.

Smith's analysis of the critical treatment of black women writers powerfully incorporates anecdotes and excerpts from critical articles to demonstrate the silencing of black women writers and black lesbians. Smith outlines the principles of a black feminist criticism that acknowledges the coexistence of black and female identity; examines the intersections of race, sex, and class in those identities; and functions in conjunction with a black feminist movement to overcome heterosexism and black lesbian silence. Smith recognizes that white feminism and white lesbian-feminism have been relatively privileged discourses and encourages white women to adopt "a sane accountability to all the women who write and live on this soil." She calls on black feminist literary criticism to reflect the specific realities of black lesbian lives, providing an example with a lesbian-feminist reading of Toni Morrison's *Sula*.

Daly, Mary, Audre Lorde, Judith McDaniel, Adrienne Rich, and Julia Penelope Stanley. "The Transformation of Silence into Language and Action" (Lesbians and Literature Panel of the MLA Convention, Chicago, December 1977). *Sinister Wisdom* 6 (Summer 1978): 4–25.

Daly discusses the need for women to "create new words" and to reclaim "very old words" that have been used to insult and marginalize women. She considers "radical female friendship" and "female-identified erotic love" as two related ways of combating the "State of Possession" and the "State of War" that constitute life under patriarchy.

Lorde, Audre, et al. "The Transformation of Silence into Language and Action" (Lesbians and Literature Panel of the MLA Convention, Chicago, December 1977). *Sinister Wisdom* 6 (Summer 1978): 4–25; also *Woman of Power* 14 (Summer 1989): 40–41.

Lorde asserts that "It is not difference which immobilizes us, but silence." She exhorts everyone to speak about her differences, and to assume the responsibility of reading, sharing, and examining the words of silenced (lesbian, black, old, etc.) women.

McDaniel, Judith, et al. "The Transformation of Silence into Language and Action" (Lesbians and Literature Panel of the MLA Convention, Chicago, December 1977). *Sinister Wisdom* 6 (Summer 1978): 4–25.

McDaniel describes the internalized barriers to breaking the silence about one's lesbianism and the forces ranged against looking for evidence of lesbian existence in the past (via the biblical example of Naomi and Ruth). She asserts the importance of speaking aloud to challenge social conventions, stating that "Language for me is action."

Rich, Adrienne, et al. "The Transformation of Silence into Language and Action" (Lesbians and Literature Panel of the MLA Convention, Chicago, December 1977). *Sinister Wisdom* 6 (Summer 1978): 4–25.

Rich discusses "how the *unspoken* . . . becomes the *unspeakable* . . . how the nameless becomes the invisible" and urges feminists to ask questions about connections between women, particularly between black women and white women. Rich states that "All silence has a meaning," and that silence has often been in the service of racism, homophobia, and "gynophobia."

Stanley, Julia Penelope, et al. "The Transformation of Silence into Language and Action" (Lesbians and Literature Panel of the MLA Convention, Chicago, December 1977). *Sinister Wisdom* 6 (Summer 1978): 4–25.

Stanley laments the failure of many "wimmin" to understand "the language that I claim as essential to my identity" and the difficulty of describing lesbian experience in patriarchal language. She insists upon the importance of naming oneself and telling one's own story.

Desmoines, Harriet. "There Goes the Revolution . . ." (part of 1978 MLA Panel, "Lesbians and Literature: Transcending the Boundary Between the Personal and the Political," with Bertha Harris). *Sinister Wisdom* 9 (Spring 1979): 20–23.

The cofounder of *Sinister Wisdom* explains that "Lesbian writing" focuses on the many types of connections between women that do not appear in "so-called 'universal' literature." As such, lesbian writing is not "political," in that it does not engage in "Boys A versus Boys B" patriarchal politics. She argues that the word *lesbian* is taboo for people engaged in patriarchal politics – including many feminists – because it refers to the power of "the erotic tone of everything that happens between women."

Harris, Bertha. "Melancholia, and Why It Feels Good . . ." (part of 1978 MLA Panel, "Lesbians and Literature: Transcending the Boundary Between the Personal and the Political," with Harriet Desmoines). *Sinister Wisdom* 9 (Spring 1979): 24–26.

Harris's pithy cautionary tale warns lesbian-feminist writers against the "onerous inhibition" that lesbian-feminist politics can place on "writers of genuine talent." Harris suggests that writing from "lesbian sensibility" is writing against the rules – whether the literary rules of mainstream culture or the political rules of lesbian-feminist community – and cites the following authors as exemplifying this sensibility: Willa Cather, Flannery O'Connor, Mary (and Percy) Shelley, William Blake, Vladimir Nabokov.

Klepfisz, Irena. "Criticism: Form and Function in Lesbian Literature" (response to 1978 MLA Panel, "Lesbians and Literature: Transcending the Boundary Between the Personal and the Political"). *Sinister Wisdom* 9 (Spring 1979): 27–30.

Klepfisz criticizes Bertha Harris's essay "Melancholia, and Why It Feels Good . . ." for its patronizing, flippant, and belittling responses to women's and lesbians' literature. Klepfisz discusses the oppressive circumstances under which lesbian literature is created and discussed, arguing that while hard-won opportunities to practice lesbian literary criticism need not always be congratulatory, they should be constructive and respectful of the lesbian community.

Kaye(/Kantrowitz), Melanie. "Culture Making: Lesbian Classics in the Year 2000?" *Sinister Wisdom*, "Lesbian Writing and Publishing" 13 (Spring 1980): 23–34.

How does a book become a classic, and which lesbian books should we call "classics"? Kaye cites lesbian texts that have "come to seem central to who we become and what our culture becomes." She notes that coming out stories are/will be central to lesbian "classics" and calls for increasingly explicit treatments of lesbian sexuality in literature. Kaye insists that we need to deal with race, ethnicity, and class bias in lesbian-feminist writing, publishing, academics, and culture. She notes the responsibilities of women with access to print to bring lesbian "classics" into classrooms, scholarly reviews, and panels.

Bulkin, Elly. "Racism and Writing: Some Implications for White Lesbian Critics." *Sinister Wisdom*, "Lesbian Writing and Publishing" 13 (Spring 1980): 3–22.

Bulkin explains that homophobia and racism coexist and often appear simultaneously in much feminist scholarship. Bulkin, a white lesbian, attests that she always notices homophobia first, but asserts that "I/we do not have to be non-racist in order to be anti-racist." She ascribes lesbian-feminists' implicit racism to a "larger failure to be seriously critical, though supportive, of each other's work," and follows with a six-page critique of Mary Daly's *Gyn/Ecology*. Bulkin lists several useful questions for the white critic to ask of herself and her work.

Wittig, Monique. "The Straight Mind" (originally published as *La Pensée Straight*," *Quéstions Féministes* [février 1980]: 45–53). *Feminist Issues*, 1, no. 1 (Summer 1980): 103–11.

Wittig names the totalizing conglomeration of heterosexist disciplines, theories, and current thinking "the straight mind." In response to the straight mind's oppression of lesbian, gay, and bisexual people, Wittig demands the transformation of economics, politics and, importantly, language. She envisions the disappearance of "men" and "women" as categories of thought and language, and she praises lesbian culture for undermining heterosexist categories. She asserts that "Lesbians are not women," because "woman" is a meaningful construct only under patriarchy.

Stimpson, Catharine. "Zero Degree Deviancy: the Lesbian Novel in English." *Critical Inquiry* 8 (Winter 1981): 363–80.

Stimpson defines "lesbian" sexually and identifies two repetitive patterns in lesbian novels – "the dying fall" (narrative of suffering and condemnation) and "the enabling escape" (narrative of rebellion) – asserting that both arise from historical persecution of lesbians. She identifies silence, self-censorship, and encoding as survival tactics for lesbian writers, discussing at length *The Well of Loneliness* as an outspoken "narrative of damnation." Stimpson argues that the Kinsey Report's confirmation of widespread homosexual behavior led to two literary manifestations: "lesbian romanticism" and "lesbian realism." She notes that recent lesbian writing tends to "damn the lesbian's damnation" and often experiments with literary form and/or focuses on mother-daughter relationships.

Zimmerman, Bonnie. "What Has Never Been: An Overview of Lesbian Feminist Criticism." *Feminist Studies* 7, no. 3 (Fall 1981): 451–75.

In her rich and exhaustive essay, Zimmerman considers the historical silencing of lesbians and defines the primary task of critics as the establishment of a lesbian "canon." Central to her argument is a review of critical definitions of "lesbian" and "lesbian writing." Zimmerman warns against reductionist definitions, questions the idea of an "innately lesbian" text and a "characteristic lesbian vision," and calls for the incorporation of various critical schools. Lesbian criticism needs more specificity and the application of "rigorous historical and cross-cultural tools" if it is to be, as she hopes, nonracist, nonclassist, international, and comparatist.

Patton, E. "The Politics of Lesbian Writing: A Conversation with Elly Bulkin." *Gay Community News* 9, no. 27 (Jan. 30, 1982): 8.

Bulkin comments on lesbian fiction: genre (novel vs. short story), publishing (commercial vs. community presses), writers' responsibility to the lesbian community, and the need for critical editing and lesbian criticism. She cites feminists' "tremendous reluctance" to attempt serious criticism of one another's works and redefines criticism as accountability. She envisions a new criticism, derived from the acknowledgment of difference, which will "push" writers to deal with class, ethnicity, race, and age.

Bulkin, Elly. "An Interchange on Feminist Criticism on 'Dancing Through the Minefield.'" *Feminist Studies* 8, no. 3 (Fall 1982): 635–54.

Bulkin is one of three critics responding to Annette Kolodny's influential essay "Dancing Through the Minefield: Some Observations on the Theory, Practice, and Politics of a Feminist Literary Criticism." Bulkin considers Kolodny's essay one more example of the white, middle-class heterosexual bias that is widespread in feminist studies, and exposes the lie of Kolodny's advocacy of "a playful pluralism" in feminist criticism by pointing out the omissions in Kolodny's own work and the work she praises. Bulkin discusses the importance of white, heterosexual feminists dealing with racism and heterosexism. She advocates consciousness raising as critical method and political practice, and she provides questions useful for all feminists examining the biases in their own work.

Zimmerman, Bonnie. "Is 'Chloe Liked Olivia' a Lesbian Plot?" *Women's Studies International Forum* 6, no. 2 (1983): 169–75.

Zimmerman discusses three myths that marginalize or erase lesbianism and divide heterosexual women from their lesbian "sisters": the "Phaon myth" (of heterosexual "rescue"), the vampire or monster myth, and the myth of masculinity. She calls for all women to refute these myths, to re-read literature for lesbian subtexts, to recover the works of lesbians (particularly lesbians of color), and to use the word *lesbian* despite (or because of) the way it has been used to threaten and silence all women.

Newman, Kathy. "Re-membering an Interrupted Conversation: the Mother/Virgin Split." *Trivia* 2 (Spring 1983): 45–63.

Newman uses examples from literature to illustrate how patriarchal society allows only two male-identified roles for women – mother or virgin – and explains how women act autonomously and with other women within these roles. While the essay is not centrally concerned with lesbianism, Newman repeatedly affirms that the woman who chooses to remain a "virgin" in patriarchal terms is often choosing a creative, lesbian life.

Crowder, Diane Griffin. "Amazons and Mothers? Monique Wittig, Hélène Cixous, and Theories of Women's Writing." *Wisconsin Studies in Contemporary Literature* 24, no. 2 (Summer 1983): 117–44.

Crowder explicates Wittig's theory and practice of "lesbian writing," opposing it to Cixous's conscious reinscription of female difference in her advocacy of "*écriture féminine*." She argues that the two theories of writing exemplify two distinct, if ambivalently regarded, strands of American feminism: one that considers gender a socially constructed and therefore changeable condition of oppression (Wittig), and the other that uncritically privileges the feminine (Cixous).

Wittig, Monique. "The Point of View: Universal or Particular." *Feminist Issues* 3, no. 2 (Fall 1983): 63–69.

Recognizing the homophobic context in which lesbian and gay literature is written and received, Wittig criticizes the self-ghettoization of lesbian and gay writers who fail to universalize their "minority" point of view. She praises Djuna Barnes and Marcel Proust as experimental writers whose ability to universalize "woman" and "homosexual," respectively, raise them to the level of "literature."

Kennard, Jean E. "Ourself Behind Ourself: A Theory for Lesbian Readers." *Signs*, "The Lesbian Issue" 9, no. 4 (Summer 1984): 647–62.

Citing the necessity for a reader-centered lesbian literary theory, Kennard posits a "polar reading/writing," drawing heavily from Wolfgang Iser's reader-response theory and Joseph Zinker's Gestalt theory. "Polar reading/writing" is based upon the recognition and acceptance of the "other within oneself." Kennard discusses what we mean by lesbianism and writes that lesbians can become most fully lesbian by acknowledging the heterosexual part in themselves. She suggests that we don't need a lesbian literary theory, but rather a universal method of reading that necessarily includes lesbian and other marginalized readers without excluding dominant-identified readers.

Dollimore, Jonathan. "The Dominant and the Deviants: A Violent Dialectic." *Critical Quarterly* 28, no. 1/2 (Spring/Summer 1986): 179–92.

If, as Michel Foucault suggests, deviancy is a social construction produced by the dominant culture, how then can deviancy resist or subvert dominant power structures? Dollimore discusses the deviant/dominant relation in terms of oppositions that seem to govern literary representations of homosexuality: inversion/subversion, authenticity/inauthenticity, inclusion/exclusion. He considers Radclyffe Hall's *The Well of Loneliness* a text that retains the dominant categories of authenticity, integrity, and inclusion, comparing it to *Rubyfruit Jungle*, which reverses the dominant oppositions by treating heterosexuals as "perverts" and homosexuals as "normal." Dollimore asserts that Oscar Wilde, Jean Genet, and Joe Orton subvert the oppositions themselves, inverting the dominant rather than appropriating it.

Cramer, Patricia. "Building a Tradition for Lesbian Feminist Literary Criticism: An Annotated Bibliography." *Feminist Teacher* 2, no. 3 (1987): 20–22.

An annotated list of five books, nine essays, and two special issues of journals intended to "provide a sampling of the range and content of recent lesbian feminist scholarship and criticism."

Fetterley, Judith F. "Writes of Passing." *Gossip* (Great Britain) 5 (n.d.): 21–28, and *Gay Studies Newsletter* 14, no. 1 (March 1987).

Fetterley asserts the danger to lesbians of perpetuating lesbian invisibility by "passing" as heterosexual. She discusses lesbian writers and works with lesbian characters that "pass" in mainstream culture, including

Sarah Orne Jewett, Willa Cather, Alice Walker's *The Color Purple*, and Lisa Alther's *Other Women*. Fetterley opposes these works to a "butch/bulldagger text" like *The Well of Loneliness* and moves on to a discussion of what is "missing" from the many explicitly lesbian books published since 1970 – namely, eroticism that is "integral" to the text – stating that "it is . . . our task to inscribe the unrecognized and unrecognizable."

Lesselier, Claudie (translated by Mary Jo Lakeland from a paper delivered November 1986 at the conference "Homosexualité, homosocialité, et urbanité," held at the Sorbonne). "Social Categorizations and Construction of a Lesbian Subject." *Feminist Issues* 7 (Spring 1987): 89–94.

Lesselier discusses "a time of great invisibility of lesbians and lesbianism" in France, from the late 1930s to the late 1960s. Drawing on literature and oral history, she concludes that the "social discourses" of both dominant culture and lesbian subculture influence individuals' recollections. She discusses lesbians' conscious use of silence as a protective strategy, as well as lesbians' unwillingness to describe themselves with the stigmatized labels that came into public discourse in the early twentieth century.

Alexander, Kate. "Lesbian Reading." *Gossip* (Great Britain) 6 (1988): 37–43.

Alexander argues in favor of writing and reading self-consciously lesbian books "that are a reflection and a celebration of ourselves and the many ways we choose to live," as opposed to remaining satisfied with ambiguous relationships between women in mainstream or closeted books and films. Referring to her own and other lesbians' experiences, Alexander cites *The Well of Loneliness* and Gillian Hanscombe's *Between Friends* as two examples of lesbian literature's power to strengthen and shape lesbian identity. She also discusses a perceived critical "backlash" from homophobic, nonlesbian feminists, against the freedom to write openly as and about lesbians.

Gomez, Jewelle. "Imagine a Lesbian . . . a Black Lesbian . . ." *Trivia* 12 (Spring 1988): 45–60.

A decade after Barbara Smith's groundbreaking essay "Toward a Black Feminist Criticism," Gomez considers the role and reception of the essay and applies its principles to black lesbian literature. Gomez cites the barriers black lesbian writers face to being published and reviewed, and she calls for a responsible feminist criticism that considers black lesbian writing in all of its contexts – cultural, literary, and historical. Gomez discusses a combination of short stories and novels as exemplary works that reject the norms of academic, Euro-American language and structure in order to "open up the meaning of race and sex in this society."

Allen, Jeffner. "Poetic Politics: How the Amazons Took the Acropolis." *Hypatia* 3, no. 2 (Summer 1988): 107–22.

Allen examines the "poetic politics" of "textual violence" – the displacement of phallocentric language and its universalist claims with a multiplicity of female languages. "Lacunary feminine language," according to the models of Monique Wittig and Hélène Cixous, uses metaphors, gaps, and silences in order to seize control of the production of meaning, disrupt textual history, and produce new textual worlds. All female speech acts are thus political acts of resistance, and all form part of an "amazon intertextuality" in which the texts of female freedom, by placing more and more female-defined signs in relation to one another, "make vanish patriarchal signifiers and signification."

Penelope, Julia. "Lesbians Reviewing/Reviewing Lesbians." *Feminist Studies* 14, no. 3 (Fall 1988): 606–9.

One of several short pieces in a "Symposium" on feminist book reviewing, Penelope's essay asserts the role of reviewing in publicizing new books and in generating serious, if heated, discussion about them. Penelope notes that the critic is vulnerable to censure, but she argues for the importance of honest criticism and acknowledgment that reviewing entails responsible value judgment. Penelope assumes "a critical, active, argumentative audience," in which the reviewer's opinion is only one among many.

Farwell, Marilyn R. "Toward a Definition of the Lesbian Literary Imagination." *Signs* 14, no. 1 (Autumn 1988): 100–118.

Following Adrienne Rich and Monique Wittig, Farwell posits the tremendous potential of the "metaphoric" use of the term *lesbian* to define female creativity as primarily sexual and autonomous, though also situated in a community of women readers and writers. Farwell summarizes the lesbian and feminist debate over generalized use of *lesbian* to define women whose sexual behavior is not explicitly lesbian. The article gives an overview of traditional male heterosexual metaphors for creativity – androgyne, lover/muse, and mother – as well as unsuccessful feminist and lesbian attempts to reclaim them (including Virginia Woolf's invocation of androgyny, but focused on critics in the 1970s and '80s).

Case, Sue-Ellen. "Towards a Butch-Femme Aesthetic." *Discourse: Journal for Theoretical Studies in Media and Culture* 11, no. 1 (Fall–Winter 1988–89): 55–73.

Situated within theater/film criticism, this essay takes up the theoretical problem of the female subject position, posed as an impossibility by Foucauldian theory. Case goes beyond Teresa de Lauretis's unanswered call for a "feminist" subject position ("The Technology of Gender," 1984), arguing that the lesbian roles of butch and femme – seen historically as an instance of subversive homosexual "camp" and likened to the coupled self ("j/e") in Monique Wittig's *The Lesbian Body* – offer the most promising possibilities for a female subject position endowed with agency.

Anzaldúa, Gloria. "Border Crossings." *Trivia*, "Two-Part Issue – The 3rd International Feminist Bookfair – Part II: Language/Difference: Writing in Tongues" 14 (Spring 1989): 46–51.

Transcribed fragments of a talk given in fall 1988, in which Anzaldúa discusses the role of women/lesbians of color writing from multiple, simultaneous perspectives, symbolized by the socially marginal or "border" position to which dominant culture relegates them. Anzaldúa emphasizes the decision of many radical women of color to write for themselves and each other, refusing to interpret their cultural differences for white readers. She discusses the barriers to publication for women of color and working-class women, and the "writer's block" created by internalized oppression.

References

Abel, Elizabeth. 1981. (E)merging identities: the dynamics of female friendship in contemporary fiction by women. *Signs* 6, 3:413–35.

———, (ed). 1982. *Writing and Sexual Difference*. Chicago: U of Chicago P.

Adams, Hazard (ed). 1971. *Critical Theory since Plato*. New York: Harcourt Brace Jovanovich.

Addelson, Kathryn Pyne. 1981. "On compulsory heterosexuality and lesbian existence": defining the issues. *Signs* 7, 1.

Aeschylus. 1959. *The Eumenides*. In *The Orestian Trilogy*. Trans. Philip Vellacott. New York: Penguin.

Alcoff, Linda. 1988. Cultural feminism versus post-structuralism: the identity crisis in feminist theory. *Signs* 13, 3:405–36.

Allen, Jeffner (ed). 1988. Poetic politics: how the Amazons took the Acropolis. *Hypatia* 3, 2:107–22; reprinted this volume.

———. 1990. *Lesbian Philosophies and Cultures*. Albany, N.Y.: SUNY Press.

Allen, Sally B., and Joanna Hubbs. 1980. Outrunning Atalanta: feminine destiny in alchemical transmutation. *Signs* 6, 2:210–29.

Alther, Lisa. 1984. *Other Women*. New York: Knopf.

Andermatt, Verena. 1979. Hélène Cixous and the uncovery of a feminine language. *Women and Literature* 7, 1:38–48.

Anderson, Bonnie S., and Judith P. Zinsser. 1988. *A History of Their Own*, vol. 1. New York: Harper & Row.

Apologie de la secte anandryne. 1784. In *L'espion anglais ou correspondance secrète entre Milord All'Eye et Milord All'Ear*. London: John Adamson, vol. 10.

Arnold, June. 1975. *Sister Gin*. London: The Women's Press.

———. 1976. Lesbian fiction. *Sinister Wisdom* 2:28–30.

Atwood, Margaret. 1984. Review of *Diving into the Wreck*. In Jane Roberta Cooper (ed.), 238–41.

Austen, Jane. [1813] 1950. *Pride and Prejudice*. In *"Pride and Prejudice" and "Sense and Sensibility"*. New York: Modern Library/Random House.

Baetz, Ruth. 1980. *Lesbian Crossroads*. Tallahassee, Fla.: Naiad.

Bakhtin, Mikhail. 1984. *Rabelais and His World*, trans. by Helen Iswolsky. Bloomington: Indiana UP.

Balakian, Anna. 1947. *Literary Origins of Surrealism: A New Mysticism in French Poetry*. New York: New York UP.

———. 1959. *Surrealism: The Road to the Absolute*. New York: Noonday.

Bamber, Linda. 1982. *Comic Women, Tragic Men: A Study of Gender and Genre in Shakespeare*. Stanford, Calif.: Stanford UP.

Barnes, Djuna. 1927. Dusie. In *American Esoterica*, New York: Macy-Masius, 75–82.

———. [1928] 1972. *The Ladies' Almanack*. New York: Harper and Row.

———. [1936] 1961. *Nightwood*. New York: New Directions.

———. 1962. *Selected Works*. New York: Farrar, Straus and Cudahy, 12–20; 21–28.

Barr, Marleen (ed.). 1981. *Future Females: A Critical Anthology*. Bowling Green, Ohio: Bowling Green State U Popular Press.

Barr, Marleen, and Nicholas Smith (eds.). 1983. *Women and Utopia*. Lanham, Md.: U Presses of America.

Barthes, Roland. [1953] 1977. *Writing Degree Zero*. Trans. Annette Lavers and Colin Smith of *Le degré zéro de l'écriture*. New York: Hill and Wang.

Bartkowski, Frances. 1989. *Feminist Utopias*. Lincoln, Neb.: U of Nebraska Press.

Baruch, Elaine Hoffman, and Ruby Rohrlich (eds.). 1984. *Women in Search of Utopia: Mavericks and Mythmakers*. New York: Schocken.

Baudelaire, Charles. 1932. Correspondances in *Oeuvres*. Bibliothèque de la Pléiade, vol. 1. Paris: NRF.

Bayard, Caroline. 1984. Post-modernisme et avant-garde au Canada, 1960–1984. *Voix et Images* 10, 1:37–58.

Baym, Nina. 1987. Review of *Women of the Left Bank* by Shari Benstock. *American Literature* 59:472–75.

Beck, Evelyn Torton (ed). 1982. *Nice Jewish Girls: A Lesbian Anthology*. Watertown, Mass.: Persephone Press.

Belsey, Catherine. 1980. *Critical Practice*. London and New York: Methuen.

Benegas, Noni. 1986. Virgile, non. *Vlasta* 4:96–98.

Bennett, Paula. 1977. The language of love: Emily Dickinson's homoerotic poetry. *Gai Saber* (Spring).

———. 1986. *My Life a Loaded Gun: Dickinson, Plath, Rich and Female Creativity*. Boston: Beacon Press.

———. 1990. *Emily Dickinson: Woman Poet*. New York: Harvest Wheatsheaf.

Bergson, Henri. 1911. *Laughter*. Trans. Cloudesley Brereton and Fred Rothwell. London and New York: Macmillan.

Benstock, Shari. 1986. *Women of the Left Bank*. Austin, Tex.: U of Texas P.

Bernikow, Louise. 1974. *The World Split Open*. New York: Vintage.

Berry, Ellen E. 1987. Left Bank and distaff. Review of *Women of the Left Bank* by Shari Benstock. *Novel* 21:99–102.

Bethel, Lorraine. 1982. "This infinity of conscious pain": Zora Neale Hurston and the black female literary tradition. In Gloria T. Hull et al. (eds.), 176–88.

Billy, Andre. 1951. *L'époque 1900*. Paris: Editions Jules Tallandier.

Bishop, Nadean. 1980. Renunciation in the bridal poems of Emily Dickinson. Unpublished paper pres ted at the National Women's Studies Association.

Blau, Herbert. 1982/1983. Disseminating Sodom. *Salmagundi* 58/59:221–51.

Boucher, Sandy. 1977. Lesbian artists. *Heresies* 3:47–48.

Bowen, Elizabeth. 1927. *The Hotel*. London: Constable.

Bowles, Gloria. 1984. Adrienne Rich as feminist theorist. In Cooper (ed.), 319–28.

Bradley, Marion Zimmer. 1976. *The Shattered Chain*. New York: Daw.

———. 1978. *The Ruins of Isis*. Norfolk, Va.: Donning.

Brady, Maureen, and Judith McDaniel. 1980. Lesbians in the mainstream: images of of lesbians in recent commercial fiction. *Conditions* 6:82–105.

Brantenberg, Gerd. 1985. *Egalia's Daughters: A Satire of the Sexes*. Seattle: The Seal Press.

Bray, Alan. 1982. *Homosexuality in Renaissance England*. London: Gay Men's Press.

Broe, Mary Lynn. 1989. My art belongs to daddy: incest as exile – the textual economics of Hayford Hall. In Mary Lynn Broe and Angela Ingram (eds.), *Women's Writing in Exile*, Chapel Hill: U of North Carolina P, 41–86.

Brontë, Charlotte. [1849] 1974. *Shirley*. Harmondsworth: Penguin.

Brossard, Nicole. [1970] 1980a. *Un livre*. Montréal: Quinze.

———. 1980b. *Amantes*. Montréal: Les Quinze; *Lovhers*, trans. Barbara Godard. Montréal: Guernica, 1986.

———. 1982. *Picture Theory*. Montréal: Nouvelle Optique.

———. 1984. *Journal intime*. Montréal: Les Herbes Rouges.

———. 1986. Le réel et plus. In *Choisir la poésie*, Trois Rivières, Québec: Des Forges.

———. 1987a. *Le désert mauve*. Montréal: l'Hexagone.

———. 1987b. *Sous la langue/Under tongue*. Montréal: l'Essentielle and Charlottetown: Gynergy Books.

———. [1977] 1988a. *L'Amèr ou le chapitre effrité*. Montréal: l'Hexagone. (Original edition, 1977.)

———. 1988b. *La lettre aérienne*. Montréal: Les Editions du Remue-Ménage.

———. 1988c. *The Aerial Letter*. Trans. Marlene Wildeman. Toronto, Ontario: The Women's Press.

———. 1988d. Memory: hologram of desire. *Trivia* 13:42–47.

Brossard, Nicole, and Roger Soublière. 1970. De notre écriture en sa résistance. *La Barre du Jour* 26:3–6.

Brown, Rita Mae. [1973] 1977. *Rubyfruit Jungle*. New York: Bantam. (Originally published by Daughters, Inc., Plainfield, Vermont.)

———. [1976] 1988. *In Her Day*. New York: Bantam.

Brownstein, Rachel. 1982. *Becoming a Heroine: Reading about Women in Novels*. Harmondsworth: Penguin.

Bulkin, Elly. 1977. An interview with Adrienne Rich: Part II. *Conditions* 2:58.

———. 1978. "Kissing against the light": a look at lesbian poetry. *Radical Teacher* 10:8.

———. 1980a. "An Old Dyke's Tale: An Interview with Doris Lunden," *Conditions* 6:26–44.

———. 1980b. Heterosexism and women's studies. *Radical Teacher* 17:25–31.

———. 1980c. Racism and writing. *Sinister Wisdom* 13:3–22.

———, (ed). 1981. *Lesbian Fiction*. Watertown, Mass.: Persephone.

———. 1982. An interchange on feminist criticism: on "Dancing Through the Minefield." *Feminist Studies* 8:635–54.

———. 1990. *Enter Password: Recovery, Re-Enter Password*. Albany, N.Y.: Turtle Books.

Bunch, Charlotte. 1975. Lesbians in revolt. In Nancy Myron and Charlotte Bunch (eds.), *Lesbianism and the Women's Movement*, Baltimore: Diana Press.

Burch, Beverly. 1987. Barriers to intimacy: conflicts over power, dependency, and nurturing in lesbian relationships. In The Boston Lesbian Psychologies Collective (eds.), *Lesbian Psychologies: Explorations and Challenges*. Urbana: U of Illinois P, 126–41.

Burke, Carolyn. 1982. Gertrude Stein, the Cone sisters, and the puzzle of female friendship. *Critical Inquiry* 8, 3:543–64.

Burney, Fanny. [1782] 1986. *Cecilia or, the Memoirs of an Heiress*. New York: Virago/Penguin.

Butler, Judith. 1990. *Gender Trouble: Feminism and the Subversion of Identity*. New York/London: Routledge.

Butler, Marilyn. 1988. Feminist criticism, late '80s style. *Times Literary Supplement*, 11–17 March:283–85.

Carr, Virginia Spencer. 1975. *The Lonely Hunter: A Biography of Carson McCullers*. New York: Doubleday/Anchor.

Carruthers, Mary J. 1979. Imagining women: notes toward a feminist poetic. *Massachusetts Review* 10, 2:281–307.

———. 1983. The re-vision of the muse: Adrienne Rich, Audre Lorde, Judy Grahn, Olga Broumas. *Hudson Review* 36, 2:293–327.

Case, Sue-Ellen. 1988/89. Towards a butch-femme aesthetic. *Discourse* 11:55–73. Reprinted in Lynda Hart (ed.), *Making a Spectacle: Feminist Essays on Contemporary Women's Theatre*. Ann Arbor: U of Michigan P, 282–99.

Causse, Michèle. 1980. Lesbiana: le nouveau commerce. 47/48. Supplement.

———. 1987. (———). Laval, Québec: Editions Trois.

———. 1988. L'interloquée. Trans. Susanne de Lotbinière-Harwood. *Trivia* 13:79–90.

Cavin, Susan. 1985. *Lesbian Origins*. San Francisco: Ism Press.

Charles, Anne. 1987. An important beginning. Review of *Women of the Left Bank* by Shari Benstock. *Gay Studies Newsletter* 14:25–26.

Chessman, Harriet S. 1987. Review of *Women of the Left Bank* by Shari Benstock. *Tulsa Studies in Women's Literature* 6:347–8.

Chodorow, Nancy. 1978. *The Reproduction of Mothering*. Berkeley, California: U of California P.

———. 1980. Gender, relation, and difference in psychoanalytic perspective. In Hester Eisenstein and Alice Jardine (eds.), 3–19.

Chopin, Kate. 1972. *The Awakening*. New York: Avon.

Christ, Carol P. 1980. *Diving Deep and Surfacing: Women Writers on Spiritual Quest*. Boston: Beacon.

Christian, Barbara. 1985. Trajectories of self-definition: placing contemporary Afro-American women's fiction. In Marjorie Pryse and Hortense Spillers (eds.), *Conjuring: Black Women, Fiction, and Literary Tradition*, Bloomington: Indiana UP, 233–48.

Christian, Paula. [1959] 1978. *Edge of Twilight*. New Milford, Conn.: Timely Books.

———. [1963] 1978. *This Side of Love*. New Milford, Conn.: Timely Books.

Chronique d'une imposture: du mouvement de libération des femmes à une marque commerciale. 1981. Paris: Association Mouvement pour les Luttes Féministes.

Cixous, Hélène. 1969. *Dedans.* Paris: B. Grasset.

———. 1975. Le rire de la Méduse. *L'Arc* 61:39–54.

———. 1976. The laugh of Medusa. Trans. Keith Cohen and Paula Cohen. *Signs* 1, 4:875–94.

———. 1977. La venue à l'écriture. In Hélène Cixous, Madeleine Gagnon, and Annie Leclerc (eds.), *La venue à l'écriture.* Paris: Editions 10/18.

———. 1979. *Vivre l'orange.* Paris: des femmes.

———. 1980a. Poetry is/and (the) political. *Bread and Roses* 2, 1:16–18.

———. 1980b. *Sorties.* Trans. Ann Liddle. In Elaine Marks and Isabelle de Courtivron (eds.).

———. 1981. Castration or decapitation? Trans. Annette Kuhn. *Signs* 7, 1:41–55.

———. 1983. *Le livre de Promethea.* Paris: Gallimard.

———. 1986. *La prise de l'école de Madhubai. In Theatre.* Paris: des femmes.

Cixous, Hélène, and Catherine Clément. 1986. *The Newly Born Woman.* Trans. Betsy Wing. Minneapolis: U of Minnesota P.

Cixous, Hélène, and Verena Andermatt Conley. 1984. Voice I . . . *Boundary* 12, 2:51–66.

Clarke, Charles, and Mary Cowden (eds.). 1864. *The Plays of Shakespeare.* 3 vols. London: Cassell, Petter, and Galpin.

Clarke, Cheryl, et al. 1983. Conversations and questions: black women on black women writers. *Conditions* 9:88–137.

Clausen, Jan. 1982. *A Movement of Poets: Thoughts on Poetry and Feminism.* Brooklyn, N.Y.: Long Haul.

Cleidemus. 1973. In Helen Diner, *Mothers and Amazons: The First Feminine History of Culture.* New York: Doubleday.

Cliff, Michelle. 1980. *Claiming an Identity They Taught Me to Despise.* Watertown, Mass.: Persephone Press.

Coleridge, Samuel Taylor. 1926. *Biographia Literaria.* J. C. Metcalf (ed.). New York: Macmillan.

Colette. 1948. *Claudine à l'école. Oeuvres complétes.* Paris: Flammarion, vol. 1.

———. 1949. Nuit blanche. In *Les vrilles de la vigne. Oeuvres complétes.* Paris: Flammarion, vol. 3.

———. 1971. *The Pure and the Impure.* Trans. Herma Briffault. Harmondsworth: Penguin.

Cook, Blanche Wiesen. 1977. Female support networks and political activism: Lillian Wald, Crystal Eastman, Emma Goldman. *Chrysalis* 3:43–60.

———. 1979. "Women alone stir my imagination": lesbianism and the cultural tradition. *Signs* 4, 4:718–39.

Cooper, Jane Roberta (ed.). 1984. *Reading Adrienne Rich: Reviews and Re-Visions, 1951–81.* Ann Arbor: U of Michigan P.

Cornwell, Anita. 1983. *Black Lesbian in White America.* Tallahassee, Fla.: Naiad.

Cory, Donald Webster. 1951. *The Homosexual in America.* New York: Paperback Library.

Cothran, Ann. 1981. *The Pure and the Impure:* codes and constructs. *Women's Studies* 8, 4:335–57.

Cotnoir, Louise, et al. 1982/1983. Entretien avec Nicole Brossard sur *Picture Theory. La Nouvelle Barre du Jour* 118/119:177–201. Interview with Nicole Brossard on *Picture Theory,* trans. Luise von Flotow-Evans. *Canadian Fiction* 47:122–35.

Craigin, Elisabeth. 1937. *Either Is Love.* New York: Harcourt, Brace.

Crompton, Louis. 1980/81. The myth of Lesbian impunity: capital laws from 1270 to 1791. *Journal of Homosexuality* 6, 1/2:11–25.

Crowder, Diane. 1983. Amazons and mothers? Monique Wittig, Hélène Cixous, and theories of women's writing. *Wisconsin Studies in Contemporary Literature* 24, 2:114–44; also published as Amazones de . . . demain?: fiction utopique féministe et lesbienne. *Amazones d'Hier/Lesbiennes d'Aujourd'hui* 2, 4 (1984):19–27.

———. 1985. Une armée d'amantes: l'image de l'amazon dans l'oeuvre de Monique Wittig. *Vlasta* 4:79–87.

Cruikshank, Margaret (ed). 1980. *The Lesbian Path.* Monterey, Calif.: Angel.

———. 1982. *Lesbian Studies: Present and Future.* Old Westbury, N.Y.: The Feminist Press.

Daly, Mary. 1973. *Beyond God the Father: Toward a Philosophy of Women's Liberation.* Boston: Beacon.

———. 1978. *Gyn/Ecology: The Metaethics of Radical Feminism.* Boston: Beacon.

———. 1984. *Pure Lust: Elemental Feminist Philosophy.* Boston: Beacon.

———. 1987. *Websters' First New Intergalactic Wickedary of the English Language.* Boston: Beacon.

Damon, Gene, Jan Watson, and Robin Jordan. 1975. *The Lesbian in Literature: A Bibliography.* Weatherby Lake, Mo.: Naiad.

Danis, Mariette. 1987. L'impossible réelle, lecture sur partielle de l'oeuvre de Nicole Brossard. *Amazones d'Hier/Lesbiennes d'Aujourd'hui* 18:33–67.

Dash, Irene G. 1981. *Wooing, Wedding, and Power: Women in Shakespeare's Plays.* New York: Columbia UP.

Davis, Madeline, and Elizabeth Lapovsky Kennedy. 1986. Oral history and the study of sexuality in the lesbian community: Buffalo, New York, 1940–1960. *Feminist Studies* 12:7–26.

Davy, Kate. 1989. Reading past the heterosexual imperative: *dress suits to hire. Drama Review* 33:153–69.

Dean, Susan Thach. 1986. Review of *Women of the Left Bank* by Shari Benstock. *Library Journal* 111:97.

de Beauvoir, Simone. [1949] 1961. *The Second Sex.* New York: Bantam.

de Lauretis, Teresa. 1987. *The Technologies of Gender: Essays on Theory, Film, and Fiction.* Bloomington: Indiana UP.

———. 1988. Sexual indifference and lesbian representation. *Theatre Journal* 40:155–77.

———. 1990. Eccentric subjects: feminist theory and historical consciousness. *Feminist Studies* 16:115–50.

———, (ed.). 1986. *Feminist Studies/Critical Studies.* Bloomington: Indiana UP.

D'Emilio, John. 1983. *Sexual Politics, Sexual Communities: The Making of a Homosexual Minority in the United States, 1940–1970*. Chicago: U of Chicago P.

de Pisan, Annie, and Tristan, Anne. 1977. *Histories du M. L. F.* Paris: Calmann-Levy.

DeSalvo, Louise. 1982. Lighting the cave: the relationship between Vita Sackville-West and Virginia Woolf. *Signs* 8, 2:195–214.

DeShazer, Mary K. 1986. *Inspiring Women: Reimagining the Muse*. New York: Pergamon.

Desmoines, Harriet. 1976. Notes for a magazine II. *Sinister Wisdom* 1:27–34.

Diaz-Diocaretz, Myriam. 1992. The given and the created: the infinite cities of language. In Alice Parker and Elizabeth Meese (eds.), *Feminist Critical Negotiations*. Amsterdam: John Benjamins, 169–178.

Dickinson, Emily. 1960. *The Complete Poems of Emily Dickinson*, ed. Thomas Johnson. Boston: Little Brown and Co.

Diehl, Joanne Feit. 1980. "Cartographies of Silence": Rich's *Common Language* and the woman poet. *Feminist Studies* 6, 3:530–46.

Dolan, Jill. 1989. Desire cloaked in a trenchcoat. *Drama Review* 33:59–66.

Donovan, Josephine. 1975. *Feminist Literary Criticism: Explorations in Theory*. Lexington: UP of Kentucky.

———. 1986. Nan prince and the golden apples. *Colby Library Quarterly* 22:17–27.

Doolittle, Hilda. 1957. *Selected Poems of H.D.* New York: Grove Press.

Dorfman, Ariel. 1987. *The Last Song of Manuel Sendero*. New York: Viking.

Doughty, Frances. 1982. Lesbian biography, biography of lesbians. In Margaret Cruikshank (ed.), 115–21.

———. 1987. Modernism and marginality. Review of *Women of the Left Bank* by Shari Benstock. *The Women's Review of Books*, June: 5–7.

Downing, Christina. 1991. *Myths and Mysteries of Same-Sex Love*. New York: Continuum.

Dranch, Sherry A. 1983. Reading through the veiled text: Colette's *The Pure and the Impure*. *Contemporary Literature* 24, 2:176–89.

Duchen, Claire. 1986. *Feminism in France*. London: Routledge & Kegan Paul.

DuPlessis, Rachel Blau. 1985. *Writing Beyond the Ending: Narrative Strategies of Twentieth-Century Women Writers*. Bloomington: Indiana UP.

Dusinberre, Juliet. 1975. *Shakespeare and the Nature of Women*. New York: Barnes & Noble.

Echols, Alice. 1983. The new feminism of yin and yang. In Ann Snitow, Christine Stansell, and Sharon Thompson (eds.), *Powers of Desire: The Politics of Sexuality*. New York: Monthly Review Press, 440–59.

———. 1989. *Daring to Be Bad: Radical Feminism in America 1967–1975*. Minneapolis: U of Minnesota Press.

Eisenstein, Hester. 1983. *Contemporary Feminist Thought*. Boston: G. K. Hall.

Eisenstein, Hester, and Jardine, Alice (eds). 1980. *The Future of Difference*. Boston: G. K. Hall.

Elliot, Jeffrey M. (ed.). 1984. *Kindred Spirits: An Anthology of Gay and Lesbian Science Fiction Stories*. Boston: Alyson Publications.

Ellis, Havelock. [1897] 1936. *Studies in the Psychology of Sex*, vol. 2, *Sexual Inversion*, part 2. New York: Random House.

Ellison, Harlan (ed.). 1972. *Again, Dangerous Visions*. New York: Doubleday.

Ellman, Mary. 1968. *Thinking about Women*. New York: Harcourt Brace.

Engelbrecht, Penelope. 1990. "Lifting belly is a language": the postmodern lesbian subject. *Feminist Studies* 16, 1:85–114.

Ermarth, Elizabeth. 1983. Fictional consensus and female casualties. In Carolyn G. Heilbrun and Margaret S. Higonnet (eds.), *The Representation of Women in Fiction*. Baltimore: Johns Hopkins UP, 1–18.

Ernst, Max. 1968. Film interview in *Max Ernst: Journeys into the Subconscious*. Dir. Peter Schamoni and Carl Lamb. Northbrook, Ill.: Roland Films.

Faderman, Lillian. 1978a. Emily Dickinson's homoerotic poetry. *Higginson Journal*, 18:19–27.

———. 1978b. Emily Dickinson's letter to Sue Gilbert. *Massachusetts Review* 18:197–225.

———. 1978c. Female same-sex relationships in novels by Longfellow, Holmes and James. *New England Quarterly* 2, 3:309–32.

———. 1978d. Lesbian magazine fiction in the early twentieth century. *Journal of Popular Culture* 11, 4:800–817.

———. 1978e. The morbidification of love between women by 19th-century sexologists. *Journal of Homosexuality* 4, 1:73–90.

———. 1981. *Surpassing the Love of Men: Romantic Friendship and Love Between Women from the Renaissance to the Present*. New York: William Morrow.

———. 1982. Who hid lesbian history? In Margaret Cruikshank (ed.), 115–21.

Faderman, Lillian, and Louise Bernikow. 1978. Comment on Joanne Felt Diehl's "Come Slowly, Eden." *Signs* 4, 1:188–95.

Faderman, Lillian, and Brigitte Ericksson. 1980. *Lesbian Feminism in Turn-of-the-Century Germany*. Tallahassee, Fla.: Naiad Press.

Faderman, Lillian, and Ann Williams. 1977. Radclyffe Hall and the lesbian image. *Conditions* 1:31–41.

Farley, Pamella Tucker. 1983. That wrench of the mind. *Hysteria* 2, 1:25–30.

Feral, Josette. 1978. Antigone or the irony of the tribe. *Diacritics* (Fall): 2–14.

Ferguson, Ann. 1982. Patriarchy, sexual identity and the sexual revolution. In Nannerl O. Keohane, Michelle Z. Rosaldo, and Barbara C. Gelpi (eds.), 147–61.

———. 1990. Is there a lesbian culture? In Jeffner Allen (ed.), 63–88.

Ferguson, Ann, Jacqueline N. Zita, and Kathryn Pyne Addelson. 1981. On "Compulsory Heterosexuality and Lesbian Existence": defining the issues. *Signs* 7, 1:158–99.

Fetterley, Judith. 1978. *The Resisting Reader: A Feminist Approach to American Fiction*. Bloomington: Indiana UP.

Field, Andrew. 1983. *Djuna: The Life and Times of Djuna Barnes*. New York: G. P. Putnam's.

Fifer, Elizabeth. 1979. Is flesh advisable: the interior theater of Gertrude Stein. *Signs* 4, 3:472–83.

————. 1982. Rescued readings: characteristic deformations in the language of Gertrude Stein's plays. *Texas Studies in Literature and Language* 24, 4:394–428.

Fitting, Peter. 1985. "So We All Became Mothers": new roles for men in recent utopian fiction. *Science-Fiction Studies* 12, 2:156–83.

————. 1987. For men only: a guide to reading single-sex worlds. *Women's Studies International Forum* 14:101–17.

Forsyth, Louise H. 1981. The fusion of reflexive writing and theoretical reflection: Nicole Brossard and feminist criticism in Québec. Unpublished paper presented at the Modern Language Association, December.

Foster, Hal. 1984. (Post)modern polemics. *New German Critique* 33:67–79.

Foster, Jeannette. [1956] 1975. *Sex Variant Women in Literature*. Baltimore, Maryland: Diana.

Foucault, Michel. 1978. *The History of Sexuality*, vol. 1. Trans. Robert Hurley. New York: Vintage.

Franks, Claudia Stillman. 1982. Stephen Gordon, novelist: a reevaluation of Radclyffe Hall's *The Well of Loneliness*. *Tulsa Studies in Women's Literature* 1, 2:125–39.

Freedman, Estelle B., Barbara C. Gelpi, Susan L. Johnson, and Kathleen M. Weston (eds). 1984. *The Lesbian Issue: Essays from Signs*. Chicago and London: U of Chicago P.

Freud, Sigmund. [1933] 1965. Femininity. In James Strachey (trans. and ed.), *New Introductory Lectures on Psychoanalysis*, New York: Norton, 99–119.

Friedman, Susan. 1983. "I Go Where I Love": an intertextual study of H.D. and Adrienne Rich. *Signs* 9, 2:228–45.

Friedman, Susan, and Rachel Blau DuPlessis. 1981. The sexualities of H.D.'s *Her*. *Montemora* 8:7–30.

Frye, Joanne S. 1986. *Living Stories, Telling Lives: Women and the Novel in Contemporary Experience*. Ann Arbor: U of Michigan P.

Frye, Marilyn. 1980. Review of *The Coming Out Stories*, ed. Julia Penelope Stanley and Susan J. Wolfe. *Sinister Wisdom* 14:97–98.

————. 1983. To see and be seen: the politics of reality. In her *The Politics of Reality: Essays in Feminist Theory*. Trumansburg, N.Y.: Crossing Press, 152–74.

Fuss, Diana. 1989. *Essentially Speaking: Feminism, Nature and Difference*. New York and London: Routledge.

Garber, Eric. 1983. *Uranian Worlds: A Reader's Guide to Alternative Sexuality in Science Fiction and Fantasy*. Boston: G. K. Hall.

Garber, Linda. 1993. *Lesbian Sources: A Bibliography of Periodical Articles, 1970–1990*. New York: Garland.

Garber, Marjorie. 1989. Spare parts: the surgical construction of gender. *differences* 1:137–59.

Garner, Shirley. 1981. *A Midsummer Night's Dream*: "Jack shall have Jill; / Nought shall go ill." *Women's Studies* 9:47–63.

————. 1985. "Women together" in Virginia Woolf's *Night and Day*. In *The (M)other Tongue*, Ithaca, N.Y.: Cornell UP, 318–33.

Gearhart, Sally Miller. 1979. *The Wanderground*. Watertown, Mass.: Persephone.

Gilbert, Sandra M. 1983. Soldier's heart: literary men, literary women, and the great war. *Signs* 8, 3:422–50.

Gilbert, Sandra M., and Gubar, Susan. 1979a. *The Madwoman in the Attic: The Woman Writer and the Nineteenth-Century Literary Imagination.* New Haven, Conn.: Yale UP.

———, (eds). 1979b. *Shakespeare's Sisters: Feminist Essays on Women Poets.* Bloomington: Indiana UP.

———. 1989. *No Man's Land: The Place of the Woman Writer in the Twentieth Century,* vol. 2, *Sexchanges.* New Haven/London: Yale UP.

Giroux, Henry A. 1990. Rethinking the boundaries of educational discourse: modernism, postmodernism, and feminism. *College Literature* 17:1–50.

Godwin, William. [1927] 1969. *Memoirs of Mary Wollstonecraft.* W. Clark Durant (ed.). New York: Haskell House.

Goldin, Frederick. 1967. *The Mirror of Narcissus.* New York: Cornell UP.

Gombrich, E. H. 1961. *Art and Illusion: A Study in the Psychology of Pictorial Representation.* New York: Pantheon.

Gould, Karen. 1990. *Writing in the feminine: feminism and experimental writing in Québec.* Carbondale and Edwardsville: Southern Illinois UP.

Grahn, Judy. 1981. Boys at the rodeo. In Elly Bulkin (ed.), 11–16.

———. 1984. *Another Mother Tongue.* Boston: Beacon.

———. 1985. *The Highest Apple: Sappho and the Lesbian Poetic Tradition.* San Francisco: Spinsters Ink.

Graves, Robert. [1948] 1973. *The White Goddess: A Historical Grammar of Poetic Myth.* New York: Farrar, Straus, & Giroux.

Greenblatt, Stephen. 1988. *Shakespearean Negotiations: The Circulation of Social Energy in Renaissance England.* Oxford: Clarendon.

Greene, Gayle, and Coppelia Kahn (eds). 1985. *Making a Difference: Feminist Literary Criticism.* London and New York: Methuen.

Grier, Barbara (comp.). 1981. *The Lesbian in Literature,* 3rd ed. Tallahassee, Fla.: Naiad.

Grigg, Q. 1987. Review of *Women of the Left Bank* by Shari Benstock. *Choice* 24:1215–16.

Gubar, Susan. 1981. Blessings in disguise: cross-dressing for female modernists. *Massachusetts Review* 22, 3:477–508.

———. 1984. Sapphistries. *Signs* 10, 1:43–62.

Gurko, Jane. 1980. The shape of sameness: contemporary lesbian autobiographical narratives. Unpublished paper presented to the Gay Rhetoric Panel at the Modern Language Association, December.

Gurko, Jane, and Sally Gearhart. 1979. The sword and the vessel versus the lake on the lake: a lesbian model of non-violent rhetoric. Unpublished paper presented at the Modern Language Association, December.

Gutherie, W. K. C. 1955. *The Greeks and Their Gods.* Boston: Beacon.

Hall, Radclyffe. [1928] 1981. *The Well of Loneliness.* New York: Bard/Avon.

Hanscombe, Gillian, and Virginia L. Smyers. 1987. *Writing for Their Lives: The Modernist Woman, 1910–1940.* Boston: Northeastern UP.

Harris, Bertha. 1973. The more profound nationality of their lesbianism: lesbian society in Paris in the 1920s. In Phyllis Birkby, Bertha Harris, Jill

Johnston, Esther Newton, and Jane O'Wyatt (eds.), *Amazon Expedition*, New York: Times Change Press, 77–88.

————. 1976. Lesbians and literature. Paper delivered to the Modern Language Association, New York.

————. 1977. What we mean to say: notes toward defining the nature of lesbian literature. *Heresies* 3:5–8.

Hartigan, Francis X. 1987. Review of *Women of the Left Bank* by Shari Benstock. *History* 15:151–52.

Hartman, Joan, and Ellen Messer-Davidow. 1984. Learning to see: feminist perspectives in literary study. Unpublished paper presented at the National Women's Studies Association, June.

Hayman, Ronald. 1987. Stein and company. Review of *Women of the Left Bank* by Shari Benstock. *Manchester Guardian* 18:21.

Heacock, Maureen. 1987. Women's identity and women's community. Unpublished manuscript.

Herodotus. 1973. In Diner, *Mothers and Amazons: The First Feminine History of Culture*. New York: Doubleday.

Herzer, Manfred. 1985. "Kertbeny and the Nameless Love," *Journal of Homosexuality* 12:1–26.

Hoagland, Sarah Lucia. 1988. *Lesbian Ethics: Toward New Value*. Palo Alto, Calif.: Institute of Lesbian Studies.

Hoagland, Sarah Lucia, and Julia Penelope (eds). 1988. *For Lesbians Only: A Separatist Anthology*. London: Onlywomen.

Hodges, Beth (ed). 1975. *Lesbian Writing and Publishing*. Special issue of *Margins*, 23.

————, (ed). 1976. *Lesbian Literature and Publishing*. Special issue of *Sinister Wisdom* 2.

Holly, Marcia. 1975. Consciousness and authenticity: toward a feminist aesthetics. In Donovan, 38–47.

Holmlund, Christine. Forthcoming. Masculinity as multiple masquerade: the "mature" Stallone and the Stallone clone. In Ina Rae Hark and Steve Cohan (eds.), *Screening the Male*, New York and London: Routledge.

Homans, Margaret. 1980. *Women Writers and Poetic Identity: Dorothy Wordsworth, Emily Brontë, and Emily Dickinson*. Princeton: Princeton UP.

————. 1983. "Her Very Own Howl": the ambiguities of representation in recent women's fiction. *Signs* 9, 2:186–205.

Howard, Jean E. 1988. Crossdressing, the theatre, and gender struggle in early modern England. *Shakespeare Quarterly* 39:418–40.

Hull, Gloria T. 1979. "Under the Days": the buried life and poetry of Angelina Weld Grimke. *Conditions* 5:20–23.

————. 1982. Researching Alice Dunbar-Nelson: a personal and literary perspective. In Gloria T. Hull et al. (eds.), 189–95.

Hull, Gloria T., Patricia Bell Scott, and Barbara Smith (eds.). 1982. *All the Women Are White, All the Men Are Blacks, But Some of Us Are Brave: Black Women's Studies*. Old Westbury, N.Y.: The Feminist Press.

Hunter, Dianne (ed). 1989. *Seduction and Theory*. Urbana: U of Illinois P.

Irigaray, Luce. 1980. When our lips speak together. Trans. and with an introduction by Carolyn Burke. *Signs* 6:66–79.

———. 1981. And one doesn't speak without the other. Trans. and with an introduction by Hélène Vivienne Wenzel. *Signs* 7:56–67.

———. 1984. *Ethique de la différence sexuelle.* Paris: Les Editions de Minuit.

———. 1985a. *Speculum of the Other Woman.* Trans. Gillian C. Gill. Ithaca, N.Y.: Cornell UP.

———. 1985b. *This Sex Which Is Not One.* Trans. Catherine Porter with Carolyn Burke. Ithaca, N.Y.: Cornell UP.

Jaggar, Alison. 1983. *Feminist Politics and Human Nature.* Totowa, N.J.: Rowman and Allanheld.

Jardine, Alice. 1980. Prelude: the future of difference. In Hester Eisenstein and Alice Jardine (eds.), xxv–xxvii.

Jardine, Lisa. 1983. *Still Harping on Daughters: Woman and Drama in the Age of Shakespeare.* New York: Barnes & Noble.

Jay, Karla. 1988. *The Amazon and the Page: Natalie Barney and Renée Vivien.* Bloomington: Indiana UP.

———. 1990. The outsider among the expatriates: Djuna Barnes' satire on the ladies of the *Almanack.* In Karla Jay and Joanne Glasgow (eds.), 204–16.

Jay, Karla, and Joanne Glasgow (eds). 1990. *Lesbian Texts and Contexts: Radical Revisions.* New York: New York UP.

Jeffreys, Sheila. 1985. *The Spinster and Her Enemies: Feminism and Sexuality 1880–1930.* Oxon: Pandora.

———. 1989. Does it matter if they did it? In *Not a Passing Phase: Reclaiming Lesbians in History 1840–1985,* London: The Women's Press, 19–28.

Jelinek, Estelle C. (ed). 1980. *Women's Autobiography.* Bloomington: Indiana UP.

Jewett, Sarah Orne. 1966. *Deephaven and Other Stories,* ed. Richard Cary. New Haven, Conn.: College and University P.

Johnson, George. 1988. Review of *Women of the Left Bank* by Shari Benstock. *New York Times Book Review,* 6 March: 32.

Johnston, Jill. 1973. *Lesbian Nation.* New York: Simon and Schuster.

Jones, Ann Rosalind. 1985. Writing the body: toward an understanding of l'écriture féminine. In Showalter (ed.), 361–77.

Jung, Carl. 1956. *Two Essays on Analytical Psychology.* Trans. R. F. C. Hull. New York: Meridian.

Kahn, Coppelia. 1981. *Man's Estate: Masculine Identity in Shakespeare.* Los Angeles/London: U of California P.

Katz, Jonathan. 1976. *Gay American History: Lesbians and Gay Men in the U. S. A.* New York: Thomas Crowell.

Katz, Susan. 1987. Speaking out against the "talking cure": unmarried women in Freud's early case studies. *Women's Studies* 13, 4:297–324.

Kaye, Melanie. 1980. Culture-making: lesbian classics. *Sinister Wisdom* 13:23–24.

Keinhorst, Annette. 1987. Emancipatory projection: an introduction to women's critical utopias. *Women's Studies International Forum* 14:91–99.

Keohane, Nannerl O., Michelle Z. Rosaldo, and Barbara C. Gelpi (eds). 1982. *Feminist Theory: A Critique of Ideology.* Chicago: U. of Chicago Press.

Kessler, Carol Farley (ed.). 1984. *Daring to Dream: Utopian Stories by United States Women, 1836–1919.* Boston: Pandora.

Kitzinger, Celia. 1987. *The Social Construction of Lesbianism.* Newbury Park, Calif.: Sage.

Klaich, Dolores. 1974. *Woman + Woman: Attitudes toward Lesbianism.* New York: William Morrow.

Kolodny, Annette. 1976. Review essay: literary criticism. *Signs* 2, 2:404–21.

———. 1980. The lady's not for spurning: Kate Millett and the critics. In Estelle C. Jelinek (ed.), 238–59.

———. 1982. An interchange on feminist criticism: on "Dancing Through the Minefield." *Feminist Studies* 8:665–75.

———. 1985. Dancing through the minefield: some observations on the theory, practice, and politics of a feminist literary criticism. In Elaine Showalter (ed.), 144–67.

Krieger, Susan. 1982. Lesbian identity and community: recent social science literature. *Signs* 8:91–108.

Kristeva, Julia. 1987. *The Kristeva Reader.* Toril Moi (ed). New York: Columbia UP.

Kupper, Susan. 1990. *Surnames for Women: A Decision-Making Guide.* Jefferson, N.C.: McFarland.

La Belle, Jenijoy. 1988. *Herself Beheld: The Literature of the Looking Glass.* Ithaca, N.Y.: Cornell UP.

Lacan, Jacques. 1982. The meaning of the phallus. In Juliet Mitchell and Jacqueline Rosen (eds.), *Jacques Lacan and the École Freudienne,* trans. Jacqueline Rose. New York and London: W. W. Norton, 74–85.

Lambert, Deborah G. 1982. The defeat of a hero: autonomy and sexuality in *My Ántonia. American Literature* 53, 4:676–90.

Lanser, Susan Sniader. 1979. Speaking in tongues: *Ladies' Almanack* and the language of celebration. *Frontiers* 4, 3:39–46.

Laqueur, Thomas. 1990. *Making Sex: Body and Gender from the Greeks to Freud.* Cambridge, Mass./London: Harvard UP.

Larsen, Nella. [1928 and 1929] 1987. *Quicksand* and *Passing,* ed. Deborah E. McDowell. New Brunswick, N.J.: Rutgers UP.

Lauritsen, John, and David Thorstad. 1974. *The Early Homosexual Rights Movement (1864–1935).* New York: Times Change.

Leduc, Violette. 1965. *La bâtarde.* Trans. Derek Coltman. New York: Farrar, Straus and Giroux.

Lefanu, Sarah. 1988. *In the Chinks of the World Machine.* London: The Women's Press.

LeGuin, Ursula K. 1985. *Always Coming Home.* New York: Harper and Row.

Lenz, Carolyn Ruth Swift, Gayle Greene, and Carol Thomas Neely (eds). 1983. *The Woman's Part: Feminist Criticism of Shakespeare.* Urbana and Chicago: U of Illinois P.

Levine, Laura. 1986. Men in women's clothing: anti-theatricality and effeminization from 1579 to 1642. *Criticism* 28:121–43.

Libertin, Mary. 1982. Female friendships in women's verse: toward a new theory of female poetics. *Women's Studies* 9, 3:291–308.

Lorde, Audre. 1984a. *Sister Outsider: Essays and Speeches by Audre Lorde.* Trumansburg, N.Y.: Crossing Press.

——. 1984b. An interview with Audre Lorde and Adrienne Rich. In *Sister Outsider,* 81–109.

——. 1984c. *Zami: A New Spelling of My Name.* Trumansburg, N.Y.: Crossing Press.

Mackinnon, Lachlan. 1988. Lesbos-sur-Seine. Review of *Women of the Left Bank* by Shari Benstock; *Writing for Their Lives,* Gillian Hanscombe and Virginia L. Smyers (eds.); and *Geniuses Together* by Humphrey Carpenter. *Times Literary Supplement,* 11–17 March: 285.

Makward, Christiane. 1976. Interview with Hélène Cixous. *Sub-Stance* 13:19–37.

——. 1978. Structures du silence/du delire. *Poetique* 35:314–24.

Marks, Elaine. 1979. Lesbian intertextuality. In George Stambolian and Elaine Marks (eds.), 353–77; reprinted this volume.

Marks, Elaine, and Isabelle de Courtivron (eds). 1980. *New French Feminisms.* Amherst: U of Massachusetts P.

Martin, Biddy, and Chandra Talpade Mohanty. 1986. Feminist politics: what's home got to do with it? In Teresa de Lauretis (ed.), *Feminist Studies/Critical Studies,* Bloomington: Indiana UP, 191–212.

Mavor, Elizabeth. [1971] 1973. *The Ladies of Llangollen: A Study in Romantic Friendship.* Harmondsworth: Penguin.

McDaniel, Judith. 1976. Lesbians and literature. *Sinister Wisdom* 2:20–23.

——. 1978. *Reconstituting the World: The Poetry and Vision of Adrienne Rich.* Argyle, N.Y.: Spinsters, Ink.

McIntyre, Vonda, and Susan Anderson (eds). 1976. *Aurora: Beyond Equality.* New York: Fawcett.

McLuskie, Kathleen. 1985. The patriarchal bard: feminist criticism and Shakespeare: *King Lear* and *Measure for Measure.* In Jonathan Dollimore and Alan Sinfield (eds), *Political Shakespeare: New Essays in Cultural Materialism.* Ithaca, N.Y., and London: Cornell UP, 88–108.

Meese, Elizabeth. 1990. Theorizing lesbian: writing – a love letter. In Karla Jay and Joanne Glasgow (eds.), *Lesbian Texts and Contexts: Radical Revisions,* New York: New York UP, 70–87.

Mesic, Penelope. 1986. Review of *Women of the Left Bank* by Shari Benstock. *Booklist* 83:380.

Michelet, Jules. [1862] 1966. *La Sorcière.* Paris: Garnier-Flammarion.

Miller, Alice. 1981. *The Drama of the Gifted Child.* New York: Basic Books.

——. 1986. *Thou Shalt Not Be Aware: Society's Betrayal of the Child.* New York: New American Library.

Miller, Isabel. 1973. *Patience and Sarah.* New York: Fawcett Crest.

Miller, Nancy K. 1980. *The Heroine's Text: Readings in the French and English Novel, 1722–1782.* New York: Columbia UP.

Millett, Kate. [1969] 1971. *Sexual Politics*. New York: Avon.

Milton, John. 1962. *Paradise Lost*, ed. Merritt Y. Hughes. New York: Macmillan.

Mitchell, Juliet, and Jacqueline Rose. 1982. *Feminine Sexuality: Jacques Lacan and the École Freudienne*. New York and London: W. W. Norton.

Moers, Ellen. 1977. *Literary Women: The Great Writers*. Garden City, N.Y.: Anchor Press/Doubleday.

Mohanty, Chandra Talpade. 1987. Feminist encounters: locating the politics of experience. *Copyright* (Fall): 30–44.

Mora, Edith. 1966. *Sappho*. Paris: Flammarion.

Moraga, Cherríe, and Gloria Anzaldúa (eds.). 1981. *This Bridge Called My Back: Writings by Radical Women of Color*. Watertown Mass.: Persephone.

Morgan, Claire (pseud. of Patricia Highsmith). [1952] 1984. *The Price of Salt*. Tallahassee, Fla.: Naiad.

Morris, Adalaide. 1981. Two sisters have I: Emily Dickinson's Vinnie and Susan. *Massachusetts Review* 22, 2:323–32.

———. 1983. "The Love of Thee – A Prism Be": men and women in the bridal poems of Emily Dickinson. In Susan Juhasz (ed.), *Feminist Critics Read Emily Dickinson*. Bloomington, Indiana UP, 98–113.

Morrison, Toni. 1975. *Sula*. New York: Bantam.

Mushroom, Merril. 1987. *Daughters of Khaton*. Denver: Lace Publications.

Nachman, Elana. 1974. *Riverfinger Women*. Plainfield, Vt.: Daughters, Inc.

Naylor, Gloria. 1983. *The Women of Brewster Place*. New York: Penguin.

Near, Holly. 1976. "Imagine My Surprise." *Imagine My Surprise!* Redwood Records.

Neely, Carol Thomas. 1985. *Broken Nuptials in Shakespeare's Plays*. New Haven: Yale UP.

Nestle, Joan. 1987. *A Restricted Country*. Ithaca, N.Y.: Firebrand.

Newton, Esther. 1984. The mythic mannish lesbian: Radclyffe Hall and the new woman. *Signs* 9, 4:557–75.

Newton, Esther, and Shirley Walton. 1989. The misunderstanding: toward a more precise sexual vocabulary. In Carole S. Vance (ed.), 242–50.

Novy, Marianne L. 1984. *Love's Argument: Gender Relations in Shakespeare*. Chapel Hill, N.C., and London: U of North Carolina P.

O'Brien, Sharon. 1984. "The thing not named": Willa Cather as a lesbian writer. *Signs* 9, 4:576–99.

Olsen, Tillie. 1978, 1979. *Silences*. New York: Dell.

Orgel, Stephen. 1989. Nobody's perfect: or Why did the English stage take boys for women? *SAQ* 88:7–29.

Ostriker, Alicia. 1983. *Writing Like a Woman*. Ann Arbor: U of Michigan P.

Park, Katherine, and Robert A. Nye. 1991. Destiny is anatomy. A review of *Making Sex: Body and Gender from the Greeks to Freud*. *New Republic* (February 18): 53–57.

Parmeter, Sarah-Hope, and Irene Reti (eds). 1988. *The Lesbian in Front of the Classroom: Writings by Lesbian Teachers*. Santa Cruz, Calif.: HerBooks.

Patterson, Rebecca. 1951. *The Riddle of Emily Dickinson*. Boston: Houghton Mifflin.

Pearson, Carol. 1977. Women's Fantasies and Feminist Utopias. *Frontiers* 2, 3:50–61.

Pearson, Carol, and Katherine Pope. 1981. *The Female Hero.* New York: R. R. Bowker.

Penelope (Stanley), Julia. 1975. Uninhabited angels: metaphors for love. *Margins* 23:7–10.

———. 1979. The articulation of bias: hoof in mouth disease. Unpublished paper presented at the National Council of Teachers of English, November.

Penelope (Stanley), Julia, and Susan J. Wolfe. 1978. Toward a feminist aesthetic. *Chrysalis* 6:57–71.

———, (eds). 1980. *The Coming Out Stories.* Watertown, Mass.: Persephone.

Penelope, Julia. 1990. The lesbian perspective. In Jeffner Allen (ed.), 89–108.

Pharr, Suzanne. 1988. *Homophobia, a Weapon of Sexism.* Inverness, California: Chardon.

Phelan, Shane. 1989. *Identity Politics: Lesbian Feminism and the Limits of Community.* Philadelphia, Pennsylvania: Temple UP.

Piercy, Marge. 1976. *Woman on the Edge of Time.* New York: Fawcett Crest.

Plato. 1961. *Laws.* In Edith Hamilton and Huntington Cairns (eds.), *Collected Dialogues.* Princeton: Princeton UP.

———. 1968. *Republic.* Trans. Allan Bloom. New York: Basic Books.

Plutarch. 1914. *Plutarch's Lives,* vol. 1, *Theseus and Romulus.* Trans. Bernadotte Perrin. Cambridge, Mass.: Harvard UP.

Pope, Deborah. 1984. *A Separate Vision: Isolation in Contemporary Women's Poetry.* Baton Rouge: Louisiana State UP.

Pratt, Annis. 1981. *Archetypal Patterns in Women's Fiction,* with Barbara White, Andrea Loewenstein, and Mary Wyer. Bloomington: Indiana UP.

Pratt, Minnie Bruce. 1984. Identity: skin blood heart. In Elly Bulkin, Minnie Bruce Pratt, and Barbara Smith, *Yours in Struggle: Three Feminist Perspectives on Anti-Semitism and Racism.* Brooklyn: Long Haul Press, 11–63.

Pratt, Minnie Bruce. 1990. *Crimes Against Nature.* Ithaca, N.Y.: Firebrand.

Publishers Weekly. 1986. Review of *Women of the Left Bank* by Shari Benstock, 1 November: 61.

Questions féministes collective. 1977. Variations on common themes. *Questions Féministes* 1; reprinted in Elaine Marks and Isabelle de Courtivron (eds.), 212–30.

Rabine, Leslie W. 1985. *Reading the Romantic Heroine: Text, History, Ideology.* Ann Arbor: U of Michigan P.

Rabkin, Norman. 1981. *Shakespeare and the Problem of Meaning.* Chicago and London: U of Chicago P.

Rackin, Phyllis. 1987. Androgyny, mimesis, and the marriage of the boy heroine. *PMLA* 102:29–54.

Radicalesbians. 1970. The woman-identified woman. *The Ladder* 11/12; also in Deborah Babcox and Madeline Belkin (eds.), *Liberation Now!,* New York: Dell; *Radical Feminism,* New York: Quadrangle/New York Times Book Co., 1973; reprinted in Sarah Lucia Hoagland and Julia Penelope (eds.), 17–22.

Raymond, Janice G. 1986. *A Passion for Friends: Toward a Philosophy of Female Affection*. Boston: Beacon.

Reagon, Bernice Johnson. 1983. Coalition politics: turning the century. In Barbara Smith (ed.), *Home Girls*, New York: Kitchen Table: Women of Color Press, 356–68.

Register, Cheri. 1975. American feminist literary criticism: a bibliographical introduction. In Josephine Donovan (ed.), 1–28.

Reiter, Rayna R. (ed). 1975. *Toward an Anthropology of Women*. New York and London: Monthly Review.

Rhodes, Carolyn. 1983. Method in her madness: feminism in the crazy utopian vision of Tiptree's courier. In Marleen Barr and Nicholas Smith (eds.), 34–42.

Rich, Adrienne. 1973. Diving into the wreck. In *Diving into the Wreck: Poems 1971–72*. New York: Norton.

———. 1976. *Of Woman Born: Motherhood as Experience and Institution*. New York: Norton.

———. 1978. *The Dream of a Common Language: Poems 1974–1977*. New York: Norton.

———. 1979a. It is the lesbian in us. . . . In her *On Lies, Secrets, and Silence: Selected Prose, 1966–1978*. New York: Norton, 199–202.

———. 1979b. *On Lies, Secrets, and Silence: Selected Prose, 1966–1978*. New York: Norton.

———. 1980. Compulsory heterosexuality and lesbian existence. *Signs* 5, 4:631–60.

———. 1986a. *Blood, Bread, and Poetry: Selected Prose 1979–1985*. New York and London: Norton; Split at the root: an essay on Jewish identity, 100–123; Notes toward a politics of location, 210–31.

———. 1986b. *Your Native Land, Your Life: Poems*. New York: Norton.

Richman, Michele. 1980. Sex and signs: the language of French feminist criticism. *Language and Style* 13:62–80.

Ricouart, Janine. 1988. Problématiques de l'homoidentité chez Marie-Claire Blais et Nicole Brossard. Unpublished paper presented at the Midwest Modern Language Association, November.

Robbe-Grillet, Alain. 1963. *Pour un nouveau roman*. Paris: Gallimard.

Roberts, JR. 1980. "'leude behauior each with other vpon a bed': the case of Sarah Norman and Mary Hammond," *Sinister Wisdom* 14:57–62.

———. 1981. *Black Lesbians*. Tallahassee, Fla.: Naiad.

———. 1982. Black lesbians before 1970: a bibliographical essay. In Margaret Cruikshank (ed.), 103–9.

Roof, Judith. 1989. The match in the crocus: representations of lesbian sexuality. In Dianne Hunter (ed.).

Rosenfeld, Marthe. 1978. Linguistic experimentation in Monique Wittig's *Le corps lesbien*. Unpublished paper presented at the Modern Language Association, December.

———. 1984. The linguistic aspect of sexual conflict: Monique Wittig's *Le corps lesbien*. *Mosaic* 17, 2:235–41.

————. 1988. Splits in French feminism/lesbianism. In Sarah Lucia Hoagland and Julia Penelope (eds.), 457–66.

Rosinsky, Natalie M. 1984. *Feminist Futures: Contemporary Women's Speculative Fiction*. Ann Arbor: U of Michigan Press.

Rubin, Gayle. 1975. The traffic in women: notes on the "political economy" of sex. In Rayna R. Reiter (ed.), 157–210.

————. 1976. Introduction to *A Woman Appeared to Me* by Renée Vivien, iii–xli. Reno, Nev.: Naiad.

————. 1989. Thinking sex: notes for a radical theory of the politics of sexuality. In Carole S. Vance (ed.), 267–319.

Rule, Jane. [1964] 1987. *Desert of the Heart*. Tallahassee, Fla.: Naiad.

————. 1975. *Lesbian Images*. Garden City, N.Y.: Doubleday.

————. [1977] 1987. *The Young in One Another's Arms*. Tallahassee, Fla.: Naiad.

————. 1985. Inland passage. In her *Inland Passage*. Tallahassee, Fla.: Naiad, 211–36.

————. 1987. *Memory Board*. Tallahassee, Fla.: Naiad.

Russ, Joanna. 1972. When it changed. In Harlan Ellison (ed.).

————. 1975. *The Female Man*. New York: Bantam.

————. 1978. *The Two of Them*. New York: Berkley.

————. 1979. To write "like a woman": transformations of identity in Willa Cather. Unpublished paper presented at the Modern Language Association, December.

————. 1980. *Amor vincit foeminiam*: the battle of the sexes in science fiction. *Science Fiction Studies* 7; reprinted in Judith Spector (ed.), *Gender Studies*, Bowling Green, Ohio: Bowling Green U Popular Press, 1986, 234–49.

————. 1981. Recent feminist utopias. In Marleen Barr (ed.), 71–87.

Russo, Mary. 1986. Female grotesques: Carnival and theory. In Teresa de Lauretis (ed.), *Feminist Studies/Critical Studies*, 213–22.

Sagan, Carl. 1978. *The Dragons of Eden: Speculations on the Evolution of Human Intelligence*. New York: Ballantine.

Sahli, Nancy. 1979. Smashing: women's relationships before the fall. *Chrysalis* 8:17–27.

Salem, Randy. [1959] 1989. *Chris*. Tallahassee, Fla.: Naiad.

Saphira, Miriam (comp.). 1988. *New Lesbian Literature 1980–1988*. Auckland, New Zealand: Papers Inc.

Sappho. 1958. *Sappho*. Trans. Mary Barnard. Berkeley and Los Angeles: U of California P.

Sarraute, Nathalie. 1956. *L'Ere du soupçon: essais sur le roman*. Paris: Gallimard.

Sarton, May. 1965. *Mrs. Stevens Hears the Mermaids Singing*. New York: Norton.

Schuster, Marilyn. 1981. Strategies for survival: the subtle subversion of Jane Rule. *Feminist Studies* 7, 3:431–50.

Schwarz, Judith. 1979. *Yellow Clover:* Katharine Lee Bates and Katharine Coman. *Frontiers* 4, 1:59–67.

Scott, Joan W. 1988. Deconstructing equality versus difference: or, the uses of poststructuralist theory for feminism. *Feminist Studies* 15:33–51.

Scott, Sarah. [1762] 1986. *Millenium Hall*. New York: Virago/Penguin.

Secor, Cynthia. 1978. *Ida,* a great American novel. *Twentieth Century Literature* 24, 1:96–107.

———. 1979. Can we call Gertrude Stein a non-declared lesbian writer? Unpublished paper presented at the Modern Language Association, December.

———. 1982a. Gertrude Stein: the complex force of her femininity. In Kenneth W. Wheeler and Virginia Lee Lussier (eds.), *Women, the Arts, and the 1920s in Paris and New York.* New Brunswick, N.J.: Transaction Books, 27–35.

———. 1982b. The question of Gertrude Stein. In Fritz Fleischmann (ed.), *American Novelists Revisited: Essays in Feminist Criticism.* New York: G. K. Hall, 299–310.

Sedgwick, Eve Kosofsky. 1989. Across gender, across sexuality: Willa Cather and others. *SAQ* 88:53–72.

Seigel, Jerrold. 1987. Pilgrims in Paris. Review of *On the Left Bank* by Wambly Bald; *The Paris Edition: The Autobiography of Waverly Root,* Samuel Abt (ed.); *Four Lives in Paris* by Hugh Ford; and *Women of the Left Bank* by Shari Benstock. *New Republic,* 28 September: 30–34.

Shaktini, Namascar. 1982. Displacing the phallic subject: Wittig's lesbian writing. *Signs* 8, 1:29–44.

Sheldon, Alice (aka James Tiptree, Jr., Raccoona Sheldon). 1976. Houston, Houston, do you read? In Vonda McIntyre and Susan Anderson (eds.), 36–98.

———. 1976. Your Faces, O My Sisters! Your Faces Filled of Light! In Vonda McIntyre and Susan Anderson (eds.), 16–35.

Sherman, Sarah. 1989. *Sarah Orne Jewett, an American Persephone.* Hanover, N.H.: UP of New England.

Shinn, Thelma J. 1985. Worlds of words and swords: Suzette Haden Elgin and Joanna Russ at work. In Jane Weedman (ed.), 207–22.

Shockley, Ann Allen. [1974] 1987. *Loving Her.* Tallahassee, Fla.: Naiad.

———. 1979. The black lesbian in American literature: an overview. *Conditions* 5:133–42; reprinted in Barbara Smith (ed.), *Home Girls: A Black Feminist Anthology.* New York: Kitchen Table: Women of Color Press, 1983, 83–105.

———. 1989. *Afro-American Women Writers, 1746–1933: An Anthology and Critical Guide.* New York: Meridian/NAL.

Showalter, Elaine. 1975. Review essay: literary criticism. *Signs* 1, 2:435–60.

———. 1977. *A Literature of Their Own: British Women Novelists from Brontë to Lessing.* Princeton: Princeton UP.

———. 1981. Feminist criticism in the wilderness. *Critical Inquiry* 8, 2.

———. 1985. Introduction: The feminist critical revolution. In Elaine Showalter, (ed.), 3–17.

———. (ed.). 1985. *The New Feminist Criticism: Essays on Women, Literature and Theory.* New York: Pantheon.

Simon, Judy. 1986. Introduction to *Cecilia or, Memoirs of an Heiress.* New York: Virago/Penguin.

Simons, Margaret. 1986. Beauvoir and Sartre: the philosophical relationship. *Yale French Studies* 72:165–81.

Sinclair, May. [1919] 1980. *Mary Olivier: A Life.* New York: Dial.

Smith, Barbara. 1977. Toward a black feminist criticism. *Conditions* 2:25–44; also published in *Women's Studies International Quarterly* 2 (1979), 183–94; reprinted in Gloria T. Hull et al. (eds.), 257–75, and in Elaine Showalter (ed.), 1985, 168–185.

Smith, Elizabeth A. 1989. Butches, femmes, and feminists: the politics of lesbian sexuality. *National Women's Studies Association Journal* 1:398–421.

Smith-Rosenberg, Carroll. 1975. The female world of love and ritual: relations between women in nineteenth-century America. *Signs* 1:1–29.

Spacks, Patricia Meyer. 1976. *The Female Imagination*. New York: Avon.

Special Issue: The Androgyny Papers. 1974. *Women's Studies* 2, 2.

Stambolian, George, and Elaine Marks (eds). 1979. *Homosexualities and French Literature: Cultural Contexts/Critical Texts*. Ithaca, N.Y.: Cornell UP.

Stanley, Julia Penelope. *See* Penelope.

Stanton, Domna. 1986. Difference on trial: a critique of the maternal metaphor in Cixous, Irigaray, and Kristeva. In Nancy K. Miller (ed.), *The Poetics of Gender*, New York: Columbia, UP, 157–82.

Steakley, James D. 1975. *The Homosexual Emancipation Movement in Germany*. New York: Arno Press.

Stephenson, June. 1986. *Women's Roots, Status and Achievements in Western Civilization*. Napa, Calif.: Diemer, Smith Publishing.

Stimpson, Catharine R. 1977. The mind, the body and Gertrude Stein. *Critical Inquiry* 3, 3:489–506.

———. 1981. Zero degree deviancy: the lesbian novel in English. *Critical Inquiry* 8, 2:363–80; reprinted in Elizabeth Abel (ed.), 1982.

———. 1985. Adrienne Rich and lesbian/feminist poetry. *Parnassus* 12, 2/13, 1:249–68.

Sturgis, Susanna J. 1989. Editorial memories & visions, or why does a bright feminist like you read that stuff anyway? Introduction to Susanna J. Sturgis (ed.), *Memories and Visions: Women's Fantasy and Science Fiction*. Freedom, Calif.: Crossing Press, 3.

Tan, Amy. 1989. *The Joy Luck Club*. New York: Ballantine.

Todd, Janet M. (ed.). 1980a. *Gender and Literary Voice*. New York: Holmes & Meier.

———. 1980b. *Women's Friendships in Literature*. New York: Columbia UP.

Tompkins, Jane P. 1980. The reader in history: the changing shape of literary response. In Tompkins (ed.), *Reader-Response Criticism: From Formalism to Post-Structuralism*. Baltimore: Johns Hopkins UP.

Trinh, T. Minh-ha. 1989. *Woman, Native, Other*. Bloomington: Indiana UP.

Triton, Suzette. 1983. Recontre avec Nicole Brossard. *Vlasta* 1:33–39.

Trollope, Frances. 1856. *Fashionable Life: or, Paris and London*. London: Hurst and Blackett.

van Gulik, Robert H. 1961. *Sexual Life in Ancient China*. Leiden: E. J. Brill.

Vance, Carole S. (ed.). 1989. *Pleasure and Danger: Exploring Female Sexuality*. London/Sydney/Wellington: Pandora.

Vanderlinde, Deirdre. 1979. Gertrude Stein: *Three Lives*. Unpublished paper presented at the Modern Language Association, December.

Vincent, Sybil Korff. n.d. Nothing fails like success: Radclyffe Hall's *The Well of Loneliness*. Unpublished paper.

Wagner-Martin, Linda. 1987. The other side of modernism. Review of *Women of the Left Bank* by Shari Benstock. *American Book Review* 12, 3:20.

Walker, Alice. 1982. *The Color Purple*. New York and London: Harcourt Brace Jovanovich.

Waugh, Patricia. 1989. *Feminine Fictions: Revisiting the Postmodern*. New York and London: Routledge.

Weedman, Jane B. (ed.). 1985. *Women Worldwalkers: New Dimensions of Science Fiction and Fantasy*. Lubbock: Texas Tech.

Weeks, Jeffrey. 1987. Question of identity. In Pat Caplan (ed.), *The Cultural Construction of Sexuality*, London/New York: Tavistock Publications, 31–51.

Weir, Lorraine. 1986. From picture to hologram: Nicole Brossard's grammar of utopia. In Shirley Neuman and Smaro Kamboureli (eds.), *A Mazing Space*, Edmonton: Longspoon/NeWest, 345–52.

Weiss, Andrea, and Greta Schiller. 1988. *Before Stonewall: The Making of a Gay and Lesbian Community*. Tallahassee, Fla.: Naiad.

Wenzel, Hélène Vivienne. 1981. The text as body/politics: an appreciation of Monique Wittig's writings in context. *Feminist Studies* 7, 2:264–87.

Weston, Kath. Forthcoming. Do clothes make the woman? Gender theory and lesbian eroticism.

Wilhelm, Gale. [1935] 1984. *We Too Are Drifting*. Tallahassee, Fla.: Naiad.

———. [1938] 1985. *Torchlight to Valhalla*. Tallahassee, Fla.: Naiad.

Williams, Lynn F. 1985. "Great country for men and dogs, but tough on women and mules": sex and status in recent science fiction utopias. In Jane Weedman (ed.), 223–35.

Wilson, Jean. 1981. Nicole Brossard: fantasies and realities. *Broadside* 2, 8:10–11, 18.

Winnicott, D. W. 1985. *Playing and Reality*. Middlesex: Penguin.

Winstanley, Gerrard. 1941. The new law of righteousness. In George S. Sabine (ed.), *The Works of Gerrard Winstanley*. Ithaca, N.Y.: Cornell UP, 149–244.

Wittig, Monique. 1966. *The Opoponax*. Trans. Helen Weaver. Plainfield, Vt.: Daughters, Inc.

———. 1973a. *Le corps lesbien*. Paris: Les Editions de Minuit.

———. 1973b. *Les Guérillères*. Trans. David LeVay. New York: Avon.

———. 1974. Monique Wittig et les lesbiennes barbues. *Actuel* 38:12.

———. 1975. *The Lesbian Body*. Trans. David LeVay. New York: William Morrow.

———. 1976. *The Lesbian Body*. Trans. David LeVay. New York: Avon.

———. 1979. Paradigm. In George Stambolian and Elaine Marks (eds.).

———. 1980. The straight mind. *Feminist Issues* 1, 1:103–11.

———. 1981. One is not born a woman. *Feminist Issues*, 1, 47–54; reprinted in Alison M. Jaggar and Paula S. Rothenberg (eds.), *Feminist Frameworks: Alternative Theoretical Accounts of Relations between Women and Men*. New York: McGraw-Hill, 1984, 148–52.

———. 1982. The category of sex. *Feminist Issues* 2:63–68.

———. 1983. The point of view: universal or particular? *Feminist Issues* 3:63–70.

———. 1984a. Le lieu de l'action. *Digraphe* 32 (mars): 70–75.

———. 1984b. The Trojan horse. *Feminist Issues* 4, 2:45–50.

———. 1985a. The mark of gender. *Feminist Issues* 5:3–12.

———. 1985b. Le voyage sans fin. *Vlasta* 4: supplement.

———. 1985c. Paris-la-politique. *Vlasta* 4.

———. 1985d. *Virgile, non: un roman*. Paris: Les Editions de Minuit.

———. 1990. Homo sum. *Feminist Issues* 10:3–11.

Wittig, Monique, and Sande Zeig. 1979. *Lesbian Peoples: Material for a Dictionary*. New York: Avon.

Wolfe, Susan J. 1978. Stylistic experimentation in Millett, Johnston and Wittig. Unpublished paper presented at the Modern Language Association, December.

Wollstonecraft, Mary. [1788] 1980. *Mary, a Fiction*. In *"Mary" and "The Wrongs of Women"*. Oxford: Oxford UP.

———. [1798] 1980. *The Wrongs of Woman: Maria*. Oxford: Oxford UP.

Woodbridge, Linda. 1984. *Women and the English Renaissance: Literature and the Nature of Womankind, 1540–1620*. Urbana and Chicago: U of Illinois P.

Woolf, Virginia. [1919] 1948. *Night and Day*. New York: Harcourt, Brace & World.

———. [1925] 1953. *Mrs. Dalloway*. New York: Harcourt, Brace & World.

———. [1929] 1957. *A Room of One's Own*. New York: Harcourt, Brace & World.

———. [1927] 1964. *To the Lighthouse*. New York: Harcourt, Brace & World.

———. [1939] 1965. *The Years*. New York: Harcourt, Brace & World.

———. 1978. *The Letters of Virginia Woolf*, vol. 4, *1929–31*. Nigel Nicolson and Joanne Trautman (eds.). New York: Harcourt Brace Jovanovich.

Woolston, Florence Guy. [1919] 1982. ". . . Marriage Customs and Taboo among the Early Heterodities . . .," Appendix B in *Radical Feminists of Heterodoxy, Greenwich Village 1912–1940* by Judith Schwarz. Lebanon, N.H.: New Victoria, 95–96.

Wyatt, Thomas. 1954. Description of the contrarious passions in a lover. In Hyder E. Rollins and Herschel Baker (eds.), *The Renaissance in England*. Boston: Heath.

Yaguello, Marina. 1979. *Les mots et les femmes*. Paris: Payot.

Zavarzadeh, Mas'ud, and Donald Morton. (Post)modern critical theory and the articulations of critical pedagogies. *College Literature* 17:51–63.

Zimmerman, Bonnie. 1976. The new tradition. *Sinister Wisdom* 2:34–41.

———. 1980. "Daughters of Darkness": lesbian vampires. *Jump Cut* 24–25:23–24.

———. 1981. What has never been: an overview of lesbian feminist criticism. *Feminist Studies* 7, 3; reprinted in Gayle Greene and Coppelia Kahn (eds.), 177–210; reprinted this volume.

———. 1983. Exiting from patriarchy: the lesbian novel of development. In Elizabeth Abel, Marianne Hirsch, and Elizabeth Langland (eds.), *The Voyage In: Fictions of Female Development*. Hanover, N.H.: UP of New England, 244–57.

———. 1984. The politics of transliteration: lesbian first-person narratives. *Signs* 9:663–82; reprinted in Estelle B. Freedman et al., 251–70.

———. 1990a. "The Dark Eye Beaming": female friendship in George Eliot's fictions. In Karla Jay and Joanne Glasgow (eds.), 126–44.

———. 1990b. *The Safe Sea of Women*. Boston: Beacon.

Index